# FATHERLAND

Also by Nina Bunjevac

*Heartless*

# FATHERLAND

WITHDRAWN

## A Family History

## Nina Bunjevac

LIVERIGHT PUBLISHING CORPORATION

A Division of W. W. Norton & Company

New York · London

Copyirght © 2014 by Nina Bunjevac
First American Edition 2015

First published by Jonathan Cape Ltd., one of the publishers in The Random House Group Ltd.

For information about permission to reproduce selections from this book, write to Permissions,
Liveright Publishing Corporation, a division of W. W. Norton & Company, Inc.,
500 Fifth Avenue, New York, NY 10110

For information about special discounts for bulk purchases, please contact W. W. Norton Special Sales
at specialsales@wwnorton.com or 800-233-4830

Manufacturing by Courier Kendallville
Production manager: Anna Oler

ISBN 978-1-63149-031-6

Liveright Publishing Corporation
500 Fifth Avenue, New York, N.Y. 10110
www.wwnorton.com

W. W. Norton & Company Ltd.
Castle House, 75/76 Wells Street, London W1T 3QT

1 2 3 4 5 6 7 8 9 0

TO JACOB, MOM, DAD, PETER, SARAH, MARA, AND DEJAN
WITH ALL MY LOVE

IN LOVING MEMORY OF MY GRANDPARENTS MOMIRKA AND SPASOJA

SPECIAL THANKS TO ZORAN DJUKANOVIC, ZIKA TAMBURIC,
PAUL GRAVETT, DAN FRANKLIN AND MARC VON ARX.

MANY THANKS TO DEAR FRIENDS ANA KHACHATRYAN, DEJANA ERIC,
DAVE LAPP, JORDAN BURSACH, CHESTER BROWN, AND DALTON SHARP
FOR ALL THE ENCOURAGEMENT.

# FATHERLAND

# FATHERLAND
## PART ONE
## PLAN ★ B

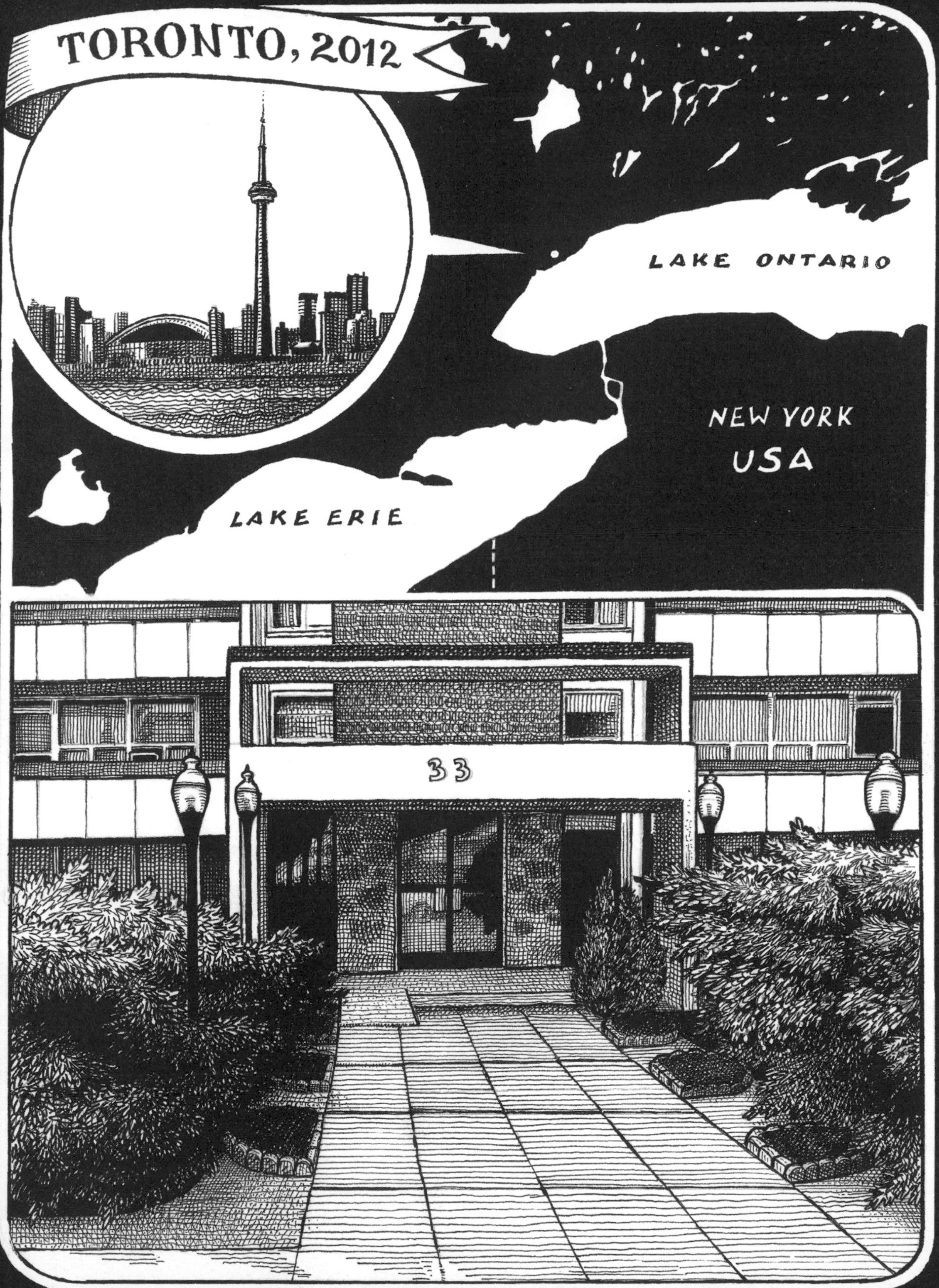
TORONTO, 2012
LAKE ONTARIO
NEW YORK
USA
LAKE ERIE
33

THE FOOD SUPPLY IS SCARCE YET IN HIGH DEMAND AS THERE ARE JUST TOO MANY MOUTHS TO FEED...

HUNGRY CHICKS BEG FOR FOOD AND ARE IN TURN PUNISHED BY THE PARENTS...

EVENTUALLY THEY WILL STOP BEGGING ALTOGETHER AND STARVE TO DEATH. OUT OF THE ROOST OF NINE ONLY TWO OR THREE COOT CHICKS WILL SURVIVE AND MAKE IT TO ADULTHOOD.

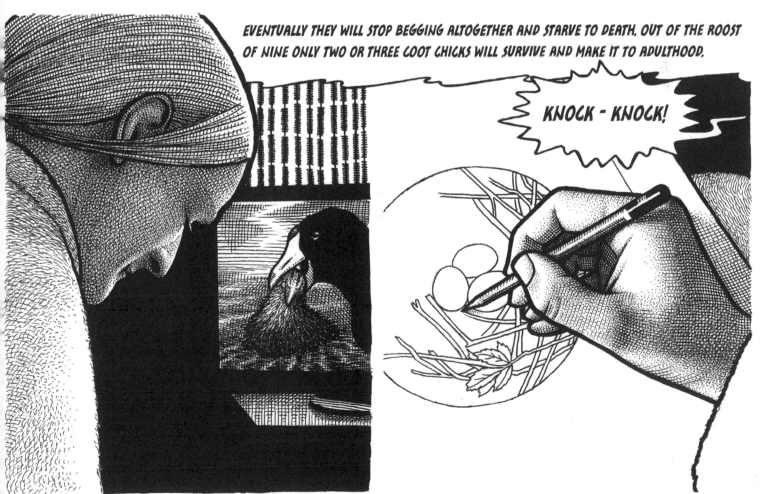

KNOCK - KNOCK!

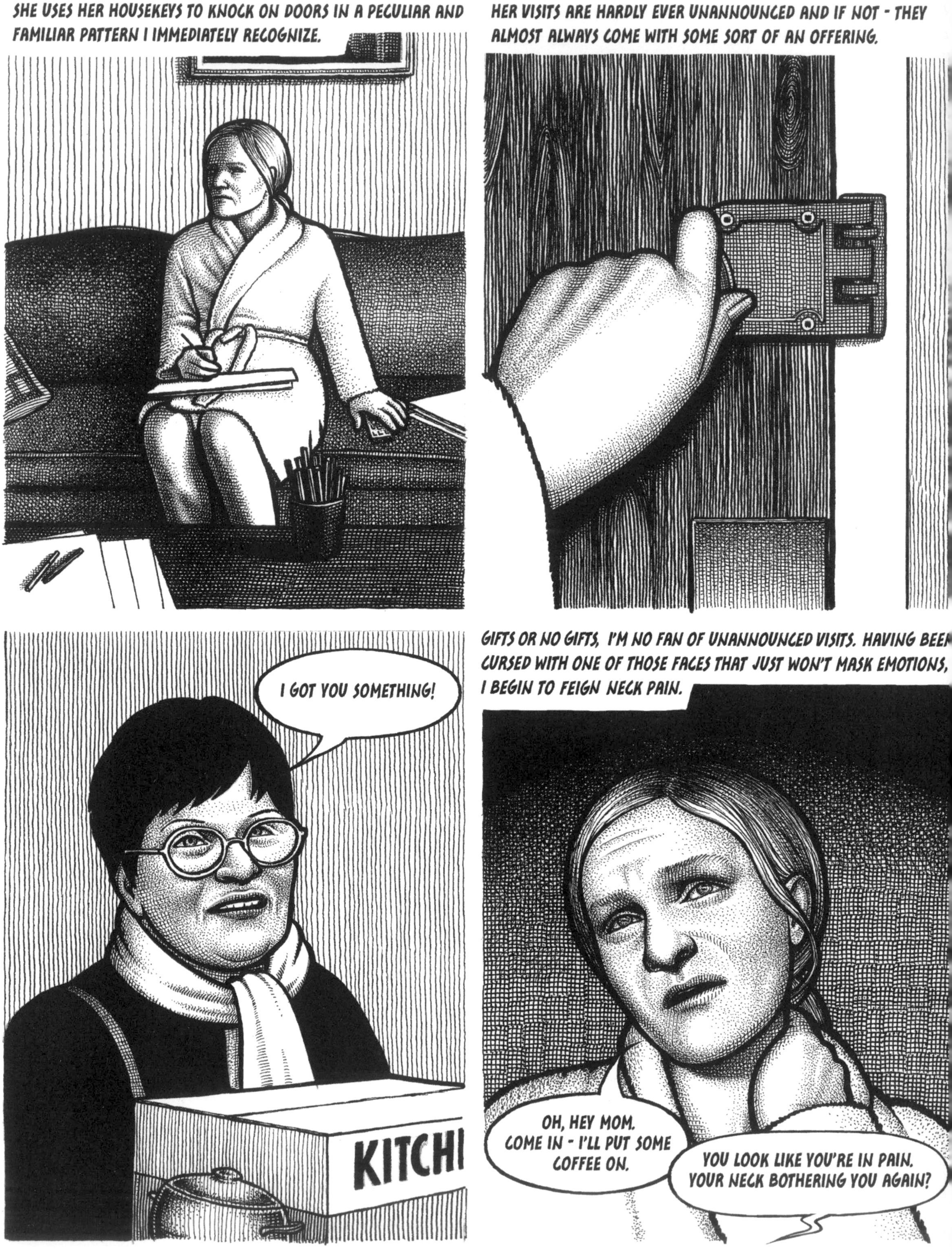
SHE USES HER HOUSEKEYS TO KNOCK ON DOORS IN A PECULIAR AND FAMILIAR PATTERN I IMMEDIATELY RECOGNIZE.
HER VISITS ARE HARDLY EVER UNANNOUNCED AND IF NOT - THEY ALMOST ALWAYS COME WITH SOME SORT OF AN OFFERING.
I GOT YOU SOMETHING!
KITCH
GIFTS OR NO GIFTS, I'M NO FAN OF UNANNOUNCED VISITS. HAVING BEEN CURSED WITH ONE OF THOSE FACES THAT JUST WON'T MASK EMOTIONS, I BEGIN TO FEIGN NECK PAIN.
OH, HEY MOM. COME IN - I'LL PUT SOME COFFEE ON.
YOU LOOK LIKE YOU'RE IN PAIN. YOUR NECK BOTHERING YOU AGAIN?

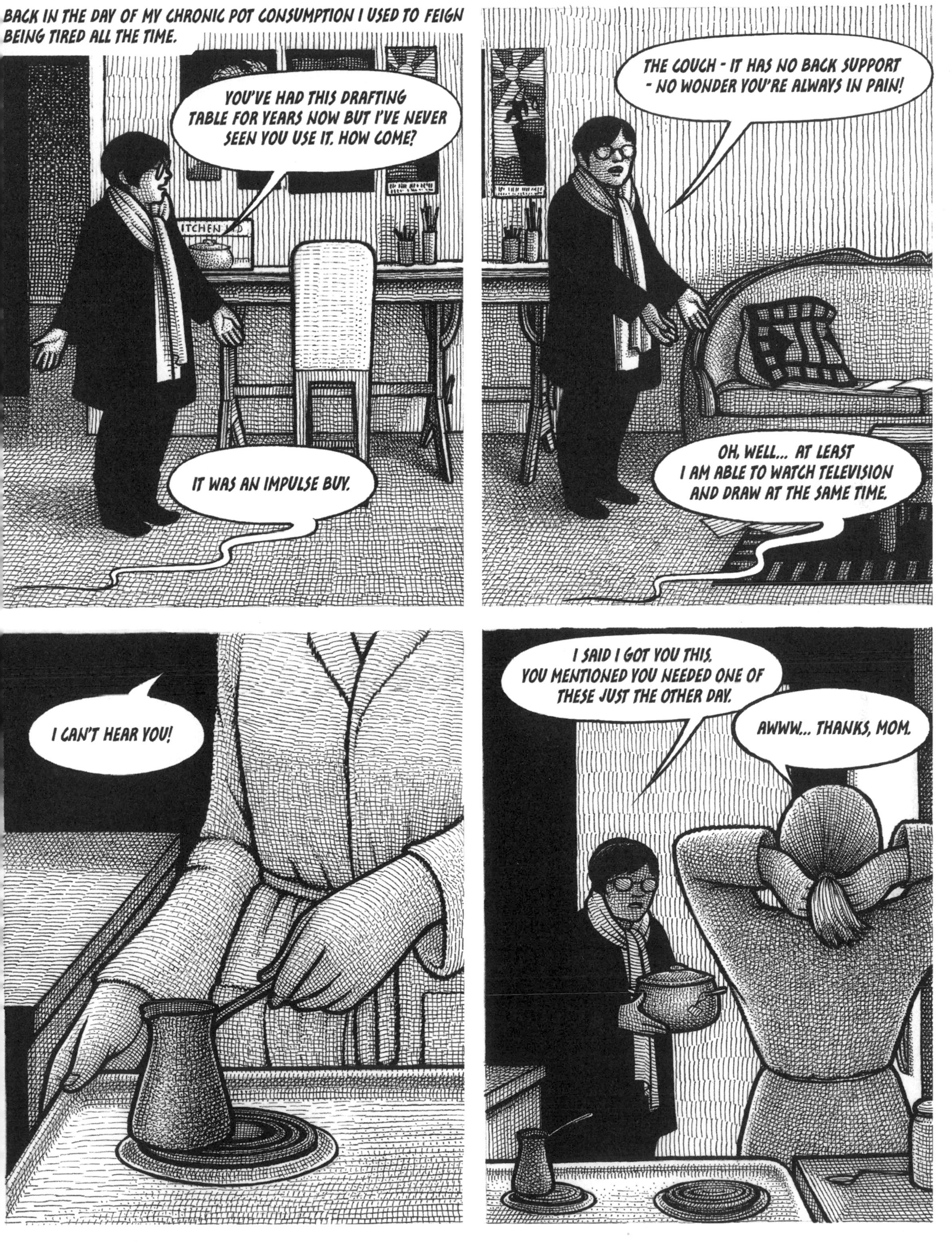
BACK IN THE DAY OF MY CHRONIC POT CONSUMPTION I USED TO FEIGN BEING TIRED ALL THE TIME.
YOU'VE HAD THIS DRAFTING TABLE FOR YEARS NOW BUT I'VE NEVER SEEN YOU USE IT. HOW COME?
IT WAS AN IMPULSE BUY.
THE COUCH - IT HAS NO BACK SUPPORT - NO WONDER YOU'RE ALWAYS IN PAIN!
OH, WELL... AT LEAST I AM ABLE TO WATCH TELEVISION AND DRAW AT THE SAME TIME.
I CAN'T HEAR YOU!
I SAID I GOT YOU THIS. YOU MENTIONED YOU NEEDED ONE OF THESE JUST THE OTHER DAY.
AWWW... THANKS, MOM.

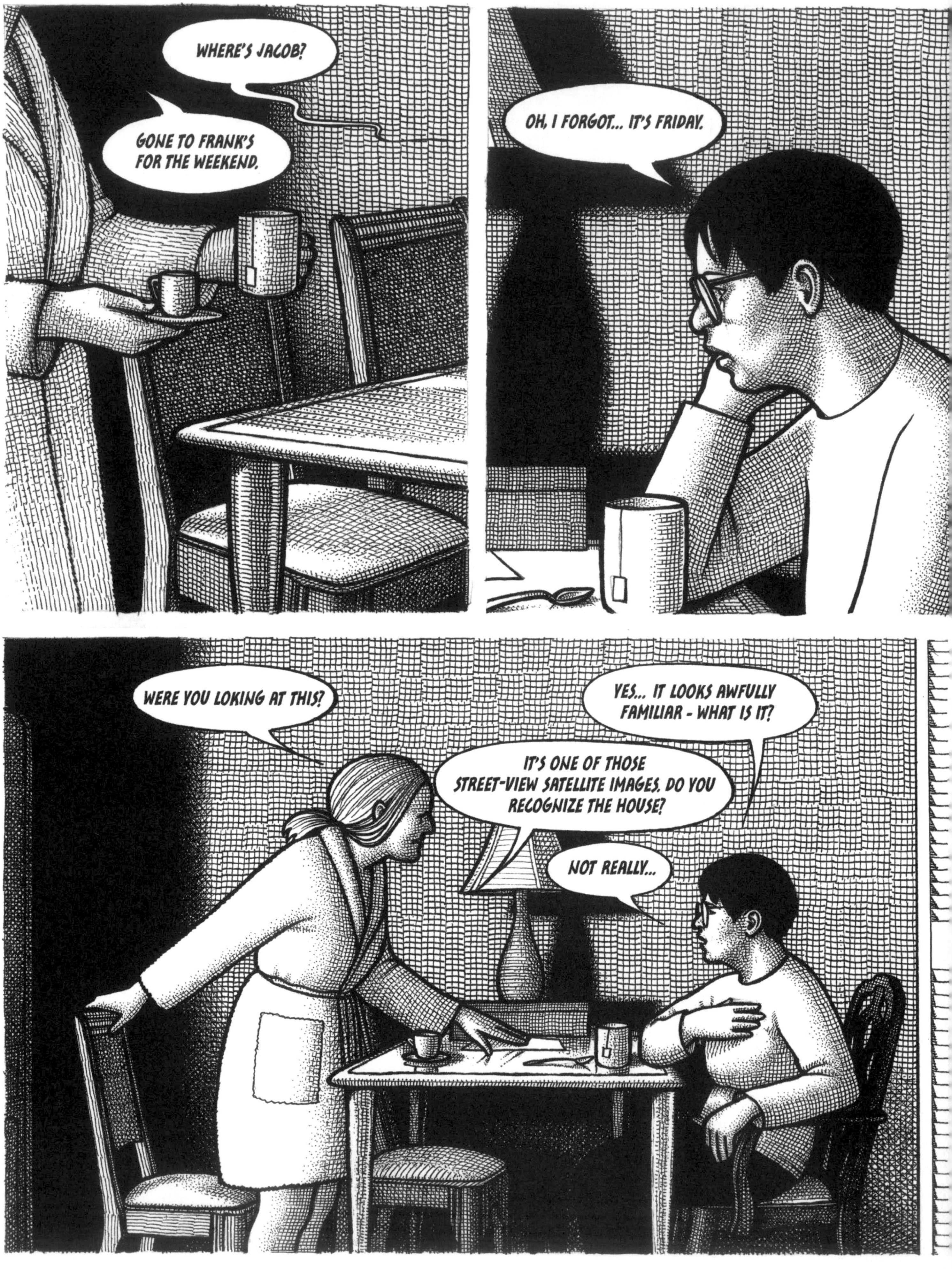
WHERE'S JACOB?
GONE TO FRANK'S FOR THE WEEKEND.
OH, I FORGOT... IT'S FRIDAY.
WERE YOU LOKING AT THIS?
YES... IT LOOKS AWFULLY FAMILIAR - WHAT IS IT?
IT'S ONE OF THOSE STREET-VIEW SATELLITE IMAGES. DO YOU RECOGNIZE THE HOUSE?
NOT REALLY...

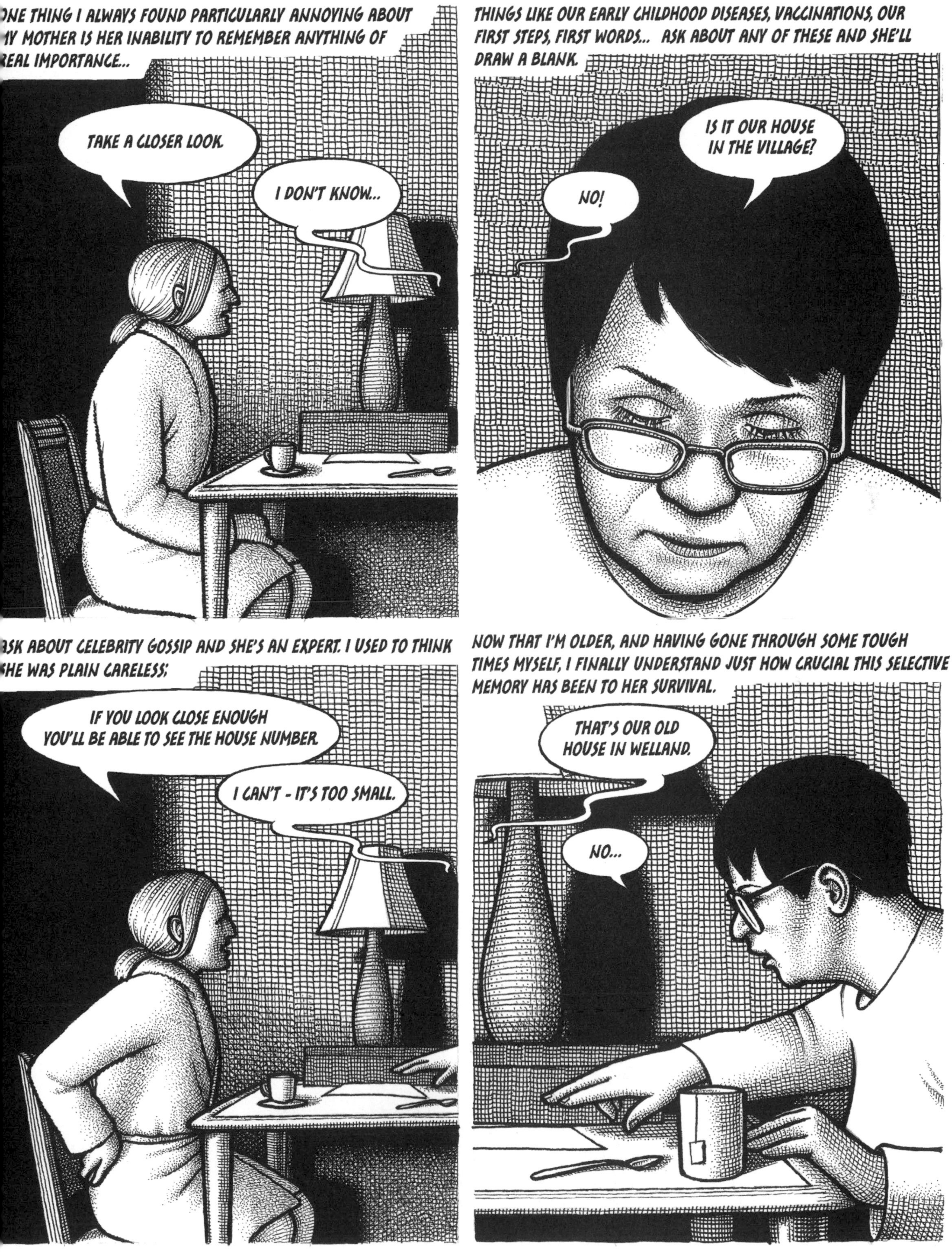
ONE THING I ALWAYS FOUND PARTICULARLY ANNOYING ABOUT MY MOTHER IS HER INABILITY TO REMEMBER ANYTHING OF REAL IMPORTANCE...
TAKE A CLOSER LOOK.
I DON'T KNOW...
THINGS LIKE OUR EARLY CHILDHOOD DISEASES, VACCINATIONS, OUR FIRST STEPS, FIRST WORDS... ASK ABOUT ANY OF THESE AND SHE'LL DRAW A BLANK.
IS IT OUR HOUSE IN THE VILLAGE?
NO!
ASK ABOUT CELEBRITY GOSSIP AND SHE'S AN EXPERT. I USED TO THINK SHE WAS PLAIN CARELESS;
IF YOU LOOK CLOSE ENOUGH YOU'LL BE ABLE TO SEE THE HOUSE NUMBER.
I CAN'T - IT'S TOO SMALL.
NOW THAT I'M OLDER, AND HAVING GONE THROUGH SOME TOUGH TIMES MYSELF, I FINALLY UNDERSTAND JUST HOW CRUCIAL THIS SELECTIVE MEMORY HAS BEEN TO HER SURVIVAL.
THAT'S OUR OLD HOUSE IN WELLAND.
NO...

BECAUSE TO HER, CHOOSING TO FORGET THIS LITTLE HOUSE OF OURS WAS A DESPERATE ATTEMPT TO SUPPRESS ALL THE MEMORIES IT ONCE HELD, GOOD AND BAD.

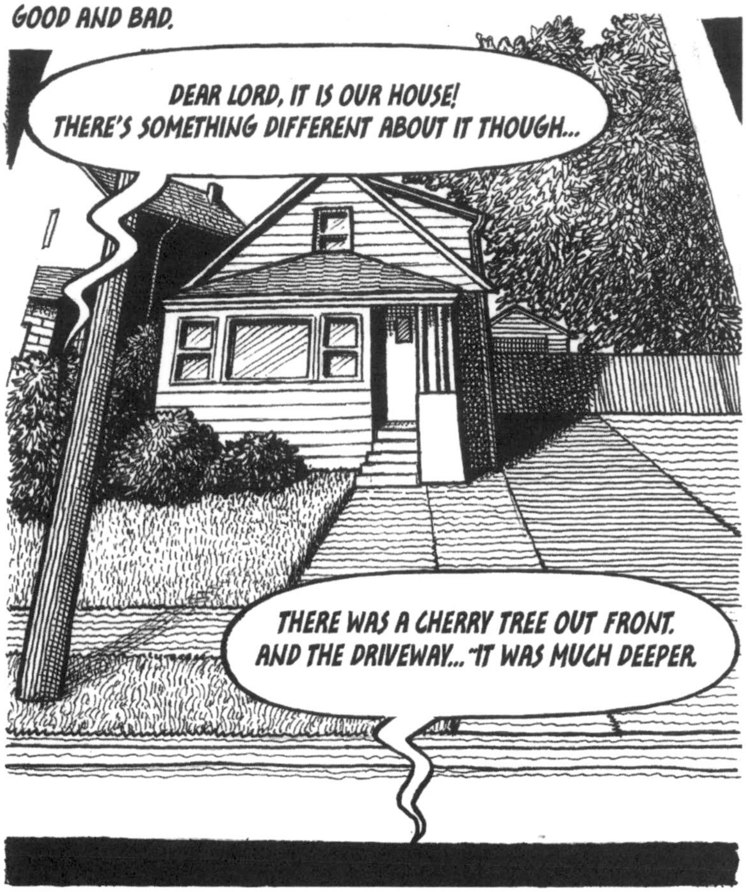
DEAR LORD, IT IS OUR HOUSE! THERE'S SOMETHING DIFFERENT ABOUT IT THOUGH...
THERE WAS A CHERRY TREE OUT FRONT. AND THE DRIVEWAY...-IT WAS MUCH DEEPER.

MEMORIES OF A LIFE REMOVED BY MORE THAN THREE AND A HALF DECADES OF TRYING DESPERATELY NOT TO LOOK BACK.

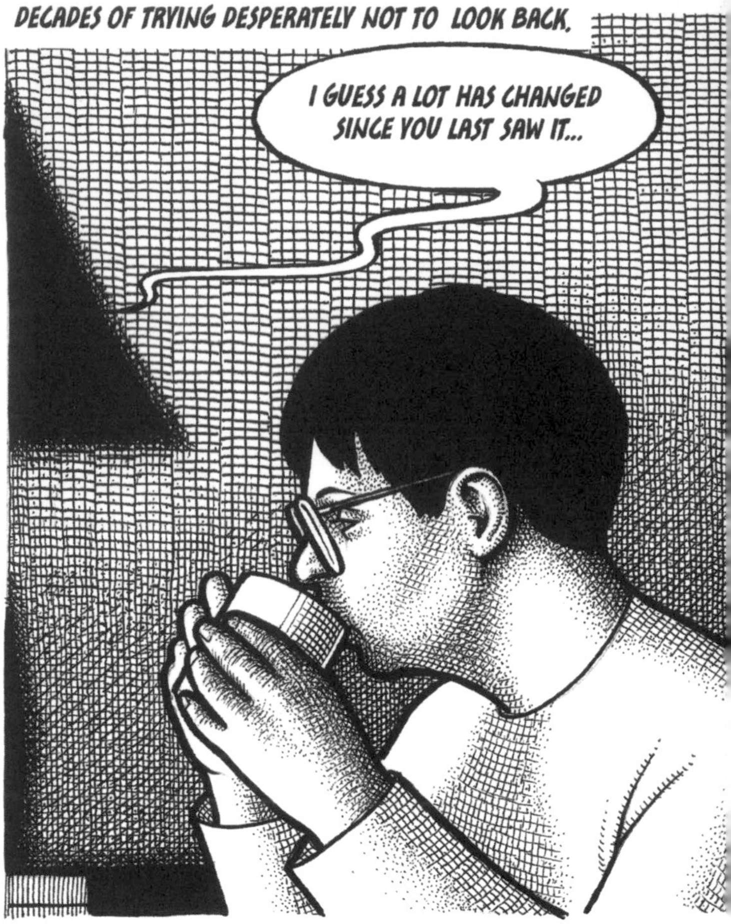
I GUESS A LOT HAS CHANGED SINCE YOU LAST SAW IT...

I HAVE NUDGED THE FLOODGATES SO NONCHALANTLY, PAUSING FOR A MERE MOMENT TO REFLECT ON THE POTENTIAL REPERCUSSIONS OF MY ACTIONS. HOW WILL SHE COPE? WILL SHE FLOAT? WILL SHE SINK?

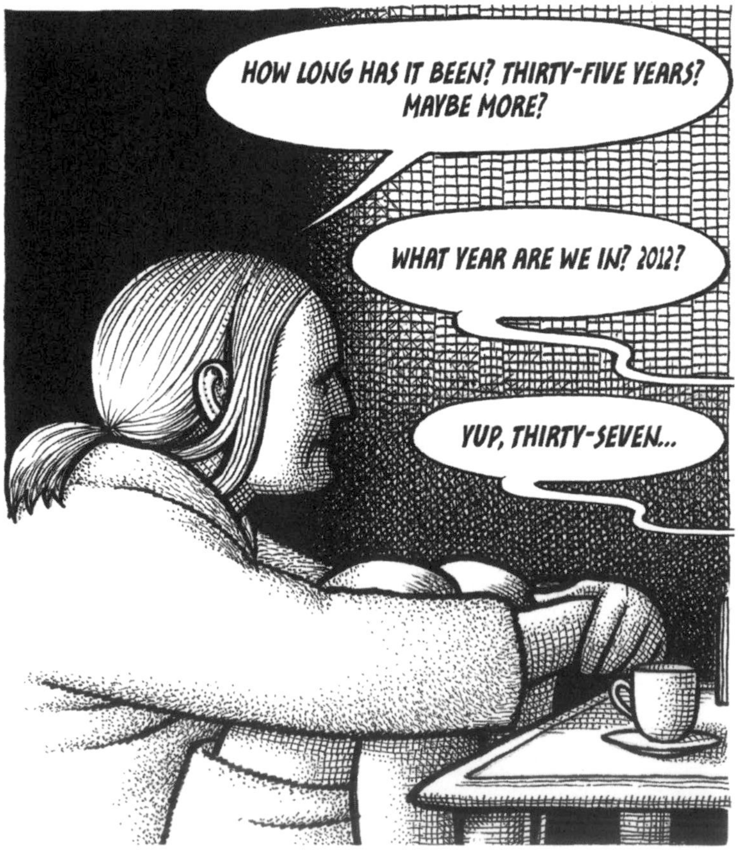
HOW LONG HAS IT BEEN? THIRTY-FIVE YEARS? MAYBE MORE?
WHAT YEAR ARE WE IN? 2012?
YUP, THIRTY-SEVEN...

AND THEN I RATIONALIZE; I TELL MYSELF: "OH, WELL, THE ABILITY TO FLOAT DOES NOT NECESSARILY GUARANTEE SURVIVAL. JUST THINK OF THOSE POOR COOT CHICKS."

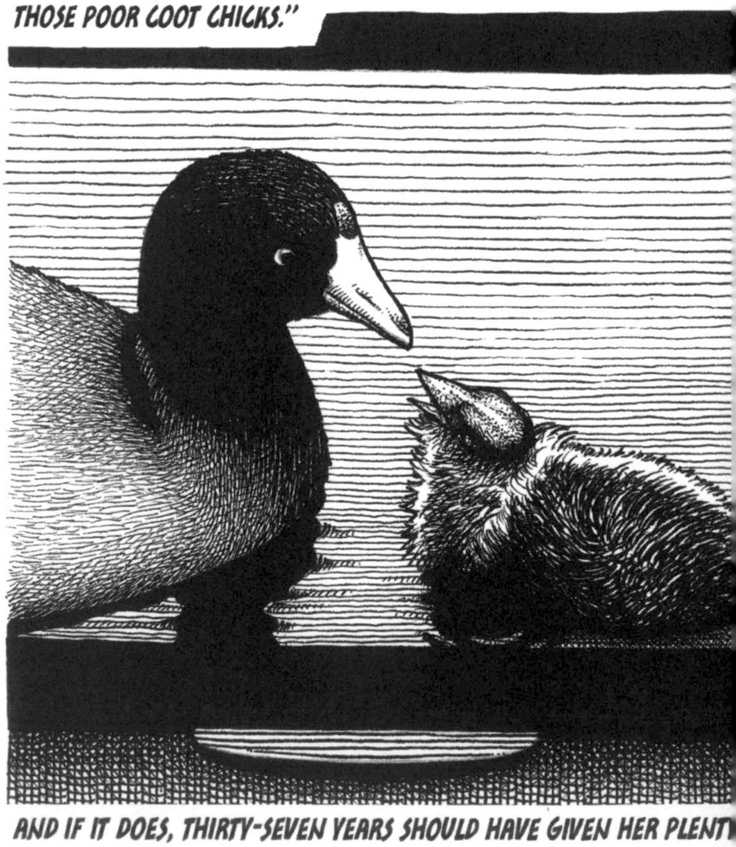

AND IF IT DOES, THIRTY-SEVEN YEARS SHOULD HAVE GIVEN HER PLENTY OF TIME TO LEARN.

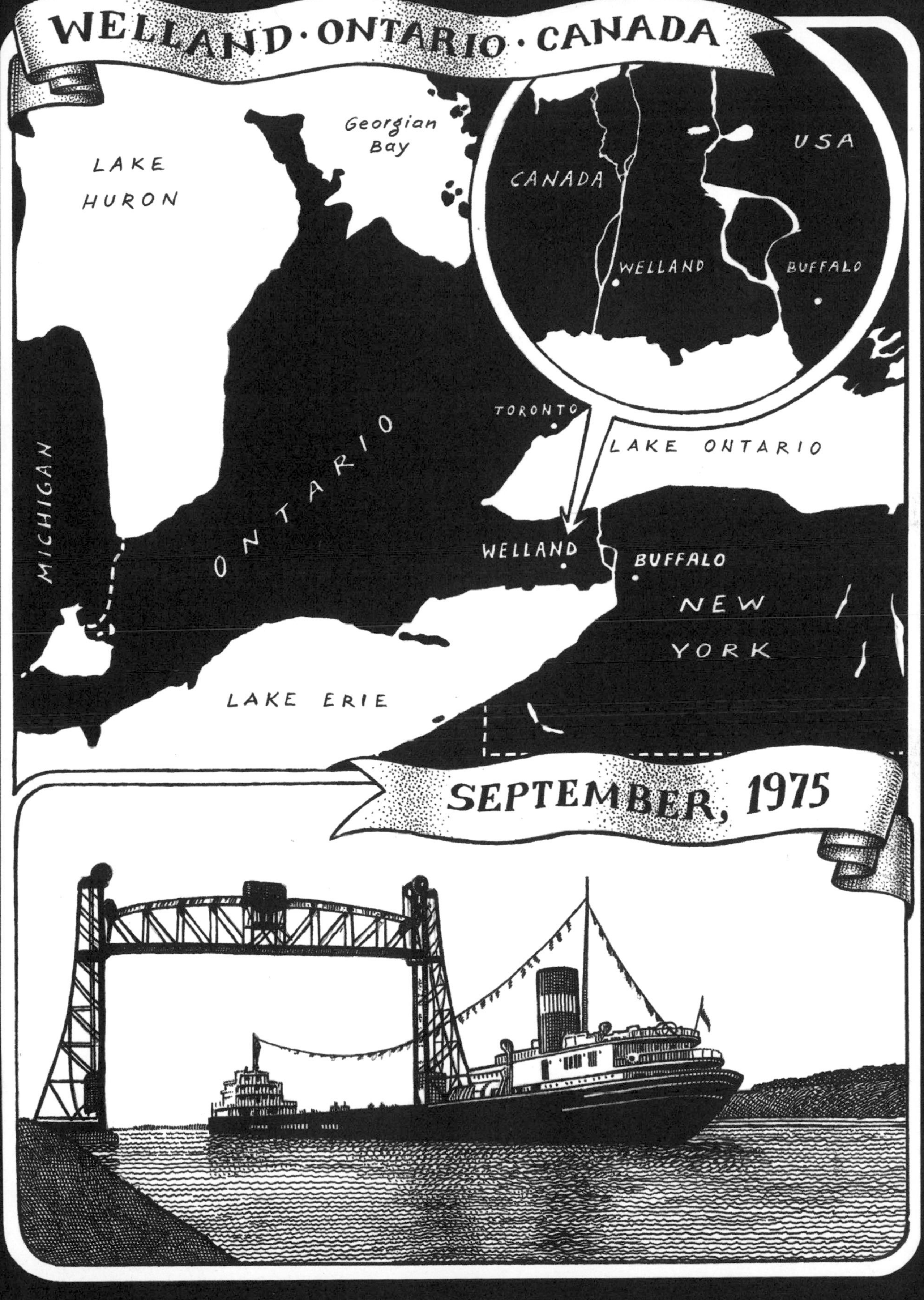
WELLAND · ONTARIO · CANADA
Georgian Bay
LAKE HURON
CANADA
USA
WELLAND
BUFFALO
TORONTO
LAKE ONTARIO
ONTARIO
MICHIGAN
WELLAND
BUFFALO
NEW YORK
LAKE ERIE
SEPTEMBER, 1975

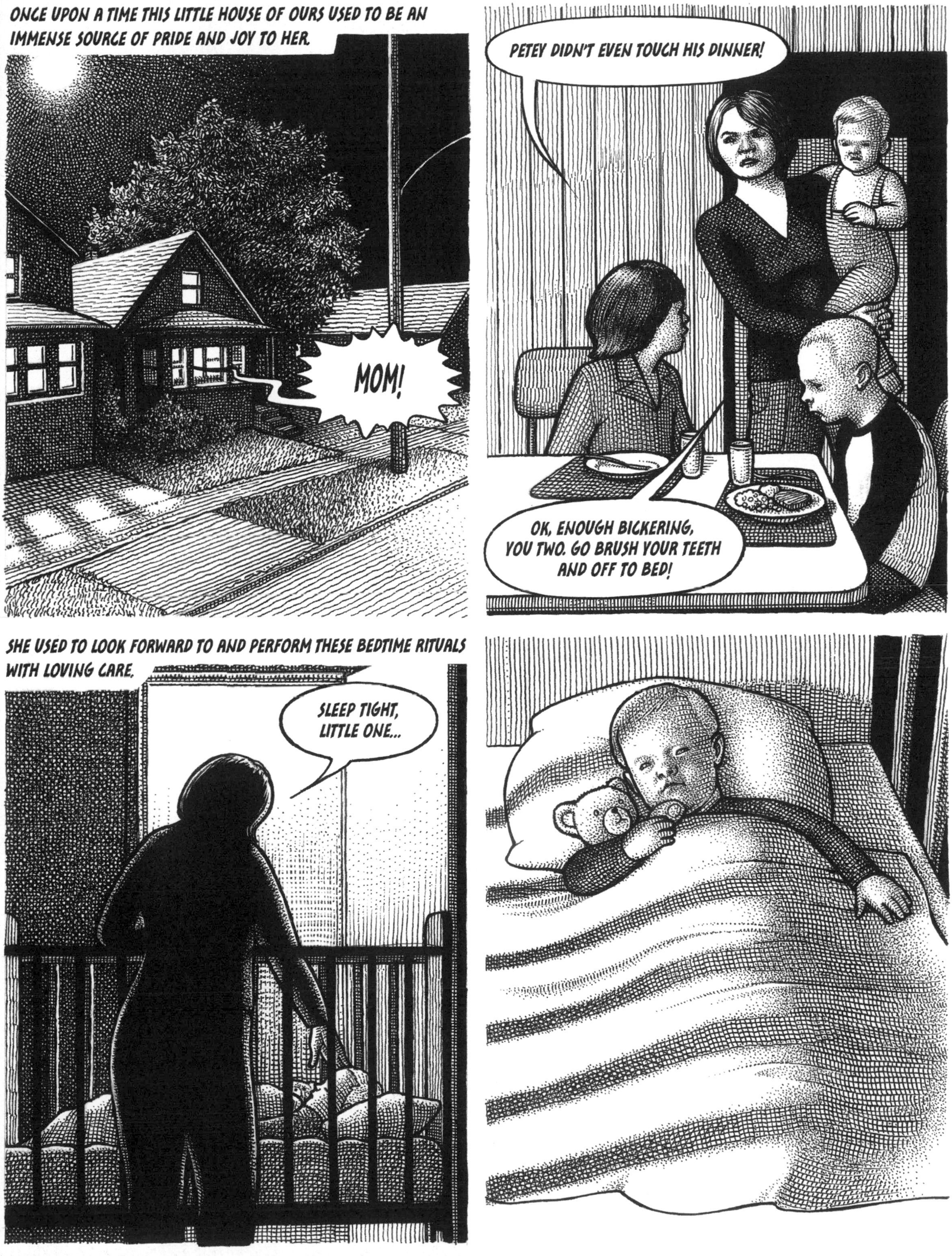
ONCE UPON A TIME THIS LITTLE HOUSE OF OURS USED TO BE AN IMMENSE SOURCE OF PRIDE AND JOY TO HER.
MOM!
PETEY DIDN'T EVEN TOUCH HIS DINNER!
OK, ENOUGH BICKERING, YOU TWO. GO BRUSH YOUR TEETH AND OFF TO BED!
SHE USED TO LOOK FORWARD TO AND PERFORM THESE BEDTIME RITUALS WITH LOVING CARE.
SLEEP TIGHT, LITTLE ONE...

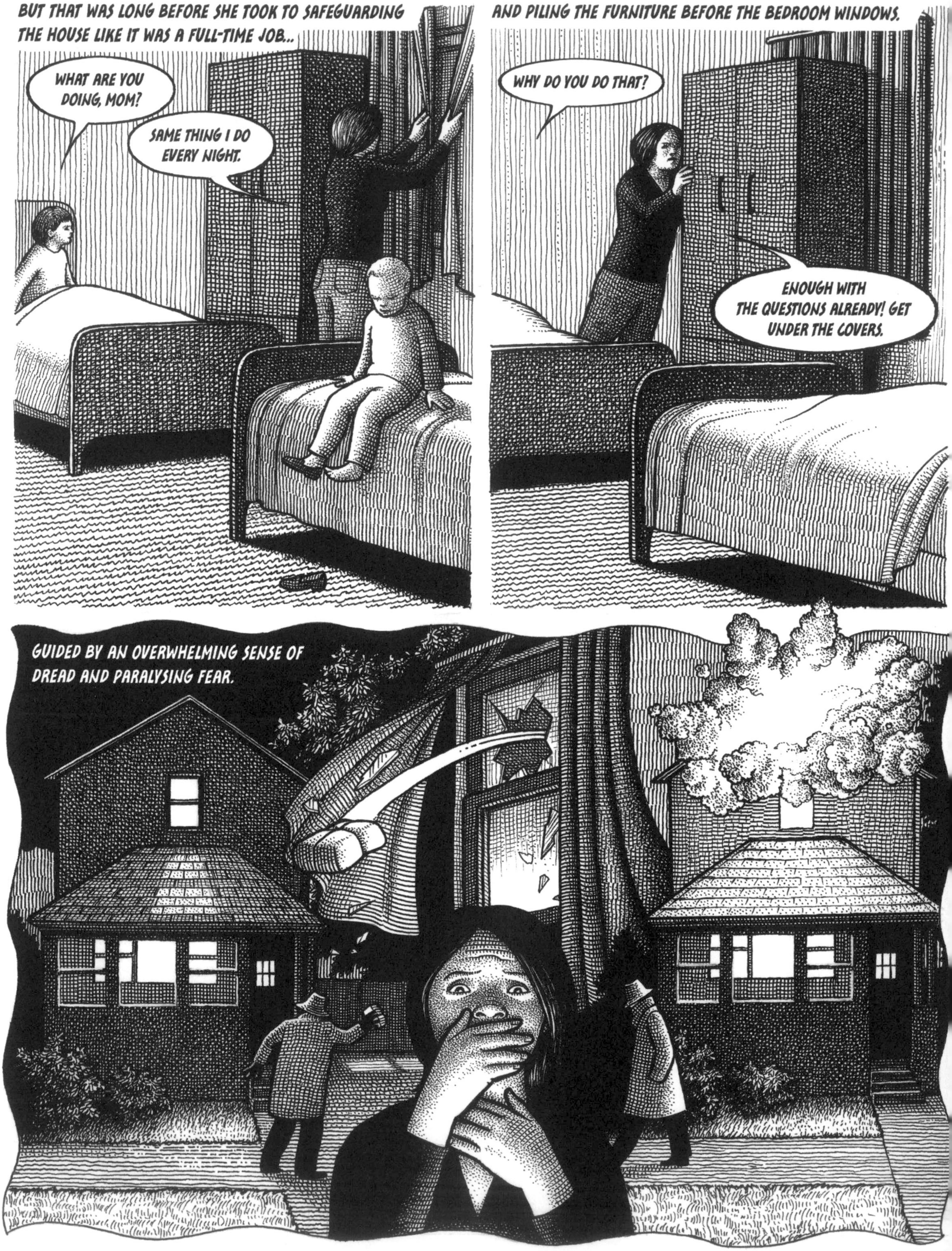
BUT THAT WAS LONG BEFORE SHE TOOK TO SAFEGUARDING THE HOUSE LIKE IT WAS A FULL-TIME JOB...
WHAT ARE YOU DOING, MOM?
SAME THING I DO EVERY NIGHT.
AND PILING THE FURNITURE BEFORE THE BEDROOM WINDOWS.
WHY DO YOU DO THAT?
ENOUGH WITH THE QUESTIONS ALREADY! GET UNDER THE COVERS.
GUIDED BY AN OVERWHELMING SENSE OF DREAD AND PARALYSING FEAR.

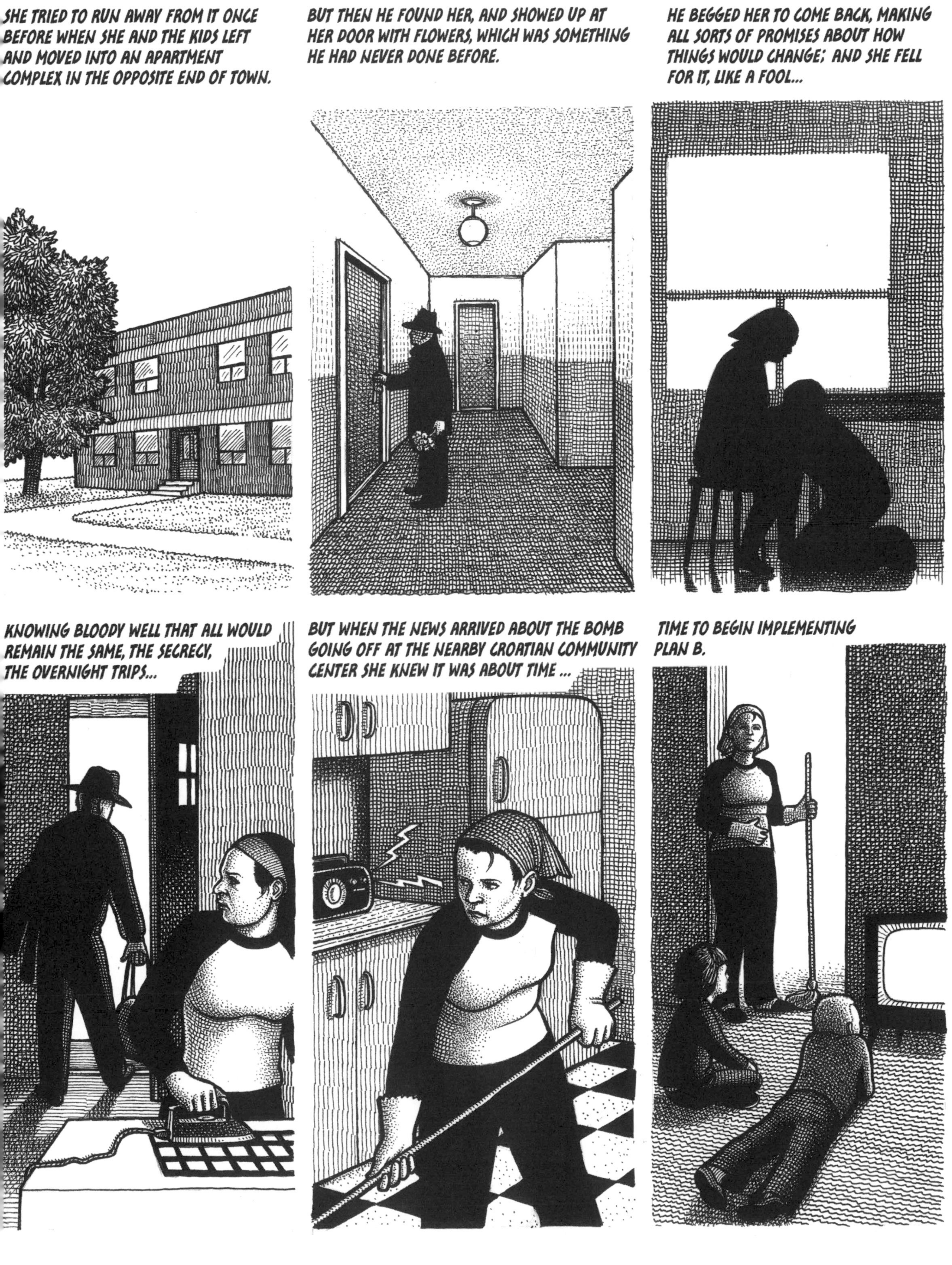
SHE TRIED TO RUN AWAY FROM IT ONCE BEFORE WHEN SHE AND THE KIDS LEFT AND MOVED INTO AN APARTMENT COMPLEX IN THE OPPOSITE END OF TOWN.
BUT THEN HE FOUND HER, AND SHOWED UP AT HER DOOR WITH FLOWERS, WHICH WAS SOMETHING HE HAD NEVER DONE BEFORE.
HE BEGGED HER TO COME BACK, MAKING ALL SORTS OF PROMISES ABOUT HOW THINGS WOULD CHANGE; AND SHE FELL FOR IT, LIKE A FOOL...
KNOWING BLOODY WELL THAT ALL WOULD REMAIN THE SAME, THE SECRECY, THE OVERNIGHT TRIPS...
BUT WHEN THE NEWS ARRIVED ABOUT THE BOMB GOING OFF AT THE NEARBY CROATIAN COMMUNITY CENTER SHE KNEW IT WAS ABOUT TIME ...
TIME TO BEGIN IMPLEMENTING PLAN B.

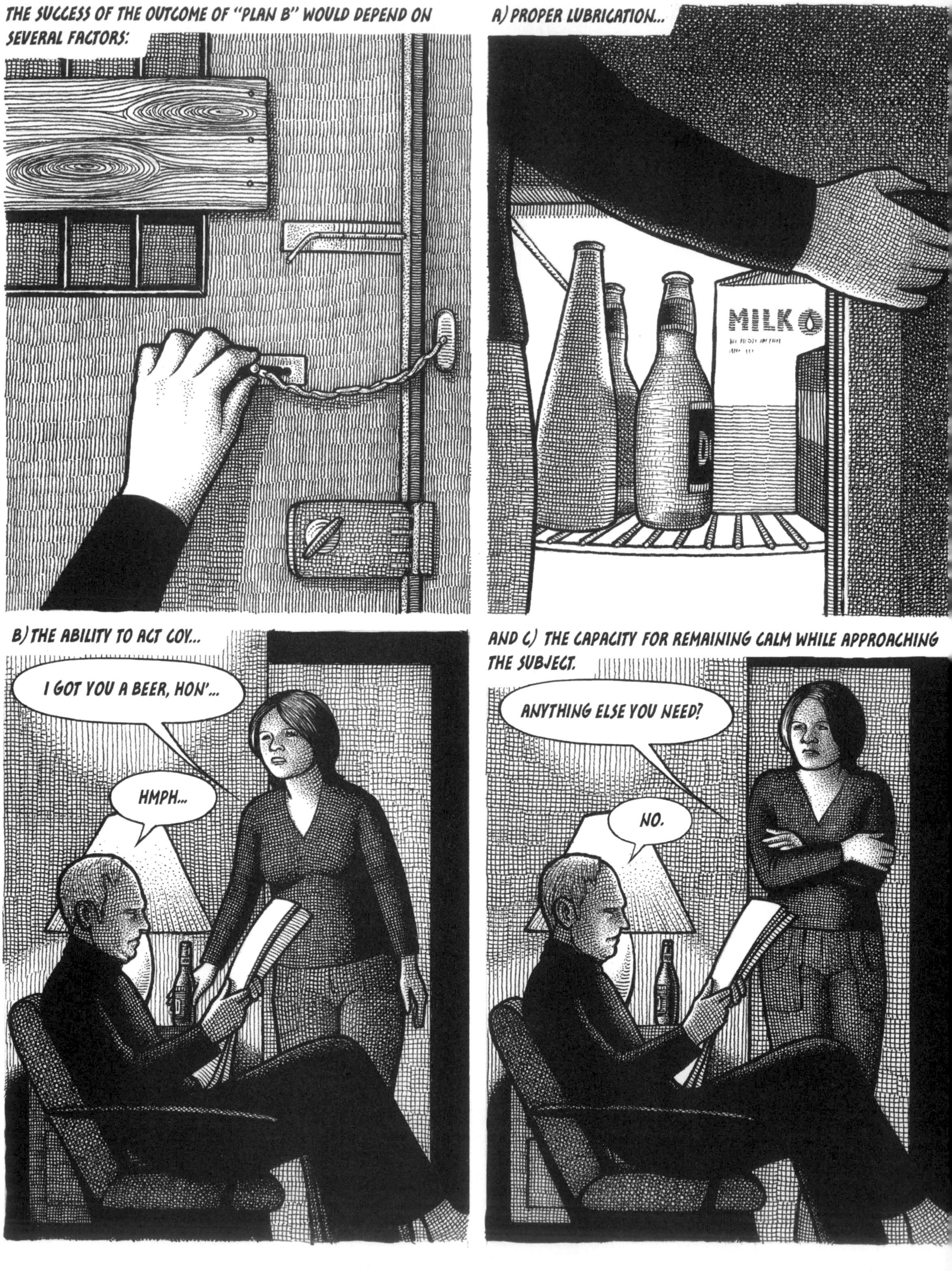
THE SUCCESS OF THE OUTCOME OF "PLAN B" WOULD DEPEND ON SEVERAL FACTORS:
A) PROPER LUBRICATION...
MILK
B) THE ABILITY TO ACT COY...
I GOT YOU A BEER, HON'...
HMPH...
AND C) THE CAPACITY FOR REMAINING CALM WHILE APPROACHING THE SUBJECT.
ANYTHING ELSE YOU NEED?
NO.

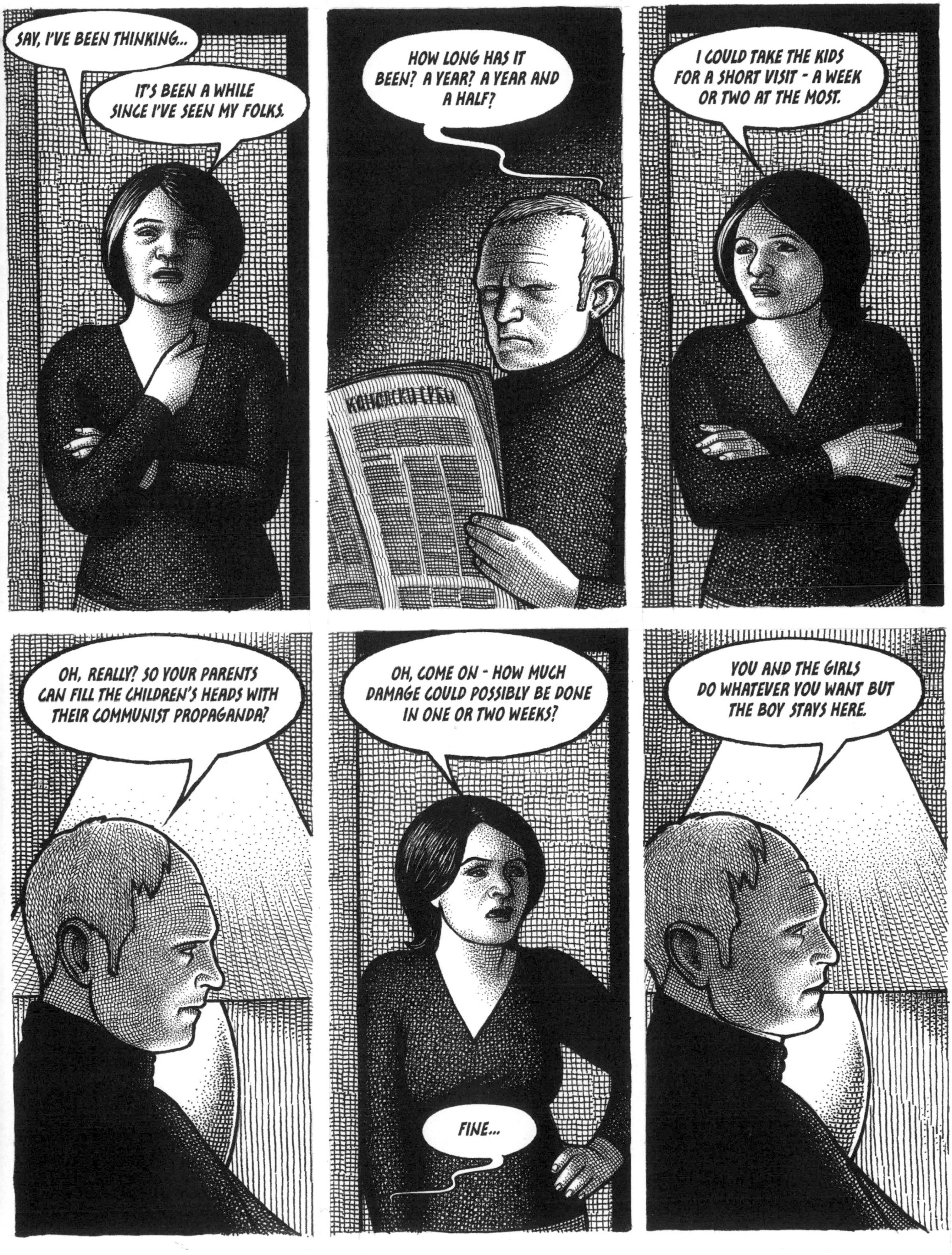
SAY, I'VE BEEN THINKING...
IT'S BEEN A WHILE SINCE I'VE SEEN MY FOLKS.
HOW LONG HAS IT BEEN? A YEAR? A YEAR AND A HALF?
I COULD TAKE THE KIDS FOR A SHORT VISIT - A WEEK OR TWO AT THE MOST.
OH, REALLY? SO YOUR PARENTS CAN FILL THE CHILDREN'S HEADS WITH THEIR COMMUNIST PROPAGANDA?
OH, COME ON - HOW MUCH DAMAGE COULD POSSIBLY BE DONE IN ONE OR TWO WEEKS?
FINE...
YOU AND THE GIRLS DO WHATEVER YOU WANT BUT THE BOY STAYS HERE.

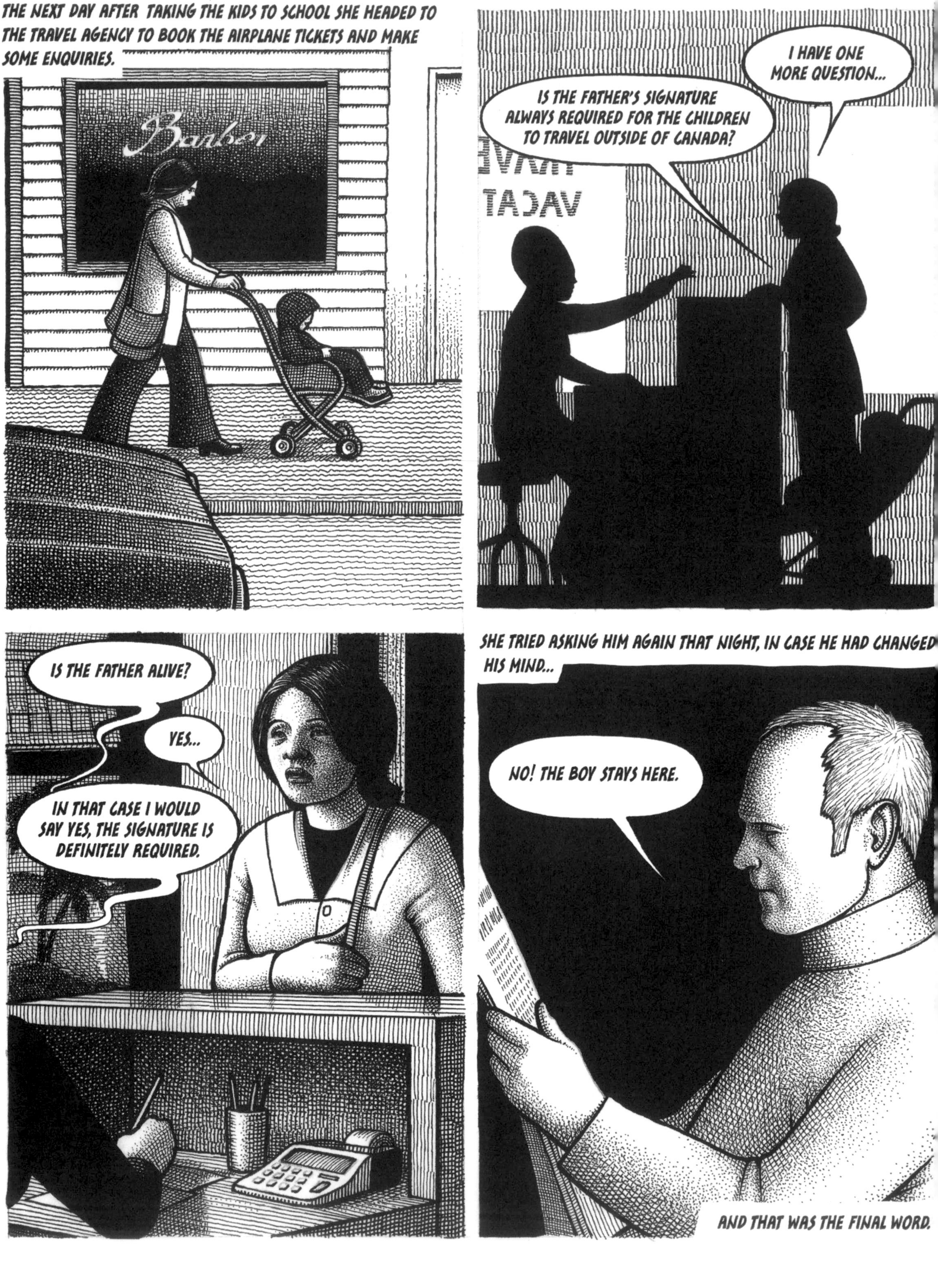
THE NEXT DAY AFTER TAKING THE KIDS TO SCHOOL SHE HEADED TO THE TRAVEL AGENCY TO BOOK THE AIRPLANE TICKETS AND MAKE SOME ENQUIRIES.
Barber
IS THE FATHER'S SIGNATURE ALWAYS REQUIRED FOR THE CHILDREN TO TRAVEL OUTSIDE OF CANADA?
I HAVE ONE MORE QUESTION...
IS THE FATHER ALIVE?
YES...
IN THAT CASE I WOULD SAY YES, THE SIGNATURE IS DEFINITELY REQUIRED.
SHE TRIED ASKING HIM AGAIN THAT NIGHT, IN CASE HE HAD CHANGED HIS MIND...
NO! THE BOY STAYS HERE.
AND THAT WAS THE FINAL WORD.

ON THE EVE OF OUR DEPARTURE WE ATE DINNER IN SILENCE.

MOM WENT ABOUT HER SAFEGUARDING BUSINESS AS USUAL

SHE FINISHED PACKING OUR SUITCASES, LIGHTLY THOUGH, WITH AUTUMN CLOTHES MOSTLY.

APART FROM CHECKING IN ON PETEY SEVERAL TIMES TOO OFTEN, SHE MANAGED TO REMAIN RELATIVELY CALM.

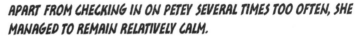

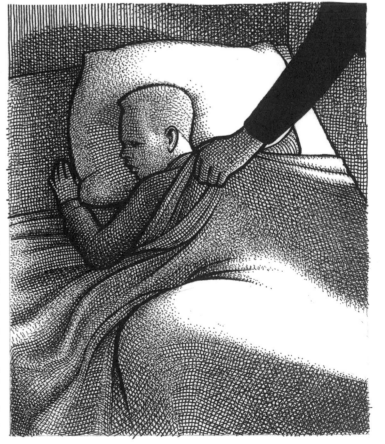

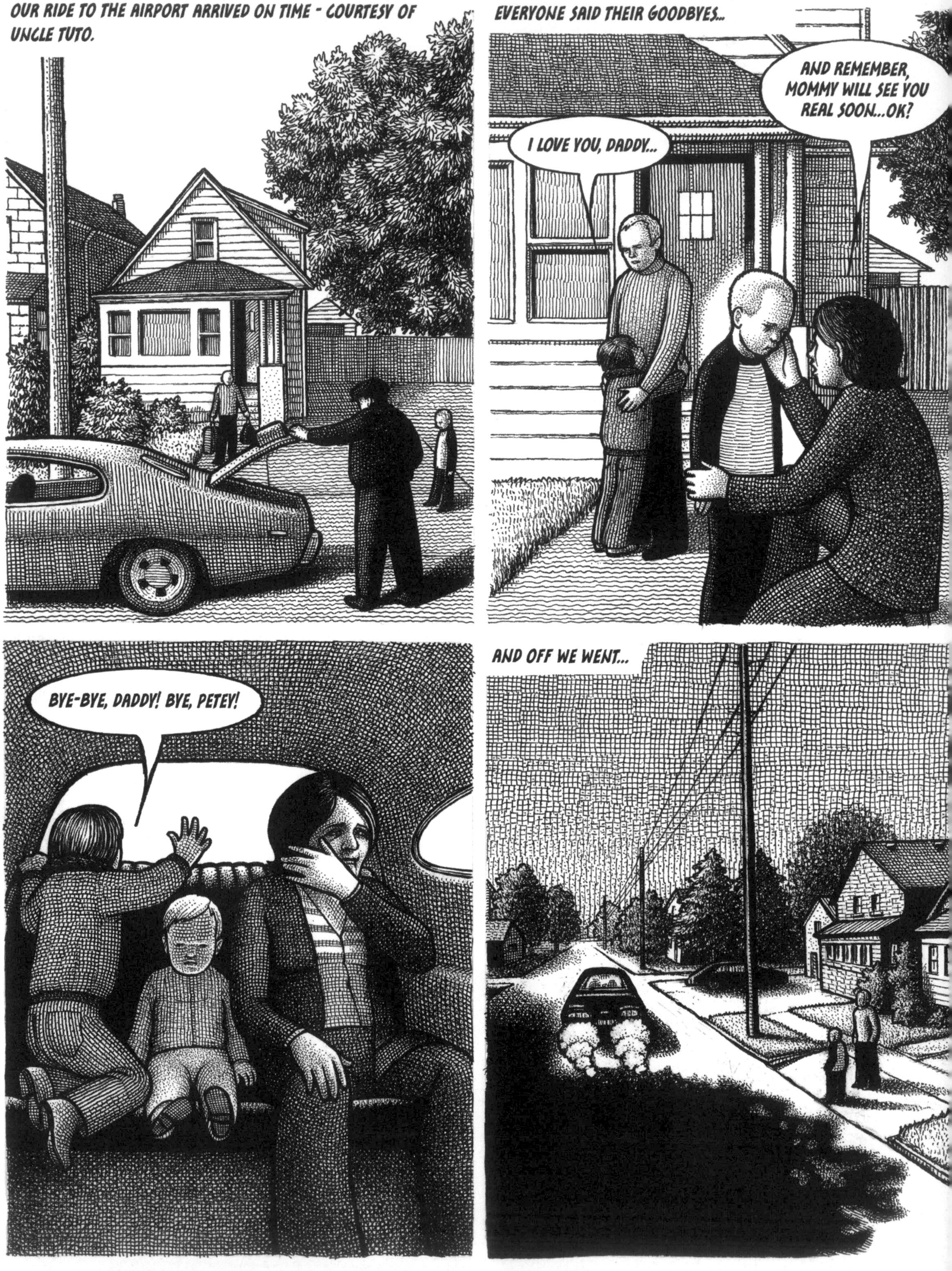
OUR RIDE TO THE AIRPORT ARRIVED ON TIME - COURTESY OF UNCLE TUTO.
EVERYONE SAID THEIR GOODBYES...
I LOVE YOU, DADDY...
AND REMEMBER, MOMMY WILL SEE YOU REAL SOON...OK?
BYE-BYE, DADDY! BYE, PETEY!
AND OFF WE WENT...

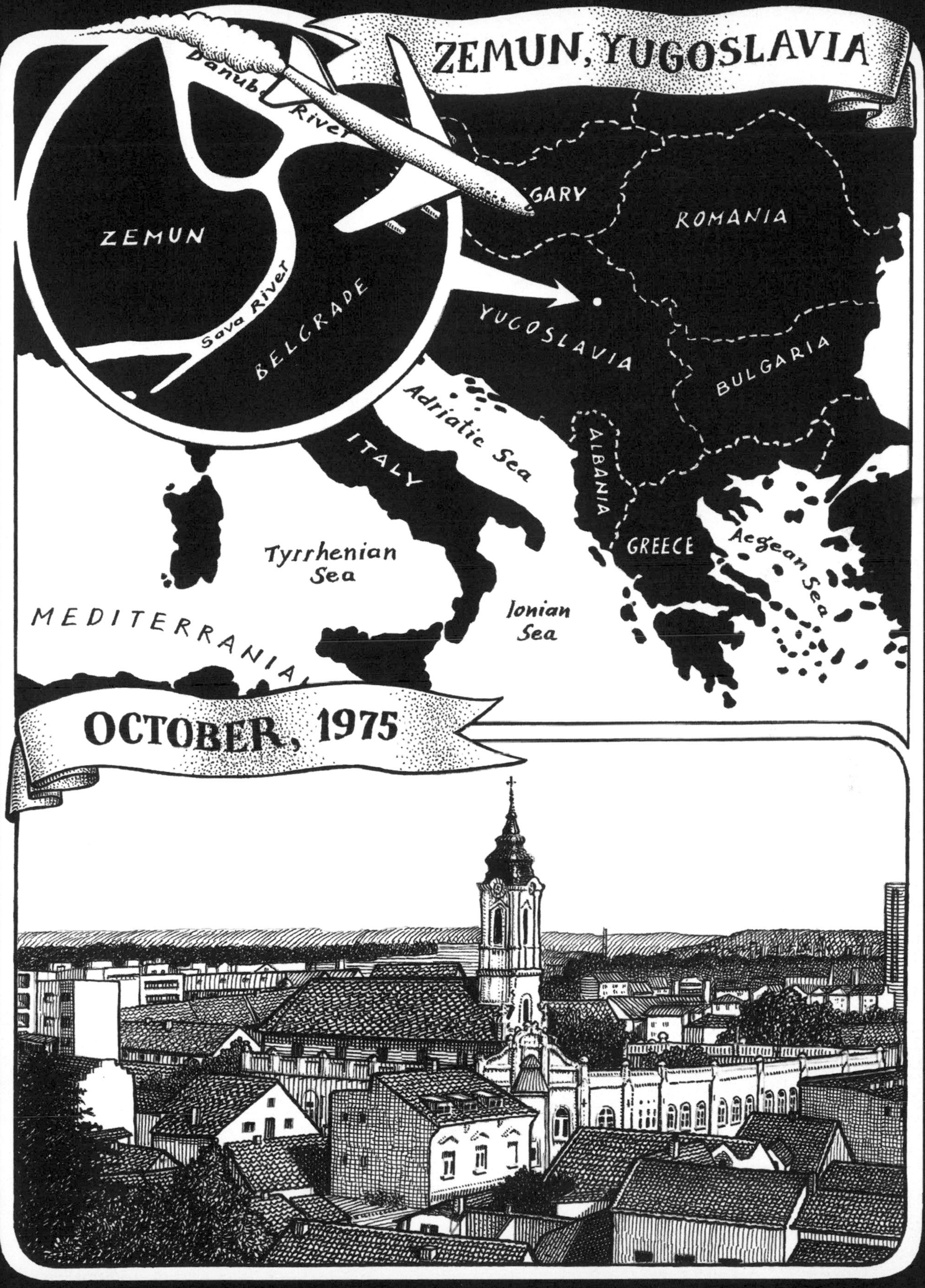
ZEMUN, YUGOSLAVIA
Danube River
ZEMUN
Sava River
BELGRADE
GARY
ROMANIA
YUGOSLAVIA
BULGARIA
Adriatic Sea
ITALY
ALBANIA
GREECE
Aegean Sea
Tyrrhenian Sea
Ionian Sea
MEDITERRANIAN
OCTOBER, 1975

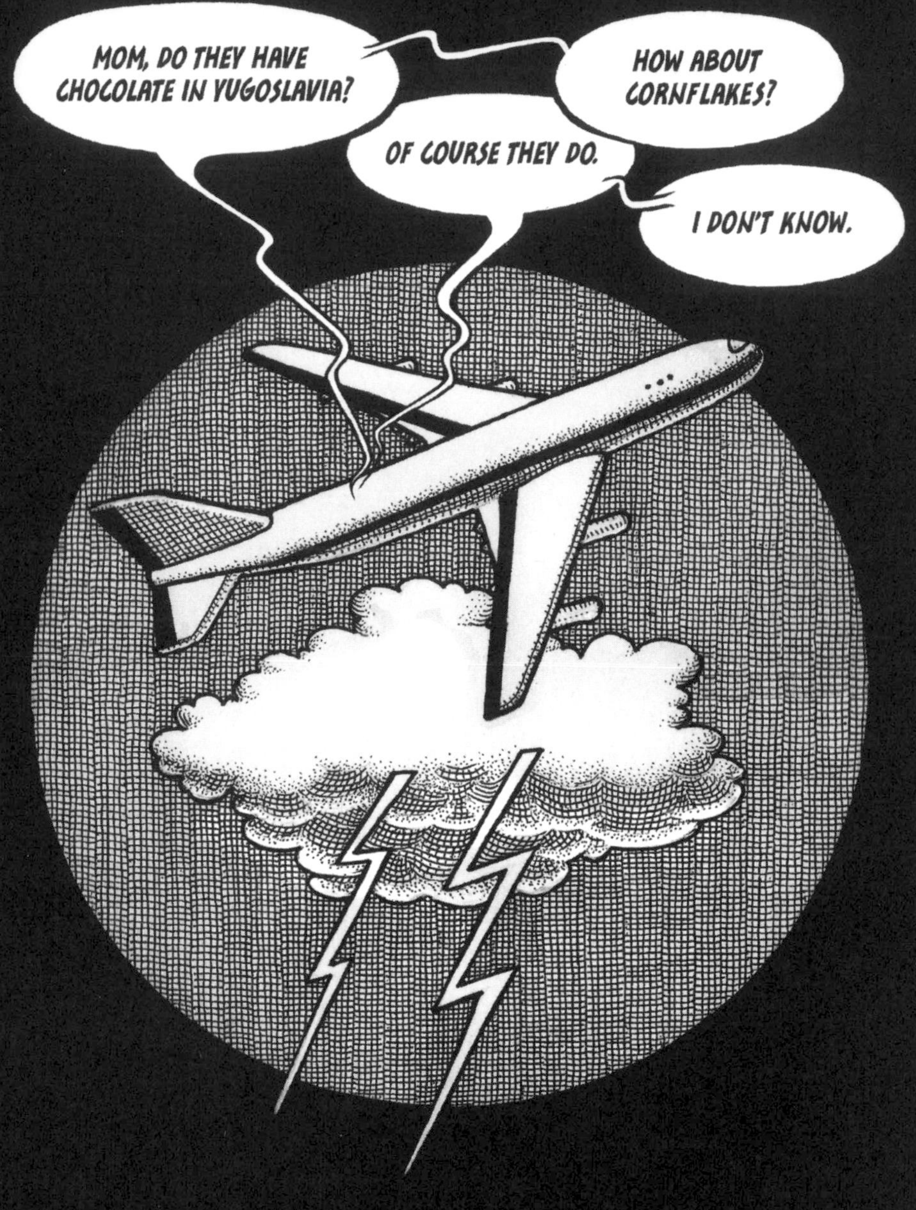

MOM, DO THEY HAVE CHOCOLATE IN YUGOSLAVIA?
OF COURSE THEY DO.
HOW ABOUT CORNFLAKES?
I DON'T KNOW.

WE ARRIVED AT THE SURČIN INTERNATIONAL AIRPORT ON AN UNUSUALLY HOT OCTOBER DAY...

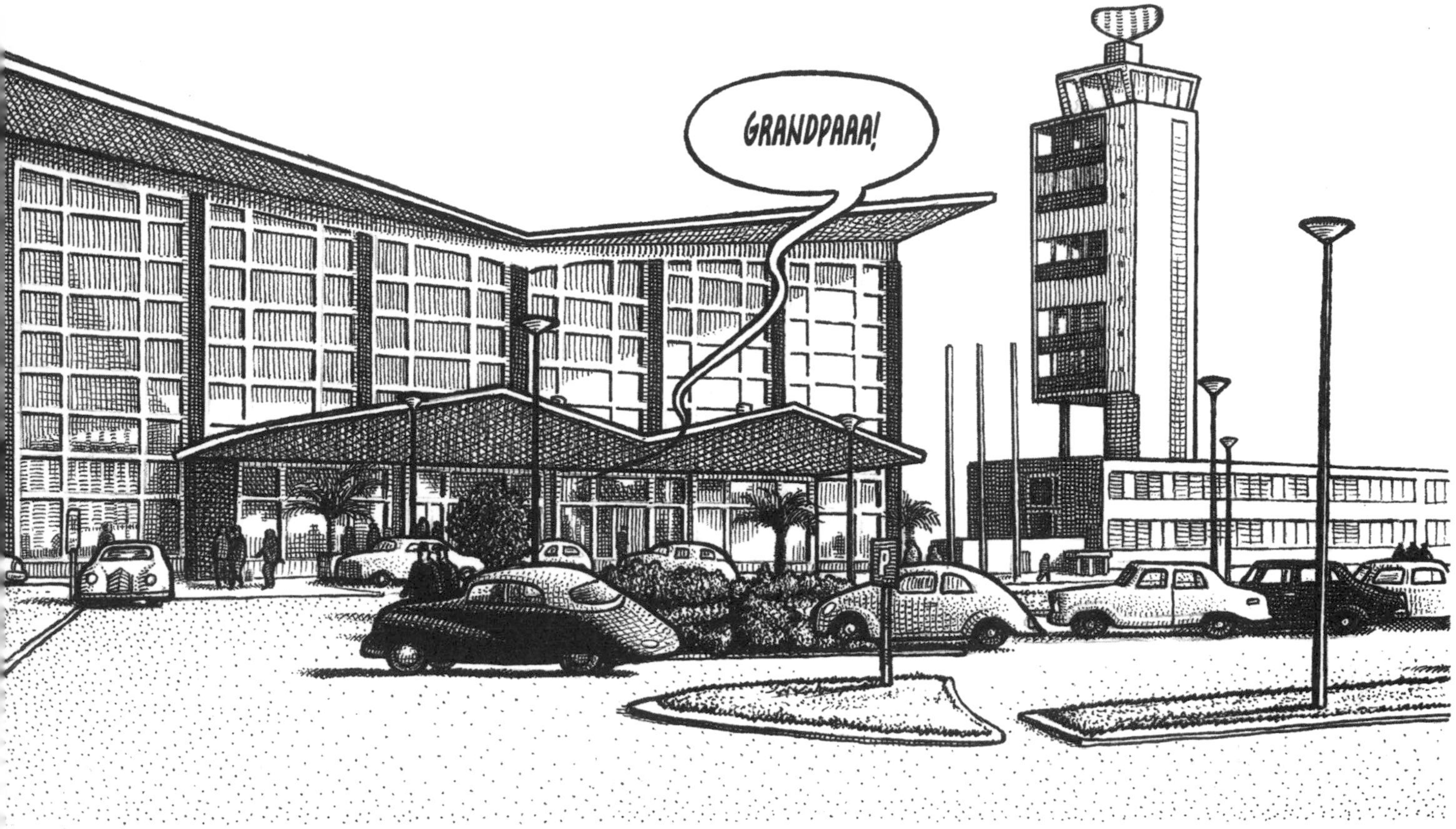
GRANDPAAA!

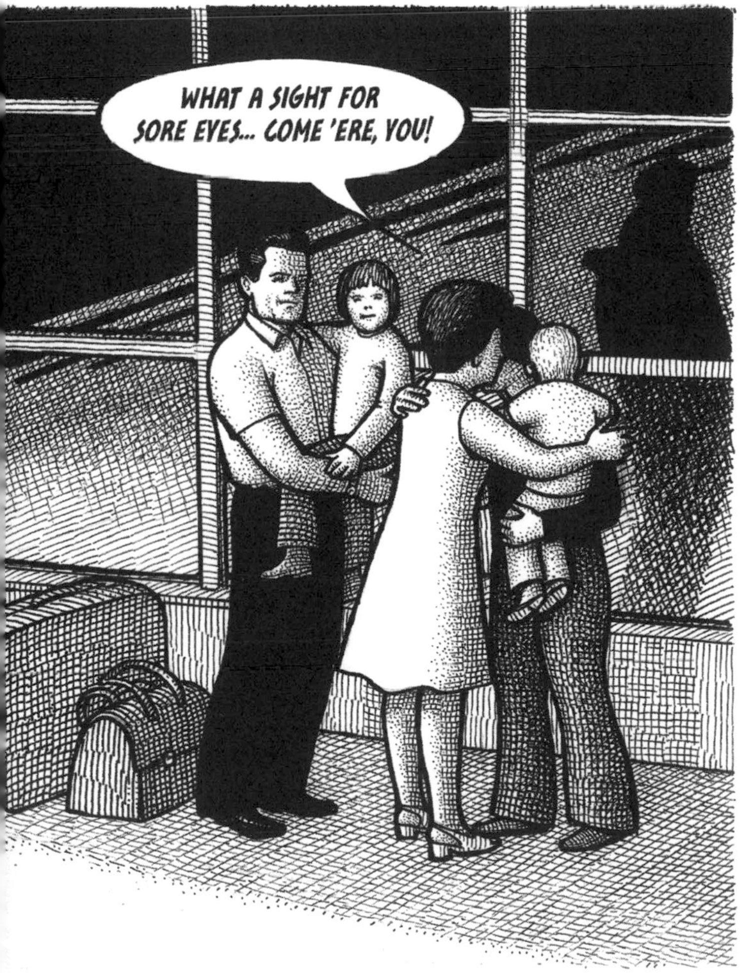
WHAT A SIGHT FOR SORE EYES... COME 'ERE, YOU!

MY GRANDMOTHER WOULD OFTEN REFER TO THIS AS ONE OF THE HAPPIEST DAYS OF HER LIFE.

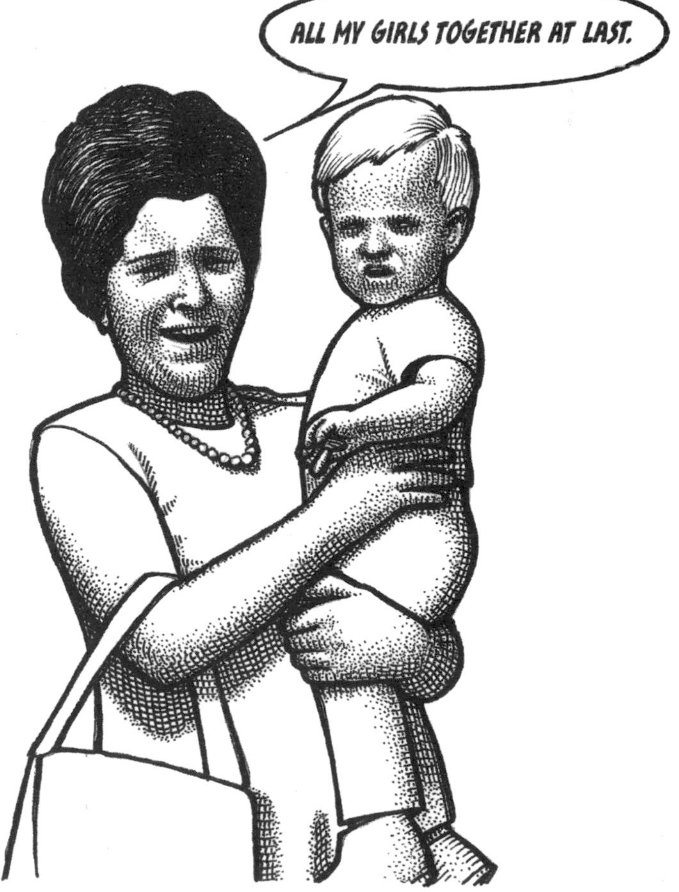
ALL MY GIRLS TOGETHER AT LAST.

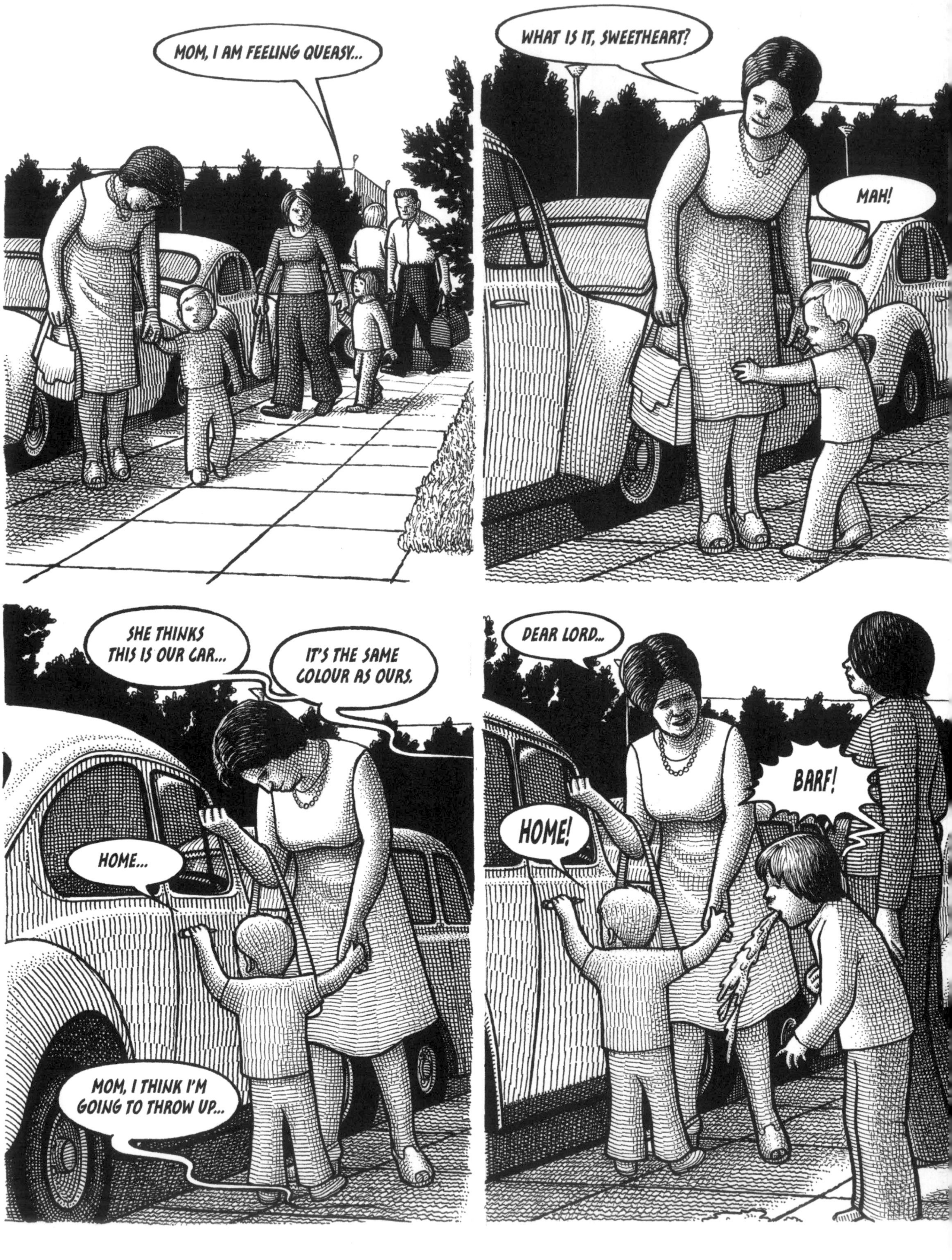
MOM, I AM FEELING QUEASY...
WHAT IS IT, SWEETHEART?
MAH!
SHE THINKS THIS IS OUR CAR...
IT'S THE SAME COLOUR AS OURS.
HOME...
MOM, I THINK I'M GOING TO THROW UP...
DEAR LORD...
HOME!
BARF!

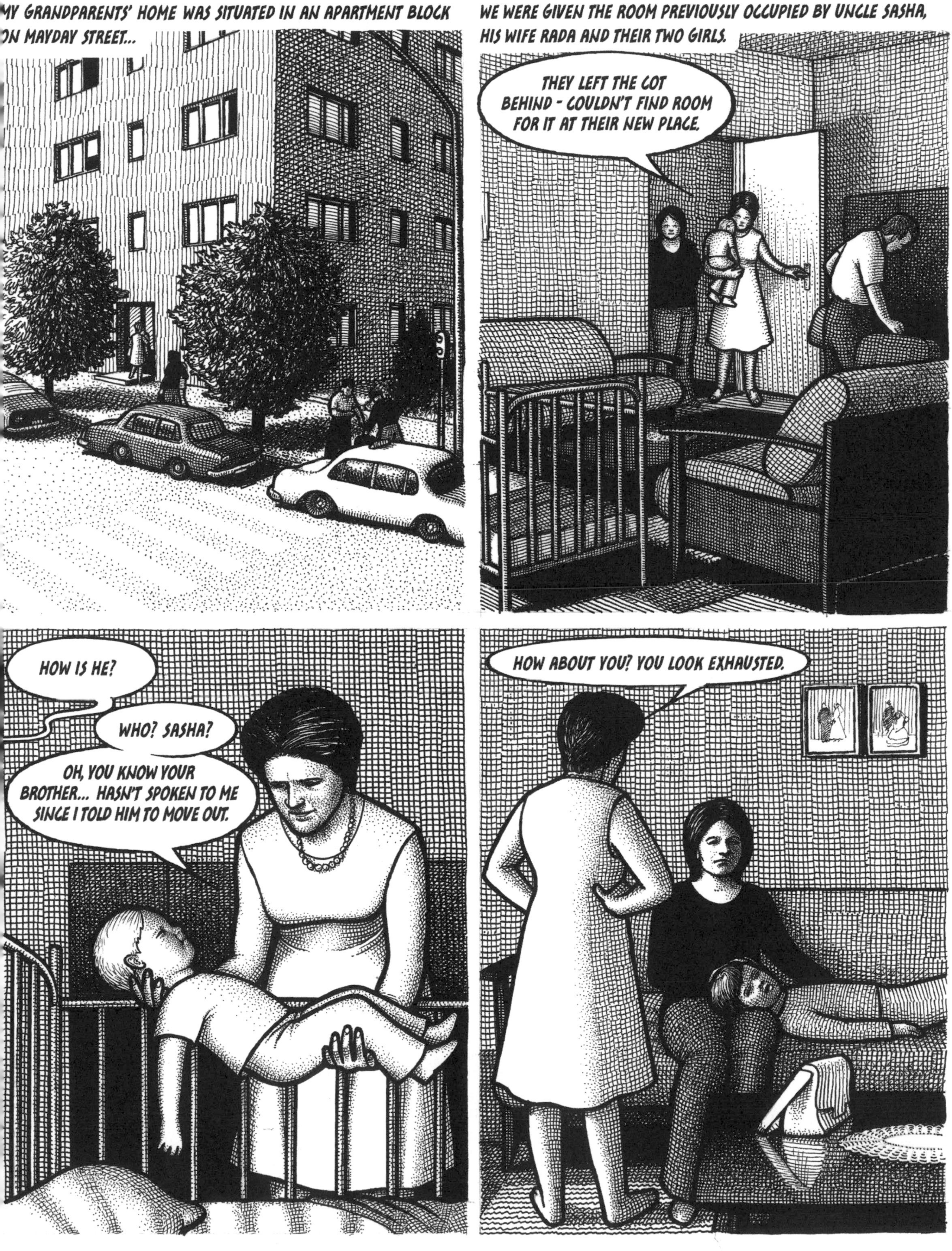
MY GRANDPARENTS' HOME WAS SITUATED IN AN APARTMENT BLOCK ON MAYDAY STREET...
WE WERE GIVEN THE ROOM PREVIOUSLY OCCUPIED BY UNCLE SASHA, HIS WIFE RADA AND THEIR TWO GIRLS.
THEY LEFT THE COT BEHIND - COULDN'T FIND ROOM FOR IT AT THEIR NEW PLACE.
HOW IS HE?
WHO? SASHA?
OH, YOU KNOW YOUR BROTHER... HASN'T SPOKEN TO ME SINCE I TOLD HIM TO MOVE OUT.
HOW ABOUT YOU? YOU LOOK EXHAUSTED.

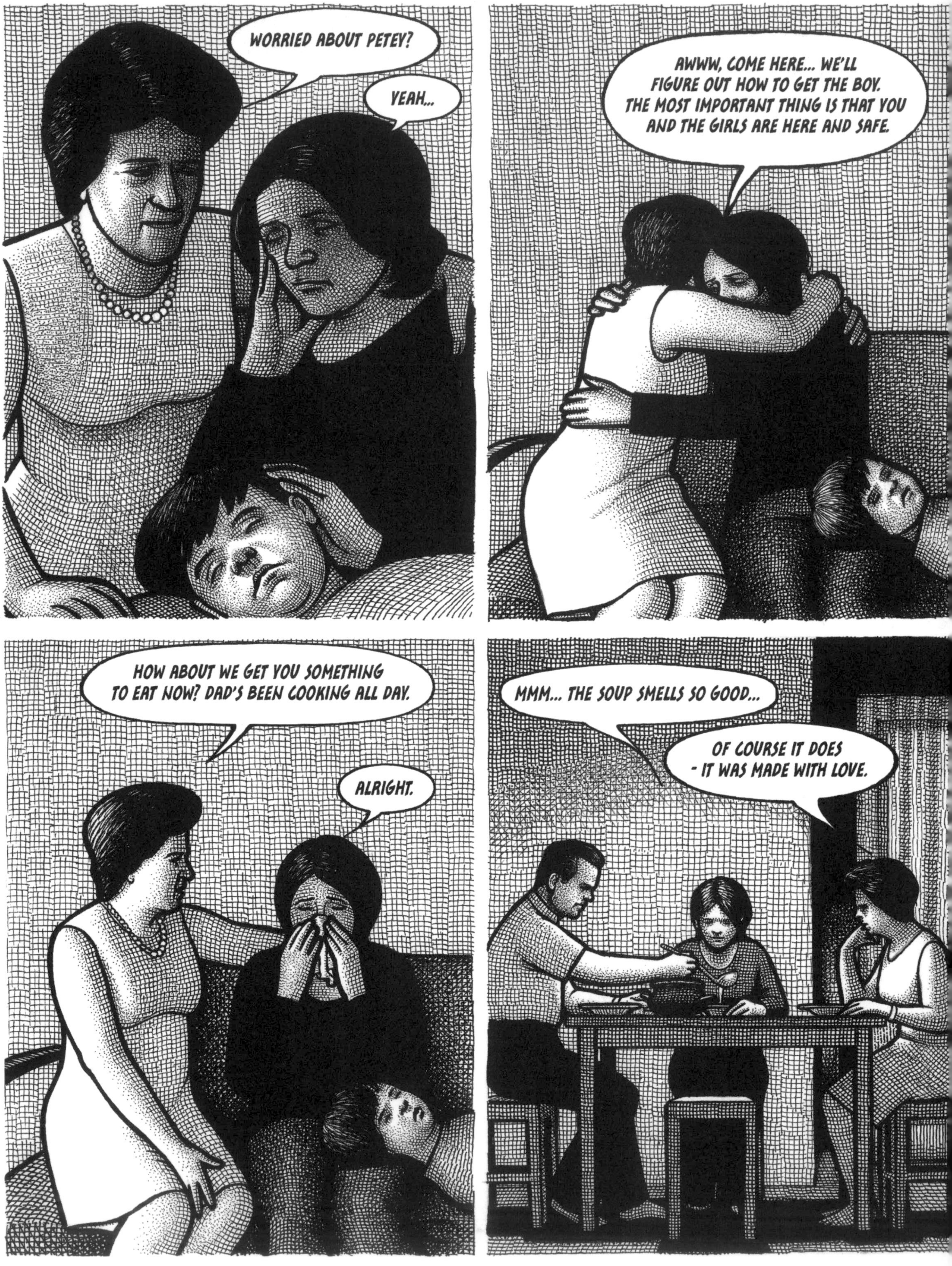
WORRIED ABOUT PETEY?
YEAH...
AWWW, COME HERE... WE'LL FIGURE OUT HOW TO GET THE BOY. THE MOST IMPORTANT THING IS THAT YOU AND THE GIRLS ARE HERE AND SAFE.
HOW ABOUT WE GET YOU SOMETHING TO EAT NOW? DAD'S BEEN COOKING ALL DAY.
ALRIGHT.
MMM... THE SOUP SMELLS SO GOOD...
OF COURSE IT DOES - IT WAS MADE WITH LOVE.

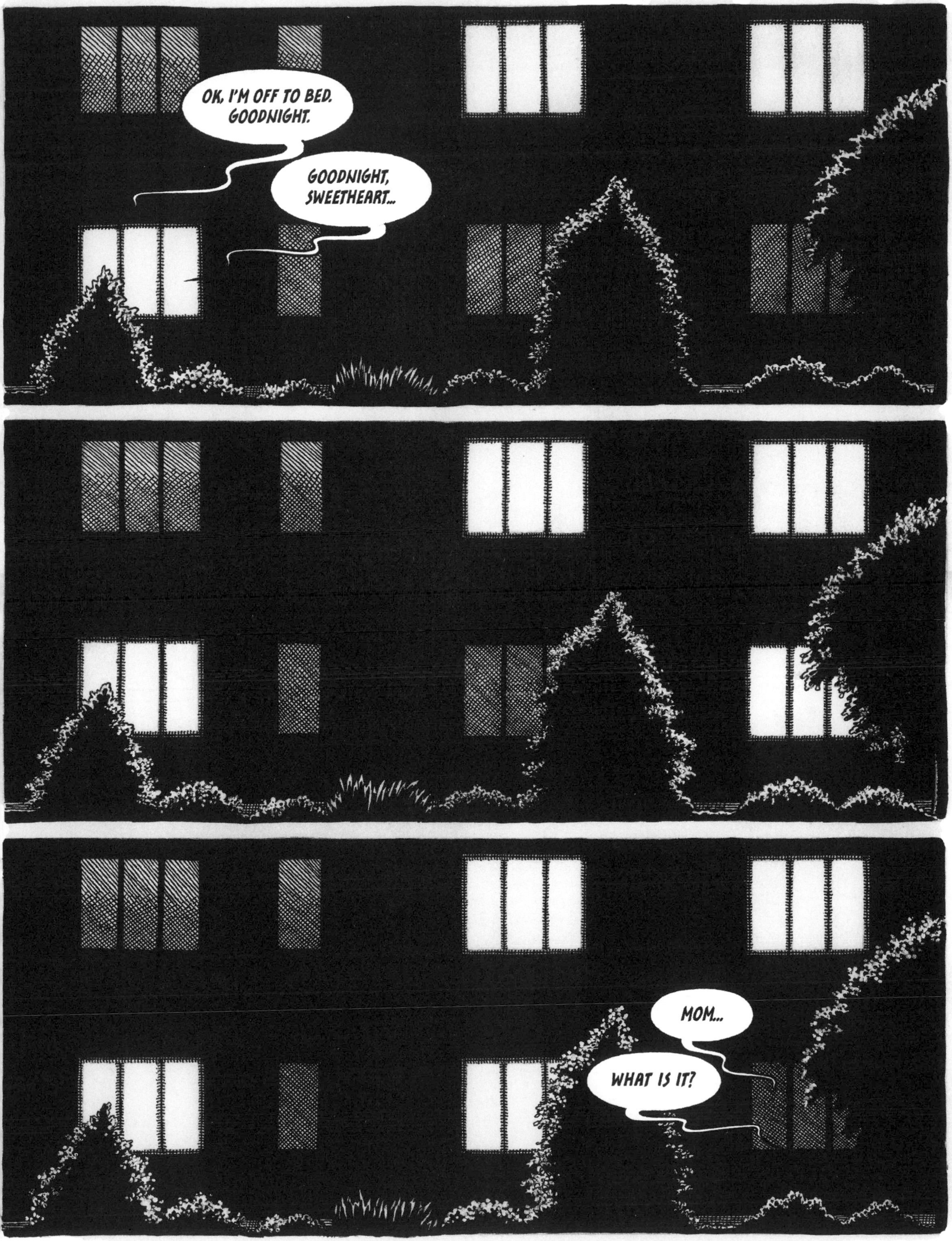
OK, I'M OFF TO BED. GOODNIGHT.
GOODNIGHT, SWEETHEART...
MOM...
WHAT IS IT?

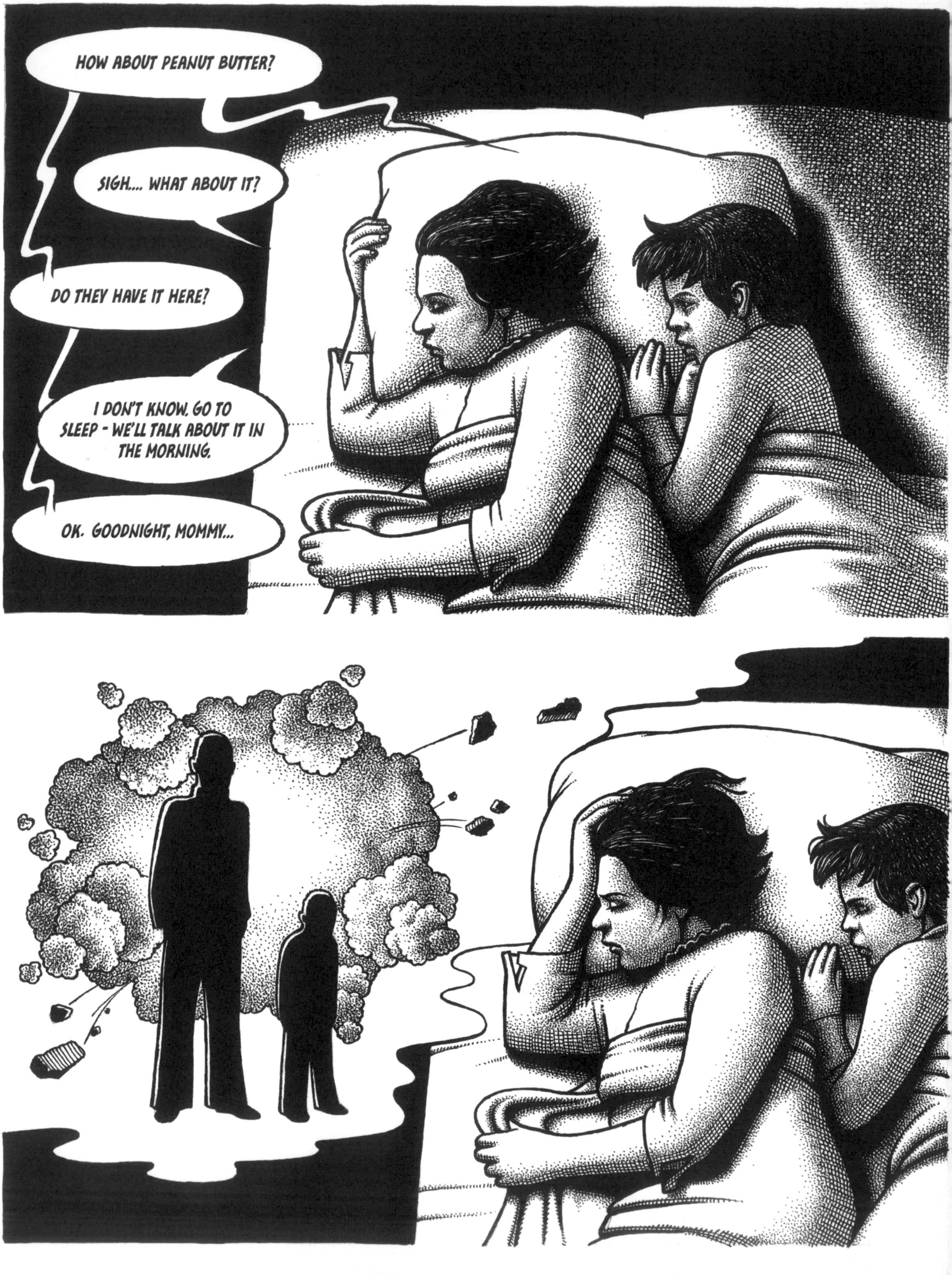
HOW ABOUT PEANUT BUTTER?
SIGH.... WHAT ABOUT IT?
DO THEY HAVE IT HERE?
I DON'T KNOW. GO TO SLEEP - WE'LL TALK ABOUT IT IN THE MORNING.
OK. GOODNIGHT, MOMMY...

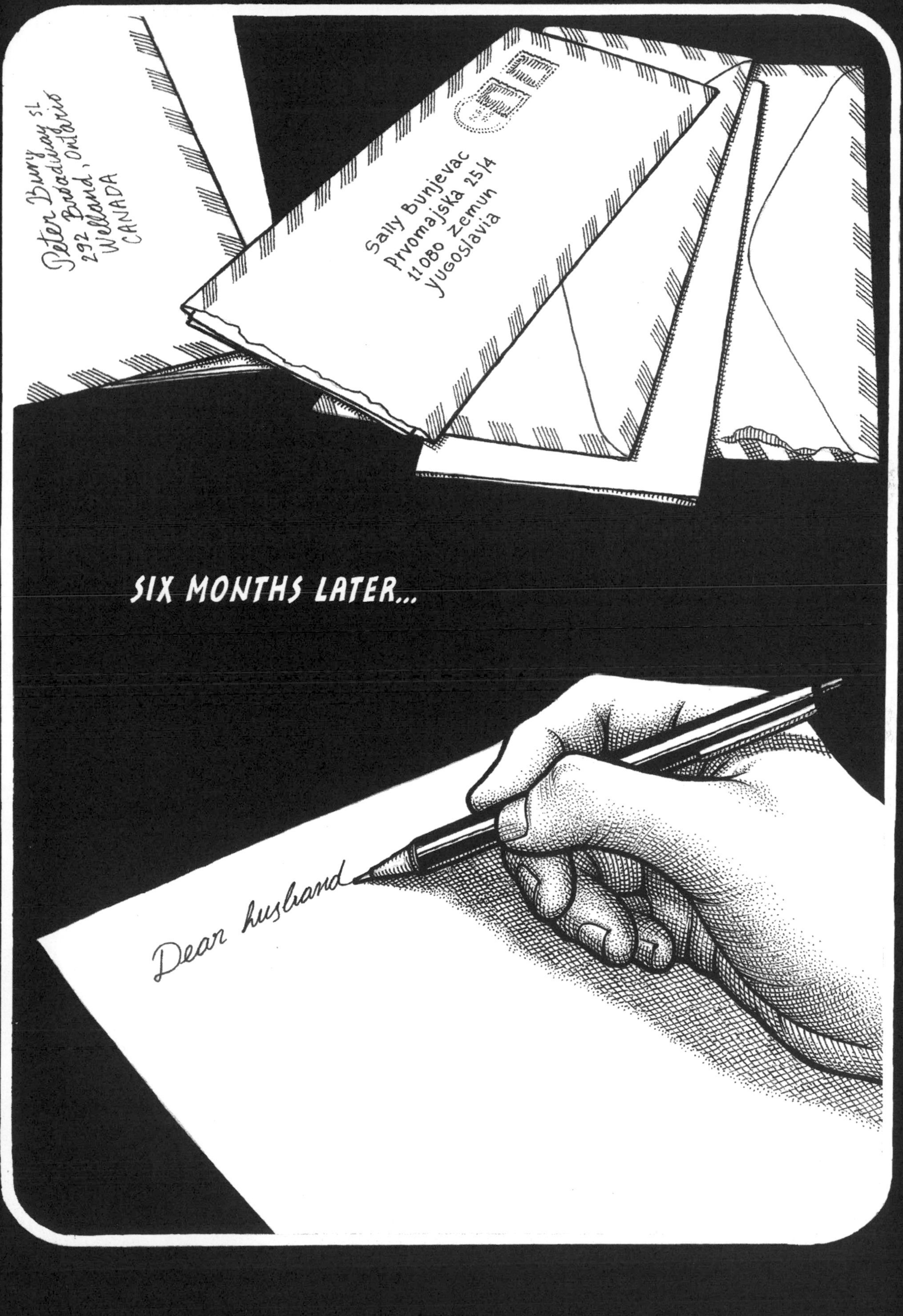
Peter Bury
292 Broadway St.
Welland, Ontario
CANADA
Sally Bunjevac
Prvomajska 25/4
11080 Zemun
YUGOSLAVIA
SIX MONTHS LATER...
Dear husband

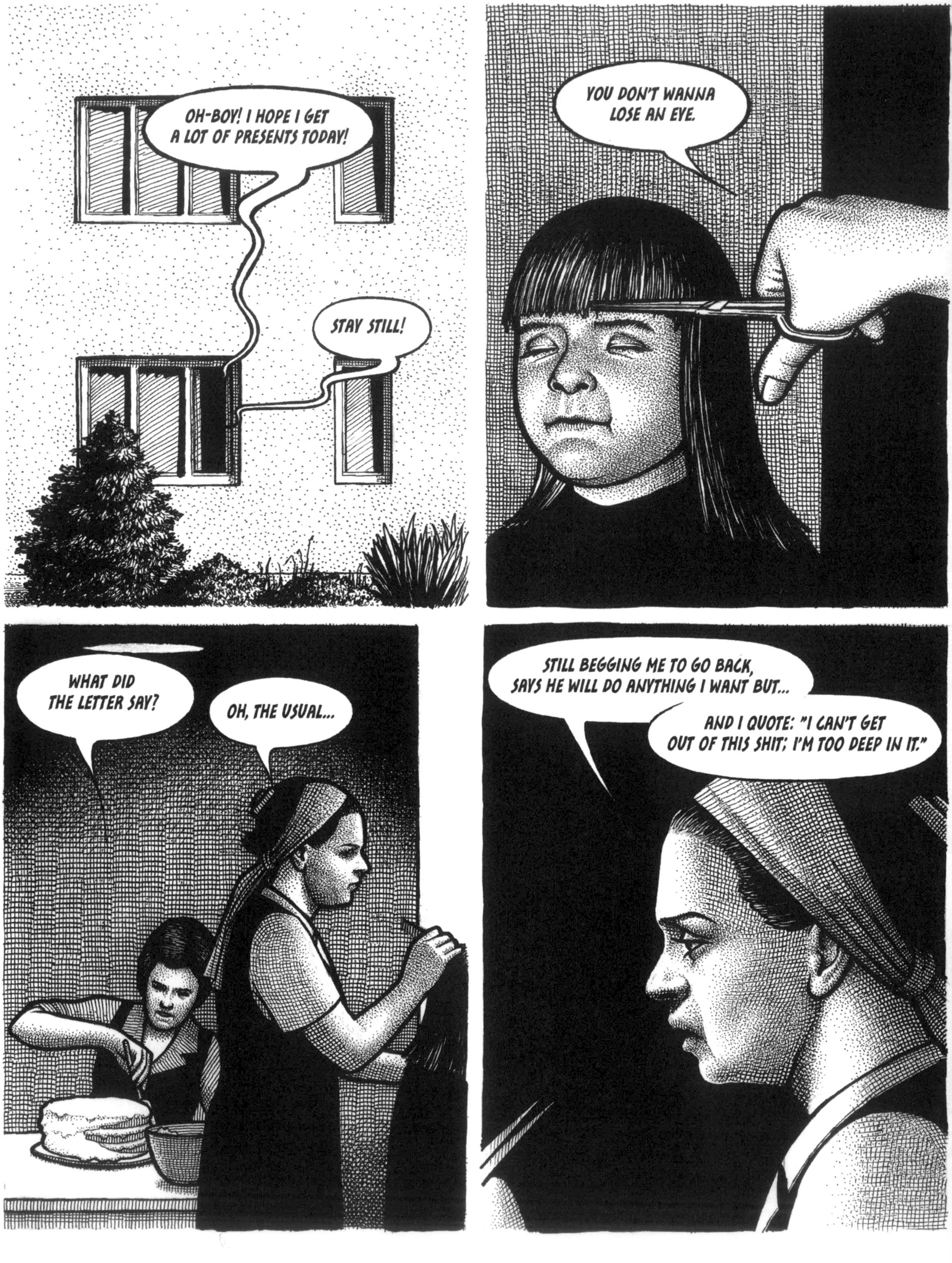
OH-BOY! I HOPE I GET A LOT OF PRESENTS TODAY!
STAY STILL!
YOU DON'T WANNA LOSE AN EYE.
WHAT DID THE LETTER SAY?
OH, THE USUAL...
STILL BEGGING ME TO GO BACK, SAYS HE WILL DO ANYTHING I WANT BUT...
AND I QUOTE: "I CAN'T GET OUT OF THIS SHIT; I'M TOO DEEP IN IT."

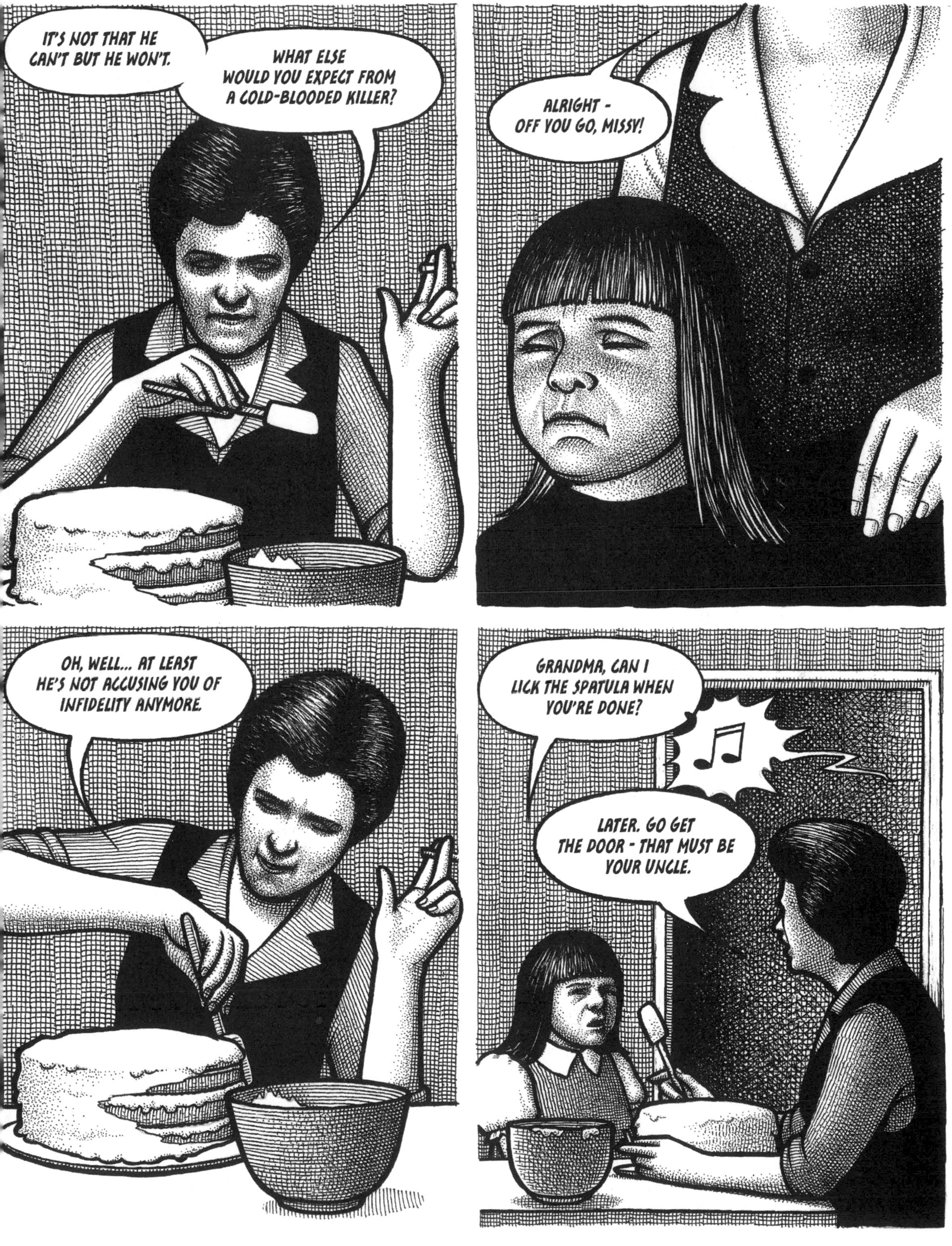
IT'S NOT THAT HE CAN'T BUT HE WON'T.
WHAT ELSE WOULD YOU EXPECT FROM A COLD-BLOODED KILLER?
ALRIGHT - OFF YOU GO, MISSY!
OH, WELL... AT LEAST HE'S NOT ACCUSING YOU OF INFIDELITY ANYMORE.
GRANDMA, CAN I LICK THE SPATULA WHEN YOU'RE DONE?
LATER. GO GET THE DOOR - THAT MUST BE YOUR UNCLE.

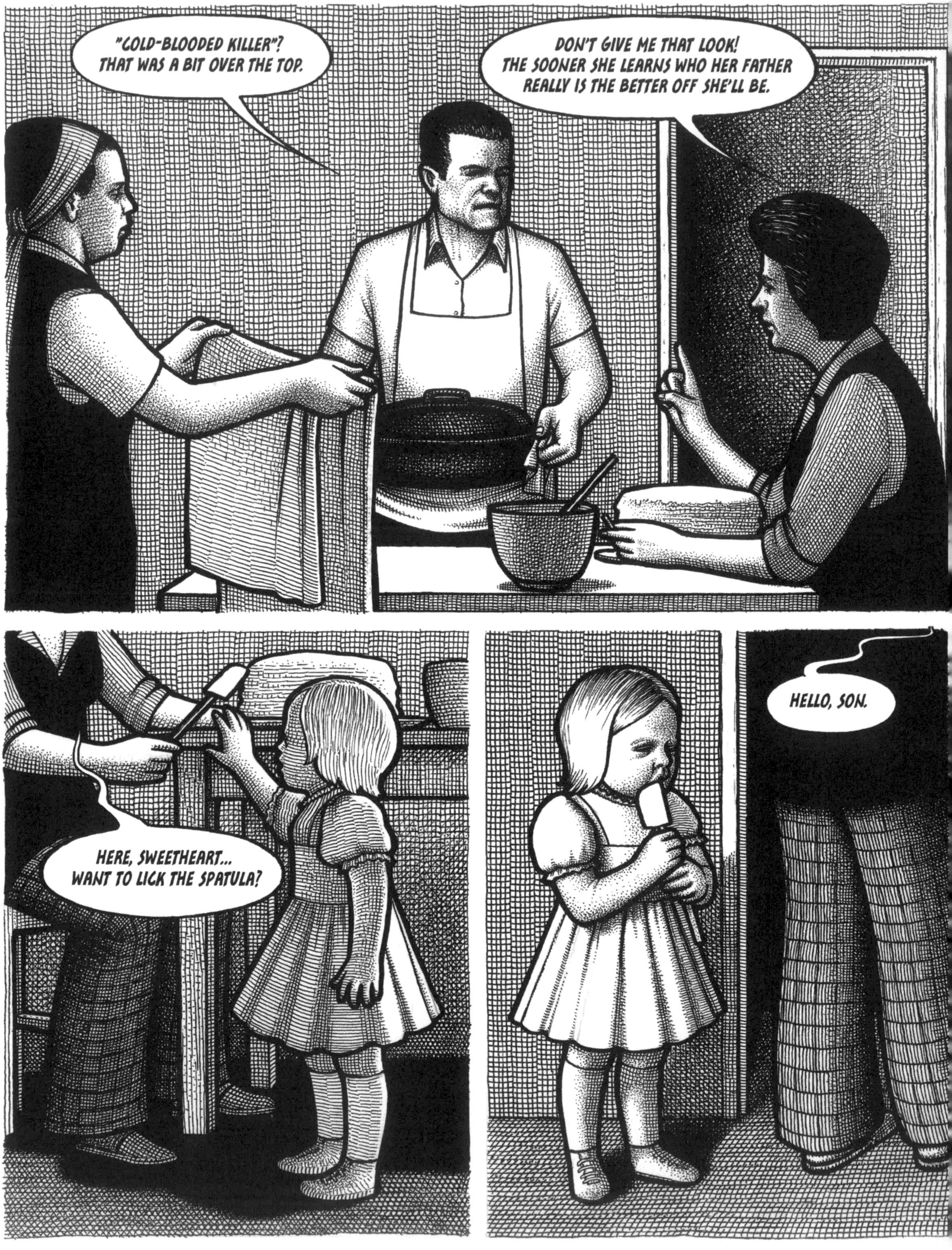
"COLD-BLOODED KILLER"? THAT WAS A BIT OVER THE TOP.
DON'T GIVE ME THAT LOOK! THE SOONER SHE LEARNS WHO HER FATHER REALLY IS THE BETTER OFF SHE'LL BE.
HERE, SWEETHEART... WANT TO LICK THE SPATULA?
HELLO, SON.

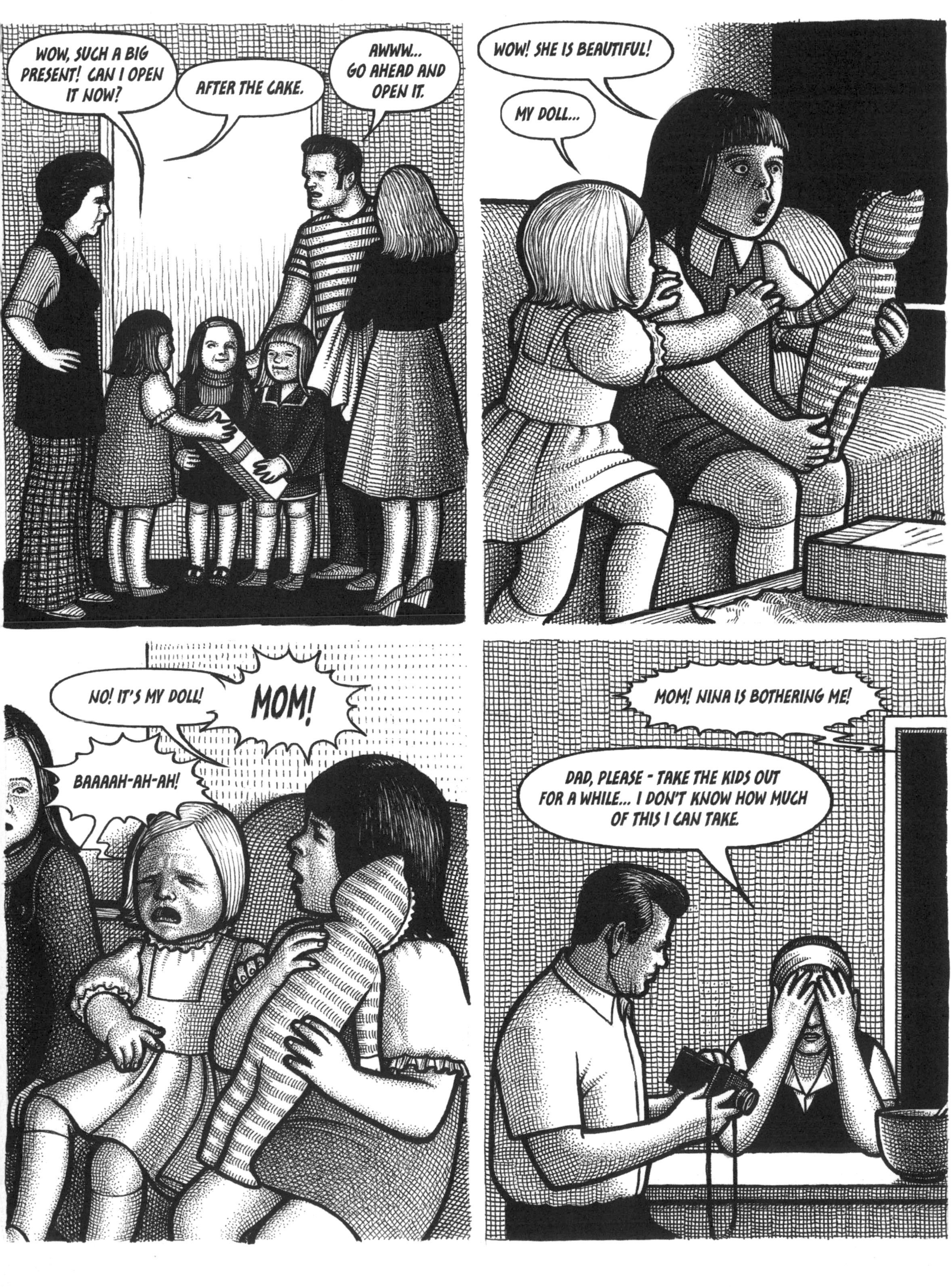
WOW, SUCH A BIG PRESENT! CAN I OPEN IT NOW?
AFTER THE CAKE.
AWWW... GO AHEAD AND OPEN IT.
WOW! SHE IS BEAUTIFUL!
MY DOLL...
NO! IT'S MY DOLL!
MOM!
BAAAAH-AH-AH!
MOM! NINA IS BOTHERING ME!
DAD, PLEASE - TAKE THE KIDS OUT FOR A WHILE... I DON'T KNOW HOW MUCH OF THIS I CAN TAKE.

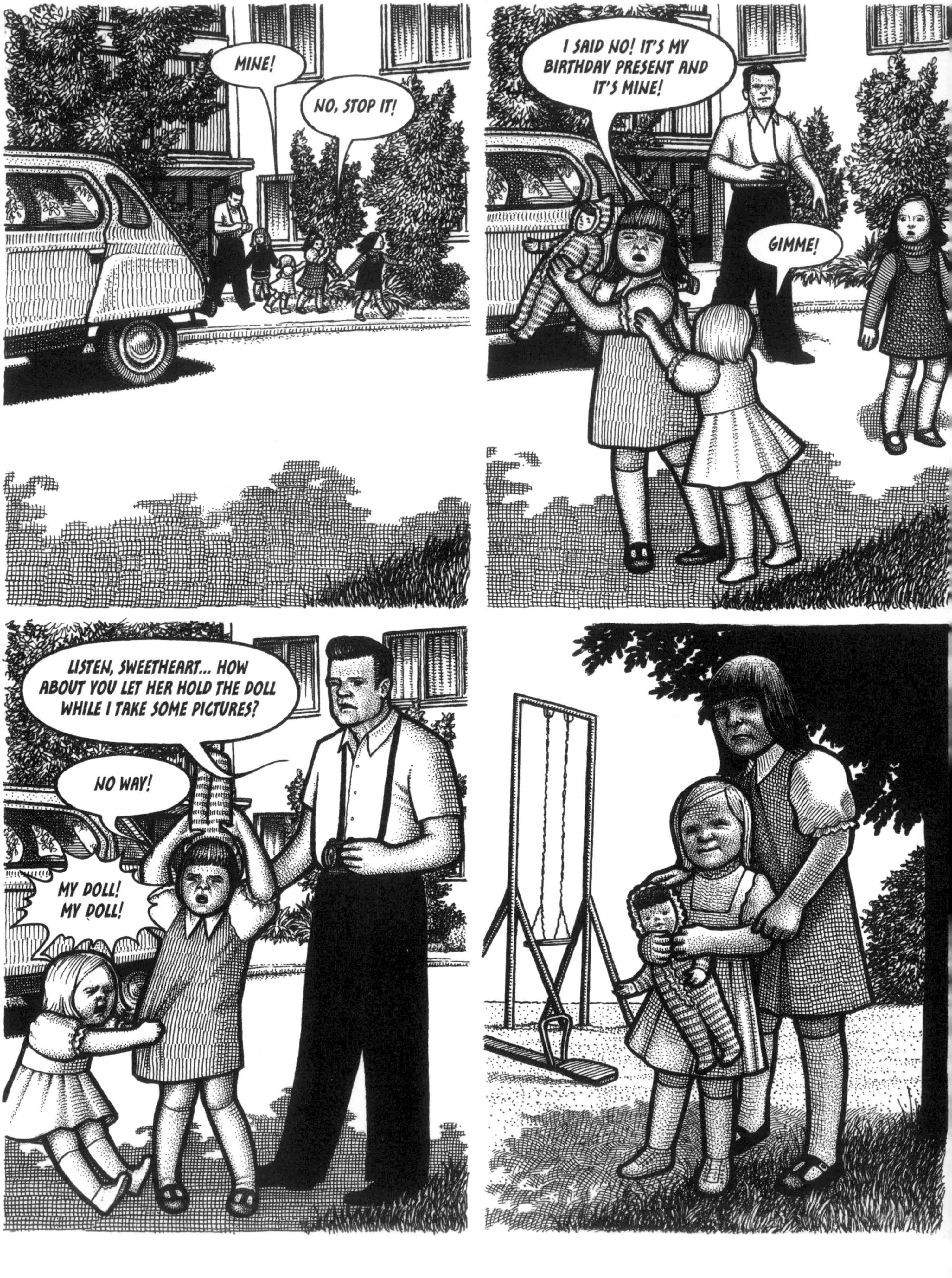
MINE!
NO, STOP IT!
I SAID NO! IT'S MY BIRTHDAY PRESENT AND IT'S MINE!
GIMME!
LISTEN, SWEETHEART... HOW ABOUT YOU LET HER HOLD THE DOLL WHILE I TAKE SOME PICTURES?
NO WAY!
MY DOLL! MY DOLL!

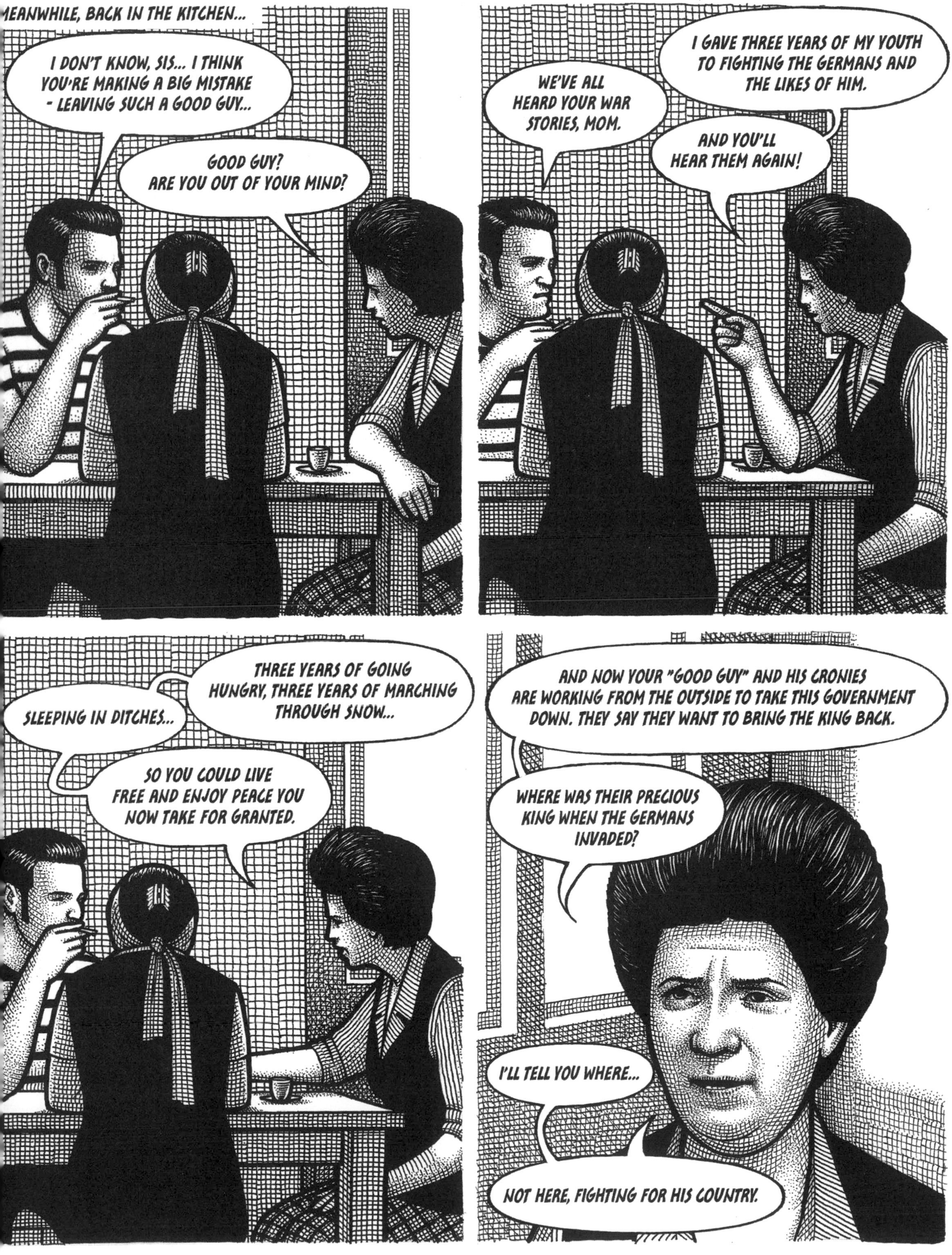
MEANWHILE, BACK IN THE KITCHEN...
I DON'T KNOW, SIS... I THINK YOU'RE MAKING A BIG MISTAKE - LEAVING SUCH A GOOD GUY...
GOOD GUY? ARE YOU OUT OF YOUR MIND?
WE'VE ALL HEARD YOUR WAR STORIES, MOM.
I GAVE THREE YEARS OF MY YOUTH TO FIGHTING THE GERMANS AND THE LIKES OF HIM.
AND YOU'LL HEAR THEM AGAIN!
SLEEPING IN DITCHES...
THREE YEARS OF GOING HUNGRY, THREE YEARS OF MARCHING THROUGH SNOW...
SO YOU COULD LIVE FREE AND ENJOY PEACE YOU NOW TAKE FOR GRANTED.
AND NOW YOUR "GOOD GUY" AND HIS CRONIES ARE WORKING FROM THE OUTSIDE TO TAKE THIS GOVERNMENT DOWN. THEY SAY THEY WANT TO BRING THE KING BACK.
WHERE WAS THEIR PRECIOUS KING WHEN THE GERMANS INVADED?
I'LL TELL YOU WHERE...
NOT HERE, FIGHTING FOR HIS COUNTRY.

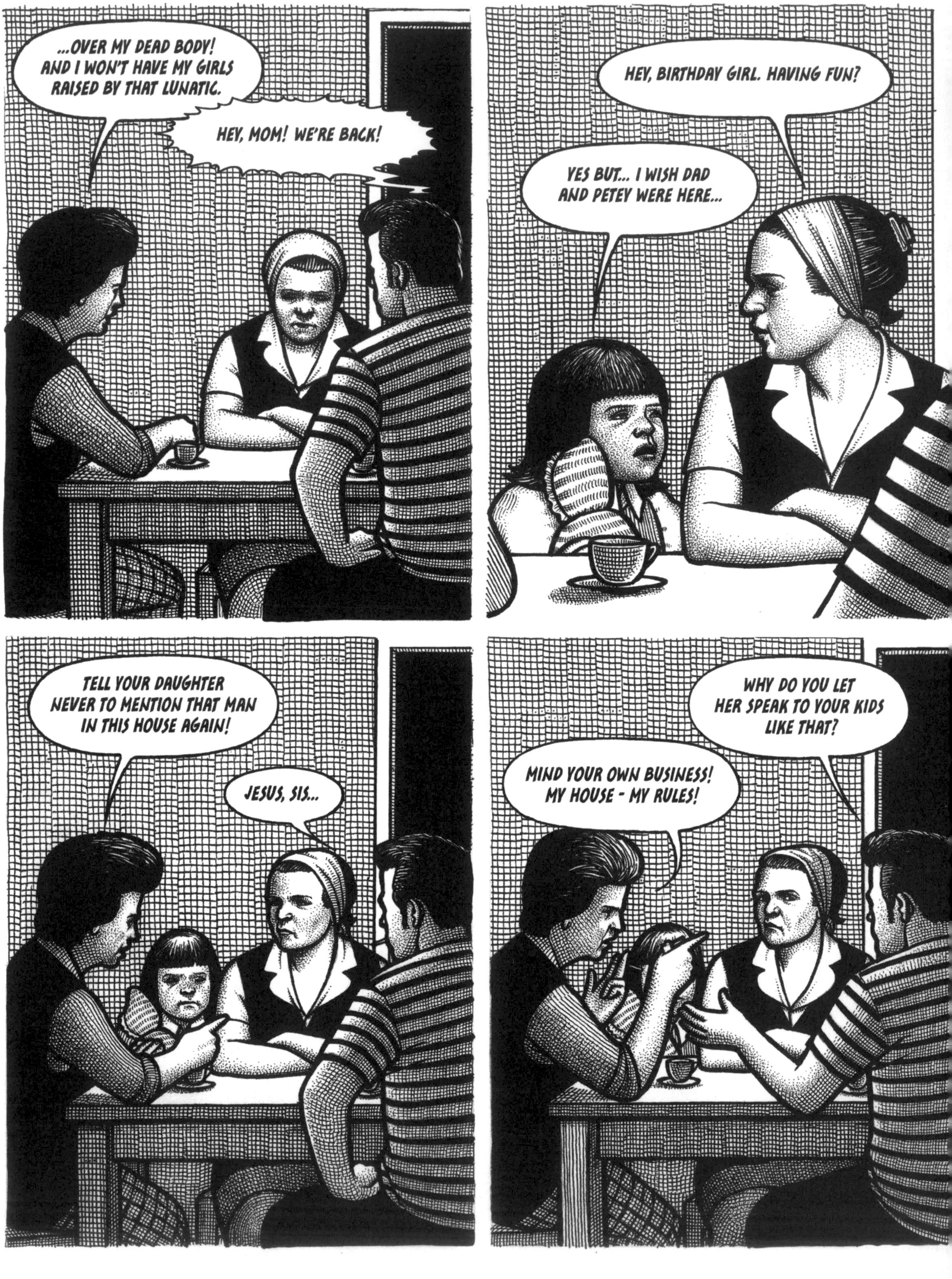
...OVER MY DEAD BODY! AND I WON'T HAVE MY GIRLS RAISED BY THAT LUNATIC.
HEY, MOM! WE'RE BACK!
HEY, BIRTHDAY GIRL. HAVING FUN?
YES BUT... I WISH DAD AND PETEY WERE HERE...
TELL YOUR DAUGHTER NEVER TO MENTION THAT MAN IN THIS HOUSE AGAIN!
JESUS, SIS...
WHY DO YOU LET HER SPEAK TO YOUR KIDS LIKE THAT?
MIND YOUR OWN BUSINESS! MY HOUSE - MY RULES!

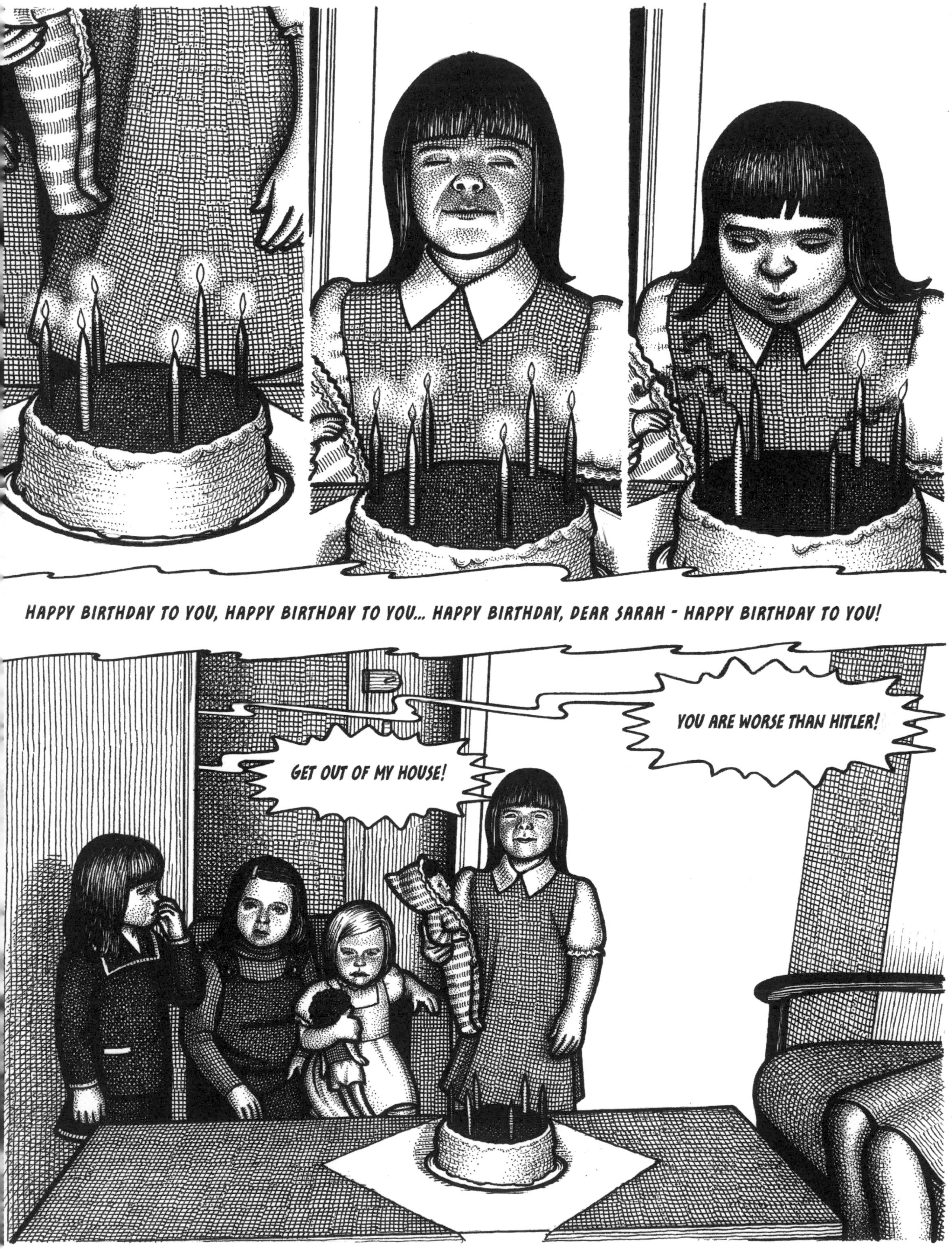
HAPPY BIRTHDAY TO YOU, HAPPY BIRTHDAY TO YOU... HAPPY BIRTHDAY, DEAR SARAH - HAPPY BIRTHDAY TO YOU!
GET OUT OF MY HOUSE!
YOU ARE WORSE THAN HITLER!

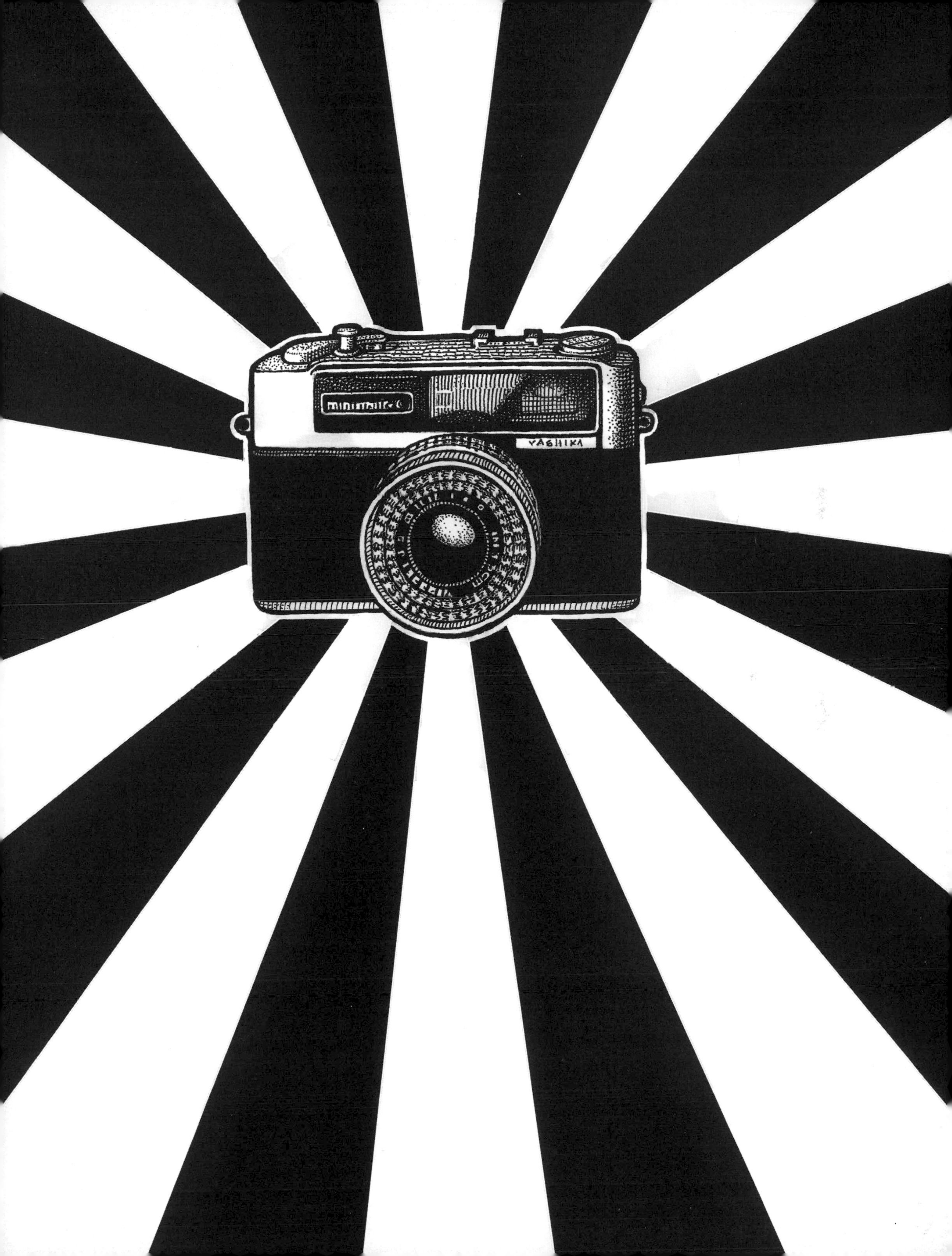
YASHICA

THE NEXT YEAR OR SO WENT BY WITHOUT MUCH TO TELL, PROVIDING NO ANECDOTES WORTHY OF REPEATING. WERE IT NOT FOR MY GRANDFATHER AND HIS HANDY CAMERA, THIS PERIOD WOULD HAVE REMAINED UNDOCUMENTED AND THUS FORGOTTEN. THE SOLE PURPOSE OF THESE PHOTOGRAPHS WAS TO SHOW MY FATHER THAT WE WERE WELL TAKEN CARE OF, AND HAPPY.

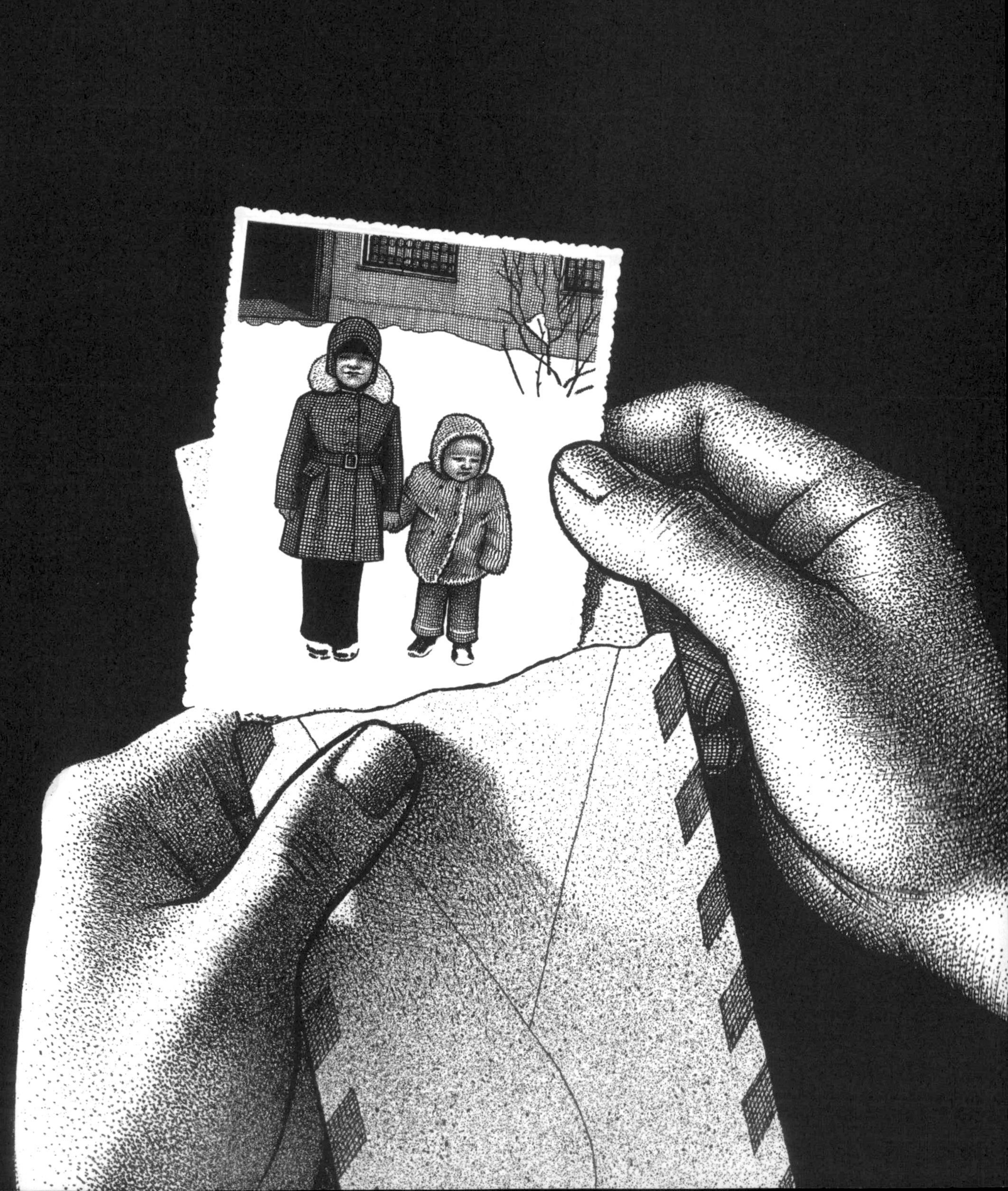

SUMMER, 1976.

AUTUMN, 1976.

WINTER, 1976 / 1977.

SPRING, 1977.

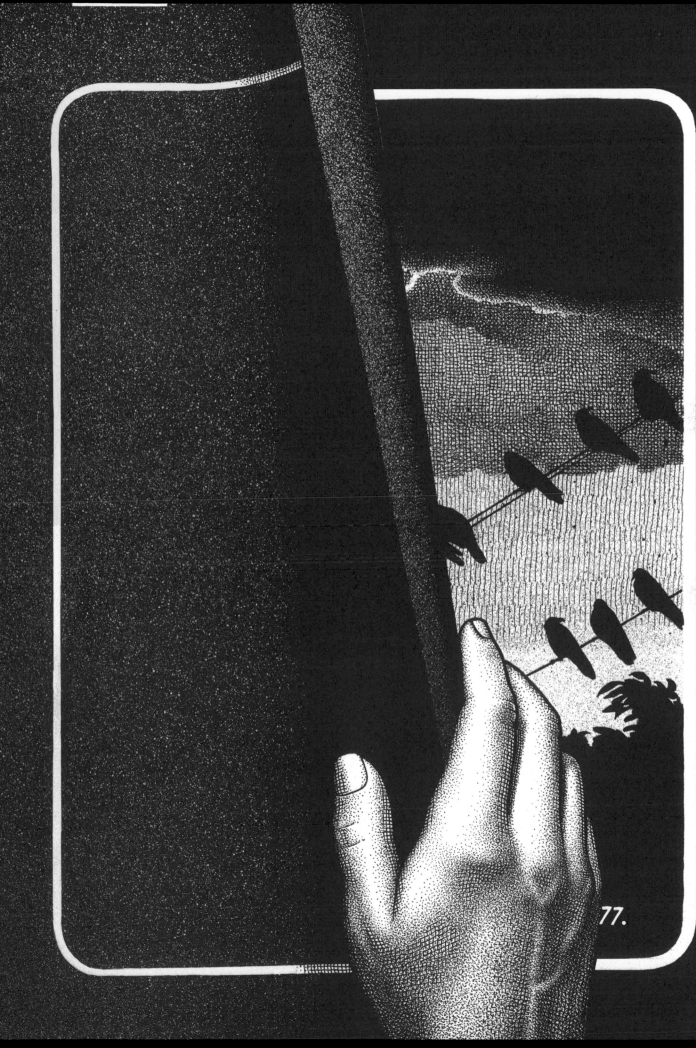

77.

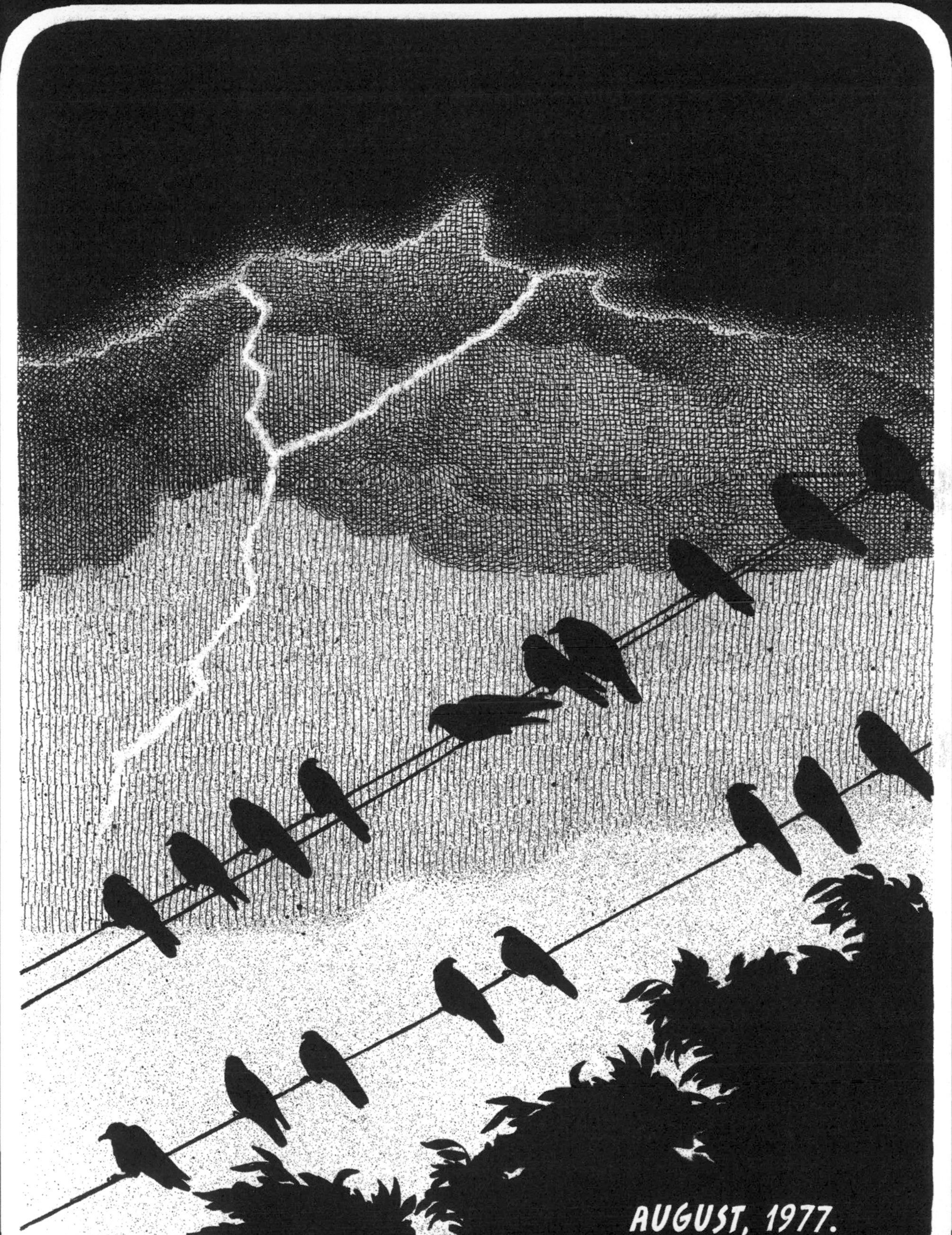
AUGUST, 1977.

IN THE BALKAN TRADITION OF DREAM INTERPRETATION, TO DREAM OF BIRDS SIGNIFIES THAT THE DREAMER IS ABOUT TO RECEIVE NEWS. DREAMING OF RAW MEAT IS OFTEN SEEN AS A SIGN OF DEATH.

ON THE NIGHT BETWEN AUGUST 27 AND 28 MY GRANDMOTHER HAD TWO DREAMS. IN THE FIRST DREAM SHE SAW A MURDER OF CROWS PERCHED ALONG THE POWER LINE. IN THE SECOND DREAM SHE SAW A MAN SLAUGHTERING A PIG. ALTHOUGH SHE COULD NOT SEE THE MAN'S FACE, SHE SOMEHOW KNEW THAT IT BELONGED TO MY FATHER.

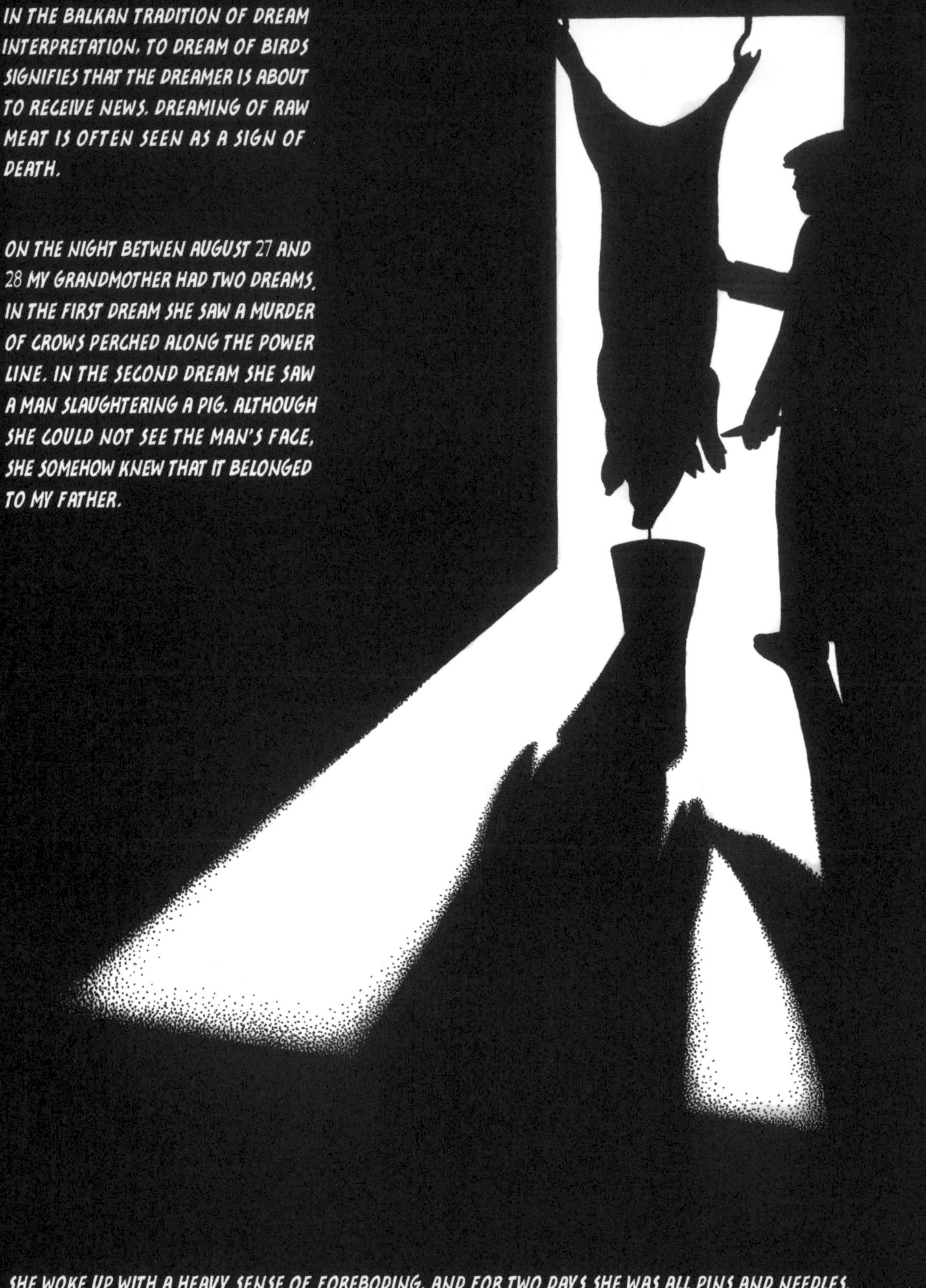

SHE WOKE UP WITH A HEAVY SENSE OF FOREBODING, AND FOR TWO DAYS SHE WAS ALL PINS AND NEEDLES. WE WEREN'T ALLOWED TO LEAVE THE HOUSE, ANSWER THE PHONE OR OPEN THE DOOR TO STRANGERS. MOM WAS GASPING FOR AIR; ON THE AFTERNOON OF DAY TWO SHE MANAGED TO NEGOTIATE TAKING THE STAIRS UP TO THE ROOF TO COLLECT THE WASHING.

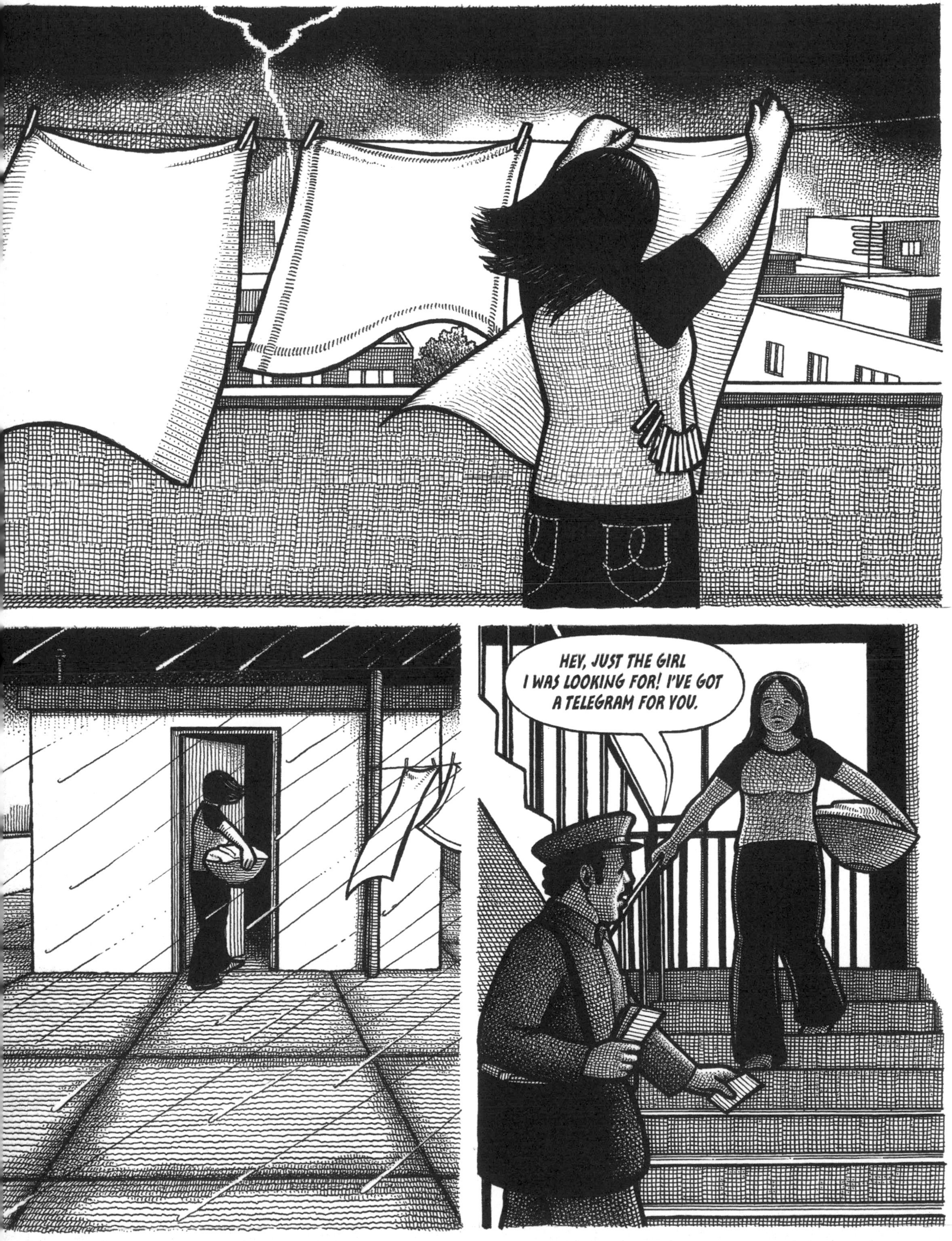
HEY, JUST THE GIRL I WAS LOOKING FOR! I'VE GOT A TELEGRAM FOR YOU.

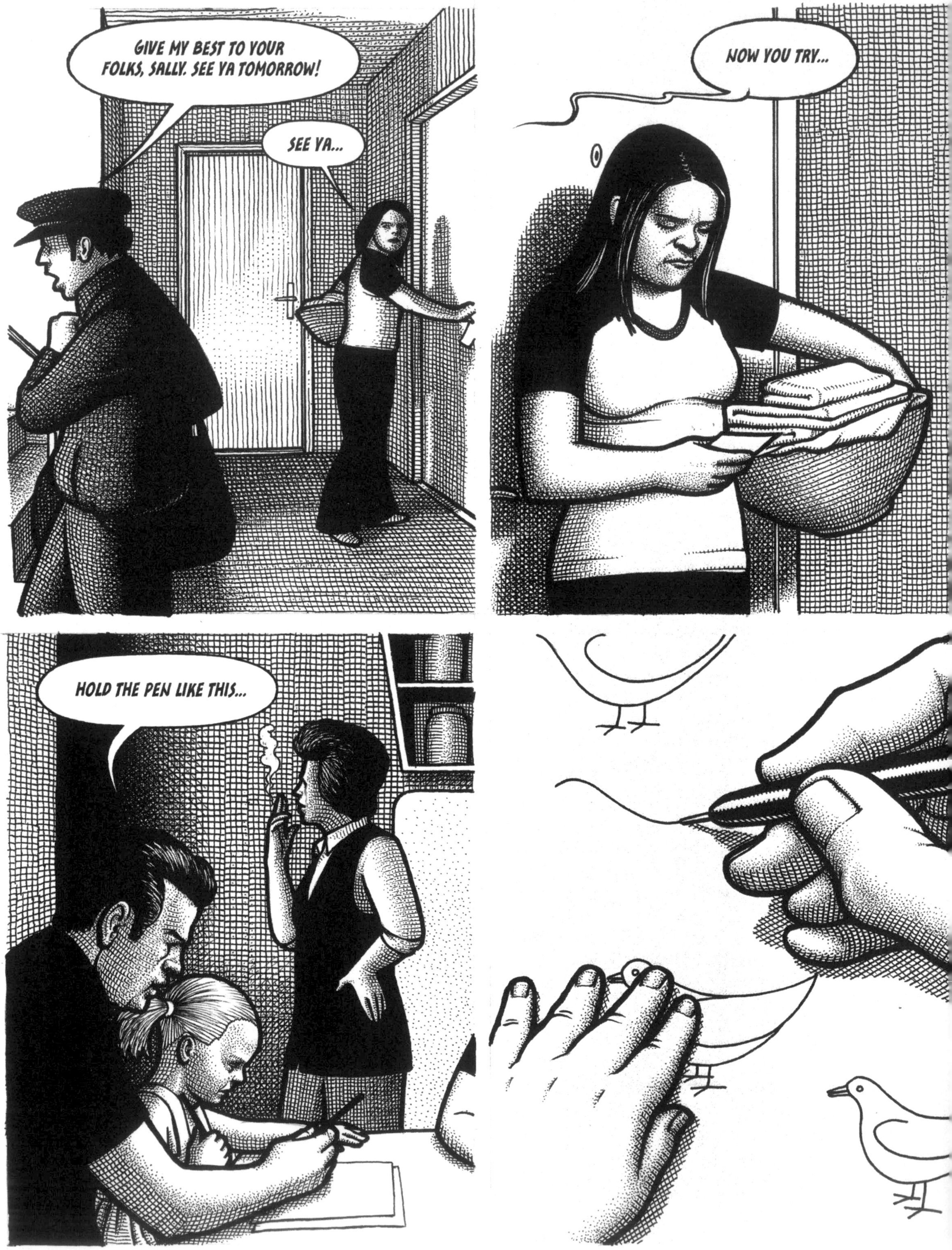
GIVE MY BEST TO YOUR FOLKS, SALLY. SEE YA TOMORROW!
SEE YA...
NOW YOU TRY...
HOLD THE PEN LIKE THIS...

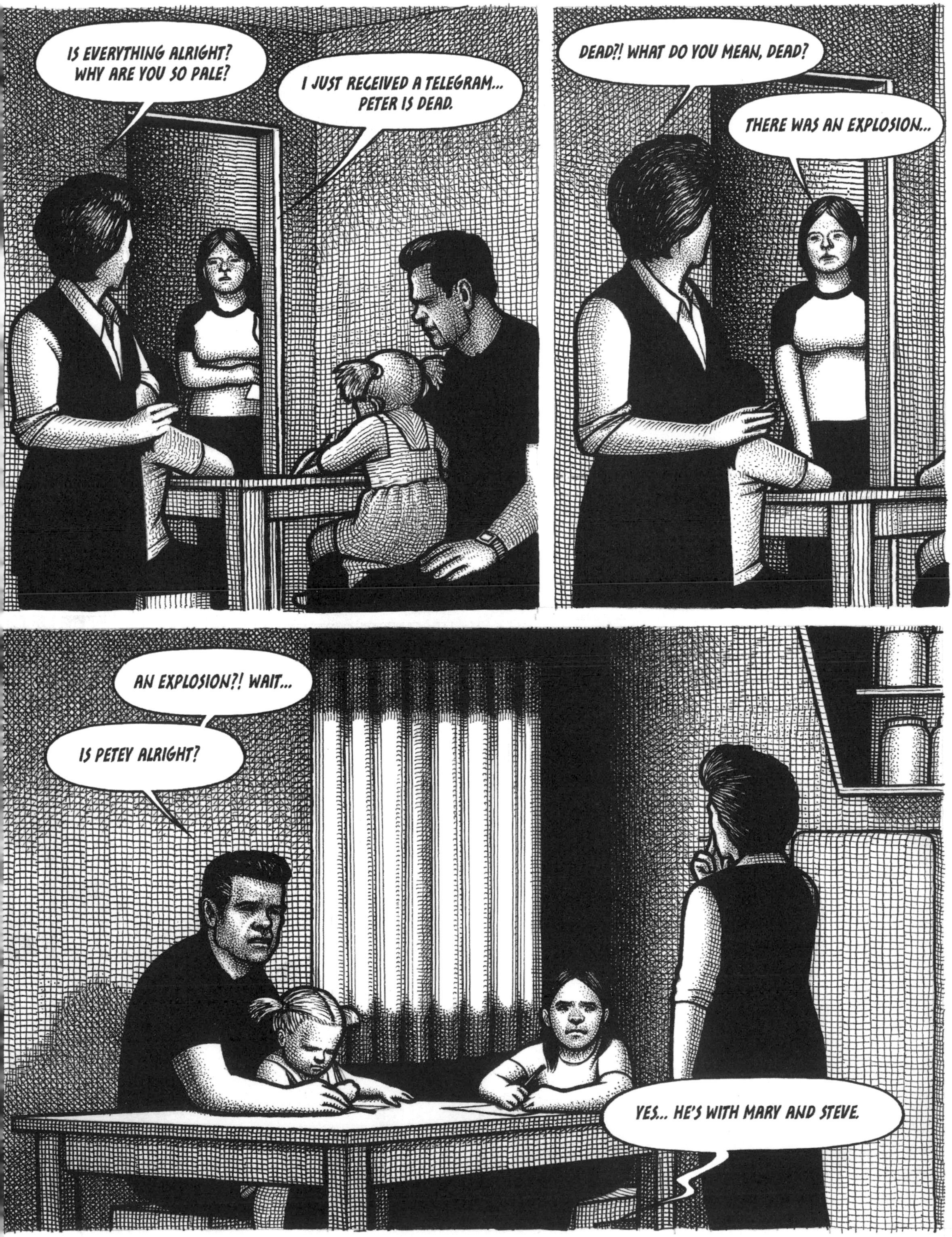
IS EVERYTHING ALRIGHT? WHY ARE YOU SO PALE?
I JUST RECEIVED A TELEGRAM... PETER IS DEAD.
DEAD?! WHAT DO YOU MEAN, DEAD?
THERE WAS AN EXPLOSION...
AN EXPLOSION?! WAIT...
IS PETEY ALRIGHT?
YES... HE'S WITH MARY AND STEVE.

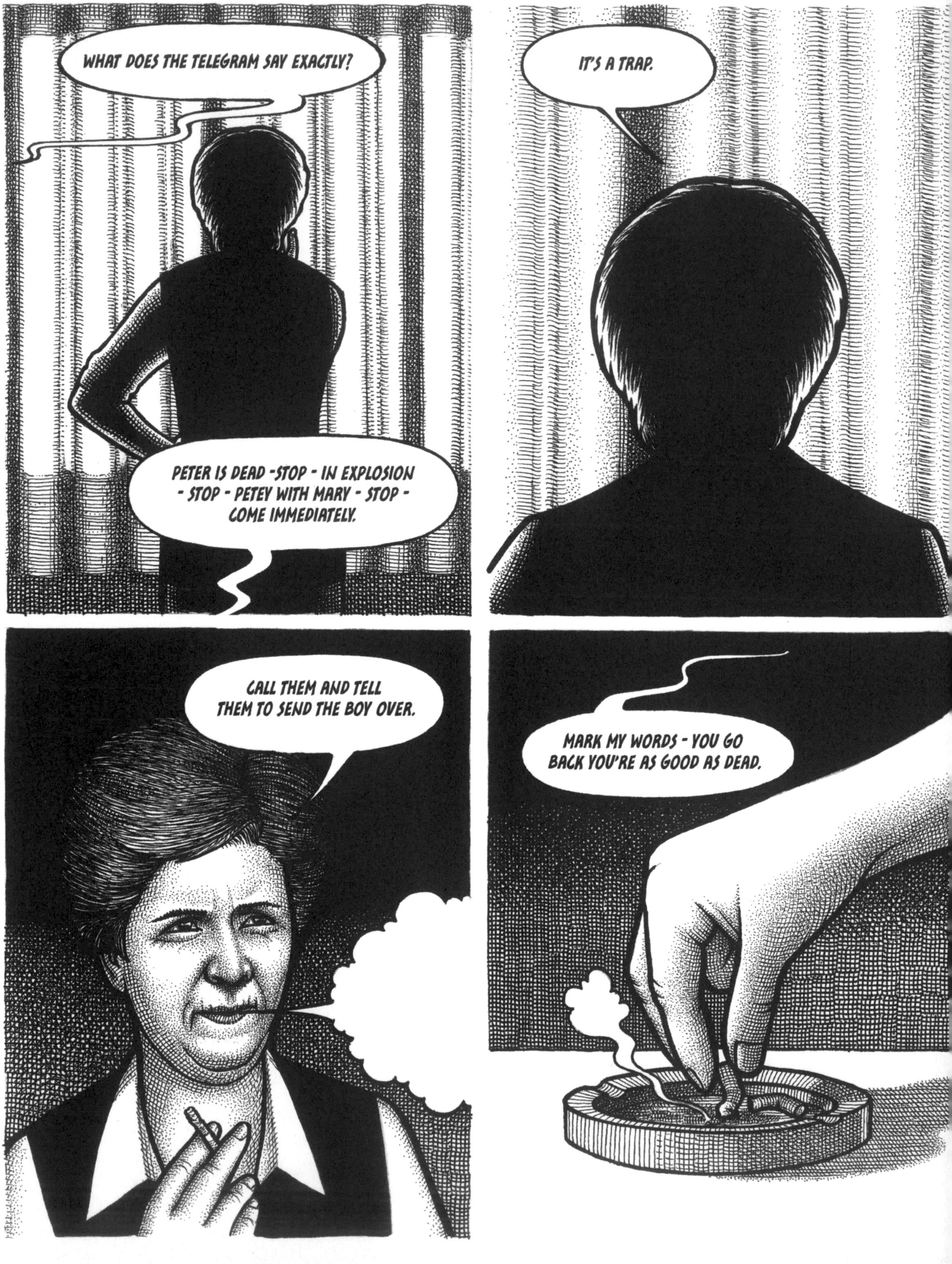
WHAT DOES THE TELEGRAM SAY EXACTLY?
PETER IS DEAD -STOP - IN EXPLOSION - STOP - PETEY WITH MARY - STOP - COME IMMEDIATELY.
IT'S A TRAP.
CALL THEM AND TELL THEM TO SEND THE BOY OVER.
MARK MY WORDS - YOU GO BACK YOU'RE AS GOOD AS DEAD.

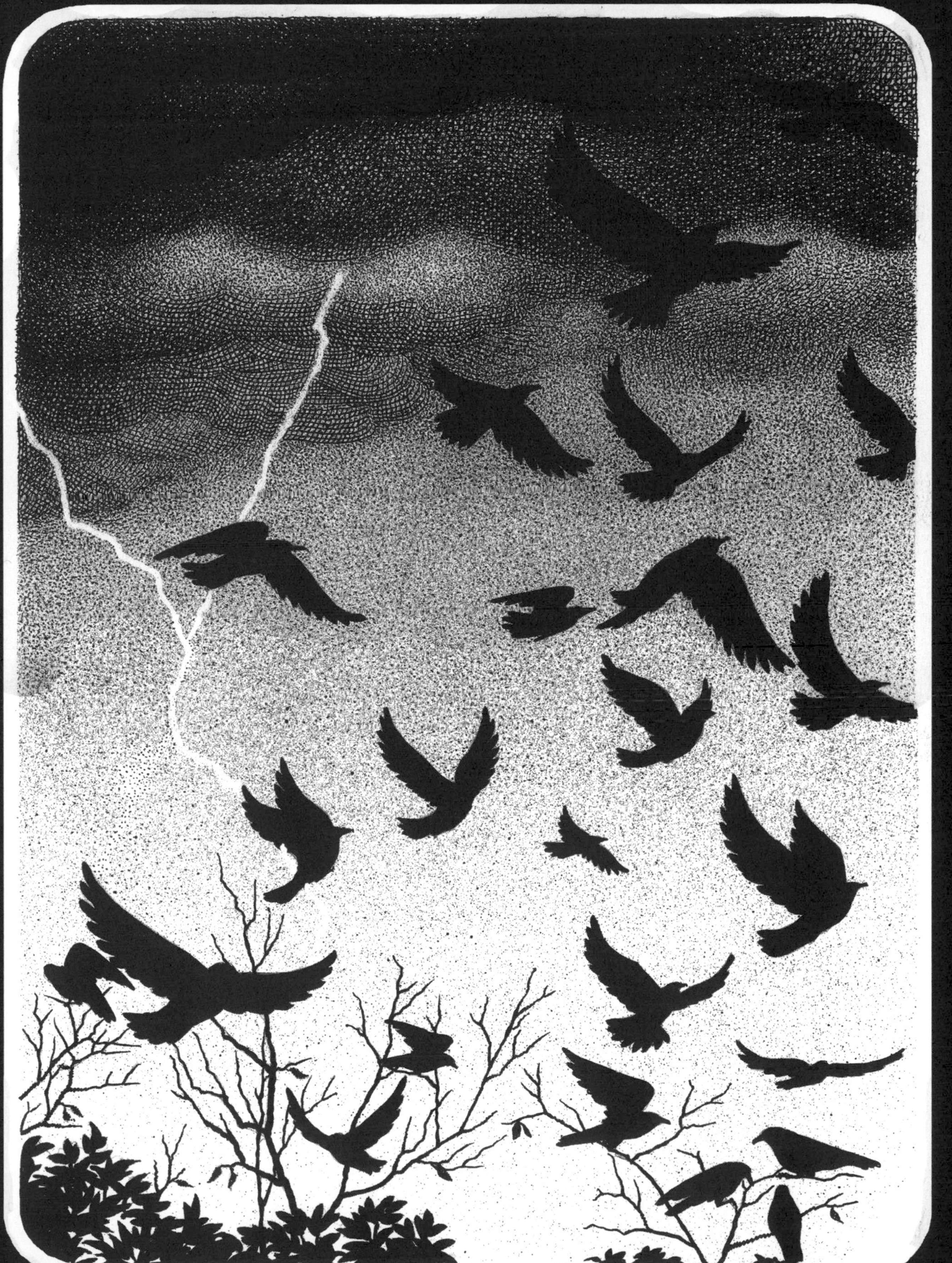

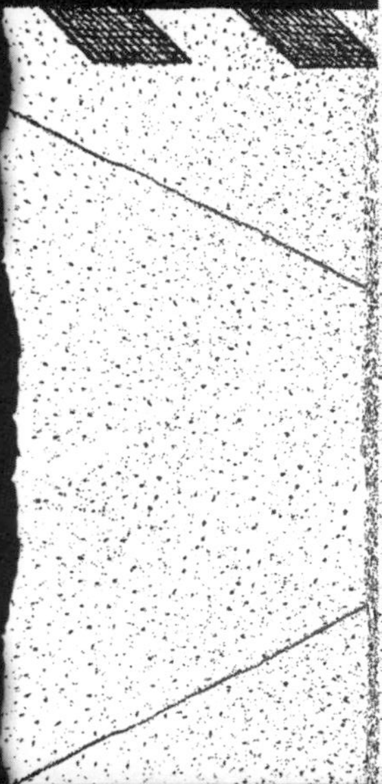

TORONTO (AP) - Three men killed in a garage explosion Monday were members of a Serbian revenge group that is planning simultaneous explosions at the homes of sympathizers with Yugoslav President Josef Tito and Yugoslav missions in six or seven cities in Canada and the United States, The Toronto Sun Reported today.

Police sources were quoted as saying their investigations indicate the three victims were manufacturing bombs in the garage. They were tentatively identified as R. P. (44,) P. K. (29), both of Toronto, and Peter Bunjevac, 41, of Welland.

Police searchers on Wednesday found a bomb hidden in a sofa in

It said the bombing campaign was planned in retaliation for the murder in Chicago in late June of Dragisa Kasikovic, editor of the anti-Communist newspaper Sloboda (Liberty) and the 9-year-old daughter of his fiancée. The Serbian community in Toronto says Kasikovich was a victim in series of political murders staged by Tito's secret police.

The Sun said the bombs were to be set off in Toronto, Hamilton, New York, Chicago and other cities with prominent Yugoslav communities.

According to the paper, a source in Toronto's Serbian community said the explosion Monday occurred because the men by

PETER BUNJEVAC   1936 - 1977

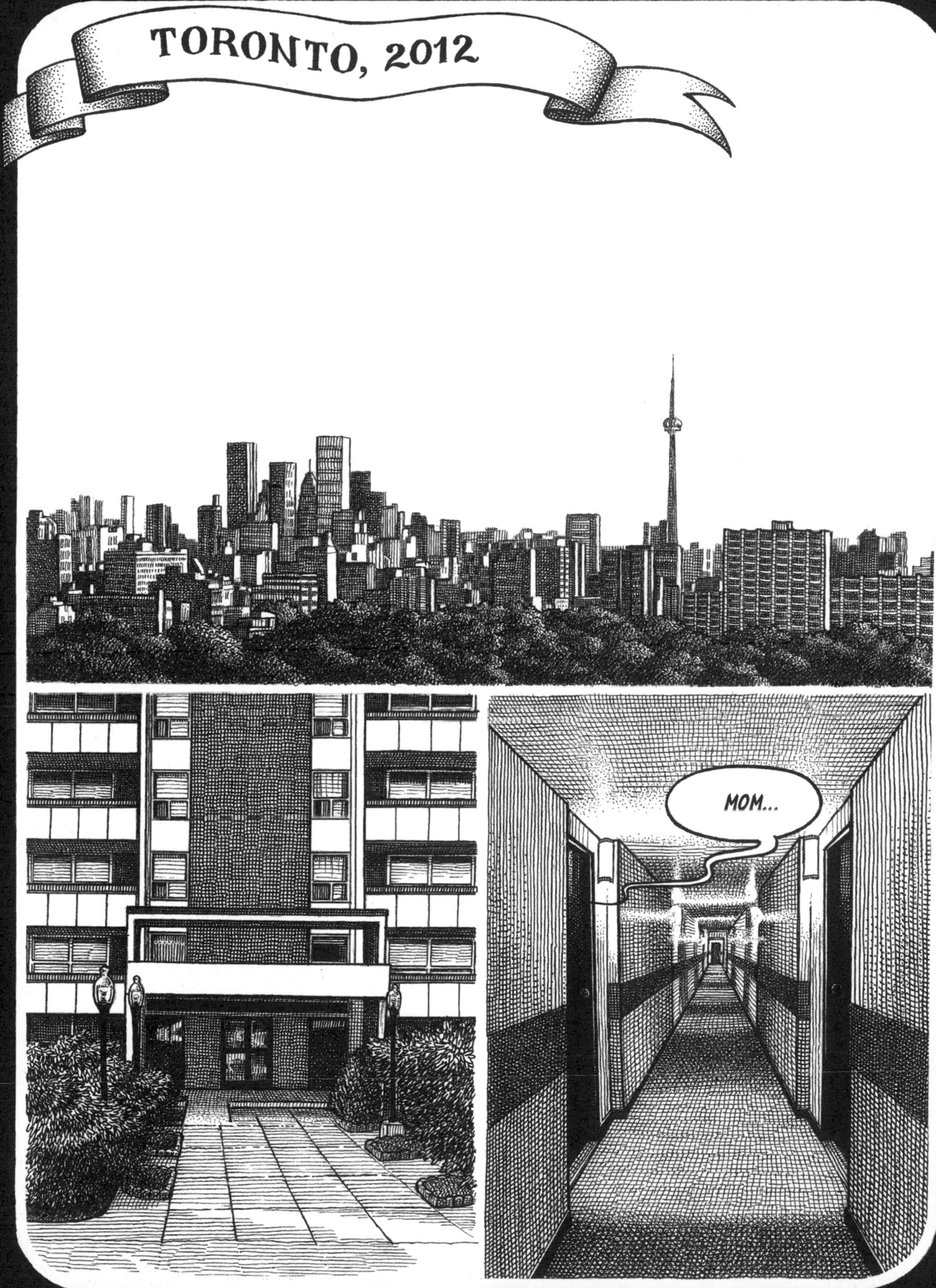
TORONTO, 2012
MOM...

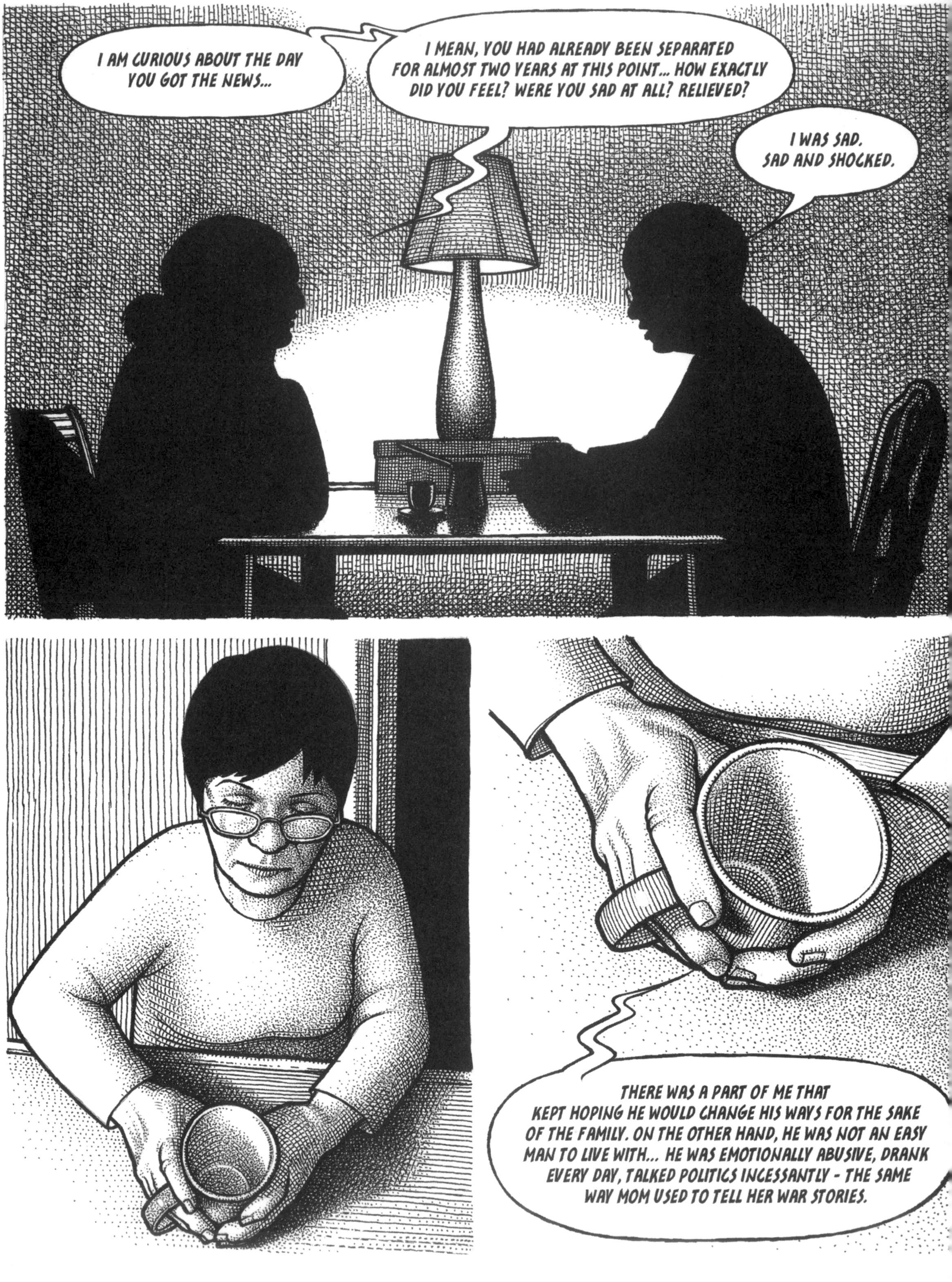
I AM CURIOUS ABOUT THE DAY YOU GOT THE NEWS...
I MEAN, YOU HAD ALREADY BEEN SEPARATED FOR ALMOST TWO YEARS AT THIS POINT... HOW EXACTLY DID YOU FEEL? WERE YOU SAD AT ALL? RELIEVED?
I WAS SAD. SAD AND SHOCKED.
THERE WAS A PART OF ME THAT KEPT HOPING HE WOULD CHANGE HIS WAYS FOR THE SAKE OF THE FAMILY. ON THE OTHER HAND, HE WAS NOT AN EASY MAN TO LIVE WITH... HE WAS EMOTIONALLY ABUSIVE, DRANK EVERY DAY, TALKED POLITICS INCESSANTLY - THE SAME WAY MOM USED TO TELL HER WAR STORIES.

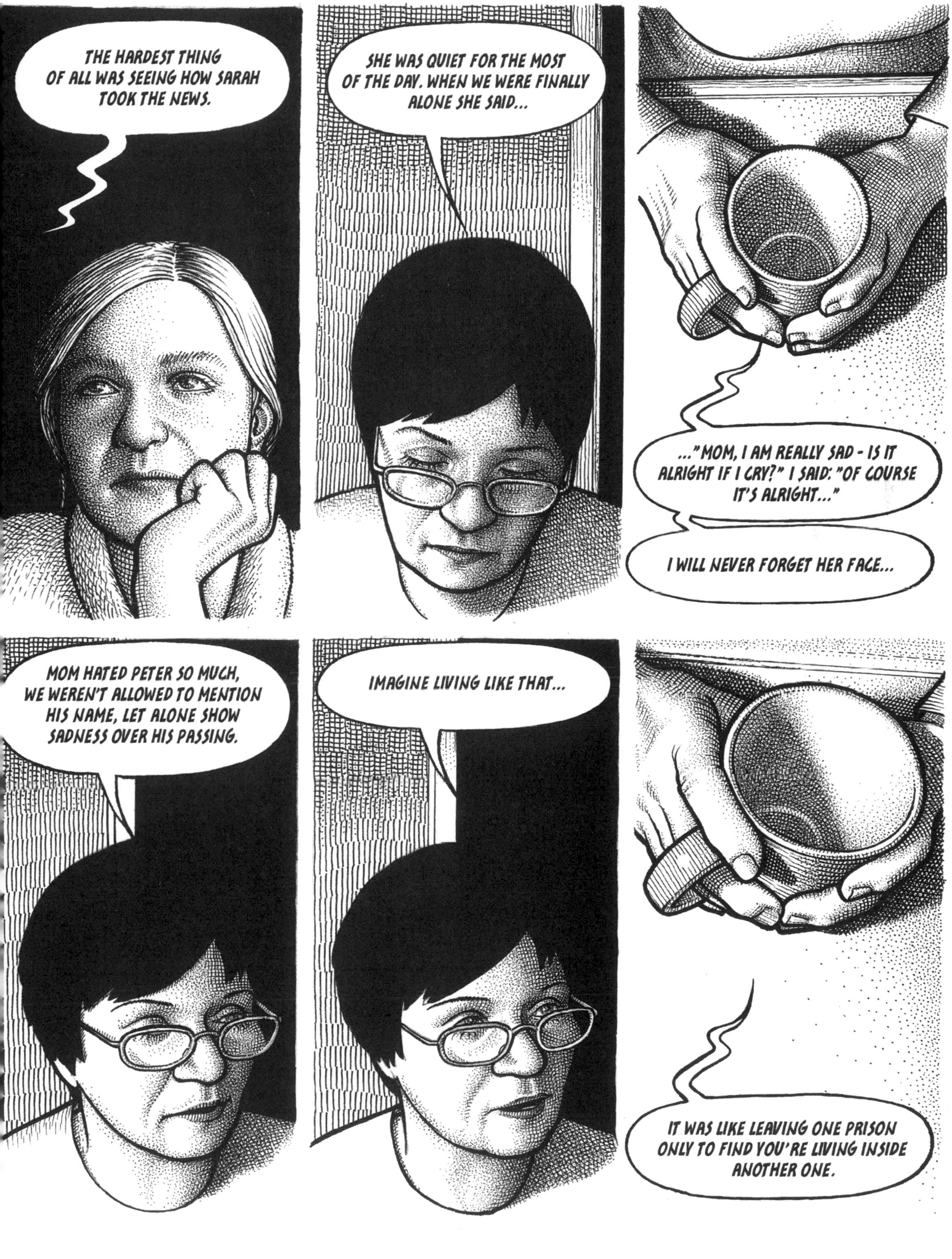
THE HARDEST THING OF ALL WAS SEEING HOW SARAH TOOK THE NEWS.
SHE WAS QUIET FOR THE MOST OF THE DAY. WHEN WE WERE FINALLY ALONE SHE SAID...
..."MOM, I AM REALLY SAD - IS IT ALRIGHT IF I CRY?" I SAID: "OF COURSE IT'S ALRIGHT..."
I WILL NEVER FORGET HER FACE...
MOM HATED PETER SO MUCH, WE WEREN'T ALLOWED TO MENTION HIS NAME, LET ALONE SHOW SADNESS OVER HIS PASSING.
IMAGINE LIVING LIKE THAT...
IT WAS LIKE LEAVING ONE PRISON ONLY TO FIND YOU'RE LIVING INSIDE ANOTHER ONE.

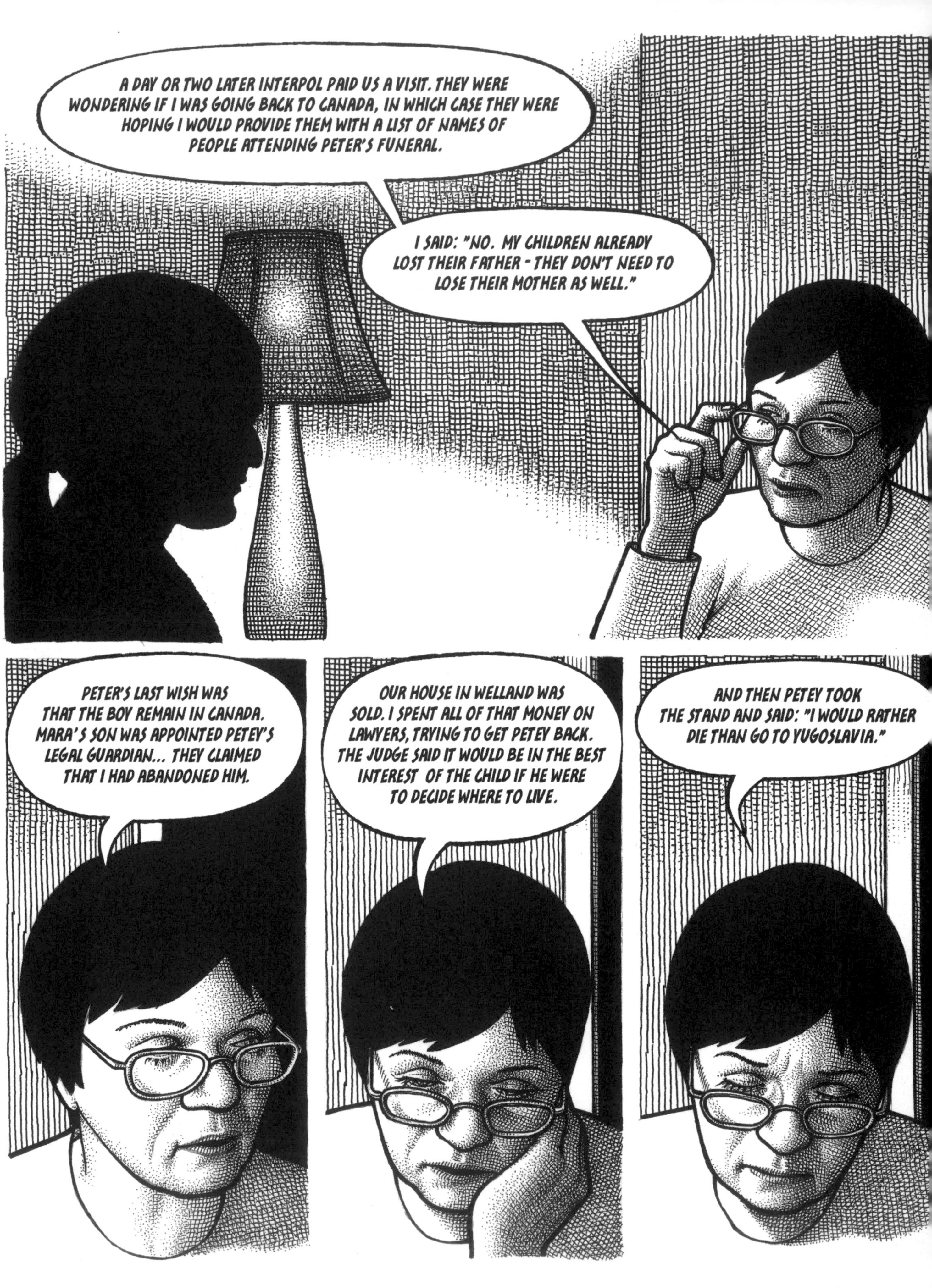
A DAY OR TWO LATER INTERPOL PAID US A VISIT. THEY WERE WONDERING IF I WAS GOING BACK TO CANADA, IN WHICH CASE THEY WERE HOPING I WOULD PROVIDE THEM WITH A LIST OF NAMES OF PEOPLE ATTENDING PETER'S FUNERAL.
I SAID: "NO. MY CHILDREN ALREADY LOST THEIR FATHER - THEY DON'T NEED TO LOSE THEIR MOTHER AS WELL."
PETER'S LAST WISH WAS THAT THE BOY REMAIN IN CANADA. MARA'S SON WAS APPOINTED PETEY'S LEGAL GUARDIAN... THEY CLAIMED THAT I HAD ABANDONED HIM.
OUR HOUSE IN WELLAND WAS SOLD. I SPENT ALL OF THAT MONEY ON LAWYERS, TRYING TO GET PETEY BACK. THE JUDGE SAID IT WOULD BE IN THE BEST INTEREST OF THE CHILD IF HE WERE TO DECIDE WHERE TO LIVE.
AND THEN PETEY TOOK THE STAND AND SAID: "I WOULD RATHER DIE THAN GO TO YUGOSLAVIA."

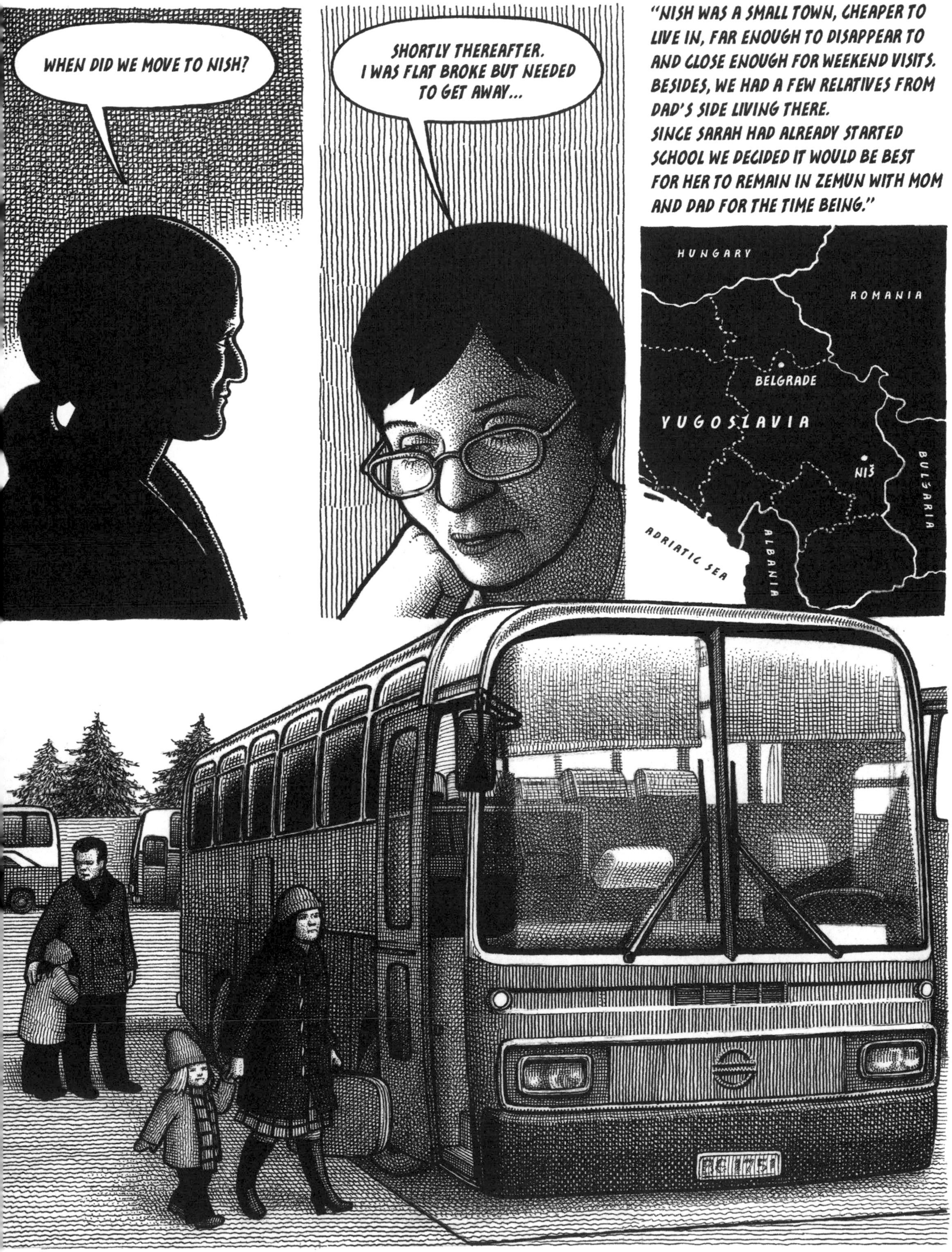

WHEN DID WE MOVE TO NISH?
SHORTLY THEREAFTER. I WAS FLAT BROKE BUT NEEDED TO GET AWAY...
"NISH WAS A SMALL TOWN, CHEAPER TO LIVE IN, FAR ENOUGH TO DISAPPEAR TO AND CLOSE ENOUGH FOR WEEKEND VISITS. BESIDES, WE HAD A FEW RELATIVES FROM DAD'S SIDE LIVING THERE. SINCE SARAH HAD ALREADY STARTED SCHOOL WE DECIDED IT WOULD BE BEST FOR HER TO REMAIN IN ZEMUN WITH MOM AND DAD FOR THE TIME BEING."
HUNGARY
ROMANIA
BELGRADE
YUGOSLAVIA
NIŠ
BULGARIA
ADRIATIC SEA
ALBANIA

"DAD TOOK ON A NIGHTSHIFT JOB TO HELP US FINANCIALLY BUT IT WASN'T NEARLY ENOUGH. WE COULD HARDLY MAKE ENDS MEET. THE UNEMPLOYMENT WAS AT A RECORD HIGH, I HAD NO WORK EXPERIENCE AND NO PROPER EDUCATION... IT TOOK ME THREE YEARS TO FIND WORK..."

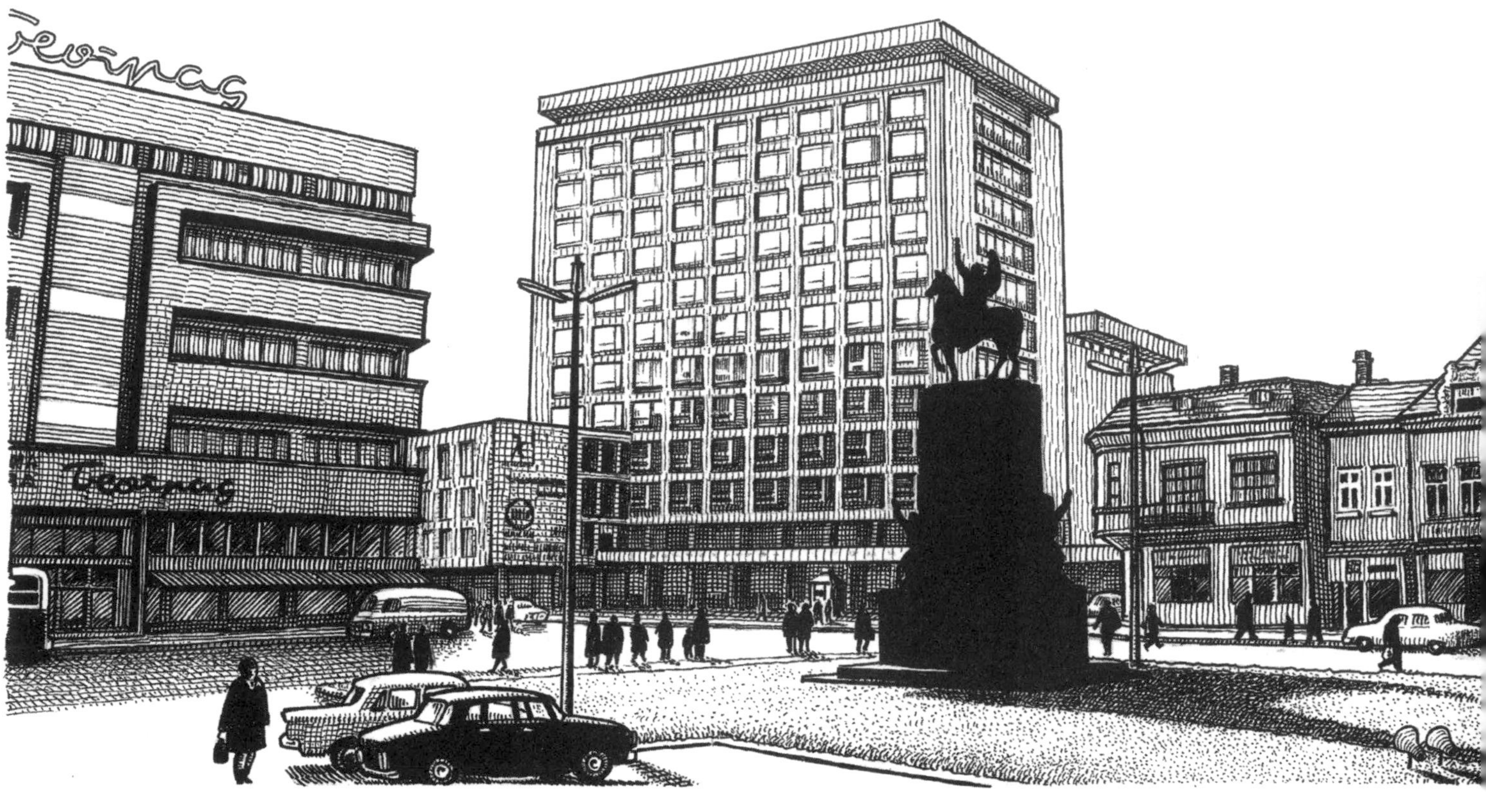

"THREE YEARS OF MOVING FROM ONE MOLDY BASEMENT TO THE NEXT..."

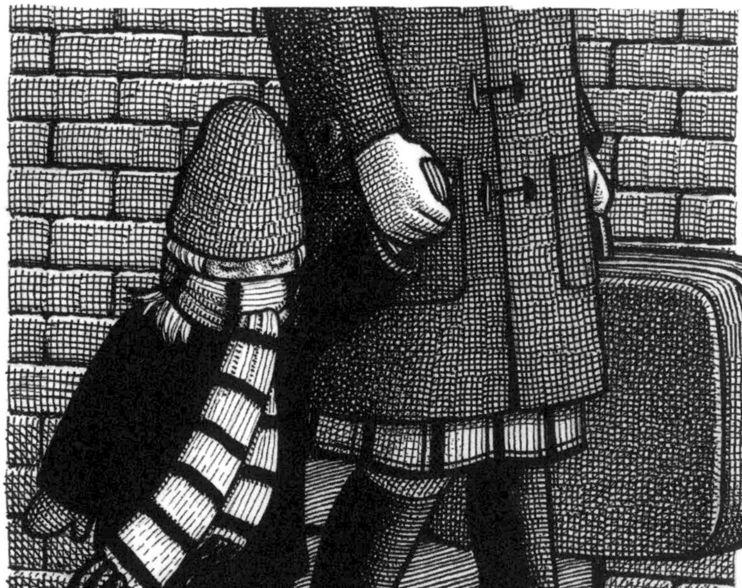

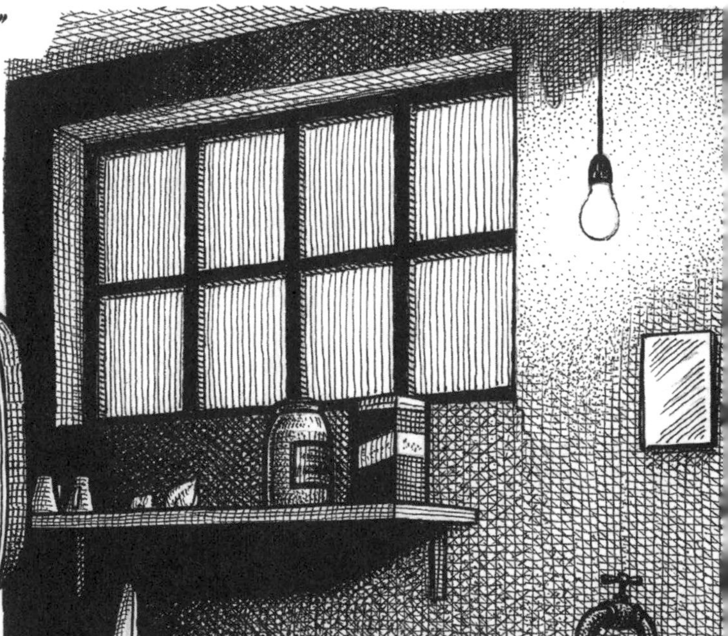

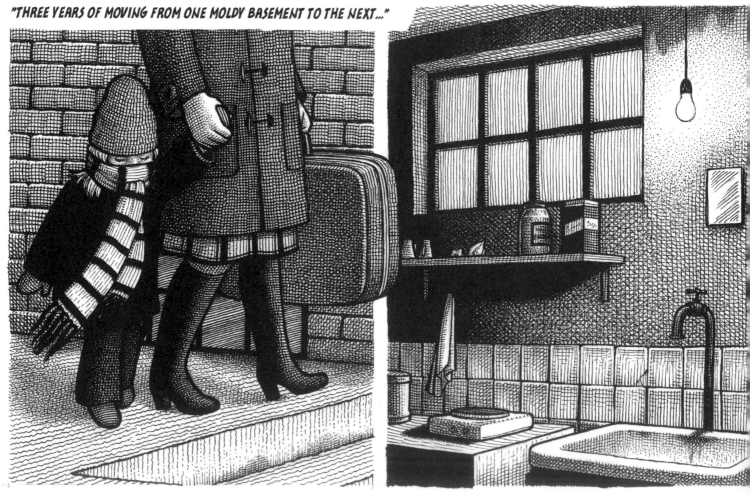

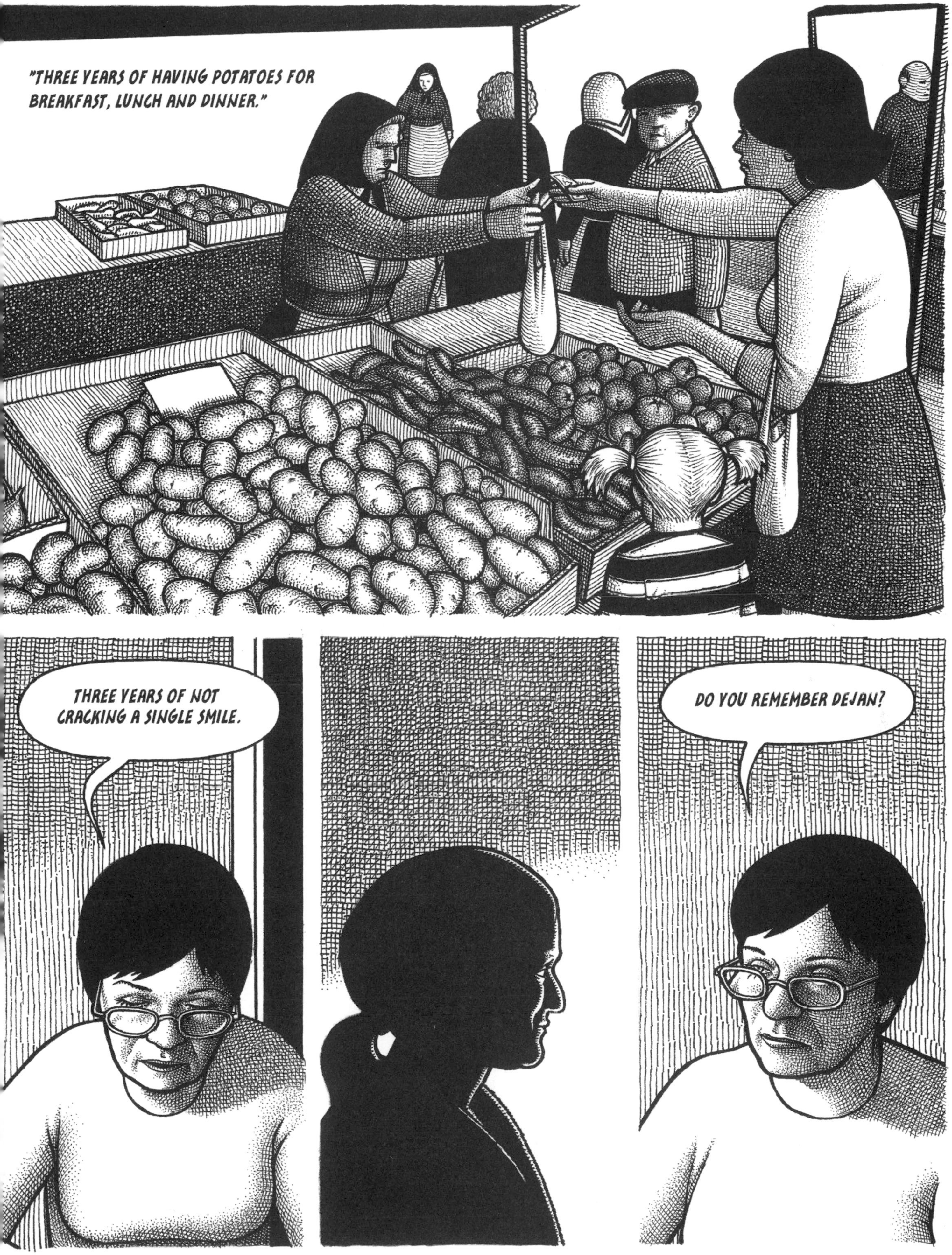
"THREE YEARS OF HAVING POTATOES FOR BREAKFAST, LUNCH AND DINNER."
THREE YEARS OF NOT CRACKING A SINGLE SMILE.
DO YOU REMEMBER DEJAN?

I REMEMBER DEJAN QUITE WELL. HE AND MOM DATED FOR ABOUT THREE YEARS BACK IN THE DAY...

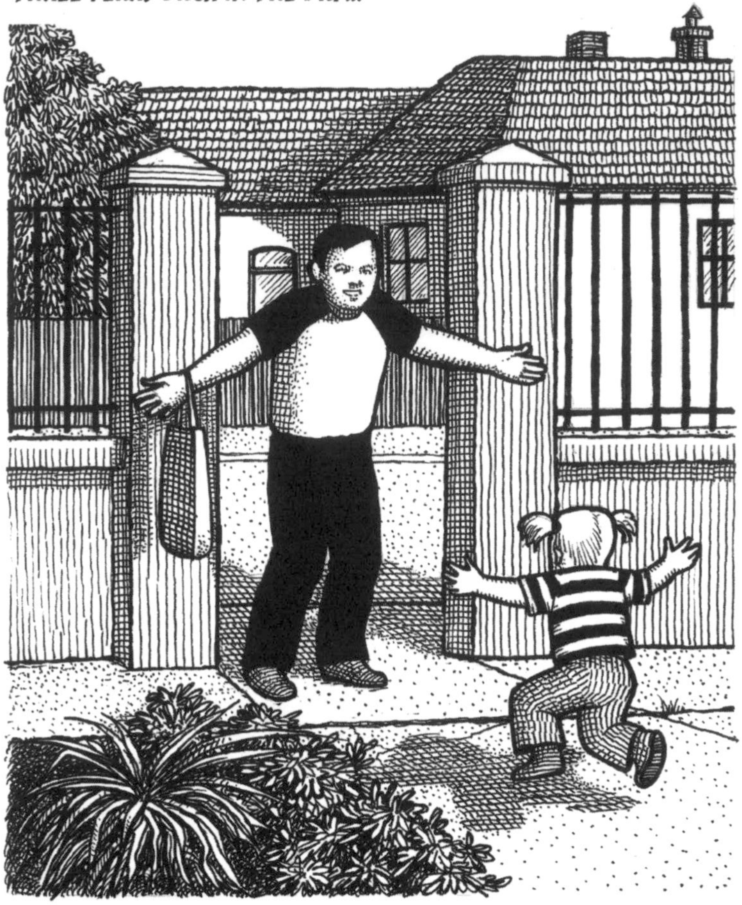

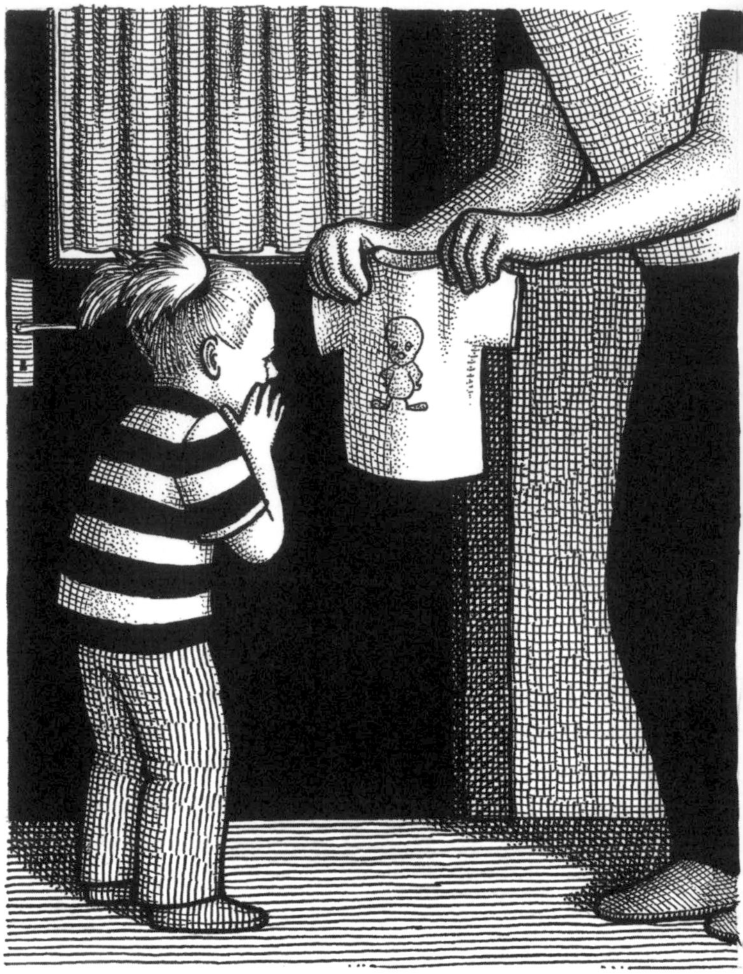

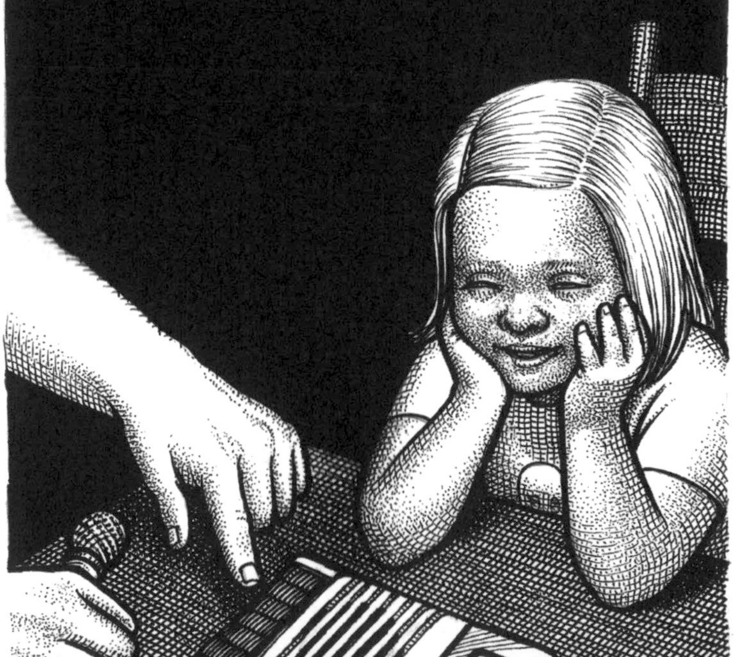

LONG ENOUGH TO LEAVE SOME LASTING MEMORIES.

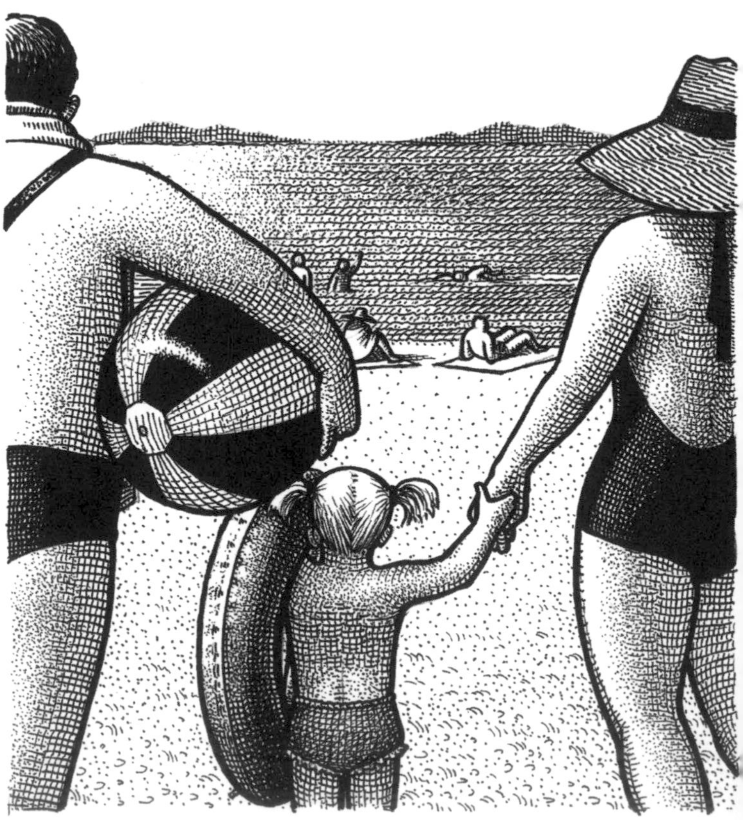

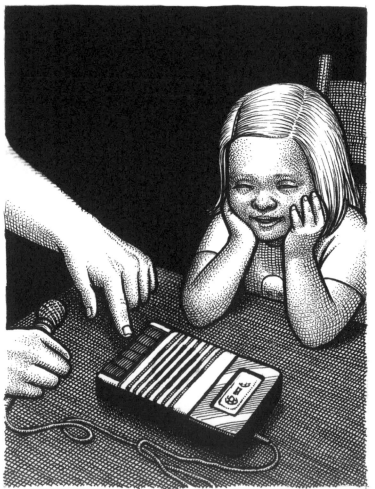

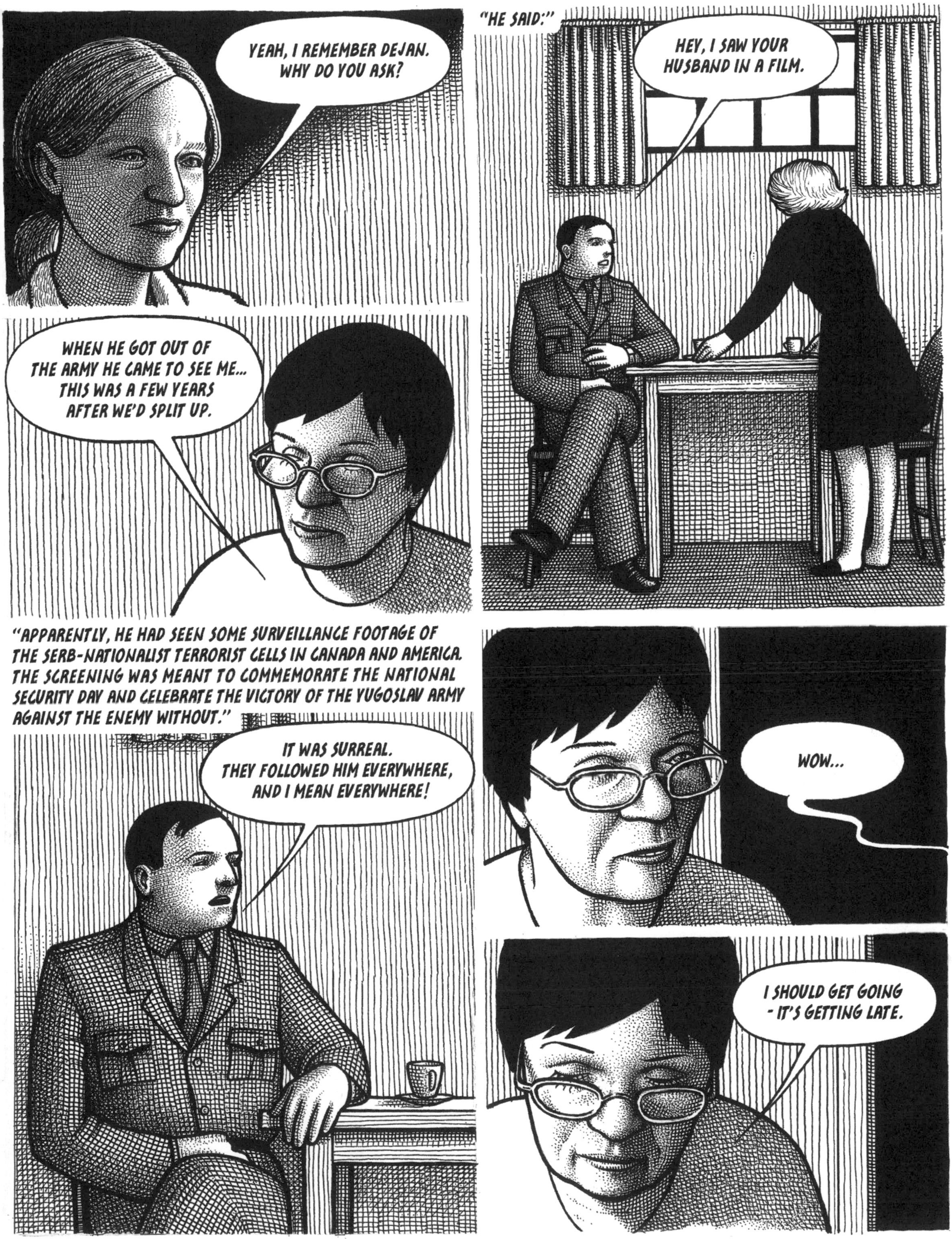

YEAH, I REMEMBER DEJAN. WHY DO YOU ASK?
WHEN HE GOT OUT OF THE ARMY HE CAME TO SEE ME... THIS WAS A FEW YEARS AFTER WE'D SPLIT UP.
"HE SAID:"
HEY, I SAW YOUR HUSBAND IN A FILM.
"APPARENTLY, HE HAD SEEN SOME SURVEILLANCE FOOTAGE OF THE SERB-NATIONALIST TERRORIST CELLS IN CANADA AND AMERICA. THE SCREENING WAS MEANT TO COMMEMORATE THE NATIONAL SECURITY DAY AND CELEBRATE THE VICTORY OF THE YUGOSLAV ARMY AGAINST THE ENEMY WITHOUT."
IT WAS SURREAL. THEY FOLLOWED HIM EVERYWHERE, AND I MEAN EVERYWHERE!
WOW...
I SHOULD GET GOING - IT'S GETTING LATE.

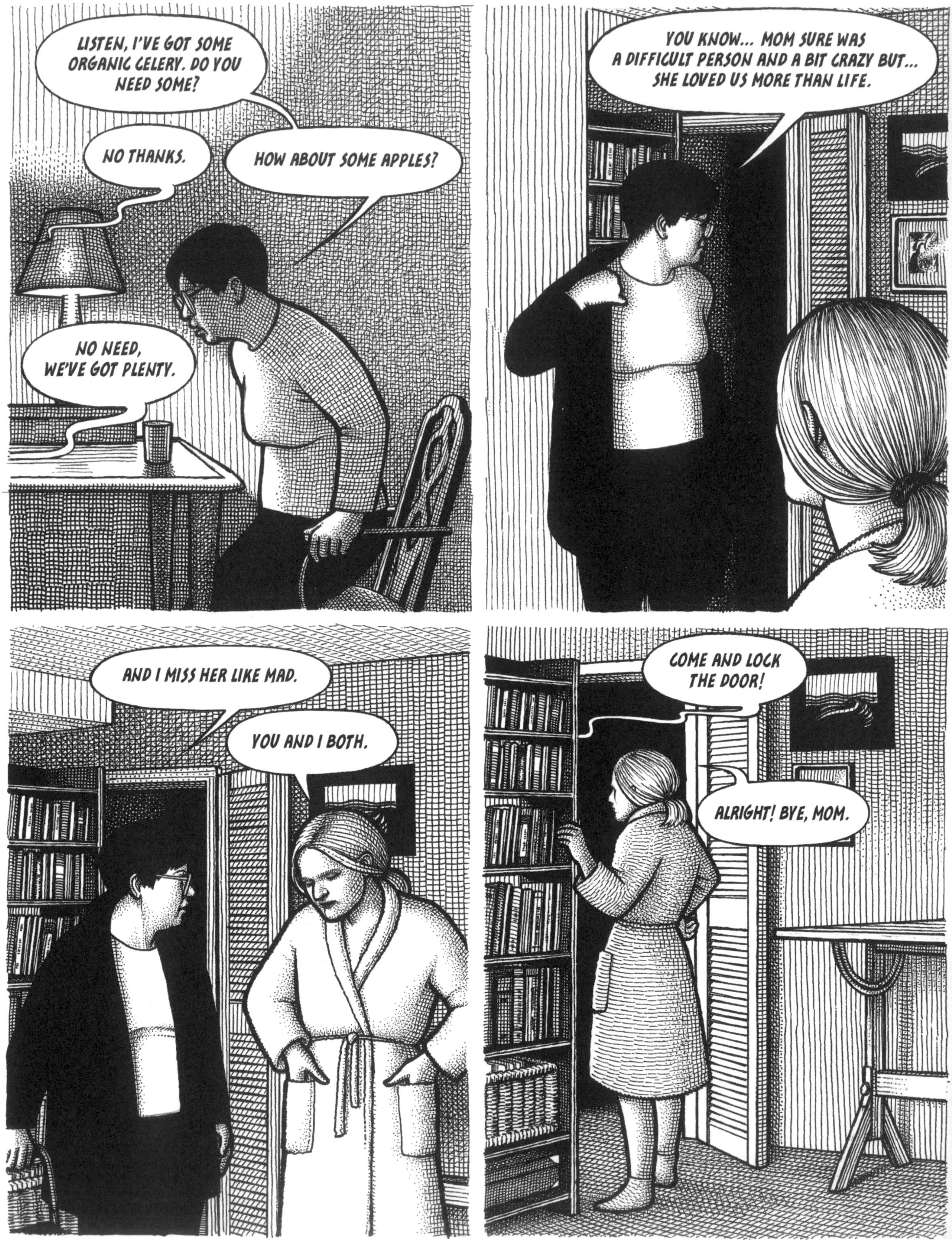
LISTEN, I'VE GOT SOME ORGANIC CELERY. DO YOU NEED SOME?
NO THANKS.
HOW ABOUT SOME APPLES?
NO NEED, WE'VE GOT PLENTY.
YOU KNOW... MOM SURE WAS A DIFFICULT PERSON AND A BIT CRAZY BUT... SHE LOVED US MORE THAN LIFE.
AND I MISS HER LIKE MAD.
YOU AND I BOTH.
COME AND LOCK THE DOOR!
ALRIGHT! BYE, MOM.

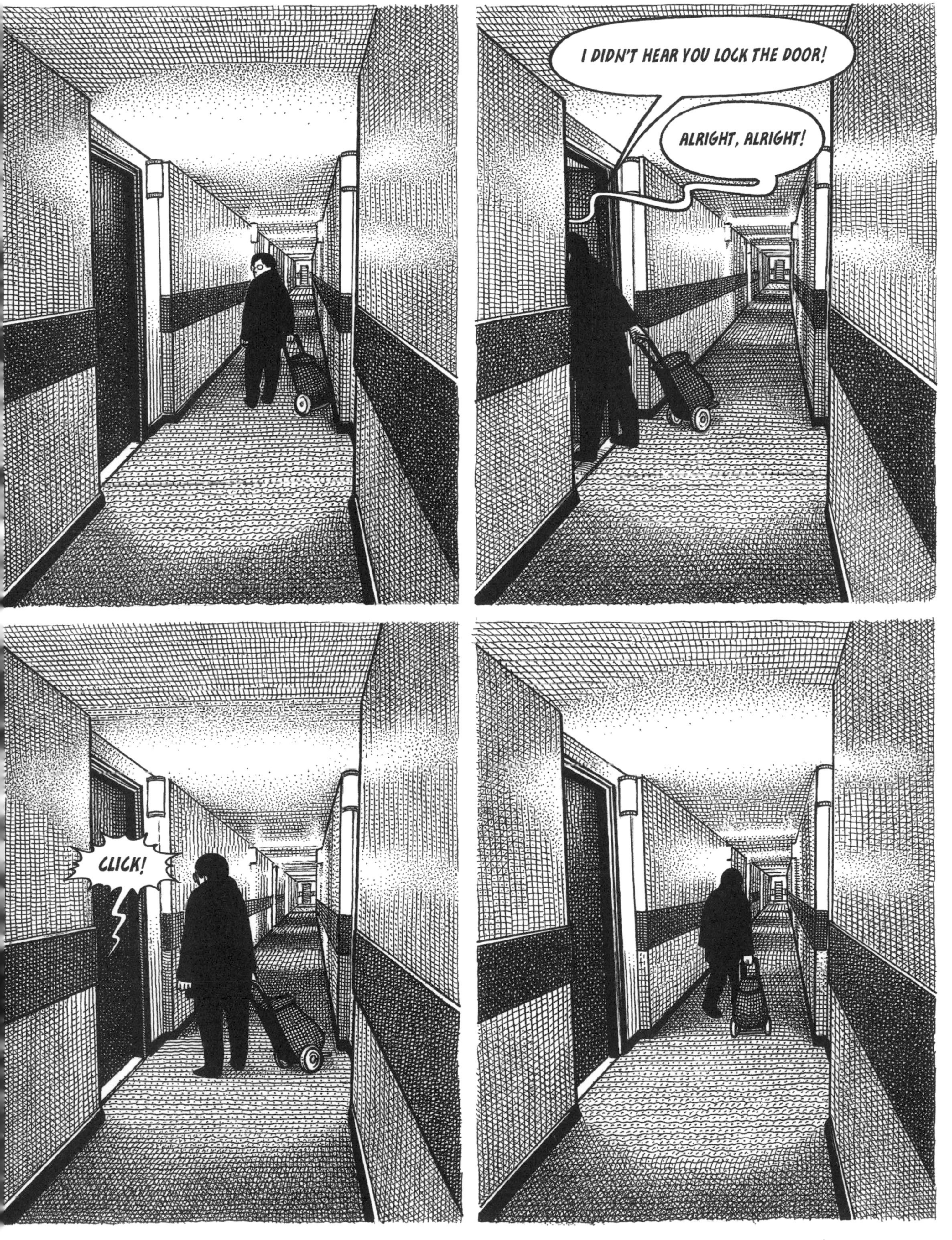
I DIDN'T HEAR YOU LOCK THE DOOR!
ALRIGHT, ALRIGHT!
CLICK!

# FATHERLAND
## PART TWO
# EXILE

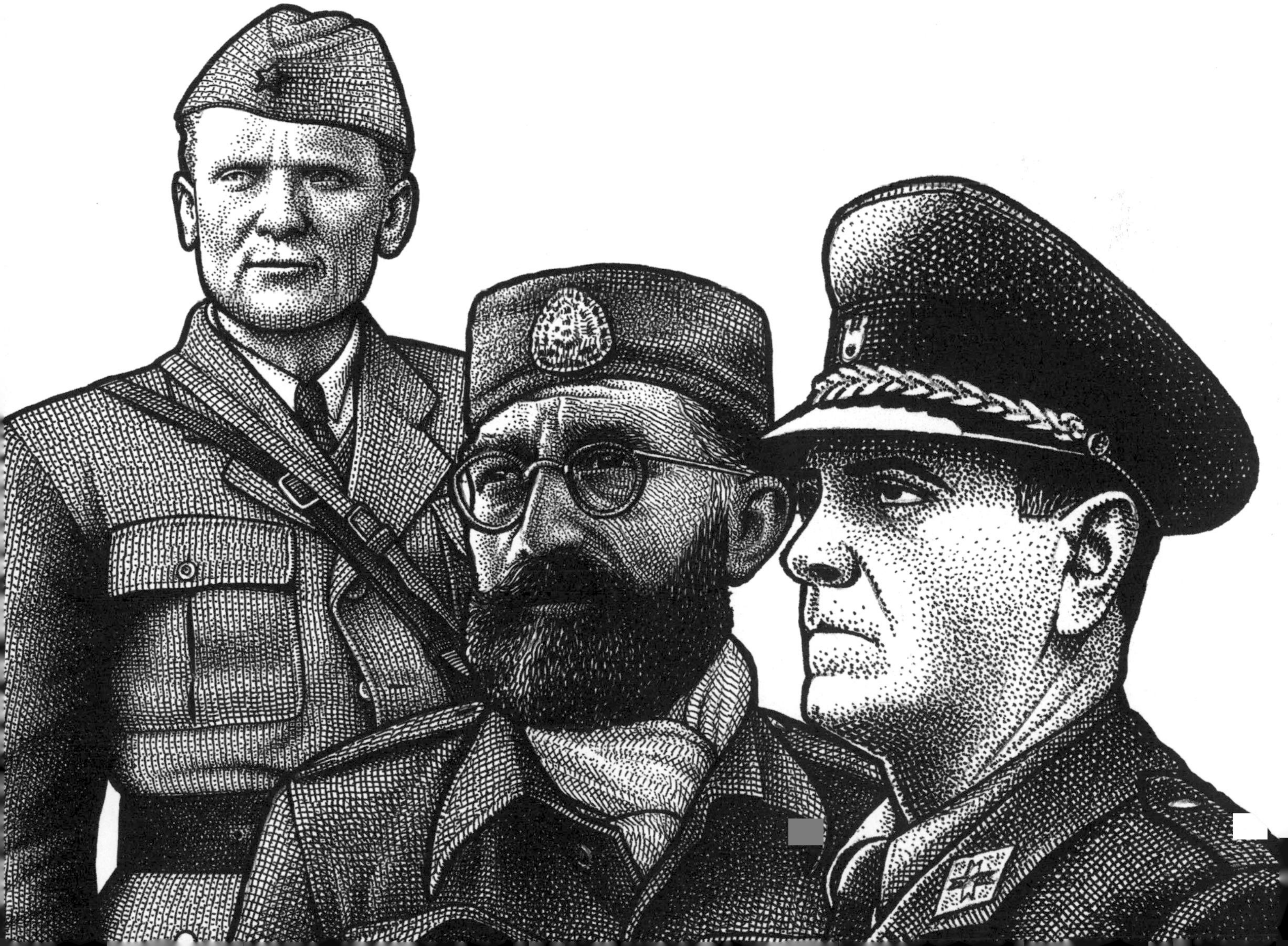

# CHILDHOOD

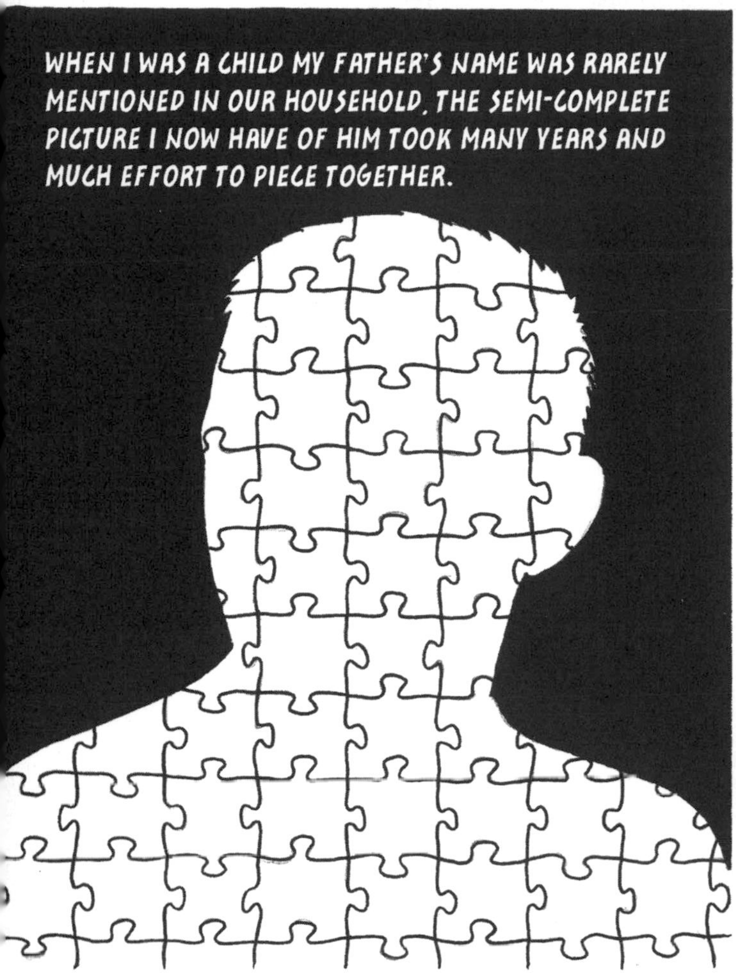
WHEN I WAS A CHILD MY FATHER'S NAME WAS RARELY MENTIONED IN OUR HOUSEHOLD. THE SEMI-COMPLETE PICTURE I NOW HAVE OF HIM TOOK MANY YEARS AND MUCH EFFORT TO PIECE TOGETHER.

HE WAS BORN IN 1936, TO SERBIAN PARENTS STANA AND DJURO...

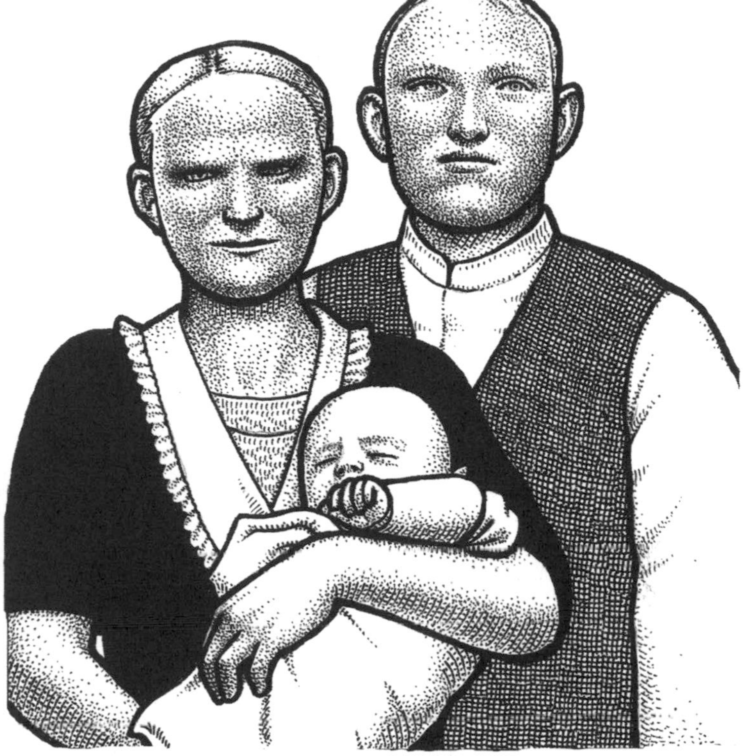

IN THE SMALL CROATIAN VILLAGE OF BOGIĆEVCI...

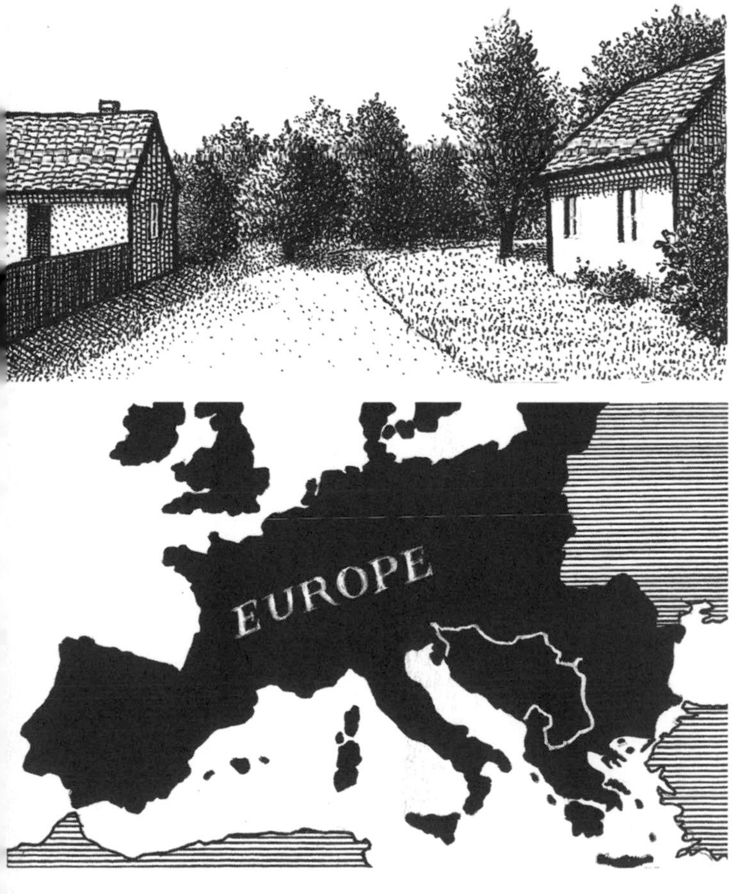
EUROPE

SITUATED IN WHAT WAS THEN CALLED THE KINGDOM OF YUGOSLAVIA.

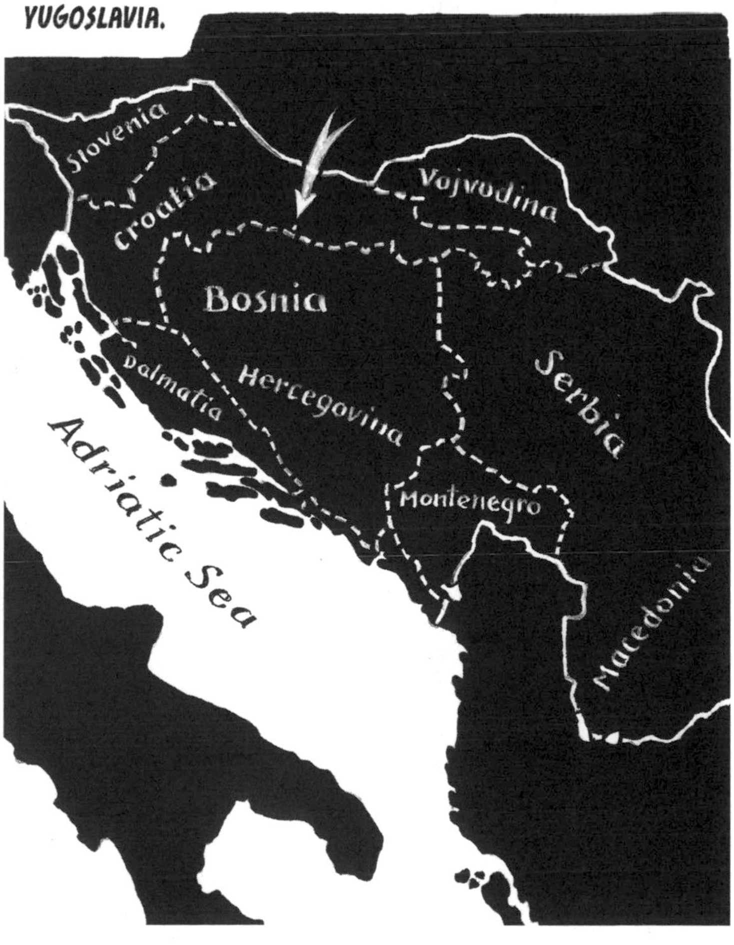
Slovenia
Croatia
Vojvodina
Bosnia
Dalmatia
Hercegovina
Serbia
Adriatic Sea
Montenegro
Macedonia

HIS FATHER DJURO WAS BORN IN GARY, INDIANA...

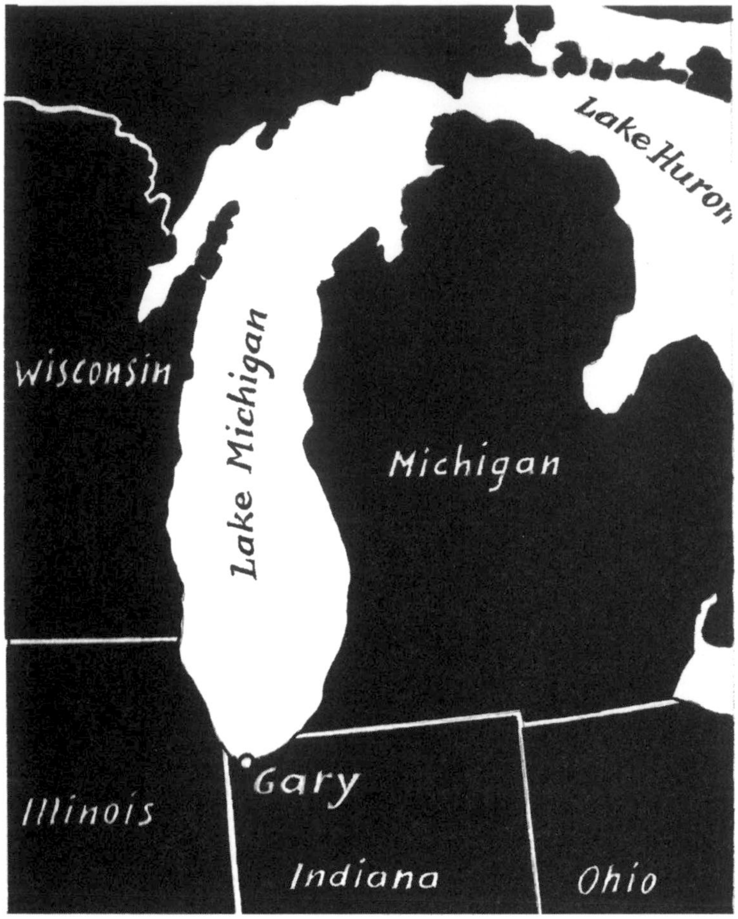
Lake Huron
Wisconsin
Lake Michigan
Michigan
Gary
Illinois
Indiana
Ohio

TO PEPO AND KATA WHO HAD IMMIGRATED TO AMERICA AT THE TURN OF THE CENTURY. KATA WAS A HOMEMAKER...

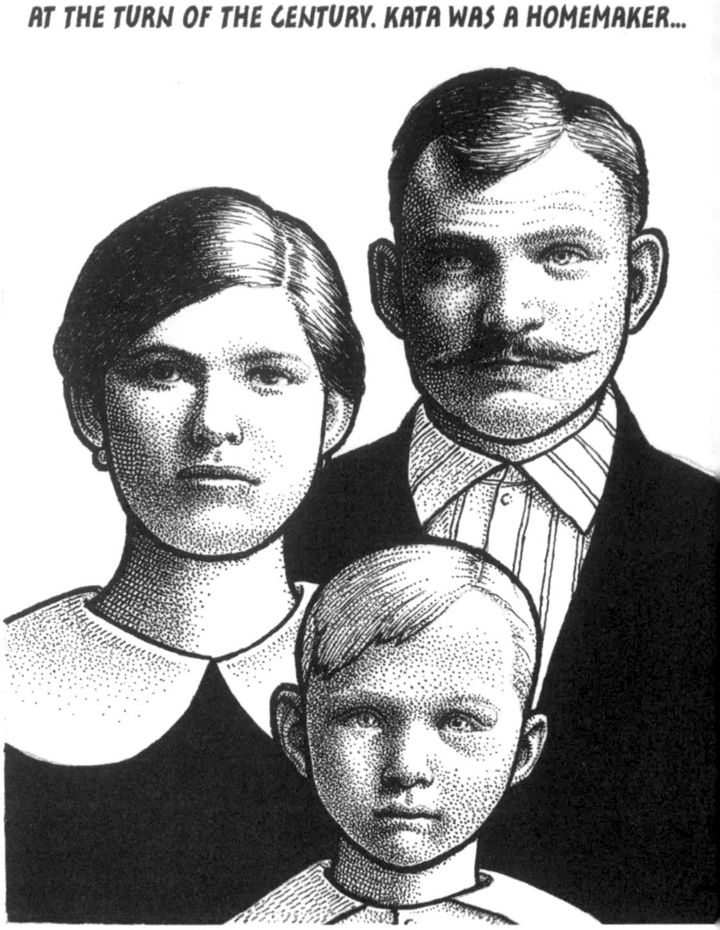

WHILE PEPO WAS EMPLOYED AS A SKILLED LABORER AT THOMPSON STEEL.

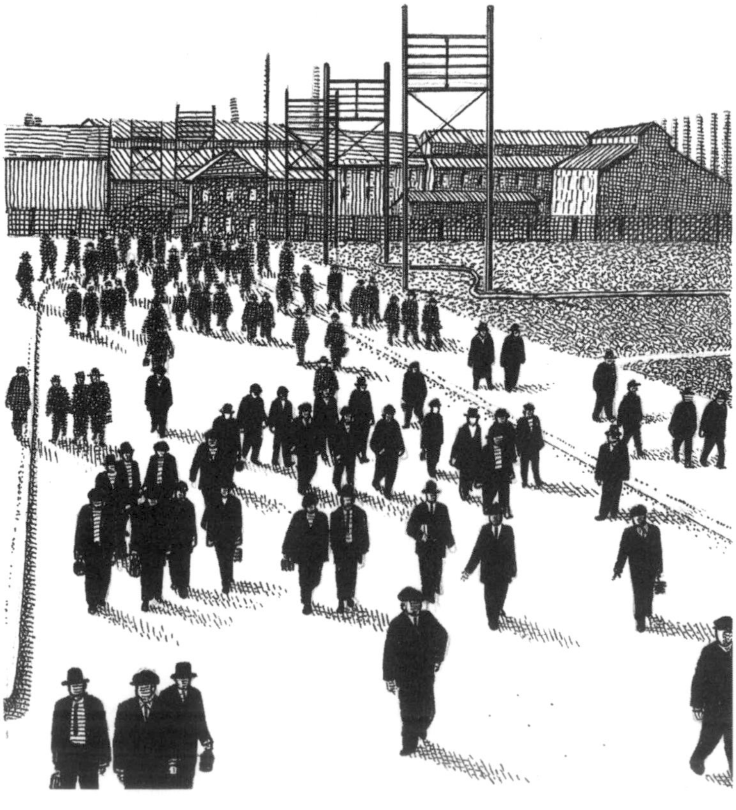

WHEN YOUNG DJURO WAS DIAGNOSED WITH TUBERCULOSIS...

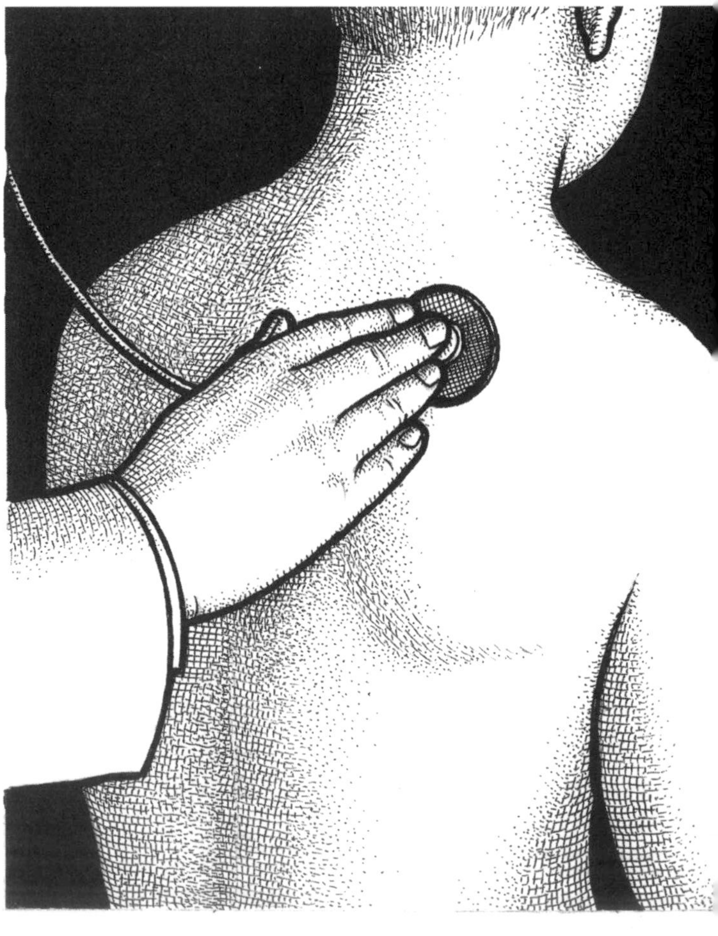

THE FAMILY RETURNED TO THEIR NATIVE VILLAGE, HOPING THAT THE FRESH COUNTRY AIR WOULD AID IN HIS RECOVERY. I OFTEN WONDER HOW DJURO FELT AT THIS POINT, HAVING BEEN RAISED IN AN AMERICAN CITY AND THEN, ALL OF A SUDDEN...

FINDING HIMSELF KNEE-DEEP IN THE OLD WORLD MUD...

HOMESICK AND ISOLATED, ON A LONG ROAD TO RECOVERY.

AND ALTHOUGH HE DID EVENTUALLY TRIUMPH OVER THE ILLNESS...

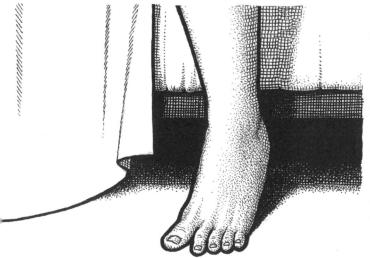

HE WAS UNABLE TO COPE WITH THE EMOTIONAL PAIN.

DJURO'S REPUTATION AS THE VILLAGE DRUNKARD DID NOT STOP MY GRANDMOTHER STANA FROM FALLING MADLY IN LOVE WITH HIM. AT FIRST SHE ADMIRED HIM FROM AFAR, HOPING AND PRAYING THAT ONE DAY HE WOULD NOTICE HER AS WELL...

AND WHEN THAT DAY FINALLY ARRIVED, SHE BEGAN PRAYING TO ONE DAY BECOME HIS WIFE...

IN SPITE OF HER MOTHER'S DISAPPROVAL.

YOU BETTER KEEP AWAY FROM THAT AMERICAN. HE WILL BRING YOU NOTHING BUT MISERY!

WITHOUT HER HUSBAND AROUND TO HELP ENFORCE DISCIPLINE STANA'S MOTHER STOOD NO CHANCE IN SAVING HER DAUGHTER FROM THE INEVITABLE.

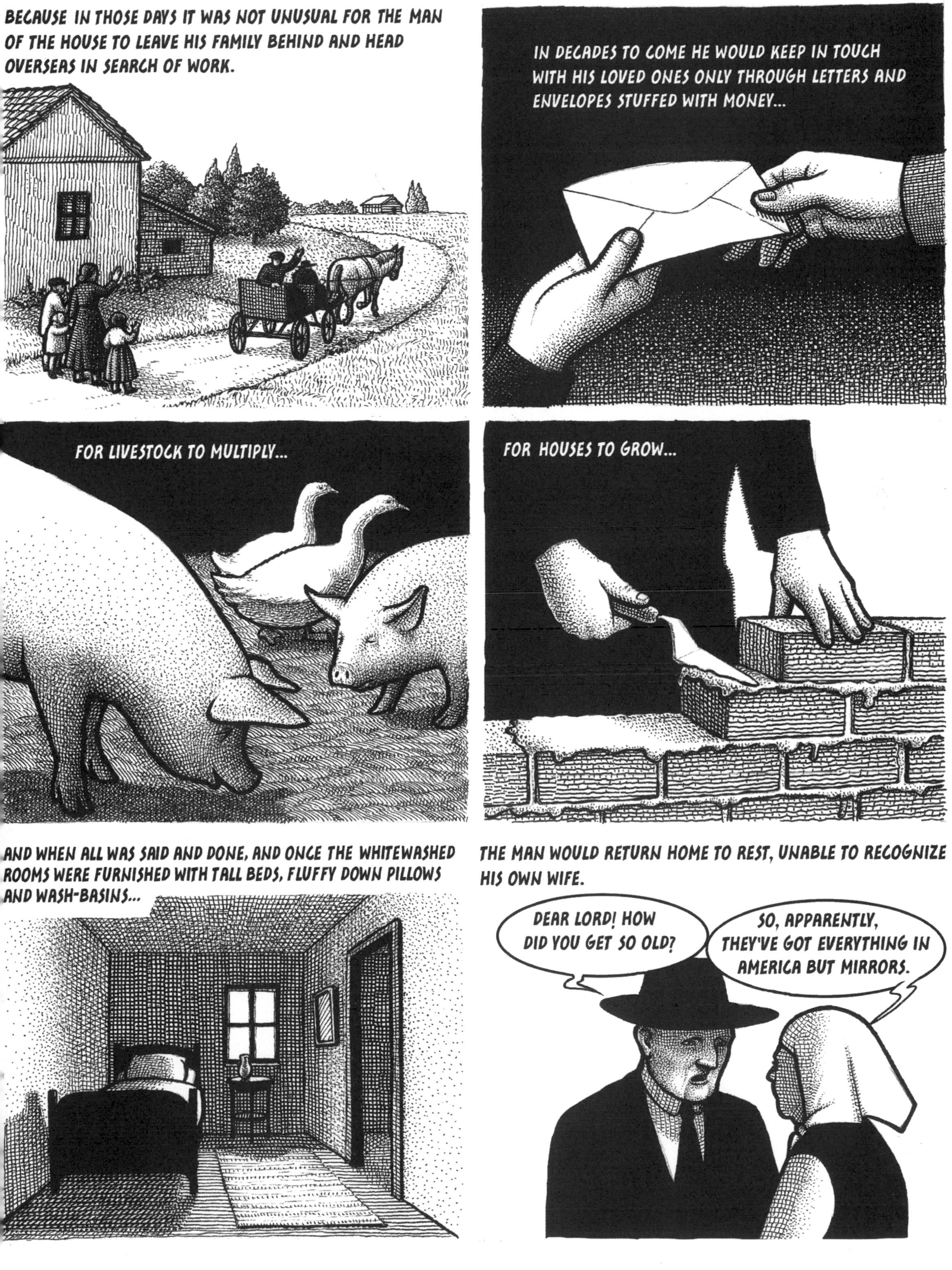
BECAUSE IN THOSE DAYS IT WAS NOT UNUSUAL FOR THE MAN OF THE HOUSE TO LEAVE HIS FAMILY BEHIND AND HEAD OVERSEAS IN SEARCH OF WORK.
IN DECADES TO COME HE WOULD KEEP IN TOUCH WITH HIS LOVED ONES ONLY THROUGH LETTERS AND ENVELOPES STUFFED WITH MONEY...
FOR LIVESTOCK TO MULTIPLY...
FOR HOUSES TO GROW...
AND WHEN ALL WAS SAID AND DONE, AND ONCE THE WHITEWASHED ROOMS WERE FURNISHED WITH TALL BEDS, FLUFFY DOWN PILLOWS AND WASH-BASINS...
THE MAN WOULD RETURN HOME TO REST, UNABLE TO RECOGNIZE HIS OWN WIFE.
DEAR LORD! HOW DID YOU GET SO OLD?
SO, APPARENTLY, THEY'VE GOT EVERYTHING IN AMERICA BUT MIRRORS.

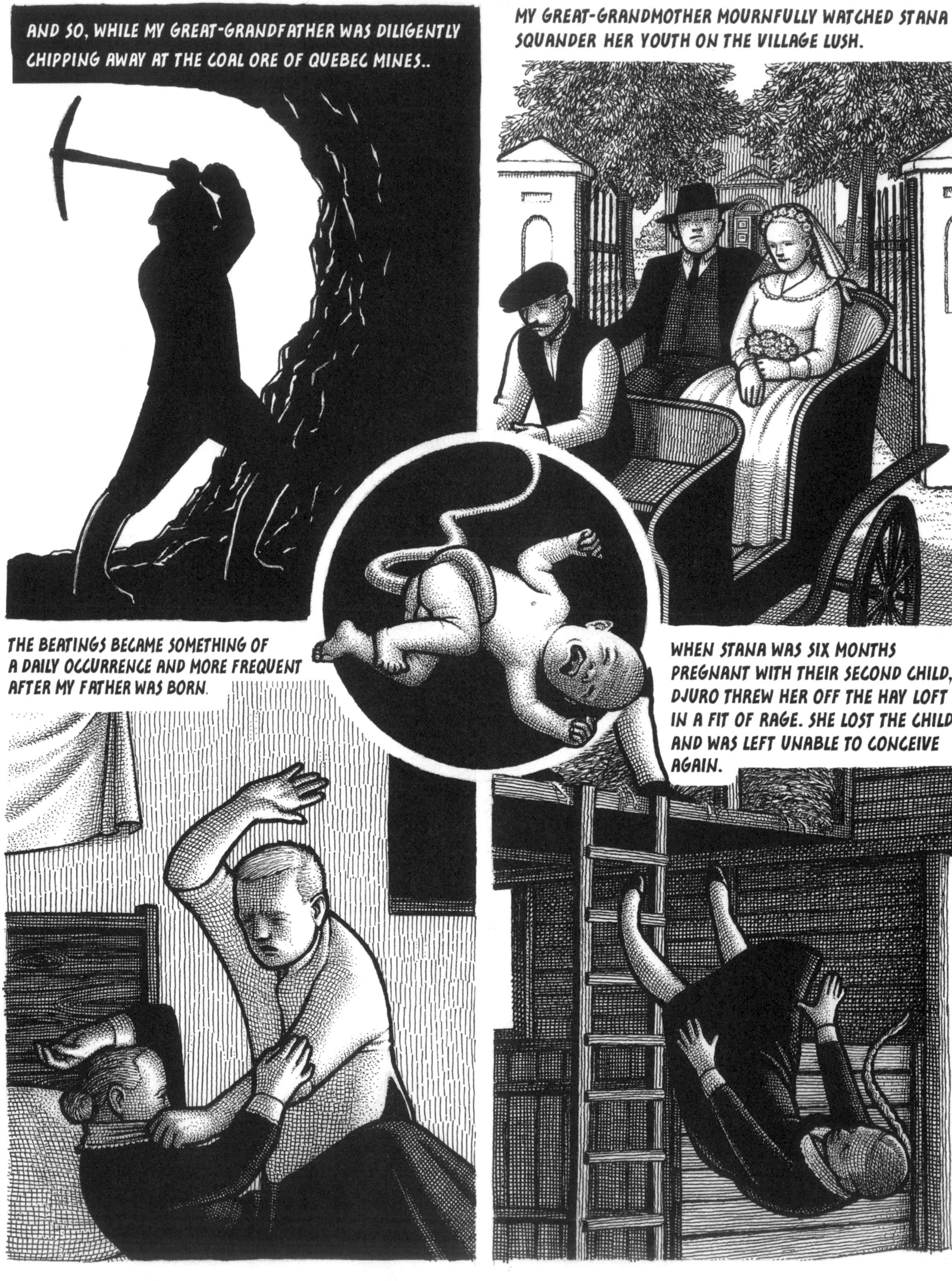
AND SO, WHILE MY GREAT-GRANDFATHER WAS DILIGENTLY CHIPPING AWAY AT THE COAL ORE OF QUEBEC MINES..
MY GREAT-GRANDMOTHER MOURNFULLY WATCHED STANA SQUANDER HER YOUTH ON THE VILLAGE LUSH.
THE BEATINGS BECAME SOMETHING OF A DAILY OCCURRENCE AND MORE FREQUENT AFTER MY FATHER WAS BORN.
WHEN STANA WAS SIX MONTHS PREGNANT WITH THEIR SECOND CHILD, DJURO THREW HER OFF THE HAY LOFT IN A FIT OF RAGE. SHE LOST THE CHILD AND WAS LEFT UNABLE TO CONCEIVE AGAIN.

ON APRIL 6, 1941, THE AXIS INVADED YUGOSLAVIA AFTER AN ANNOUNCEMENT WAS MADE THAT THE NEW YUGOSLAV GOVERNMENT WOULD NOT HONOR THE TRIPARTITE PACT WHICH PRINCE PAUL, THE REGENT OF SERBIA, HAD PREVIOUSLY SIGNED IN VIENNA ON MARCH 25TH.

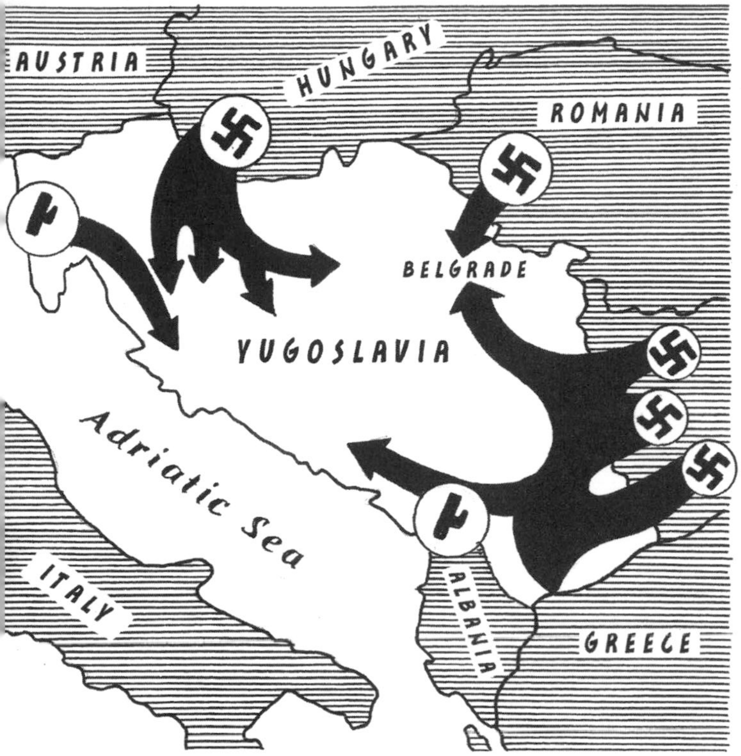
AUSTRIA
HUNGARY
ROMANIA
BELGRADE
YUGOSLAVIA
Adriatic Sea
ITALY
ALBANIA
GREECE

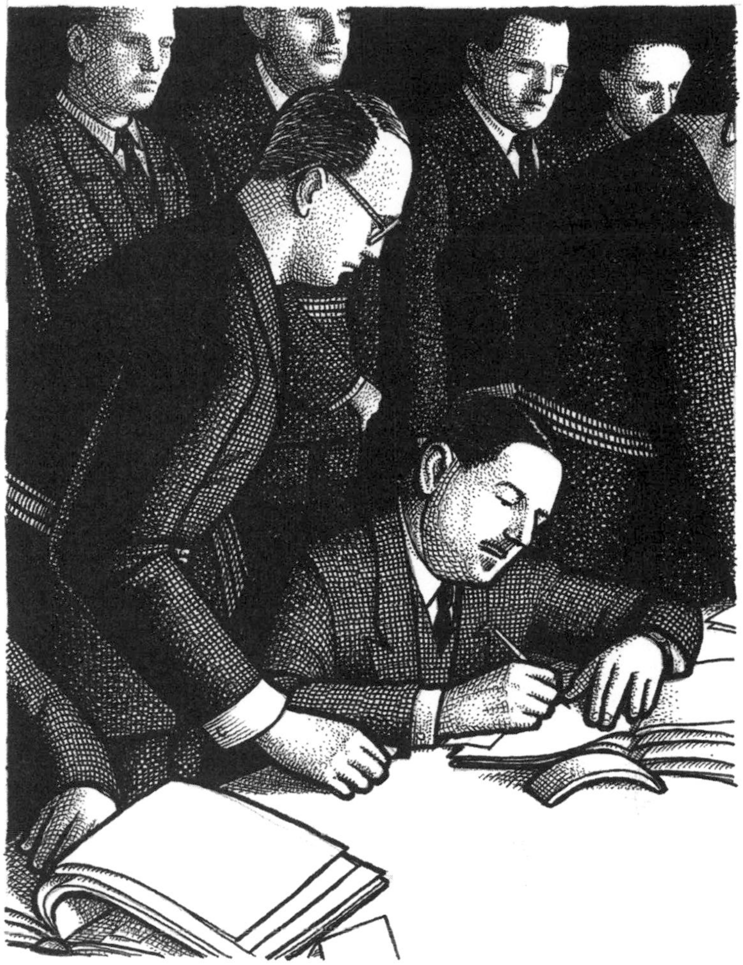

THE UNPOPULAR ACT OF SIGNING CREATED AN IMMEDIATE STIR IN THE MILITARY LEVELS OF GOVERNMENT...

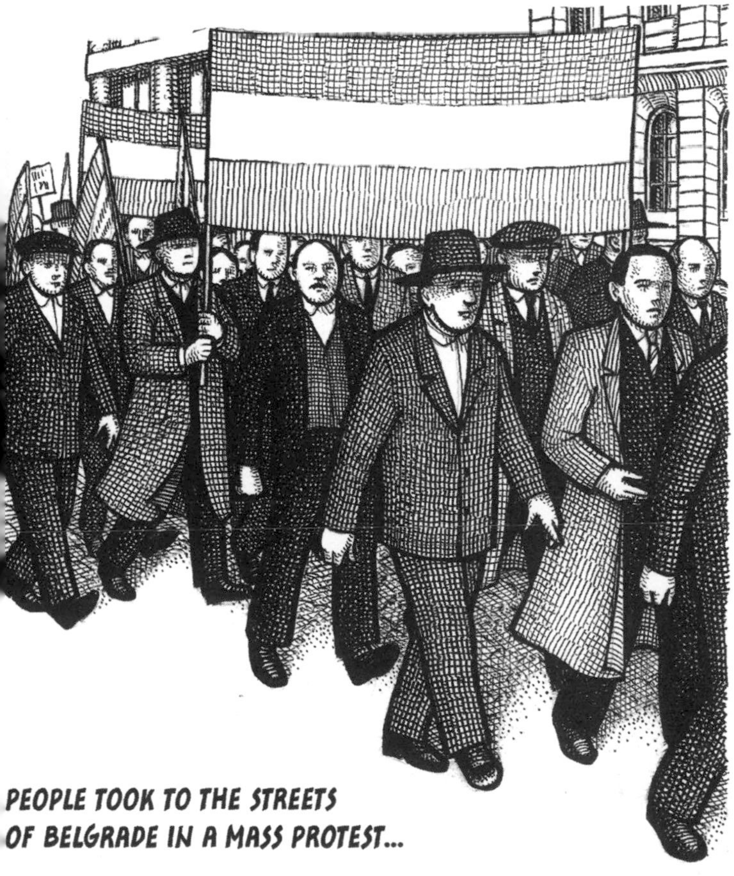

PEOPLE TOOK TO THE STREETS OF BELGRADE IN A MASS PROTEST...

RESULTING IN THE MARCH 27 MILITARY COUP D'ETAT BY WHICH THE REGENCY WAS OVERTHROWN AND THE SEVENTEEN-YEAR-OLD PRINCE PETER II PLACED IN CHARGE OF THE NEWLY FORMED GOVERNMENT.

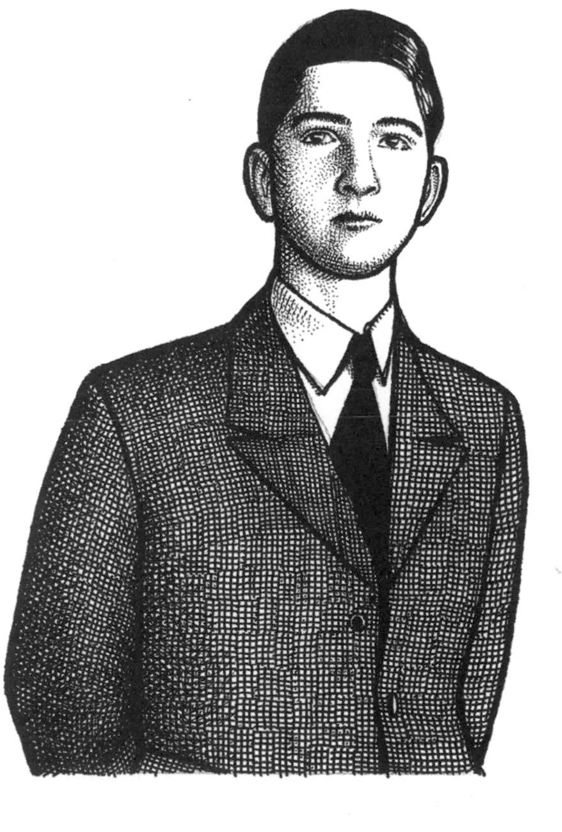

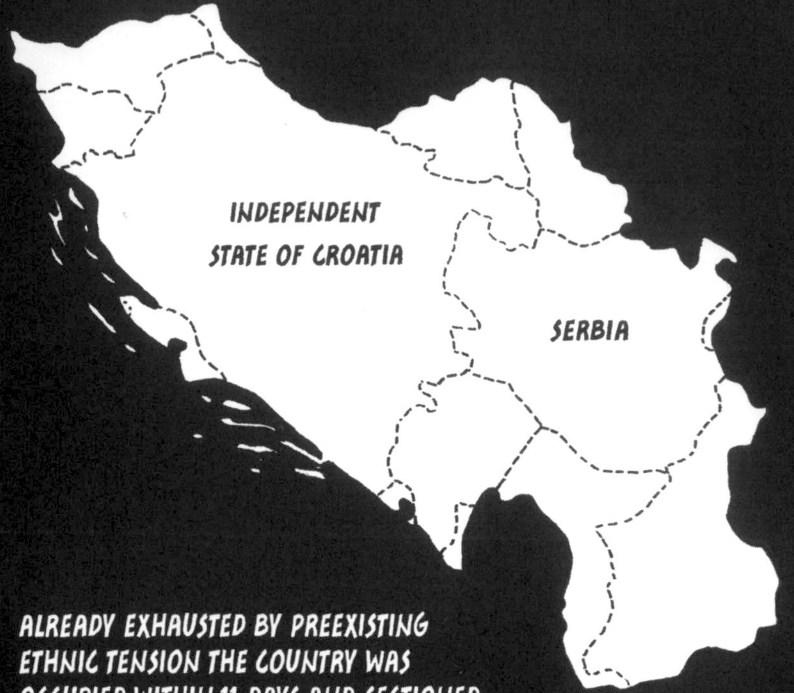
INDEPENDENT STATE OF CROATIA
SERBIA

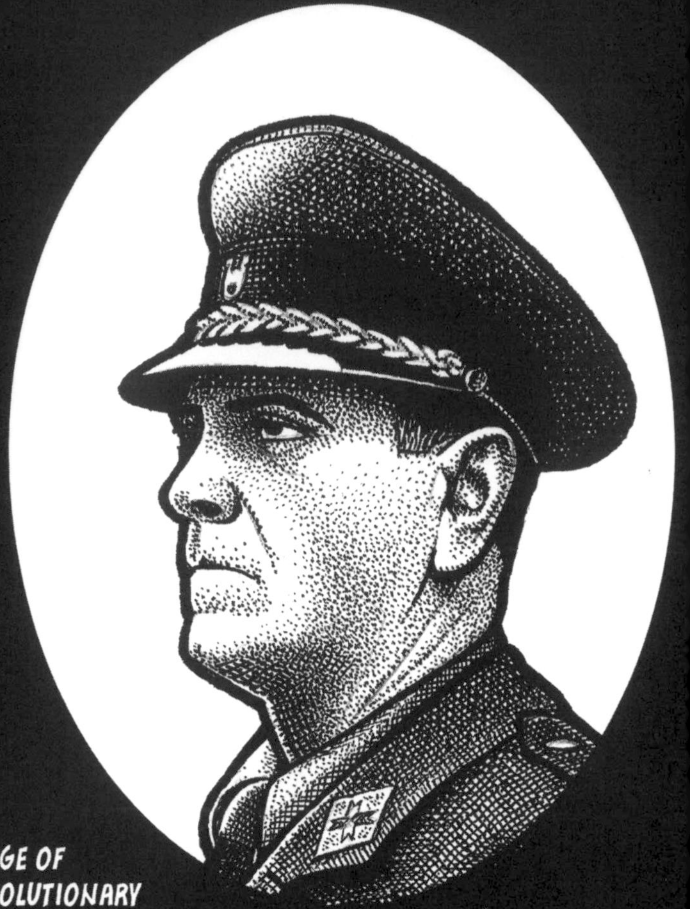

ALREADY EXHAUSTED BY PREEXISTING ETHNIC TENSION THE COUNTRY WAS OCCUPIED WITHIN 11 DAYS AND SECTIONED OFF INTO A NUMBER OF SATELLITE STATES RULED BY GERMANY, ITALY AND BULGARIA.

CROATIA BECAME A GERMAN SATELLITE STATE PLACED UNDER THE CHARGE OF THE EXILED POLITICIAN ANTE PAVELIC AND THE USTASHE MILITIA, A REVOLUTIONARY TERRORIST ORGANIZATION WHICH HE HAD FORMED WHILE LIVING IN AUSTRIA.

MEANWHILE IN SERBIA, A NAZI-BACKED PUPPET GOVERNMENT WAS ESTABLISHED, THE SO-CALLED GOVERNMENT OF NATIONAL SALVATION, HEADED BY GENERAL MILAN NEDIC.

ALMOST OVERNIGHT, A NETWORK OF DETENTION AND CONCENTRATION CAMPS BEGAN SPROUTING THROUGHOUT THE TERRITORY OF FORMER YUGOSLAVIA.

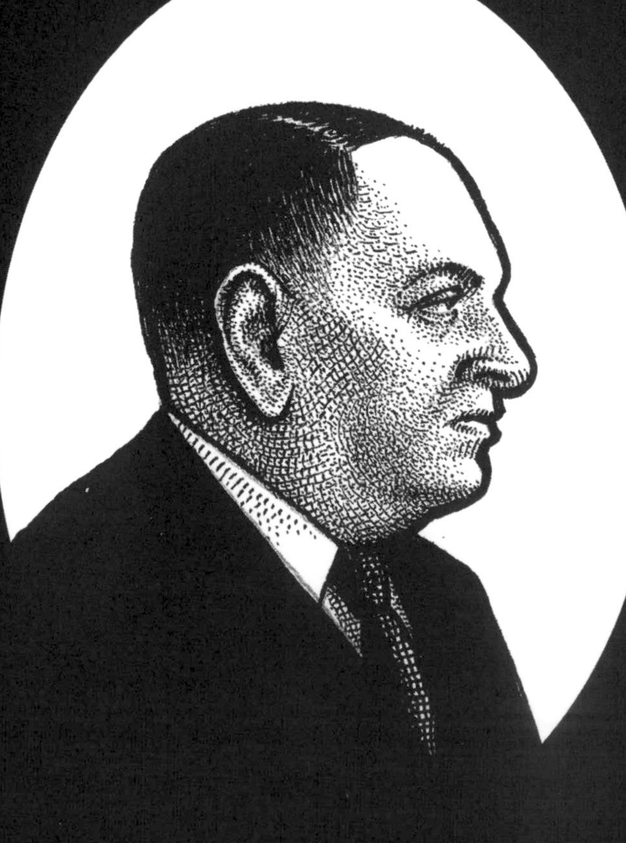

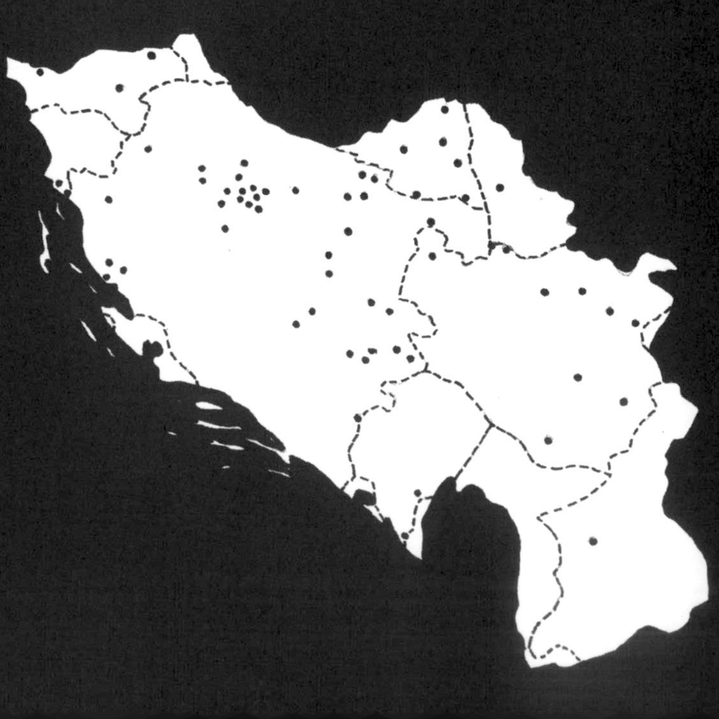

BOTH GOVERNMENTS BEGAN ASSISTING THE AXIS IN MASS-DEPORTATION AND SYSTEMATIC ELIMINATION OF JEWS, ROMAS AND COMMUNISTS. BELGRADE BECAME ONE OF THE FIRST JUDENFREI CITIES IN EUROPE.

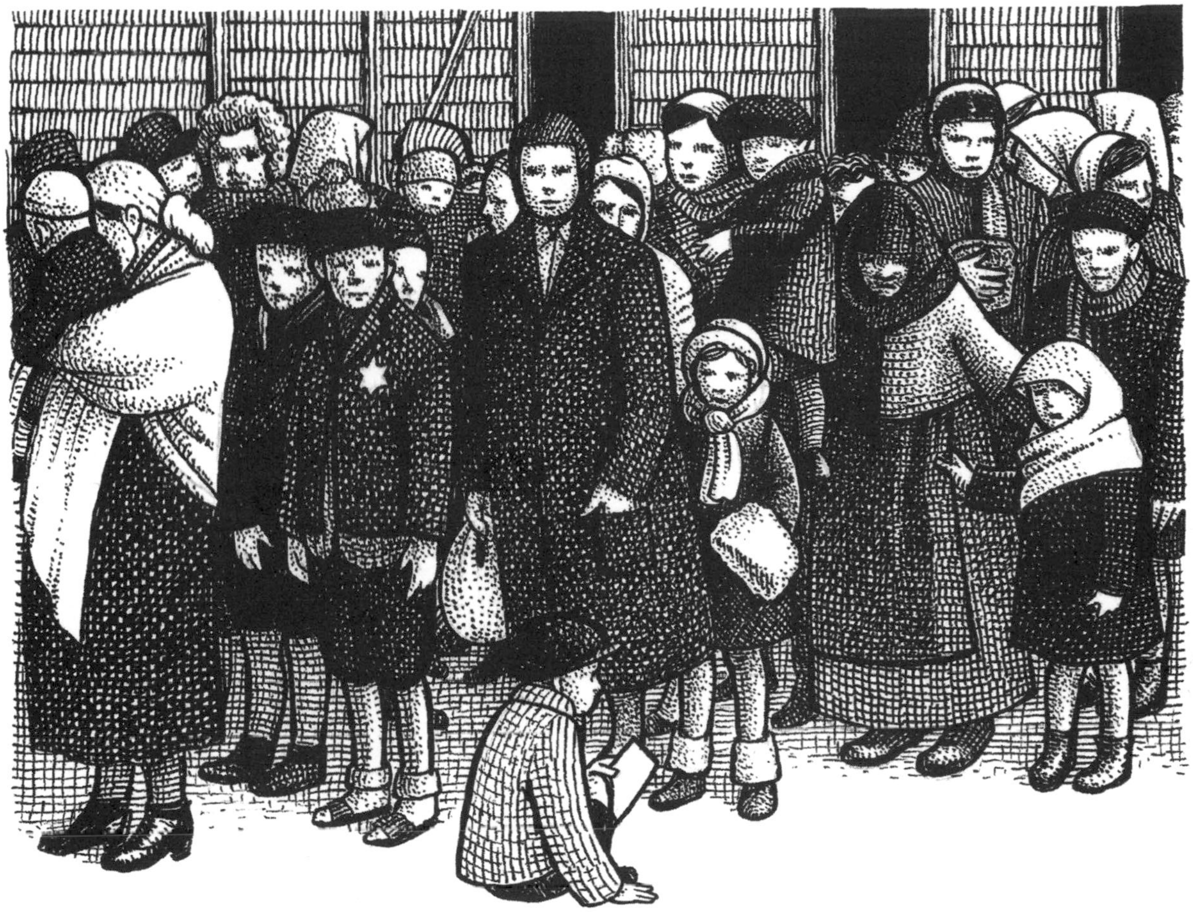

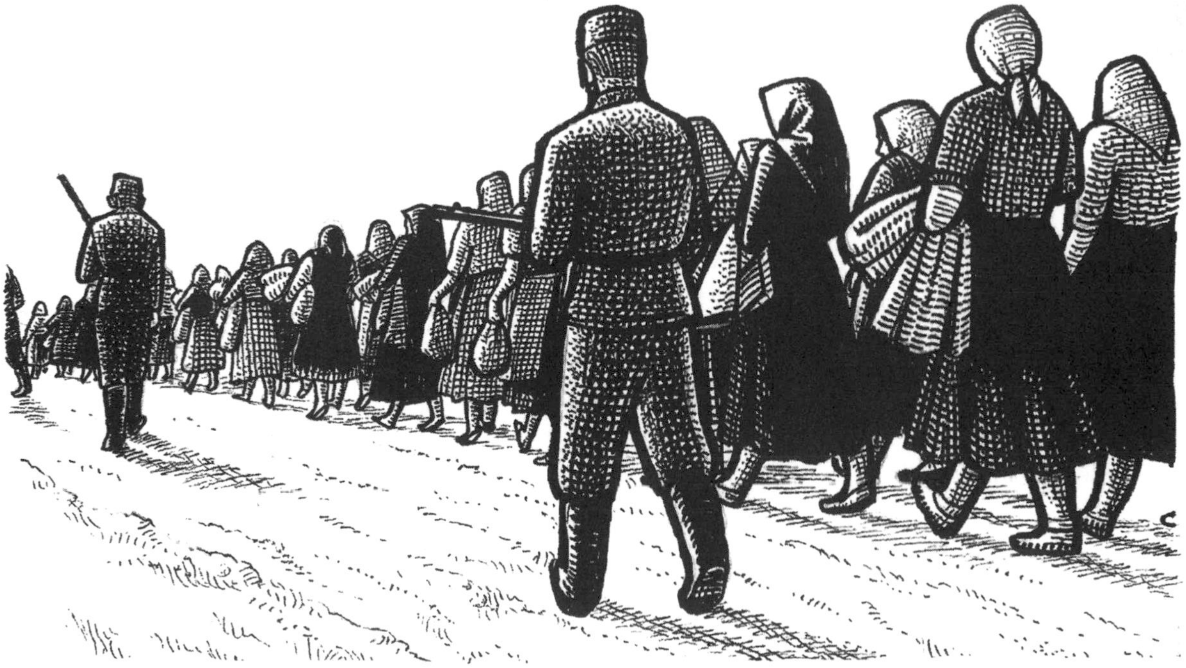

IN PAVELIC'S CROATIA ANOTHER GROUP WAS ADDED TO THE LIST OF UNDESIRABLES: THE SERBS.

A SMALL DETACHMENT OF THE YUGOSLAV ARMY LED BY GENERAL DRAZA MIHAILOVIC RETREATED INTO THE RAVNA GORA MOUNTAINS WHERE THEY FORMED THE CHETNIK DETACHMENT OF THE YUGOSLAV ARMY, COMMONLY REFERRED TO AS THE CHETNIKS.

THEIR INITIAL LONG-TERM GOAL WAS TO DEFEND THE TERRITORY FROM THE AXIS POWERS, WHILE STAYING LOYAL TO THE ROYAL HOUSE OF KARADJORDJEVIC - A TACTIC WHICH WOULD EVENTUALLY SECURE THE SUPPORT OF THE WESTERN ALLIES, PARTICULARLY THE BRITISH.

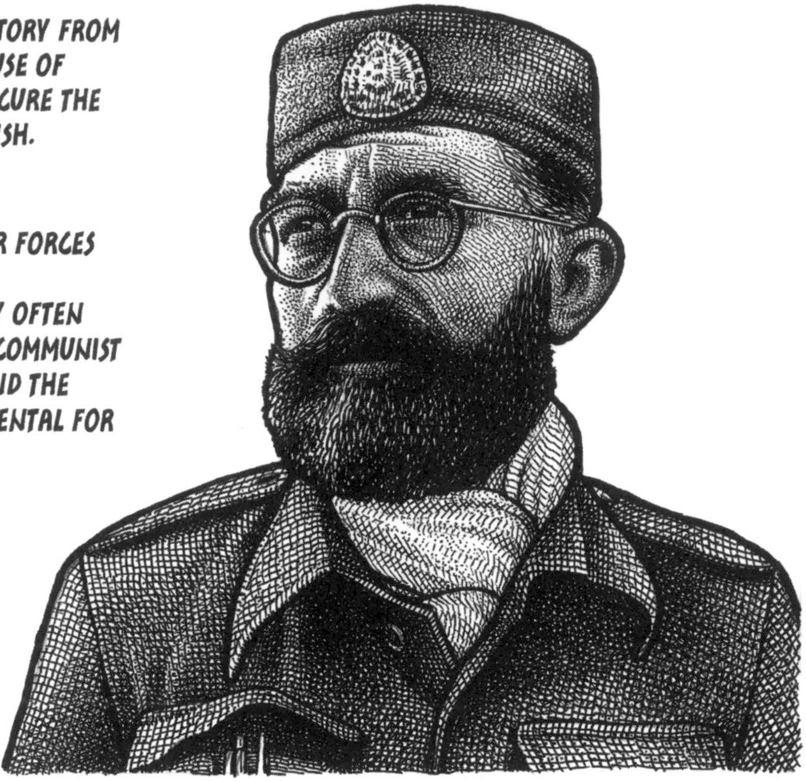

ALTHOUGH THE ALLIES INSISTED THE CHETNIKS UNIFY THEIR FORCES WITH THE PARTISANS, THEY DID SO ONLY RELUCTANTLY; FEARING A COMMUNIST POST-LIBERATION TAKEOVER THEY OFTEN COLLABORATED WITH THE AXIS IN ORDER TO DEAL WITH THE COMMUNIST THREAT. THIS NARROW-MINDED VIEW OF WAR AT LARGE AND THE POLITICAL GAME OF MUSICAL CHAIRS WOULD TURN DETRIMENTAL FOR MIHAILOVIC AND THE CHETNIKS IN THE LONG RUN.

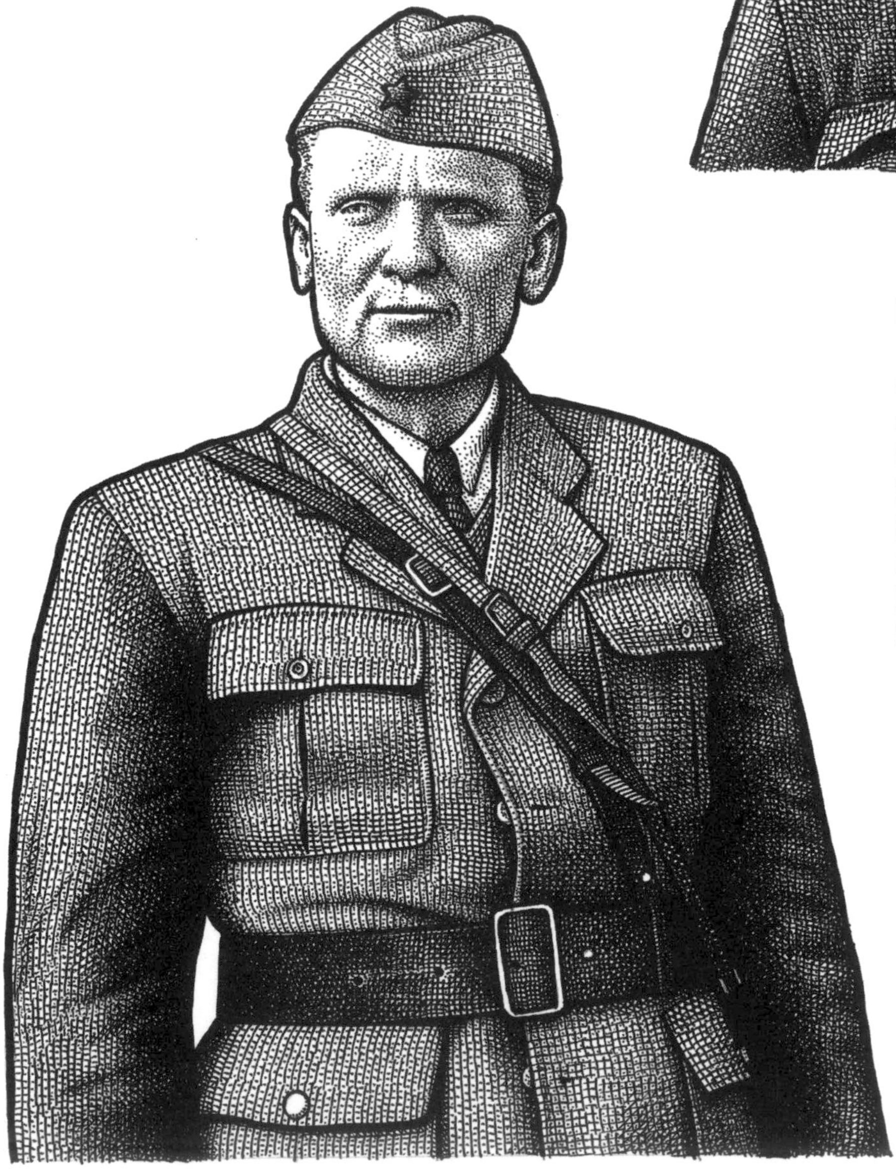

THE STRENGTH OF THE COMMUNIST RESISTANCE LED BY JOSEPH BROZ TITO WAS THE GUIDING PRINCIPLE OF EQUALITY, REGARDLESS OF NATIONALITY, GENDER OR AGE; HENCE, THE MOVEMENT SPREAD TO ALL FORMER TERRITORIES OF YUGOSLAVIA AND KEPT GROWING. THE PARTISANS FOLLOWED A STRICT MORAL CODE BOTH INTERNALLY AND EXTERNALLY, THUS EARNING THE SYMPATHY AND SUPPORT OF THE LOCAL POPULACE AND EVENTUALLY THE ALLIED FORCES.

WHEN THE WAR BROKE OUT MY GRANDFATHER WAS ALREADY ENLISTED IN THE YUGOSLAV ARMY, SERVING THE MANDATORY THREE-YEAR TERM. THERE ARE TWO VERSIONS AS TO WHAT HAPPENED TO HIM AFTER YUGOSLAVIA CAPITULATED AND THE ARMY DISSOLVED...

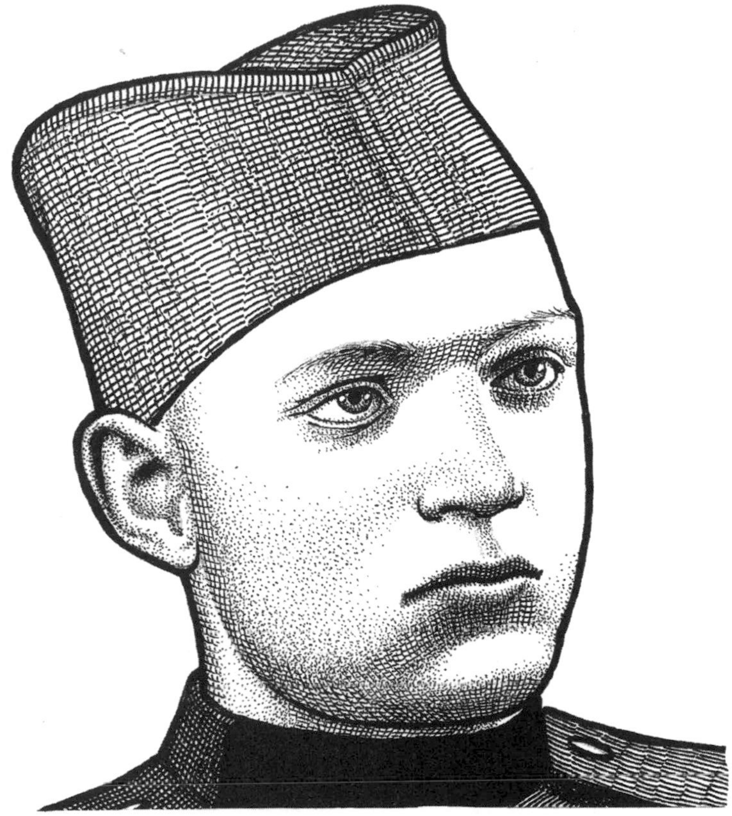

IN THE FIRST VERSION HE JOINED THE PARTISANS AND WAS CAPTURED BY GERMANS AT THE SYRMIAN FRONT IN 1945.

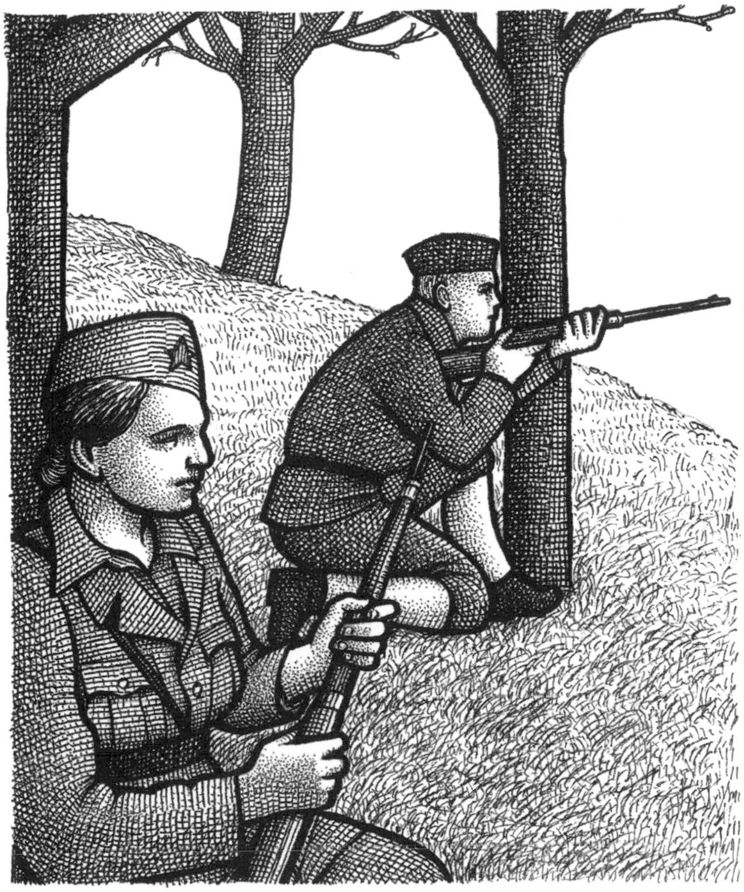

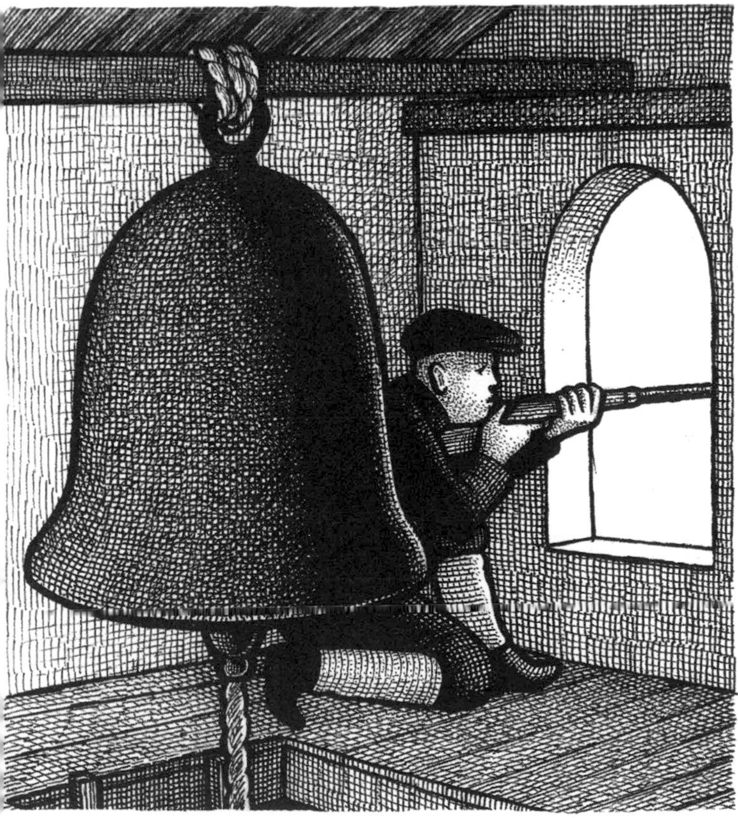

IN THE SECOND VERSION HE RETURNED HOME AND WAS CAPTURED BY THE USTASHAS AFTER HE HAD CLIMBED THE CHURCH TOWER, ATTEMPTING TO SINGLE-HANDEDLY DEFEND THE VILLAGE FROM THE APPROACHING ENEMY...

WHICHEVER HAPPENED TO BE THE CASE, DJURO WAS SUBSEQUENTLY DEPORTED TO JASENOVAC.

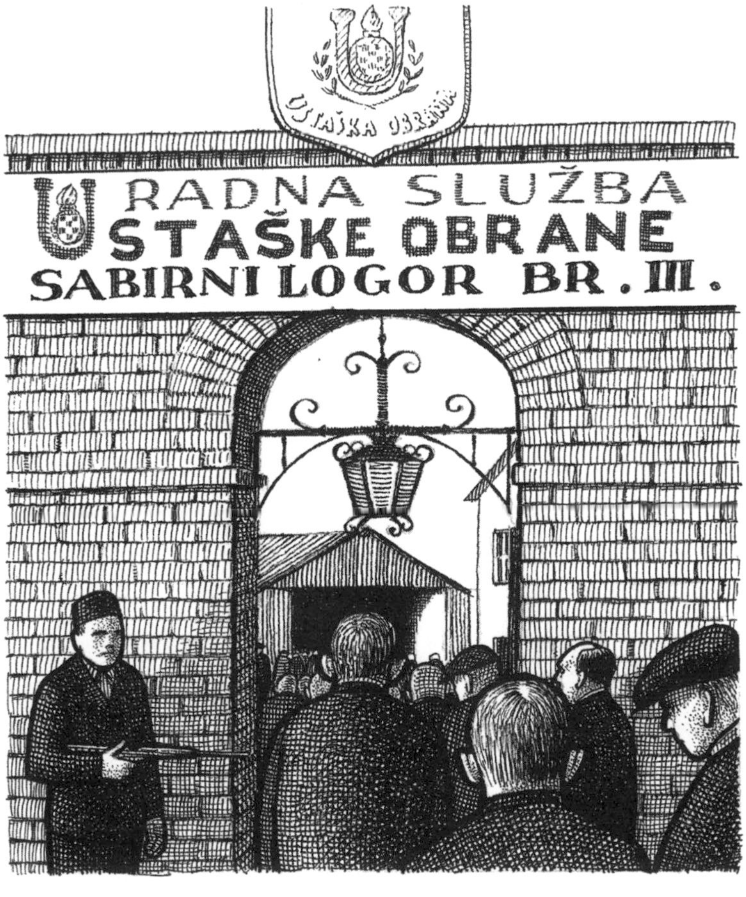
RADNA SLUŽBA
USTAŠKE OBRANE
SABIRNI LOGOR BR. III.

JASENOVAC WAS A SYSTEM OF DETENTION AND CONCENTRATION CAMPS WHICH ALSO INCLUDED A CAMP FOR WOMEN AND CHILDREN. THE TOTAL NUMBER OF ITS VICTIMS HAS BEEN DISPUTED OVER THE YEARS, RANGING BETWEEN 90000 AND 350000.
THERE WAS SOMETHING SINISTER AND VOID OF EMOTION IN THE WAY THE GERMANS ELIMINATED THEIR "UNDESIRABLES", WITH AS MUCH PASSION AS IT WOULD TAKE TO PERFECT A DIESEL ENGINE.

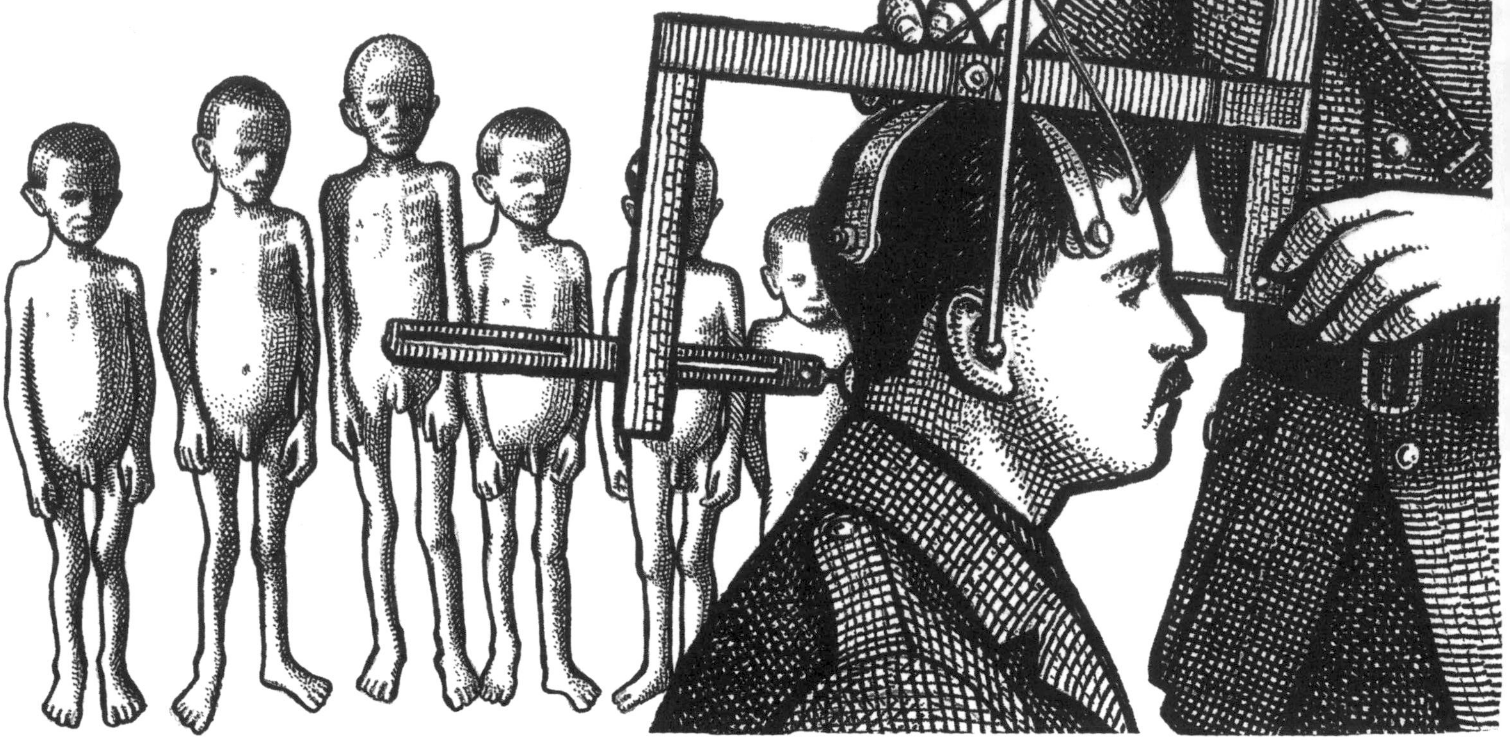

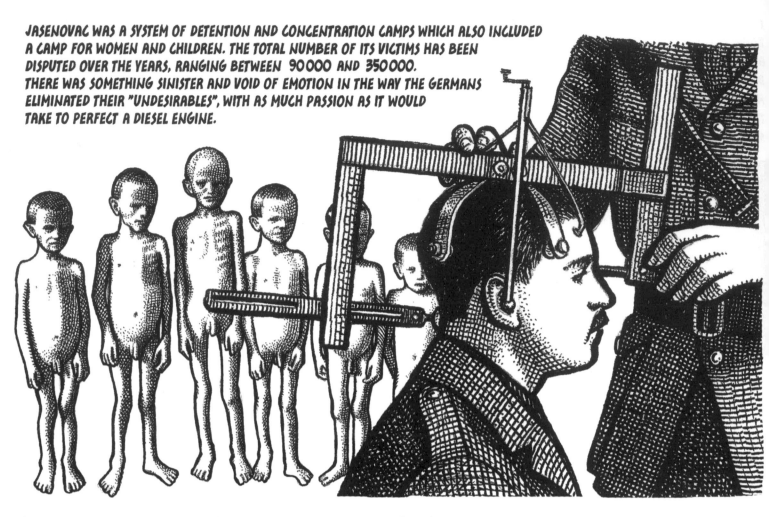

USTASHAS ON THE OTHER HAND SEEMED TO POUR THEIR HEARTS AND SOULS INTO THE HANDS-ON APPROACH TO SYSTEMATIC SLAUGHTER ...

GOING AS FAR AS TO INVENT A HANDY STRAP-ON WEAPON CALLED THE "SERBOSEK", WHICH ROUGHLY TRANSLATES TO "SERBOCUT".

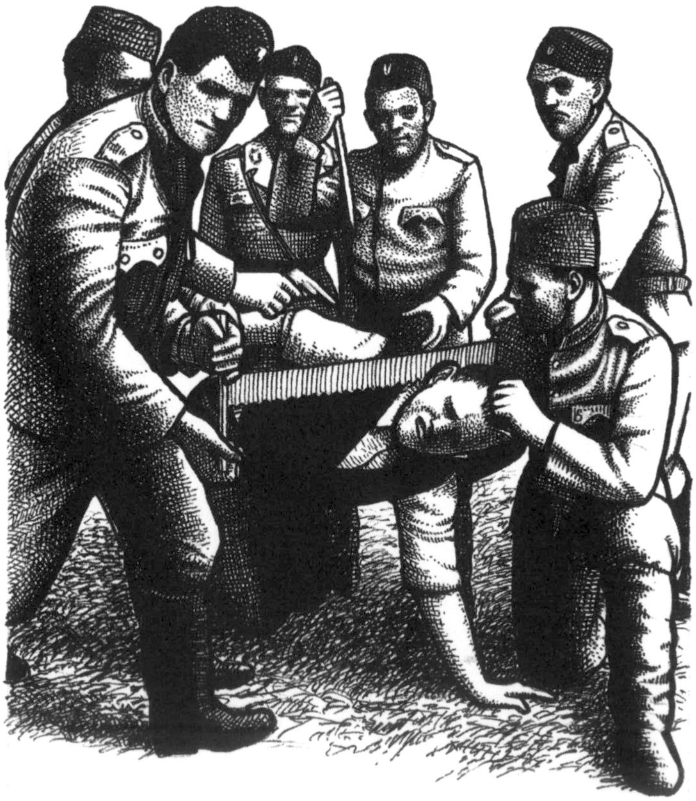

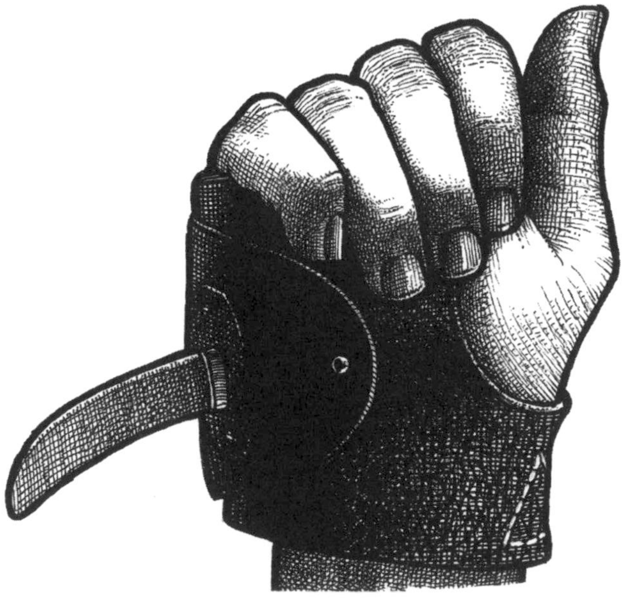

THE TERROR OF THE JASENOVAC CAMP AND THE VICIOUS TREATMENT OF ITS INMATES HAVE LEFT A LASTING MARK IN COLLECTIVE MEMORY OF THE SERBIAN MINORITY. THE FEAR OF THIS PART OF HISTORY REPEATING ITSELF ONCE AGAIN WAS TO FUEL THE UPRISING OF CROATIAN SERBS IN THE EARLY 90S, AND SERVE AS A TOOL OF MANIPULATION AND FEAR-MONGERING IN THE DECADES TO FOLLOW.

I'VE RESEARCHED THE HISTORY OF THIS REGION EXTENSIVELY, TRYING TO GET TO THE BOTTOM OF THE CONFLICT BETWEEN THE SERBS AND CROATS, BUT THE DEEPER I GO, THE FEWER THE NUMBER OF DOCUMENTED CONFLICTS BETWEEN THESE TWO ALMOST IDENTICAL GROUPS SEEM TO BE; AT LEAST, NOT PRIOR TO THE 20TH CENTURY. BOTH SEEM TO HAVE ARRIVED ON THE BALKAN PENINSULA ABOUT THE SAME TIME PERIOD, CIRCA 500 AD.

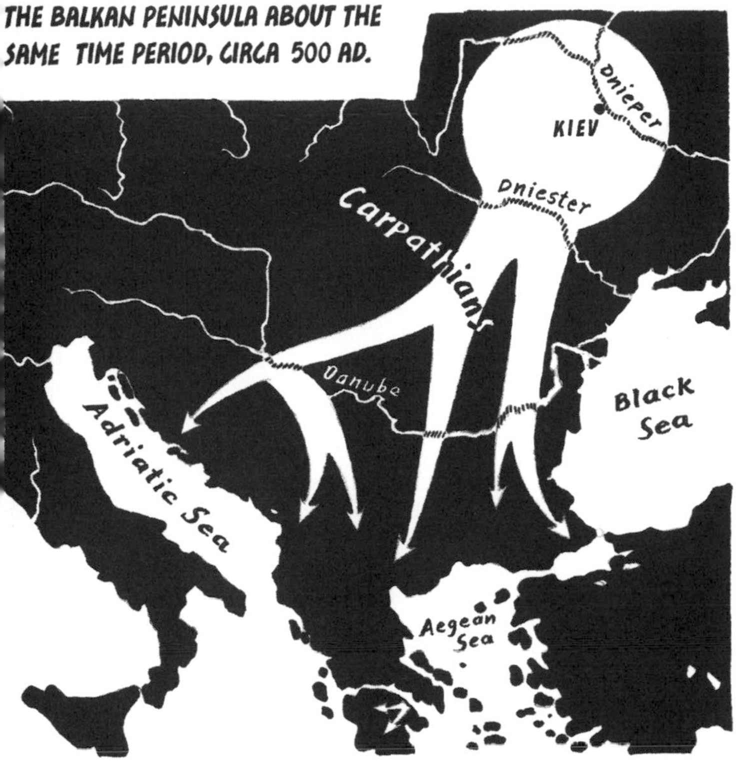
KIEV
Dnieper
Dniester
Carpathians
Danube
Black Sea
Adriatic Sea
Aegean Sea

IN ESSENCE, BOTH BELONG TO THE SAME ETHNIC GROUP, THAT OF THE SOUTHERN SLAVS. HISTORICAL ACCOUNTS DESCRIBE THEM AS NUMEROUS, DISORGANIZED, RESISTANT TO HARDSHIP AND NOT ALLOWING THEMSELVES TO BE CONQUERED OR ENSLAVED.

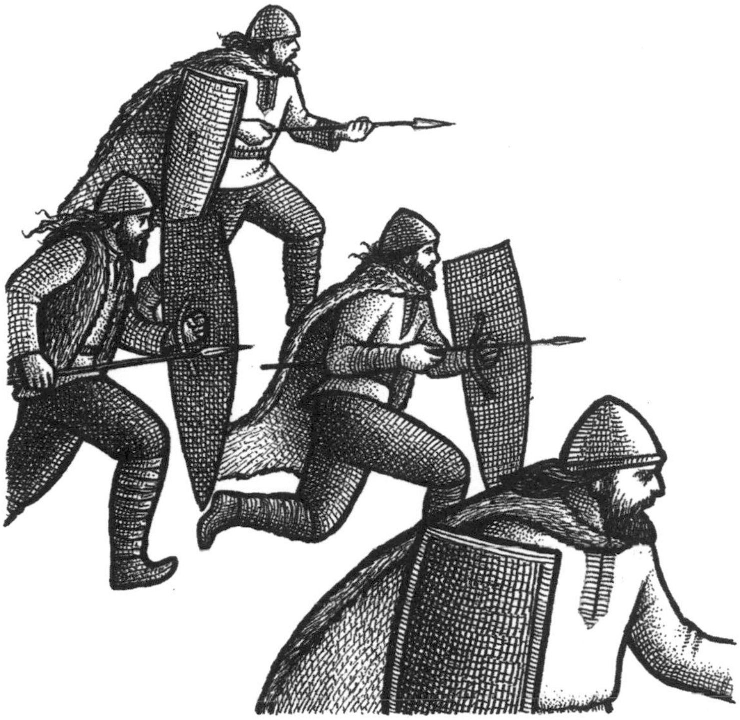

IN THE CENTURIES SUBSEQUENT TO THEIR ARRIVAL ON THE BALKAN PENINSULA, BOTH GROUPS MANAGED TO FORM SOVEREIGN STATES THAT CO-EXISTED PEACEFULLY, SPOKE THE SAME LANGUAGE, SHARED SIMILAR CUSTOMS...

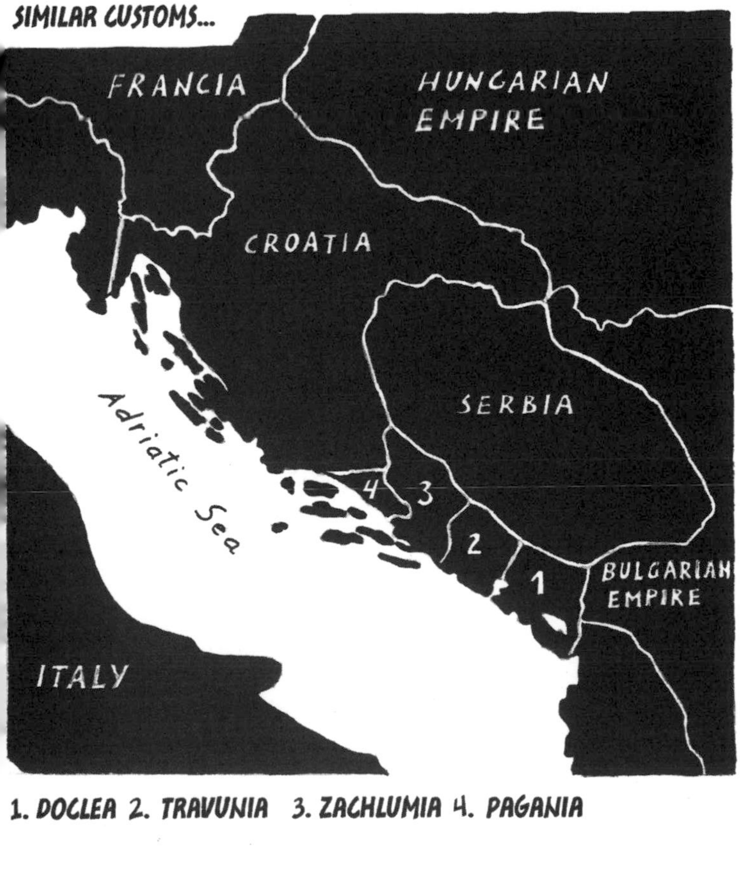
FRANCIA
HUNGARIAN EMPIRE
CROATIA
SERBIA
Adriatic Sea
4
3
2
1
BULGARIAN EMPIRE
ITALY

1. DOCLEA 2. TRAVUNIA 3. ZACHLUMIA 4. PAGANIA

AND BOTH ACCEPTED CHRISTIANITY AS THEIR OFFICIAL RELIGION CIRCA 900 AD, MOST LIKELY IN ORDER TO STRENGTHEN POLITICAL TIES WITH THEIR NEIGHBORING GIANTS; CROATIA TURNED TO ROME, AND SERBIA TO CONSTANTINOPLE. AS THE GREAT DIVIDE BETWEEN CATHOLICISM AND ORTHODOX CHRISTIANITY WIDENED, SO DID THE LINE OF DIFFERENTIATION BETWEEN THE SERBS AND THE CROATS.

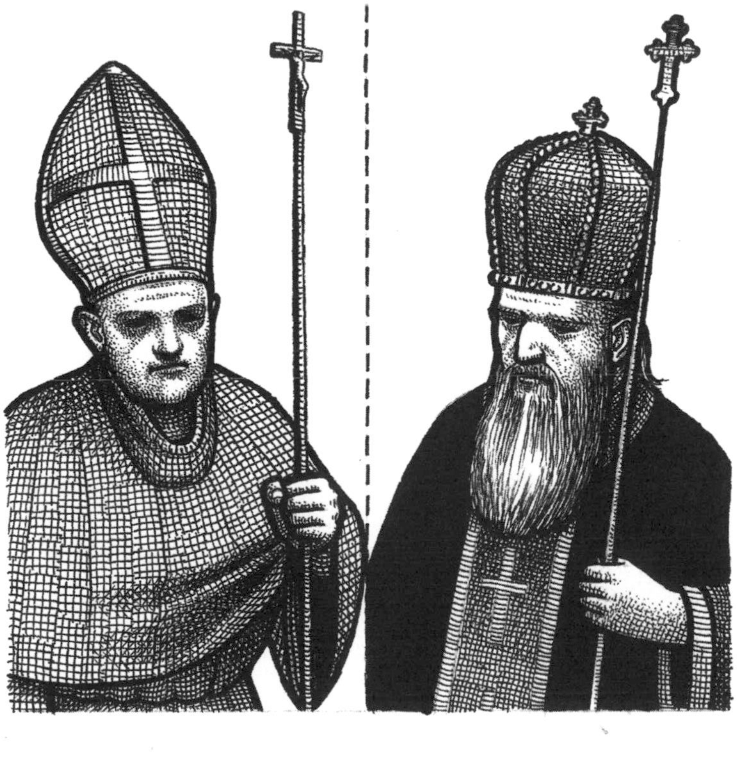

MOST OF THE CULTURAL DIFFERENCES BETWEEN THESE TWO GROUPS THAT WE KNOW OF TODAY HAVE BEEN EXACERBATED OR FURTHER INFLUENCED BY THE INVADING POWERS SUCH AS ROME, THE BYZANTINE EMPIRE, VENICE, AUSTRIA, AUSTRIA-HUNGARY AND THE OTTOMAN EMPIRE.

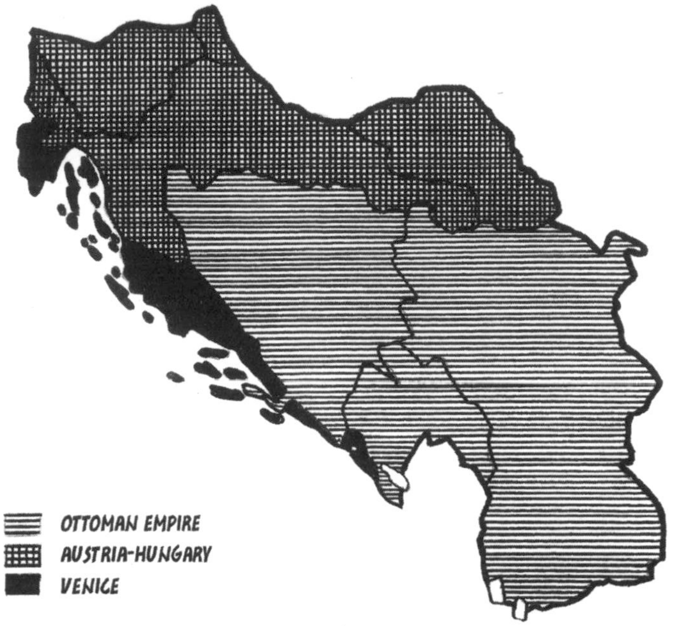
OTTOMAN EMPIRE
AUSTRIA-HUNGARY
VENICE

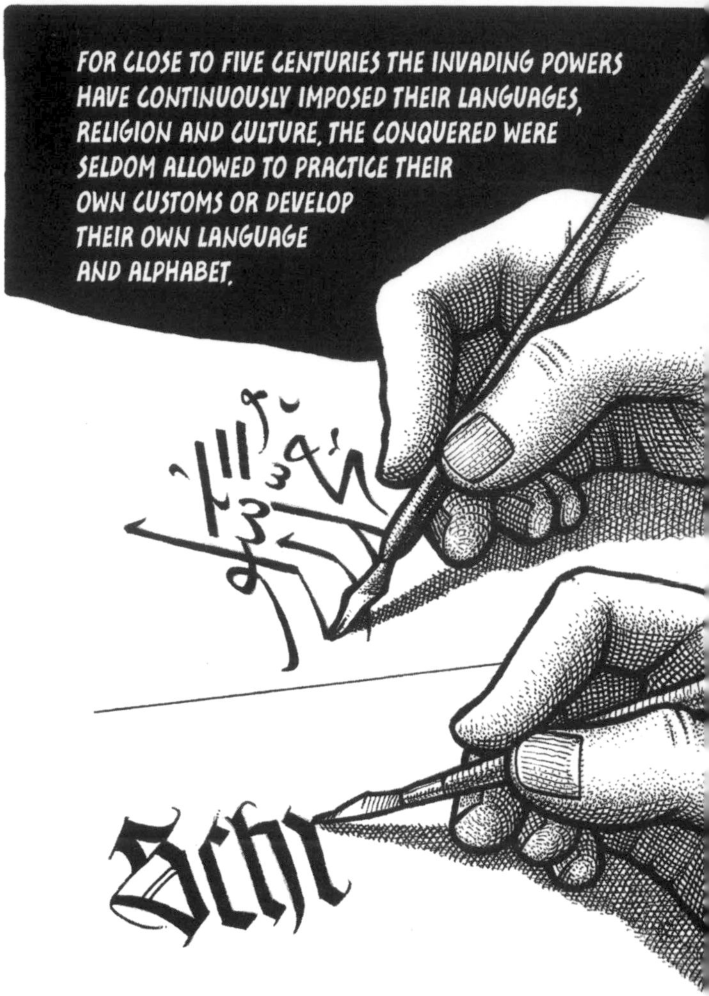
FOR CLOSE TO FIVE CENTURIES THE INVADING POWERS HAVE CONTINUOUSLY IMPOSED THEIR LANGUAGES, RELIGION AND CULTURE, THE CONQUERED WERE SELDOM ALLOWED TO PRACTICE THEIR OWN CUSTOMS OR DEVELOP THEIR OWN LANGUAGE AND ALPHABET.
Schr

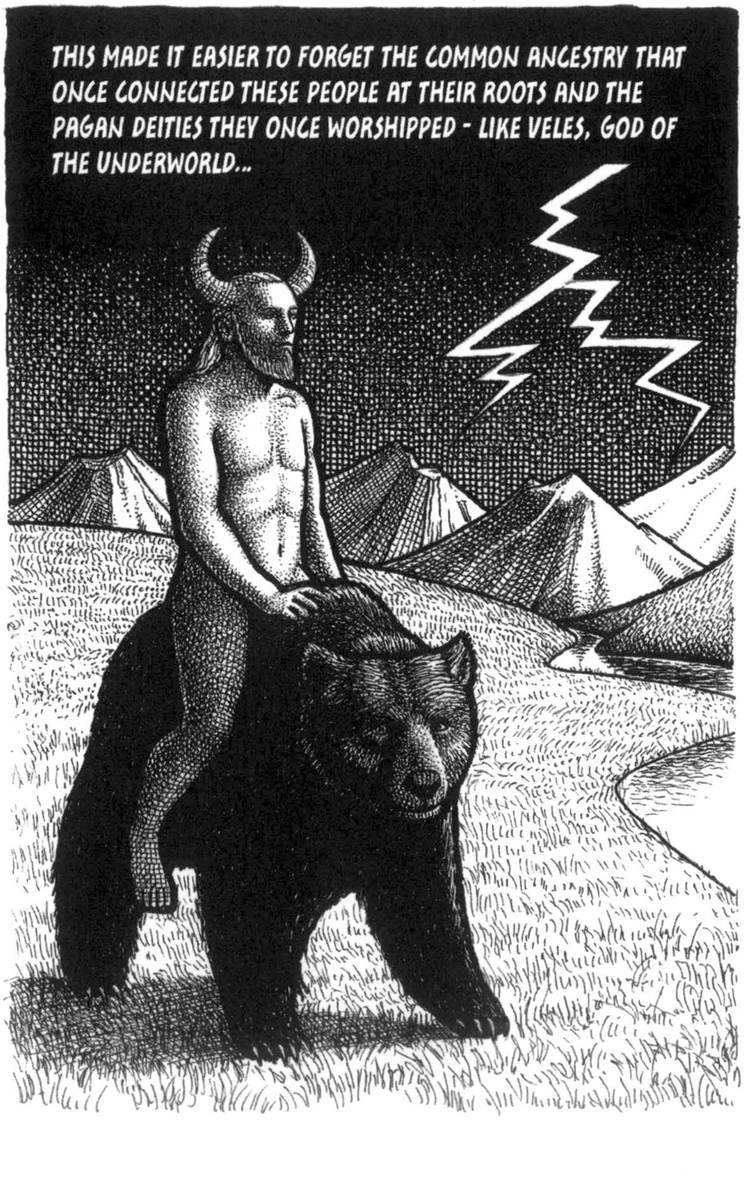
THIS MADE IT EASIER TO FORGET THE COMMON ANCESTRY THAT ONCE CONNECTED THESE PEOPLE AT THEIR ROOTS AND THE PAGAN DEITIES THEY ONCE WORSHIPPED - LIKE VELES, GOD OF THE UNDERWORLD...

WHOSE INFLUENCE SURVIVES TO THIS DAY IN THE RITUALS AND THE DRESS OF THE ZVONČARI IN CROATIA.

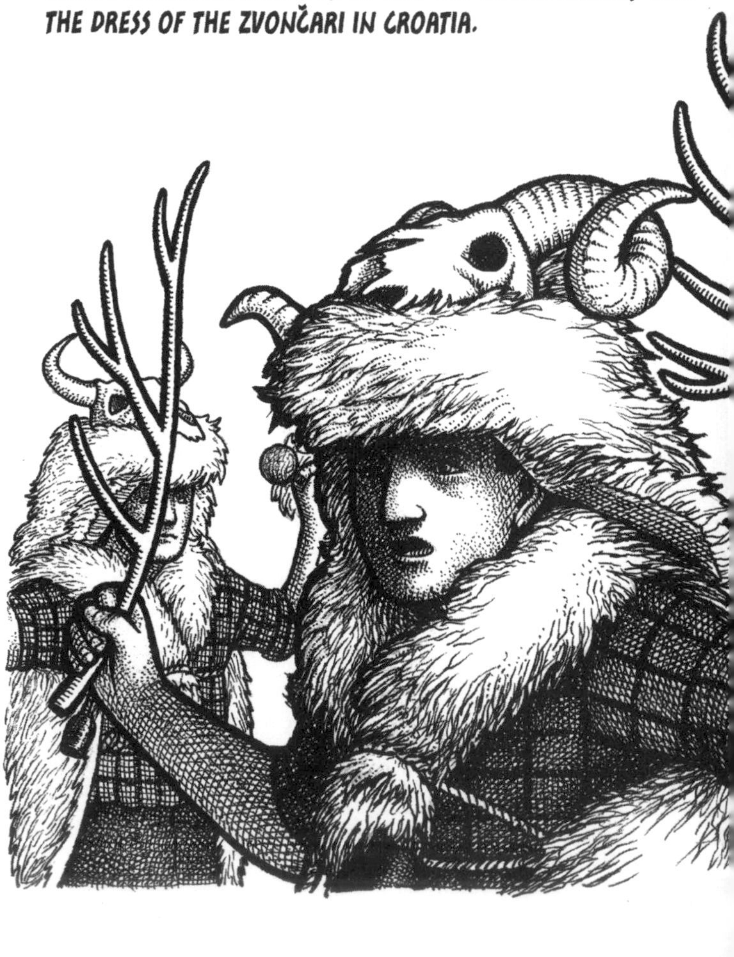

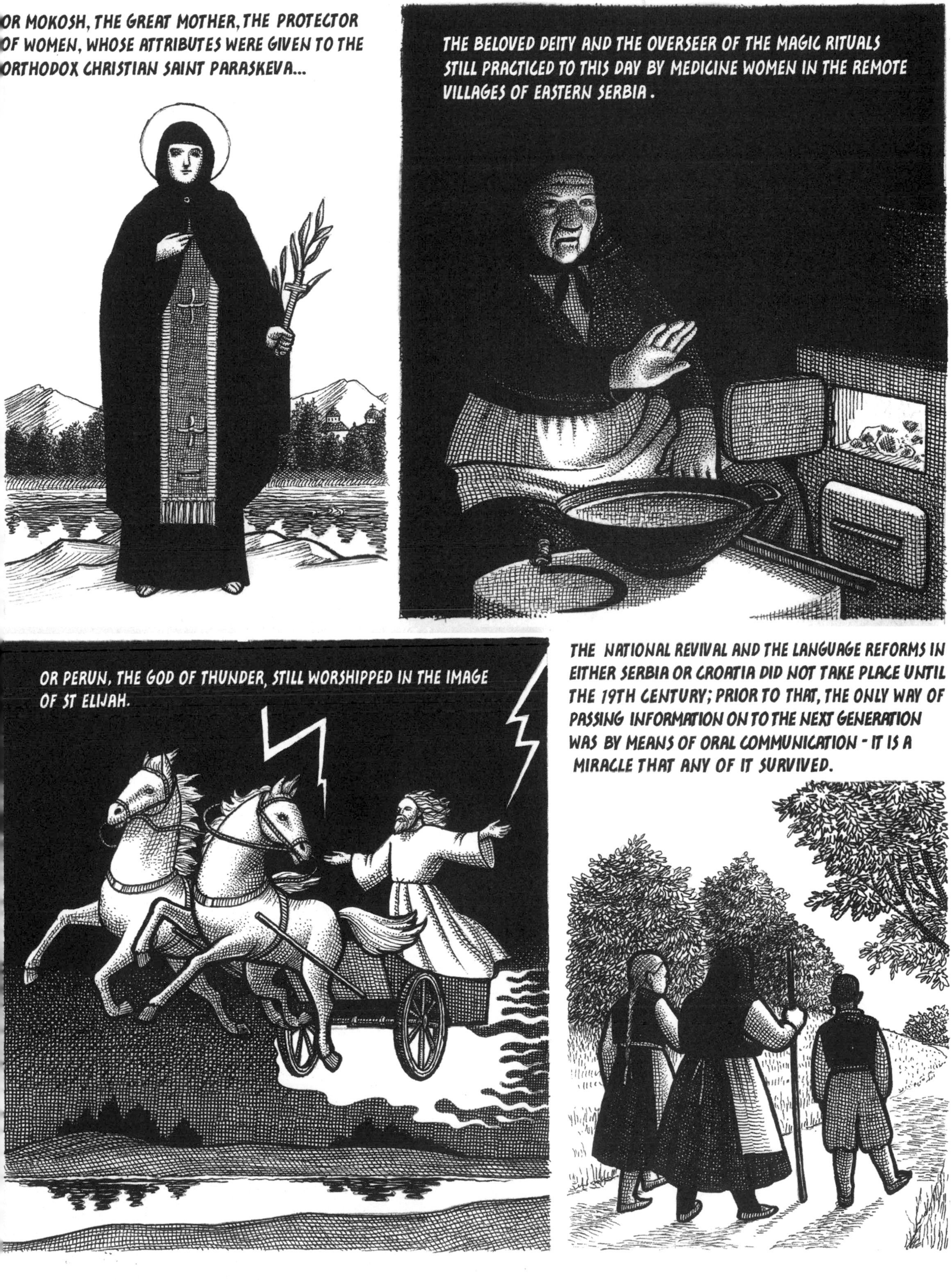
OR MOKOSH, THE GREAT MOTHER, THE PROTECTOR OF WOMEN, WHOSE ATTRIBUTES WERE GIVEN TO THE ORTHODOX CHRISTIAN SAINT PARASKEVA...
THE BELOVED DEITY AND THE OVERSEER OF THE MAGIC RITUALS STILL PRACTICED TO THIS DAY BY MEDICINE WOMEN IN THE REMOTE VILLAGES OF EASTERN SERBIA.
OR PERUN, THE GOD OF THUNDER, STILL WORSHIPPED IN THE IMAGE OF ST ELIJAH.
THE NATIONAL REVIVAL AND THE LANGUAGE REFORMS IN EITHER SERBIA OR CROATIA DID NOT TAKE PLACE UNTIL THE 19TH CENTURY; PRIOR TO THAT, THE ONLY WAY OF PASSING INFORMATION ON TO THE NEXT GENERATION WAS BY MEANS OF ORAL COMMUNICATION - IT IS A MIRACLE THAT ANY OF IT SURVIVED.

BACK IN 1941, AN OUTBREAK OF COLLECTIVE AMNESIA SEEMED TO HAVE REACHED ITS PEAK, AS MANY SERBIAN VILLAGES IN CROATIA WERE BURNED TO THE GROUND, AND MANY SERBS DEPORTED TO DEATH CAMPS, THE QUESTION THAT POSES ITSELF IS: HOW DID MY FAMILY SURVIVE?

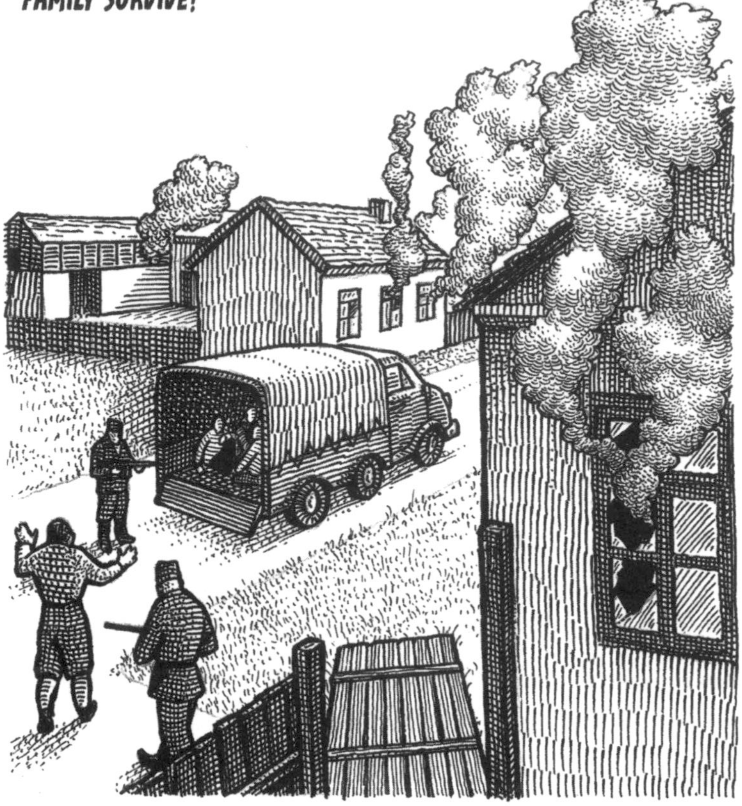

I'VE LEARNED ONLY RECENTLY THAT I MAY OWE MY EXISTENCE TO A LONELY GERMAN OFFICER STATIONED IN MY FATHER'S VILLAGE. NONE OF THE VILLAGERS SPOKE GERMAN AND HE IN TURN SPOKE NO CROATIAN, BUT A BIT OF BASIC ENGLISH, AS DID MY FATHER'S GRANDMOTHER KATA, COURTESY OF GARY, INDIANA.

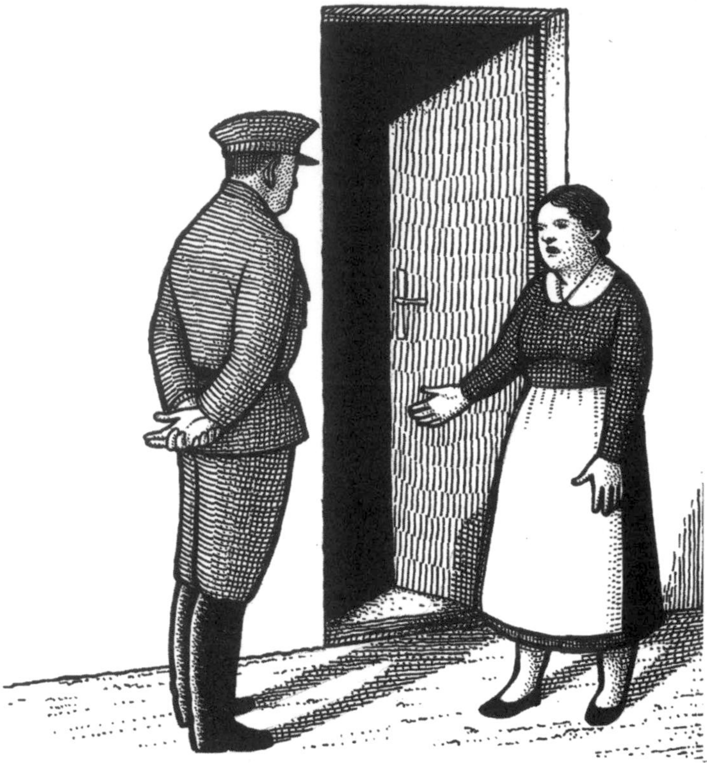

THE LONELY GERMAN WOULD OFTEN VISIT MY GREAT-GRANDMOTHER, AND THE TWO WOULD SIT AND CHAT OVER COFFEE AND CHOCOLATES, BROUGHT AS GIFTS FOR MY YOUNG FATHER.

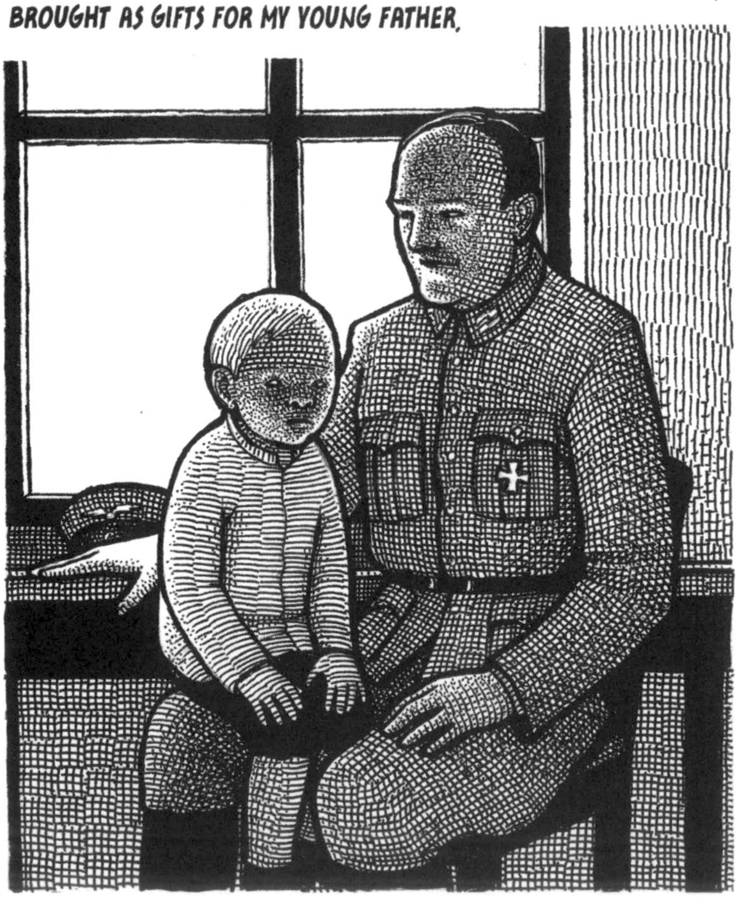

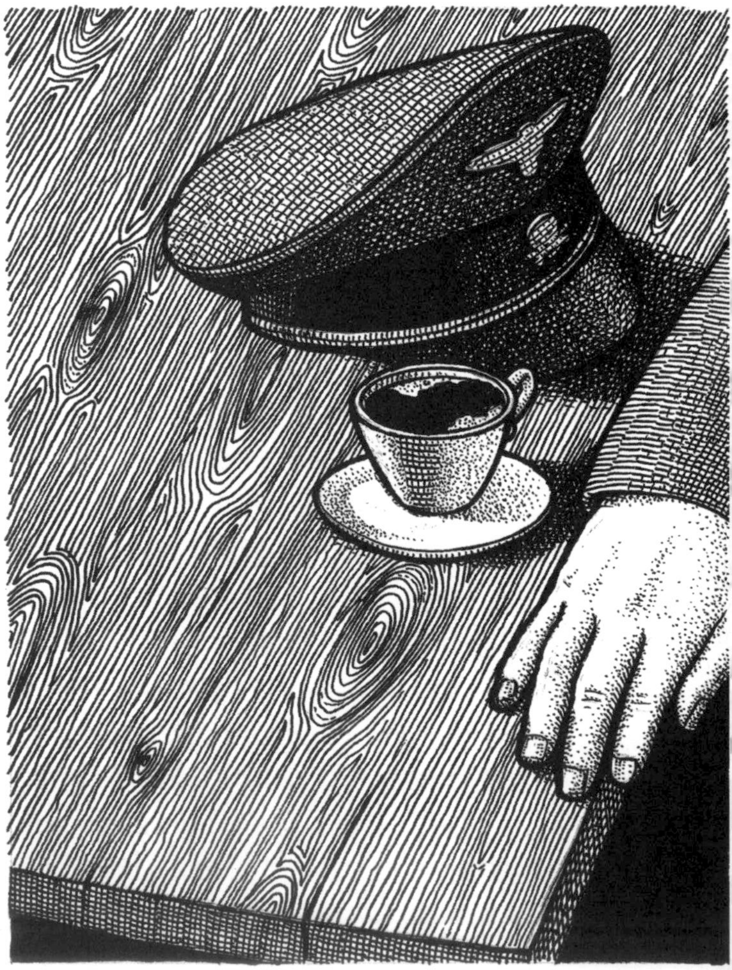

AND SO, REGARDLESS OF MY FATHER STUFFING HIS FACE WITH GERMAN CHOCOLATES, AND MY GREAT-GRANDMOTHER ENTERTAINING THE LONELY GERMAN, MY FAMILY SPENT THE REST OF THE WAR FEARING THAT THEY WOULD BE NEXT TO BOARD THE TRAIN TO JASENOVAC. IN THE MEANTIME, THE WAR RAGED ON, AND BATTLES WERE FOUGHT. IN THE EARLY SUMMER OF 1945, FOLLOWING THE BLOODY AND DECISIVE BATTLE ON THE SYRMIAN FRONT, THE COUNTRY WAS LIBERATED AT LAST.

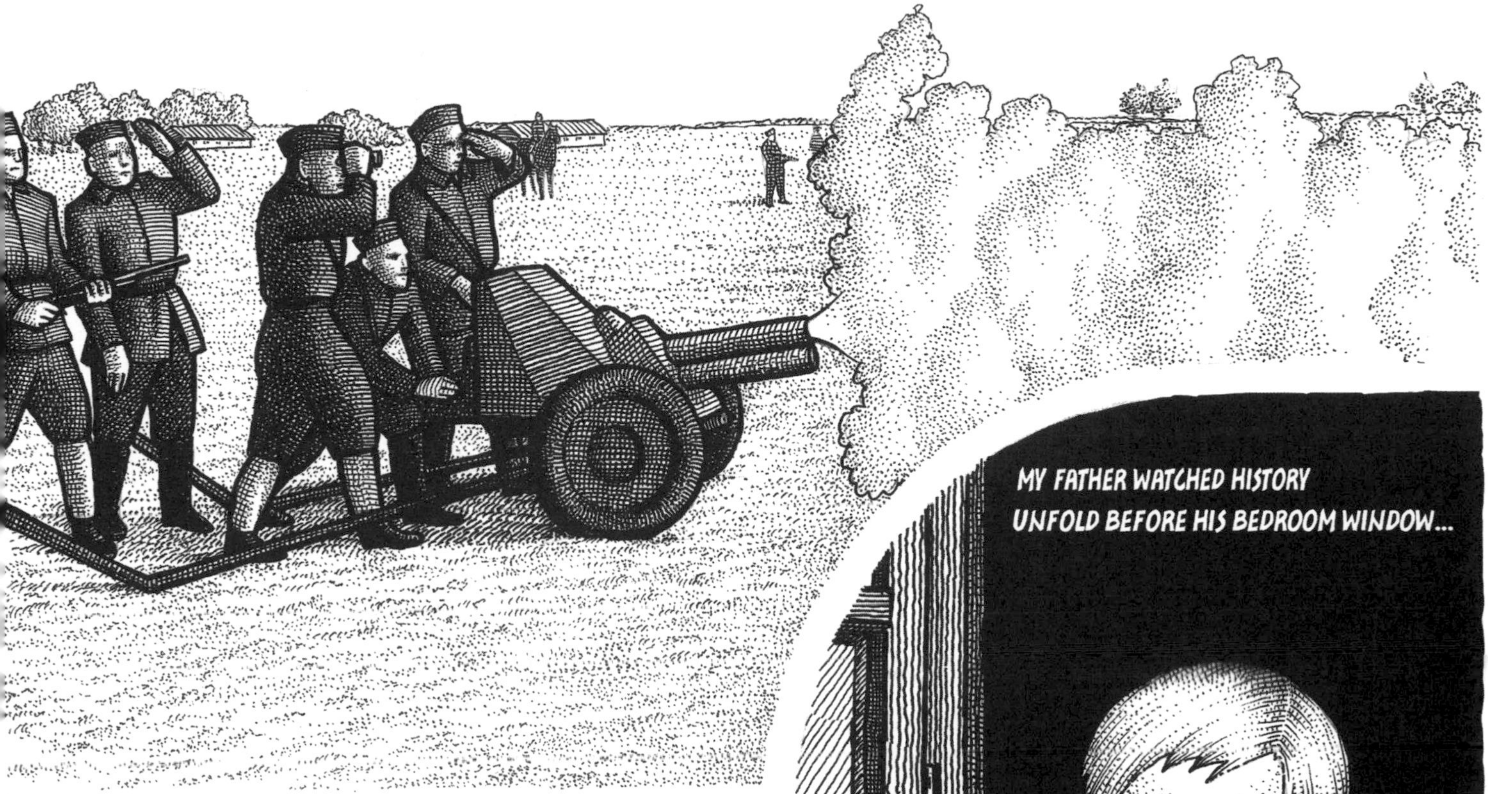

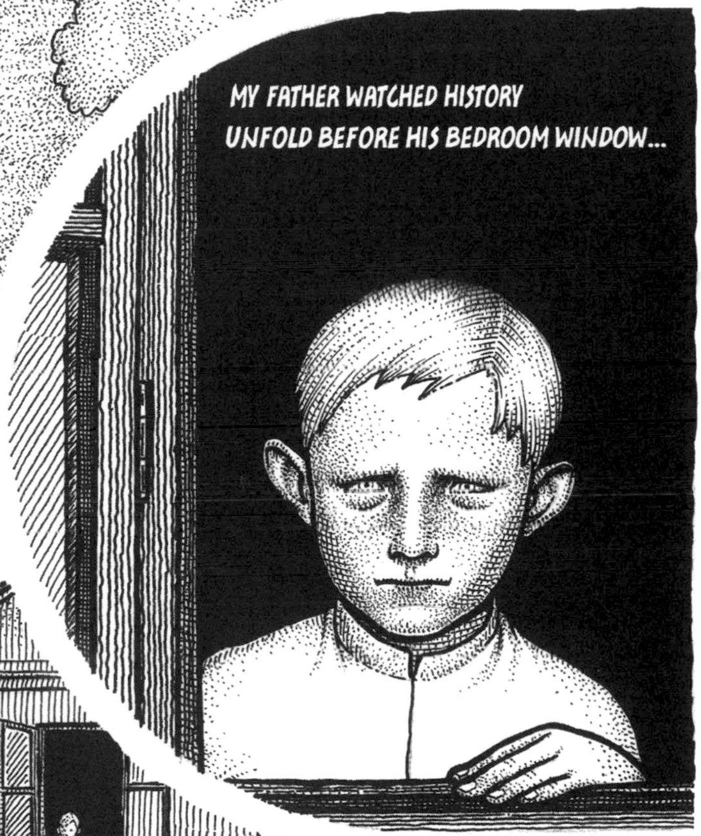
MY FATHER WATCHED HISTORY UNFOLD BEFORE HIS BEDROOM WINDOW...

AS THE NEW ARMY CAME INTO THE VILLAGE, AND THE OLD ONES LEFT. HE OBSERVED SWASTIKAS AND THE U-INSIGNIA REPLACED WITH RED STARS, WHILE EVERYTHING ELSE LOOKED PRETTY MUCH THE SAME - THE GUNS, THE UNIFORMS AND ALL...

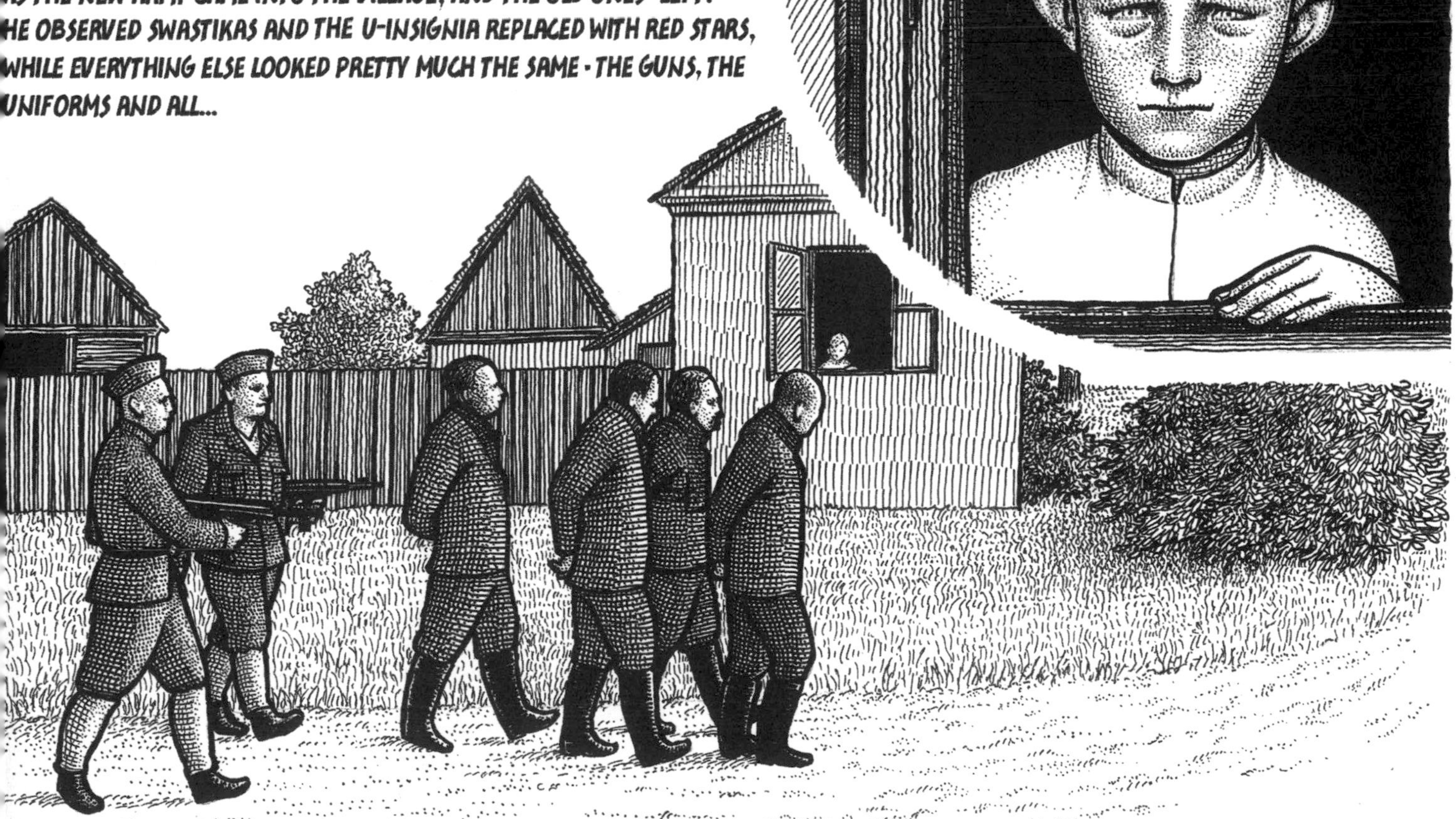

IT SEEMS AS THOUGH EVERYTHING HE HAD EVER KNOWN OR SEEN OR EXPERIENCED UP TO THIS POINT HAD BEEN WROUGHT WITH FEAR AND VIOLENCE.

THE LIBERATED COUNTRY WAS UNITED ONCE AGAIN, THIS TIME UNDER THE LEADERSHIP OF JOSEPH BROZ TITO AND THE COMMUNIST PARTY.

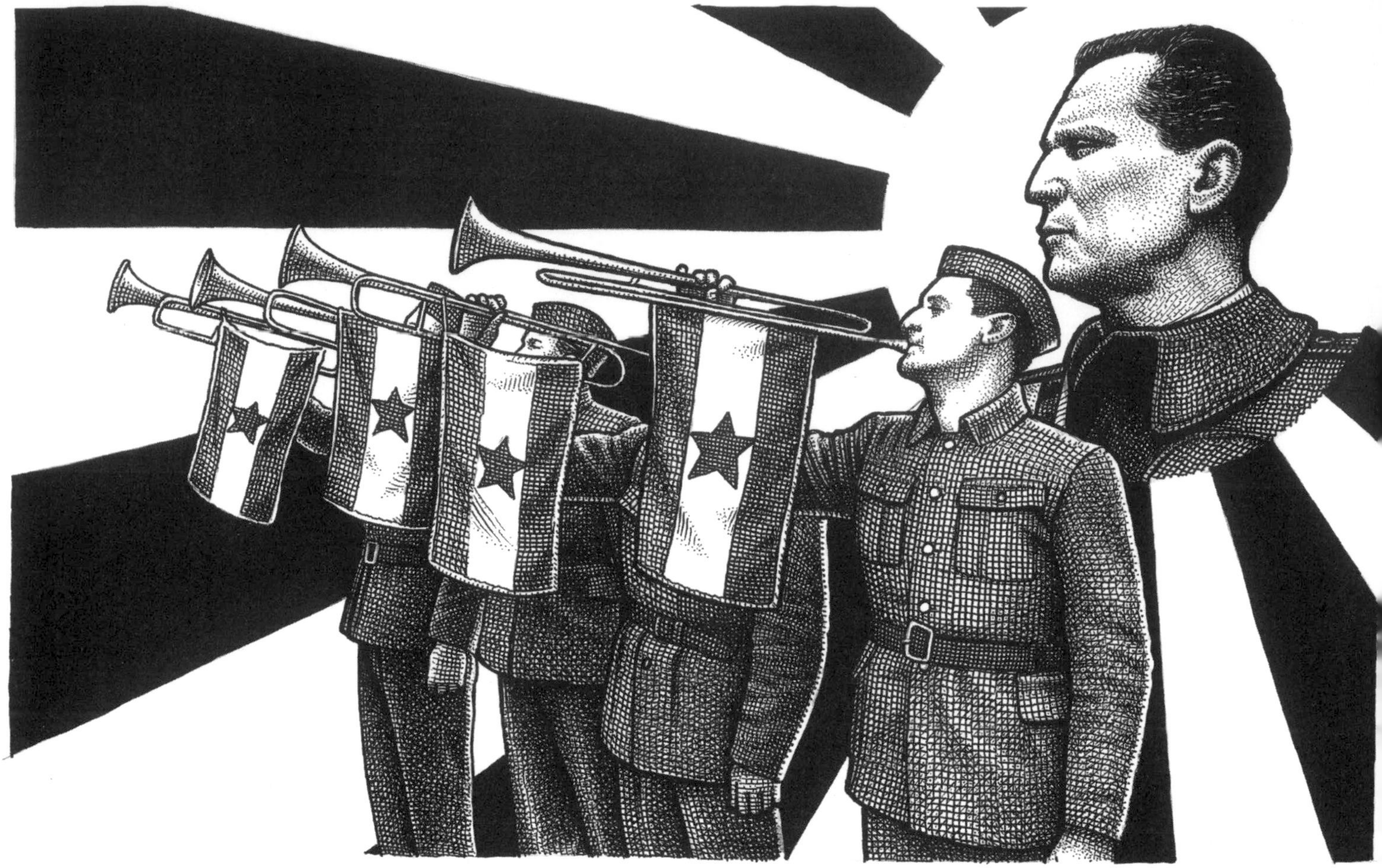

THE CHETNIK RESISTANCE LEADER DRAZA MIHAILVOIC WAS TRIED FOR TREASON AND COLLABORATING WITH THE ENEMY. HE WAS FOUND GUILTY AND EXECUTED IN 1946.

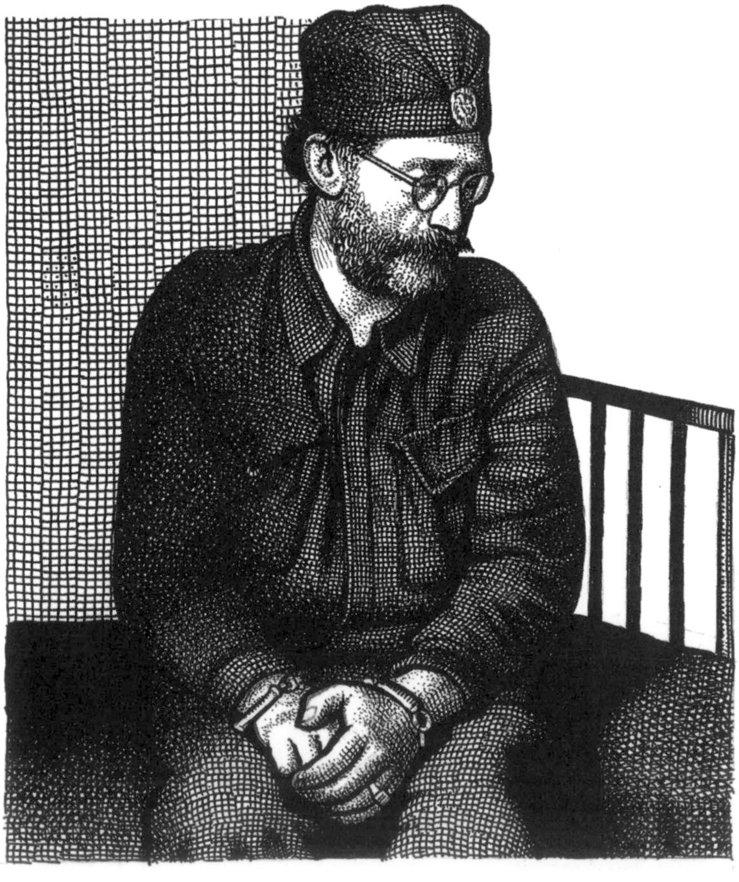

ANTE PAVELIC, THE HEAD OF THE INDEPENDENT STATE OF CROATIA, FLED TO AUSTRIA AND LATER ON TO ARGENTINA. HE SURVIVED AN ASSASSINATION ATTEMPT IN 1957 BUT EVENTUALLY DIED FROM THE INJURIES TWO YEARS LATER IN SPAIN.

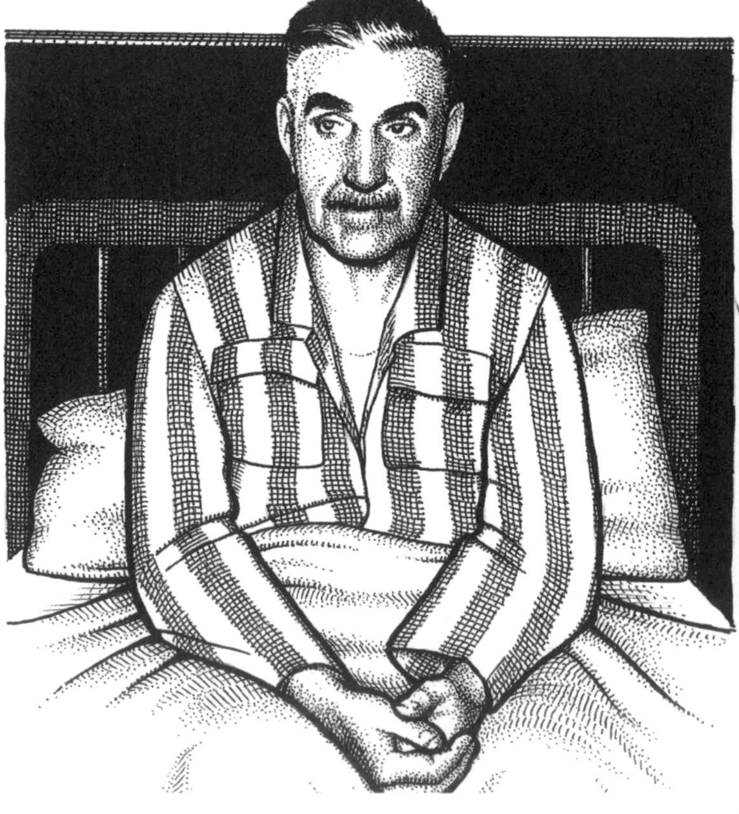

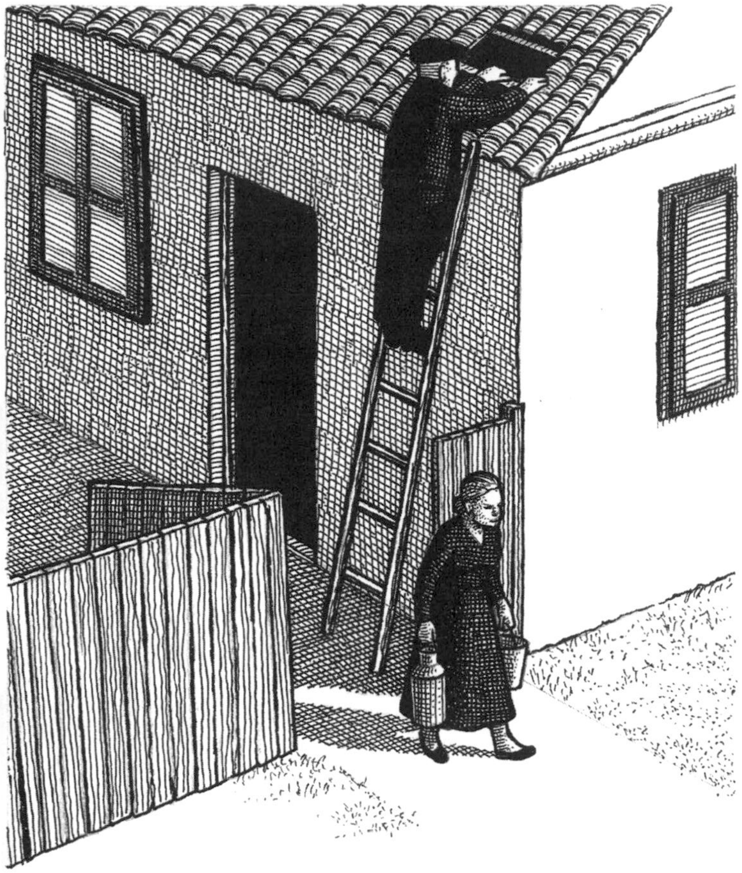

JUST AS LIFE SEEMED TO HAVE RESUMED A NORMAL COURSE TRAGEDY STRUCK AGAIN WHEN STANA'S HEALTH TOOK A TURN FOR THE WORSE.

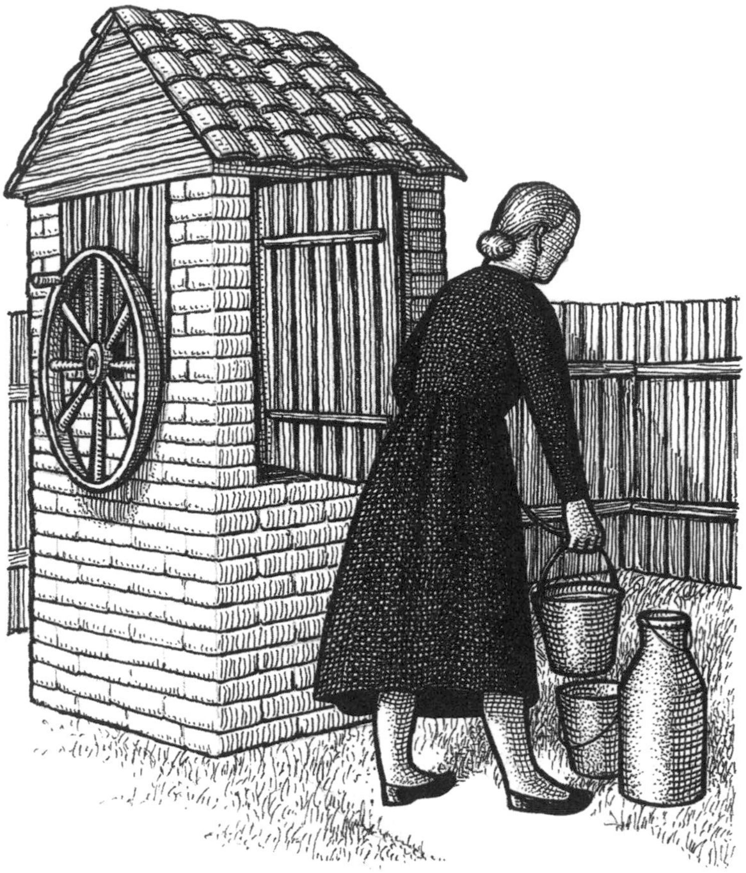

SUBJECTED TO YEARS OF STRESS AND PHYSICAL ABUSE HER BODY BECAME VULNERABLE...

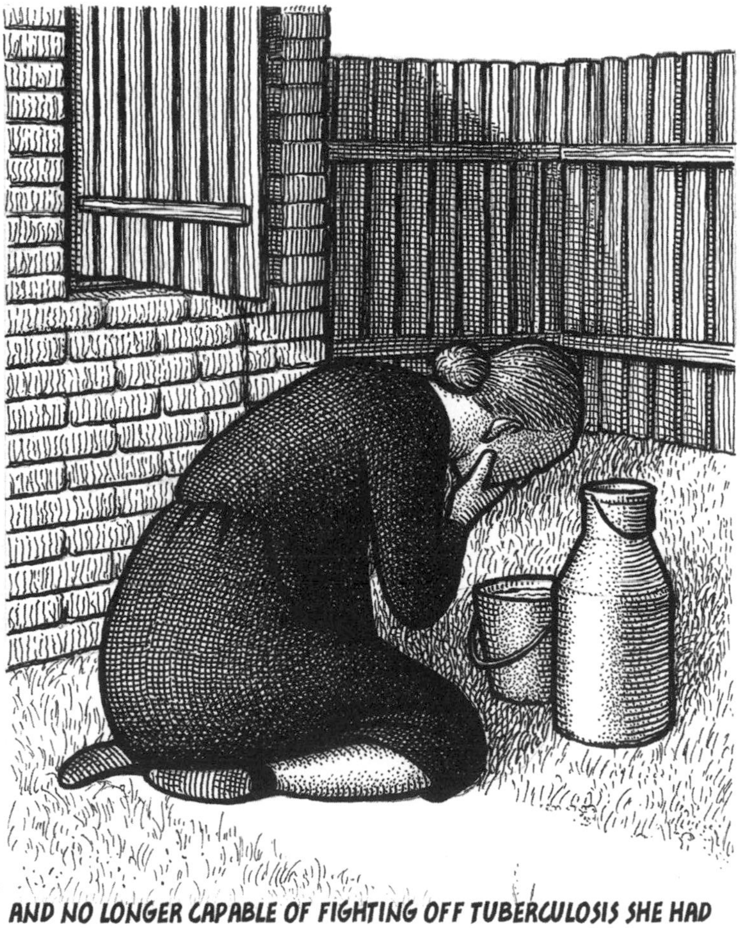

AND NO LONGER CAPABLE OF FIGHTING OFF TUBERCULOSIS SHE HAD CONTRACTED FROM DJURO IN THE EARLY DAYS OF THEIR MARRIAGE.

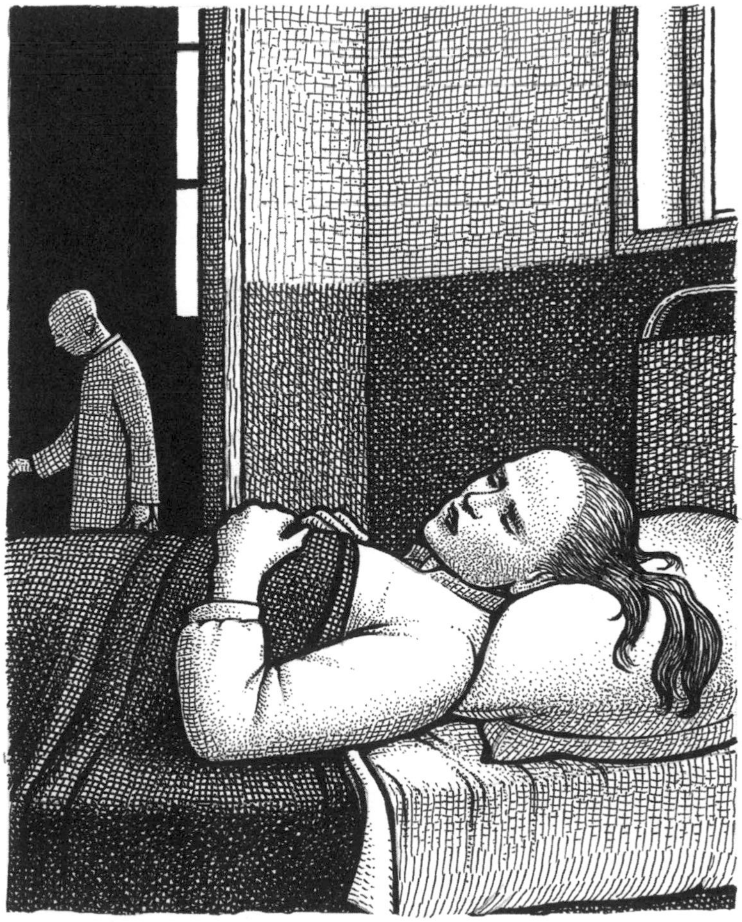

SHE WAS SENT TO A SANATORIUM IN ZAGREB...

ONLY TO RETURN HOME IN A CASKET.

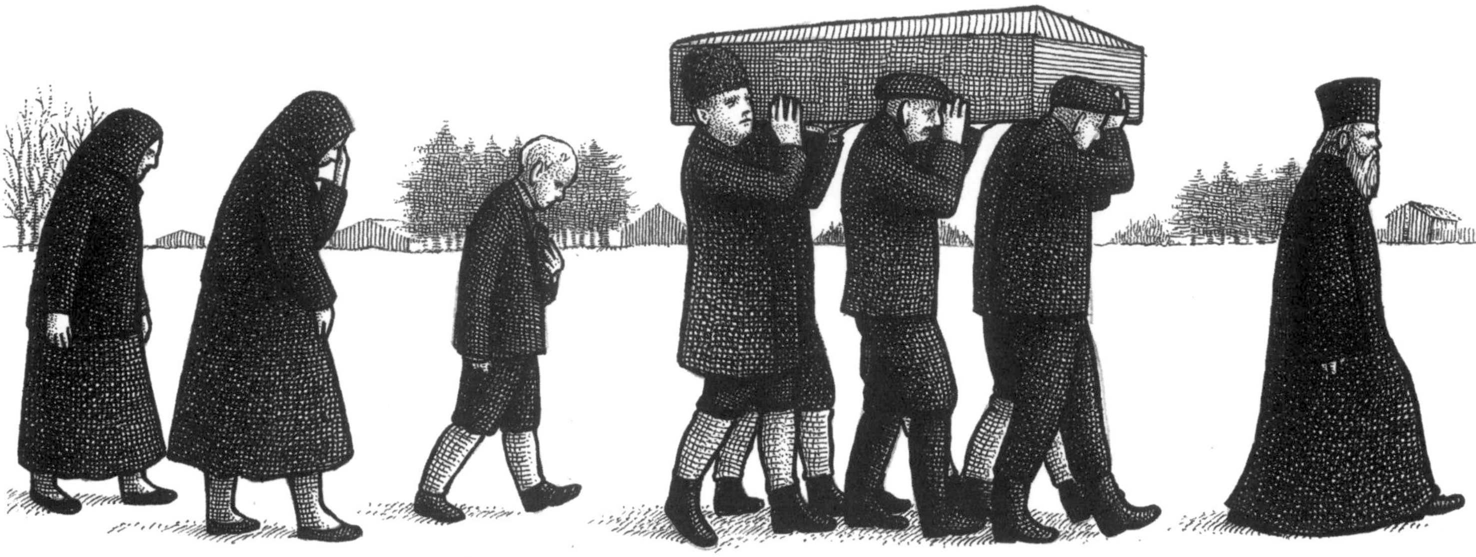

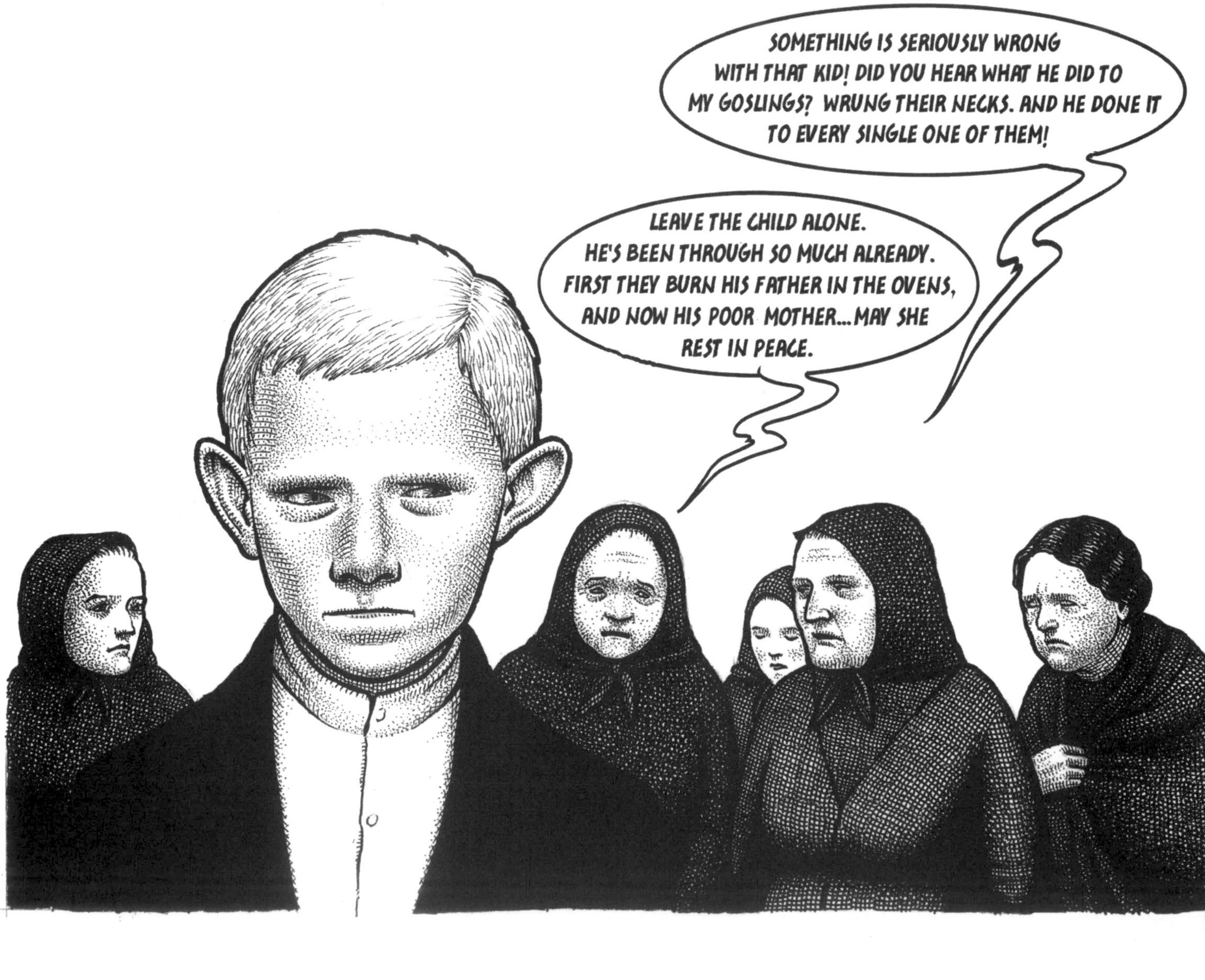
SOMETHING IS SERIOUSLY WRONG WITH THAT KID! DID YOU HEAR WHAT HE DID TO MY GOSLINGS? WRUNG THEIR NECKS. AND HE DONE IT TO EVERY SINGLE ONE OF THEM!
LEAVE THE CHILD ALONE. HE'S BEEN THROUGH SO MUCH ALREADY. FIRST THEY BURN HIS FATHER IN THE OVENS, AND NOW HIS POOR MOTHER...MAY SHE REST IN PEACE.

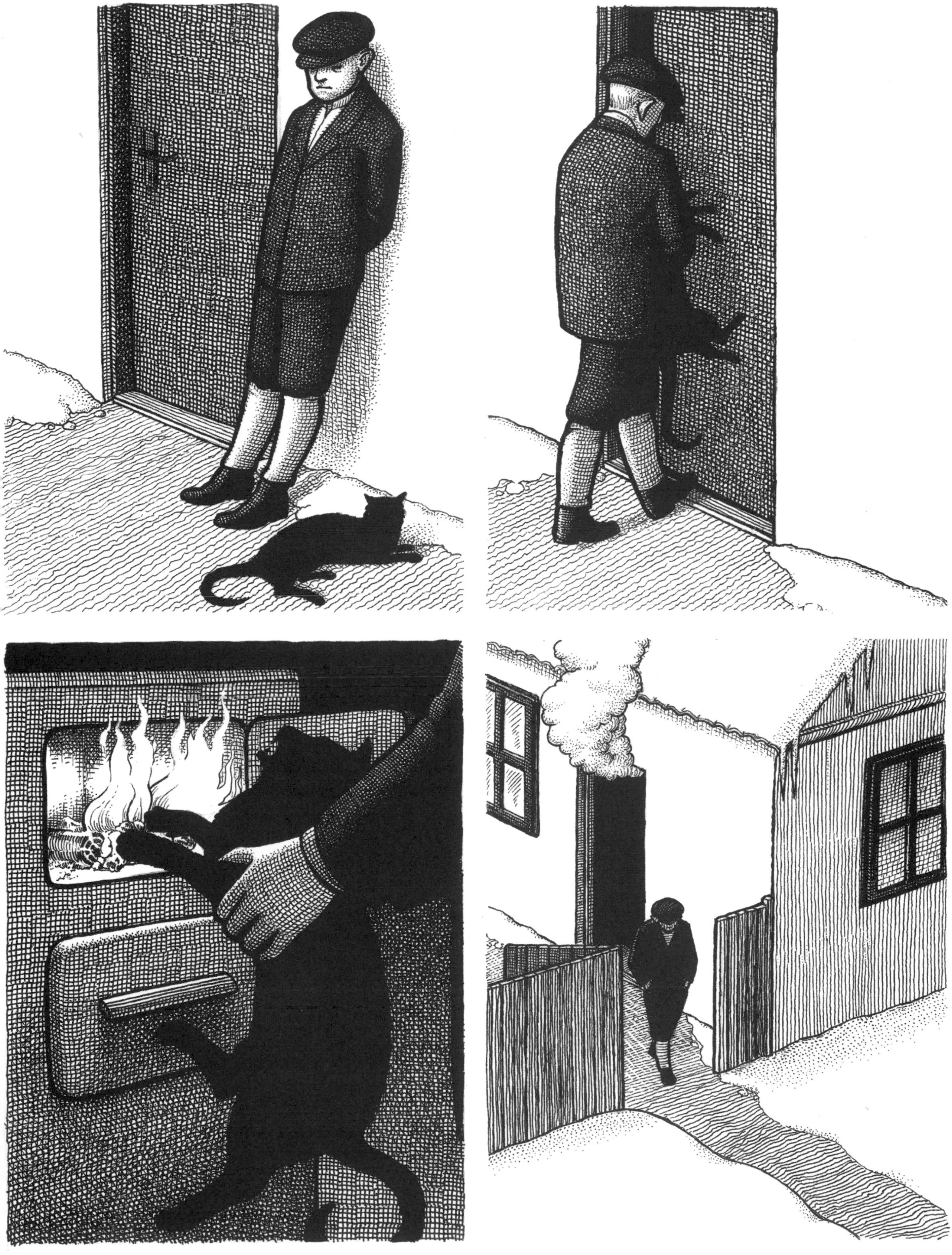

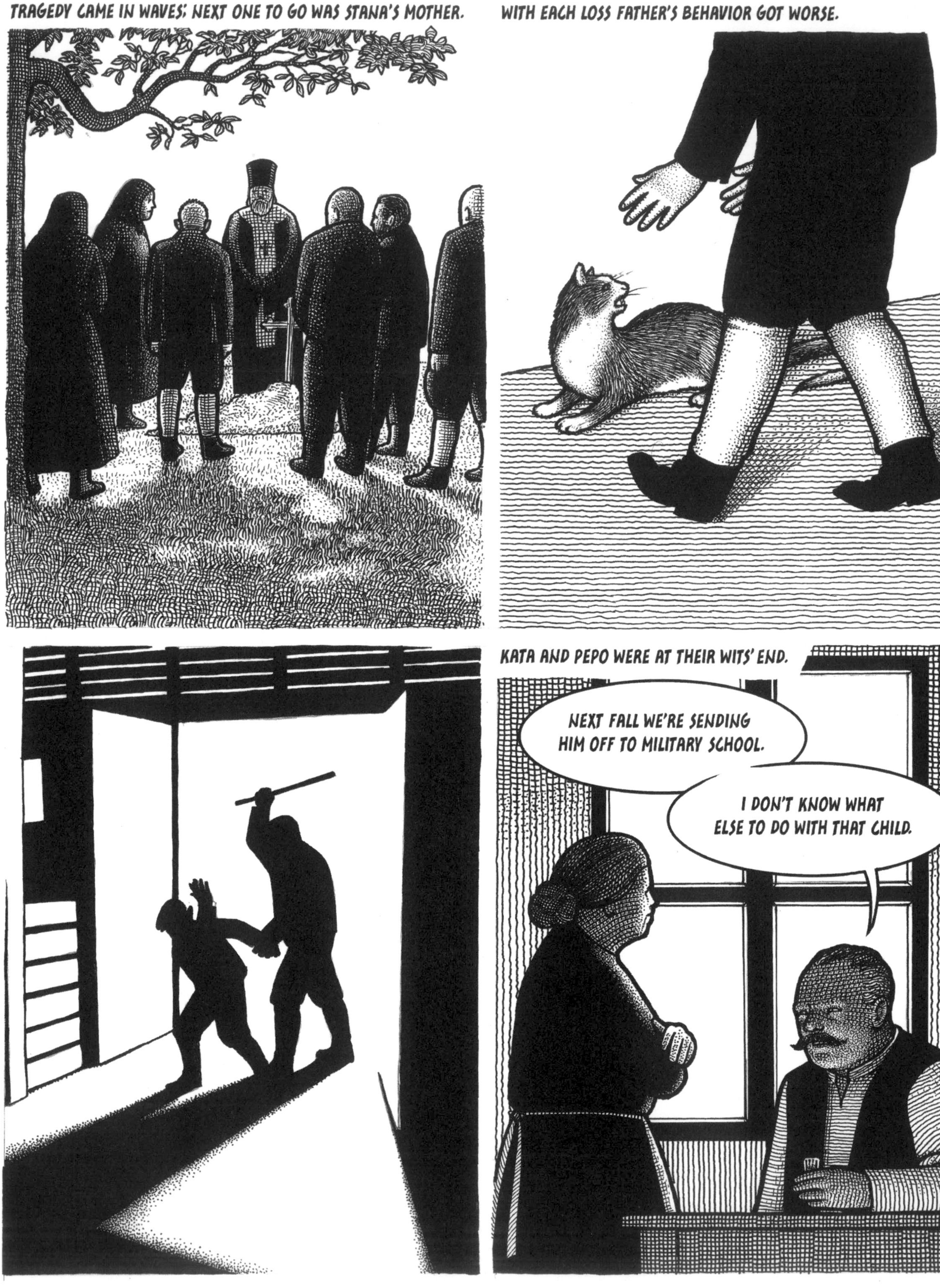
TRAGEDY CAME IN WAVES; NEXT ONE TO GO WAS STANA'S MOTHER.
WITH EACH LOSS FATHER'S BEHAVIOR GOT WORSE.
KATA AND PEPO WERE AT THEIR WITS' END.
NEXT FALL WE'RE SENDING HIM OFF TO MILITARY SCHOOL.
I DON'T KNOW WHAT ELSE TO DO WITH THAT CHILD.

STANA'S YOUNGER SISTER MARA WAS ABOUT THE ONLY PERSON WHO NEVER LOST HOPE IN HIM.

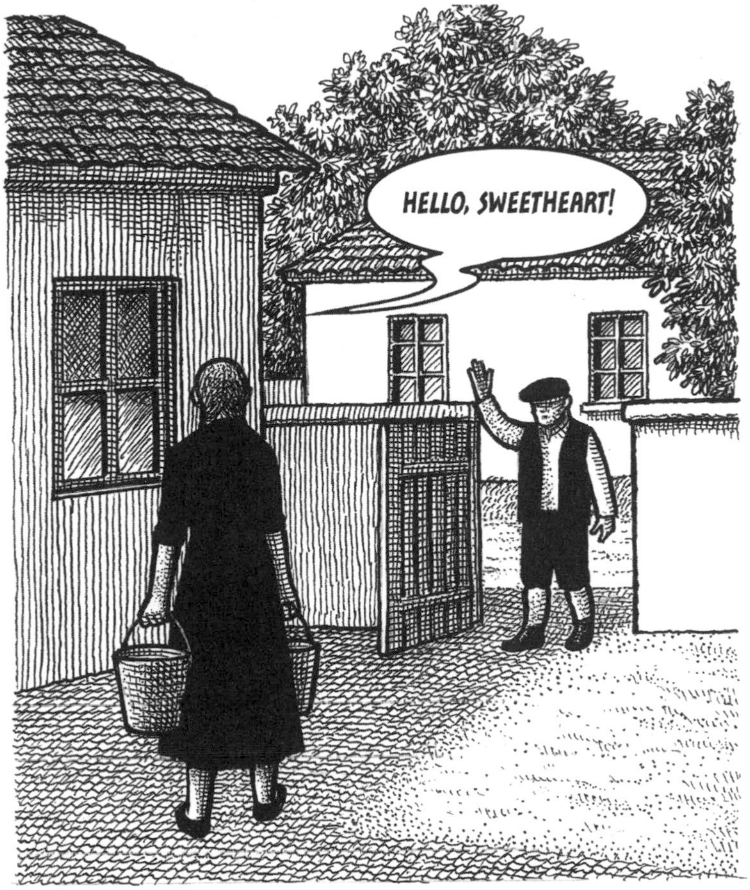
HELLO, SWEETHEART!

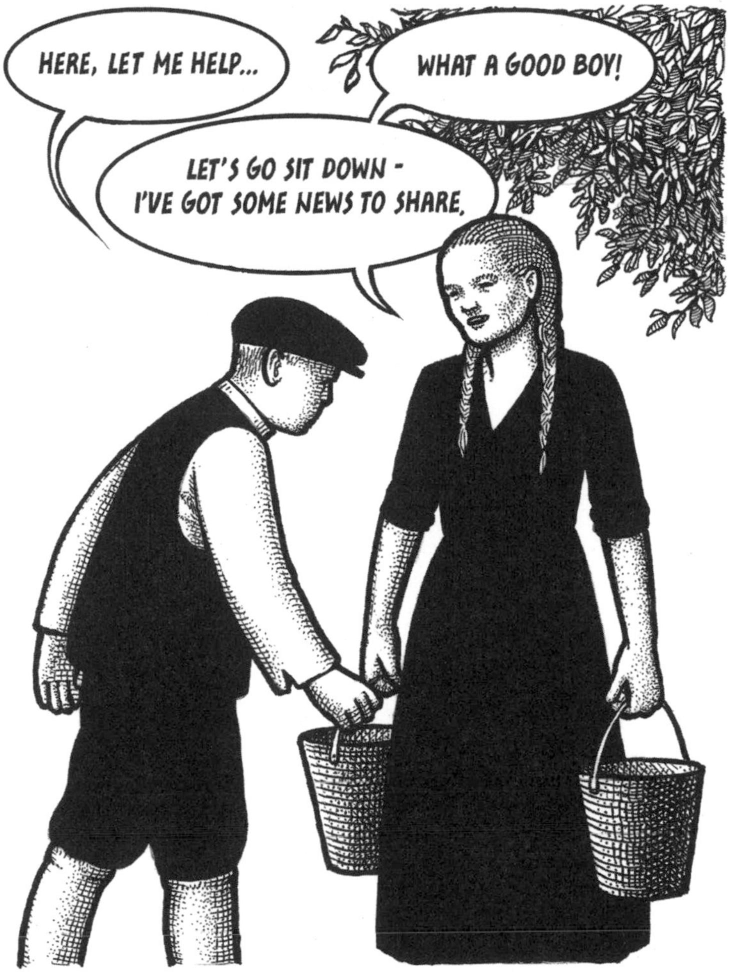
HERE, LET ME HELP...
WHAT A GOOD BOY!
LET'S GO SIT DOWN - I'VE GOT SOME NEWS TO SHARE.

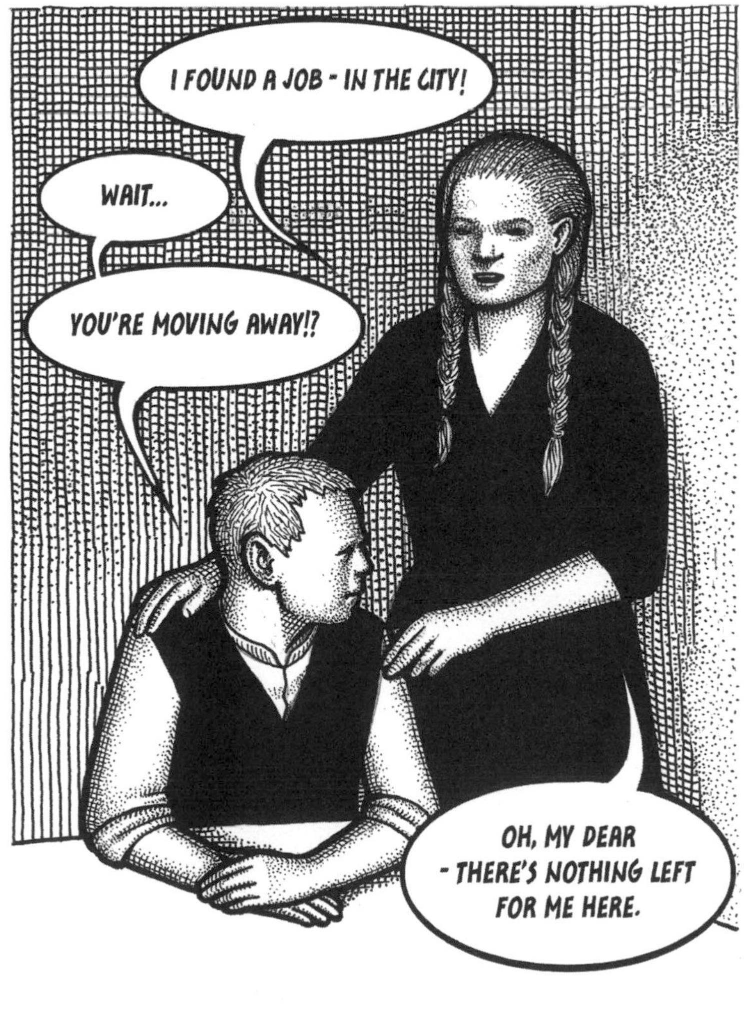
I FOUND A JOB - IN THE CITY!
WAIT...
YOU'RE MOVING AWAY!?
OH, MY DEAR - THERE'S NOTHING LEFT FOR ME HERE.

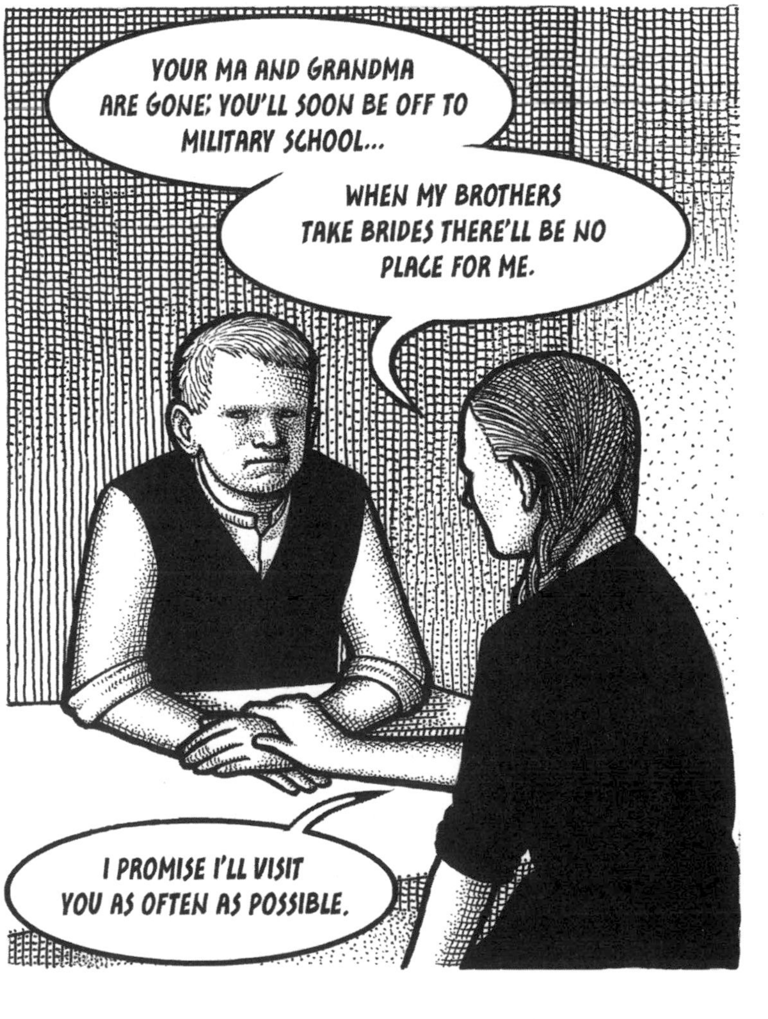
YOUR MA AND GRANDMA ARE GONE; YOU'LL SOON BE OFF TO MILITARY SCHOOL...
WHEN MY BROTHERS TAKE BRIDES THERE'LL BE NO PLACE FOR ME.
I PROMISE I'LL VISIT YOU AS OFTEN AS POSSIBLE.

NEAR THE END OF AUGUST 1949 MARA LEFT FOR NOVA GRADIŠKA.

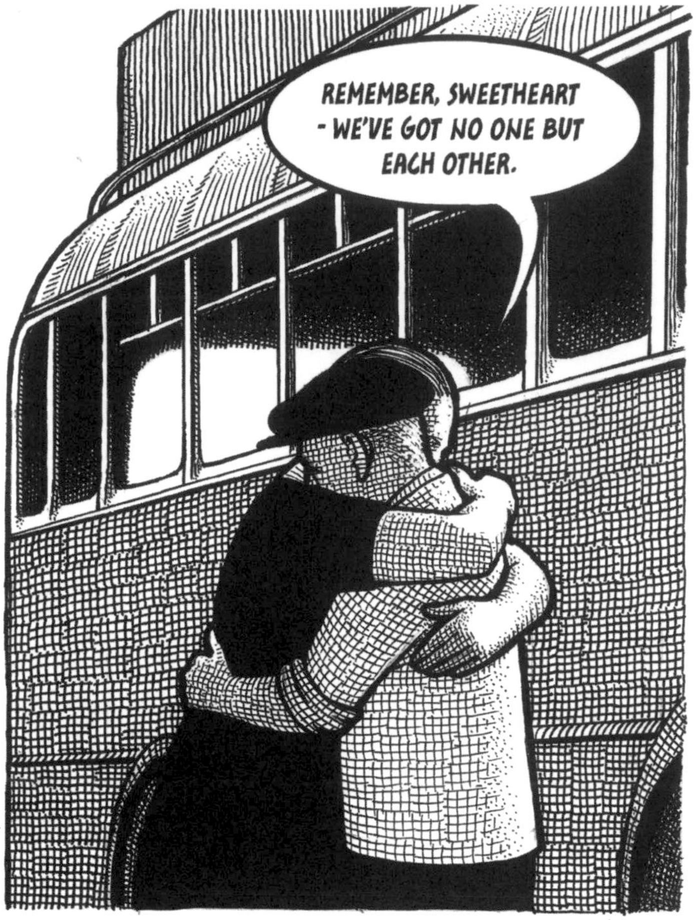
REMEMBER, SWEETHEART - WE'VE GOT NO ONE BUT EACH OTHER.

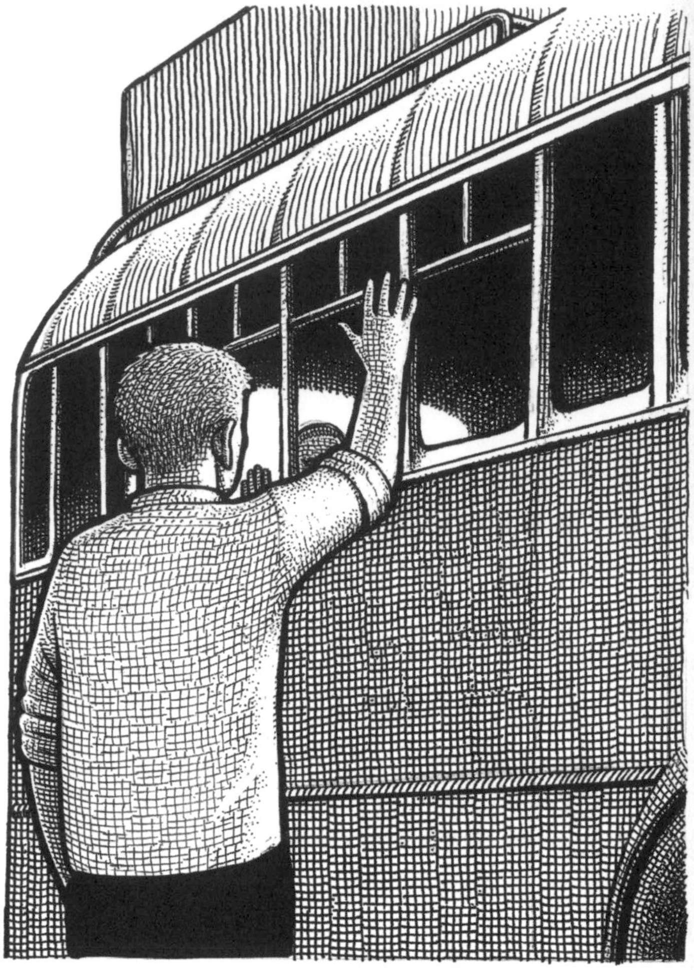

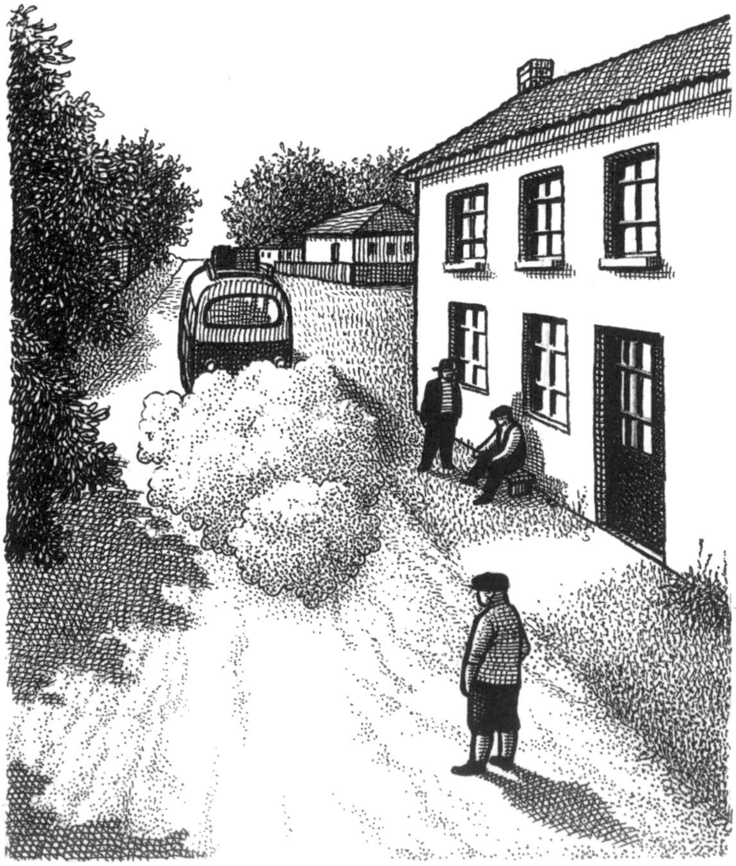

WITHIN A WEEK OR TWO OF MARA'S DEPARTURE MY FATHER WAS SHIPPED OFF TO MILITARY SCHOOL IN SPLIT.

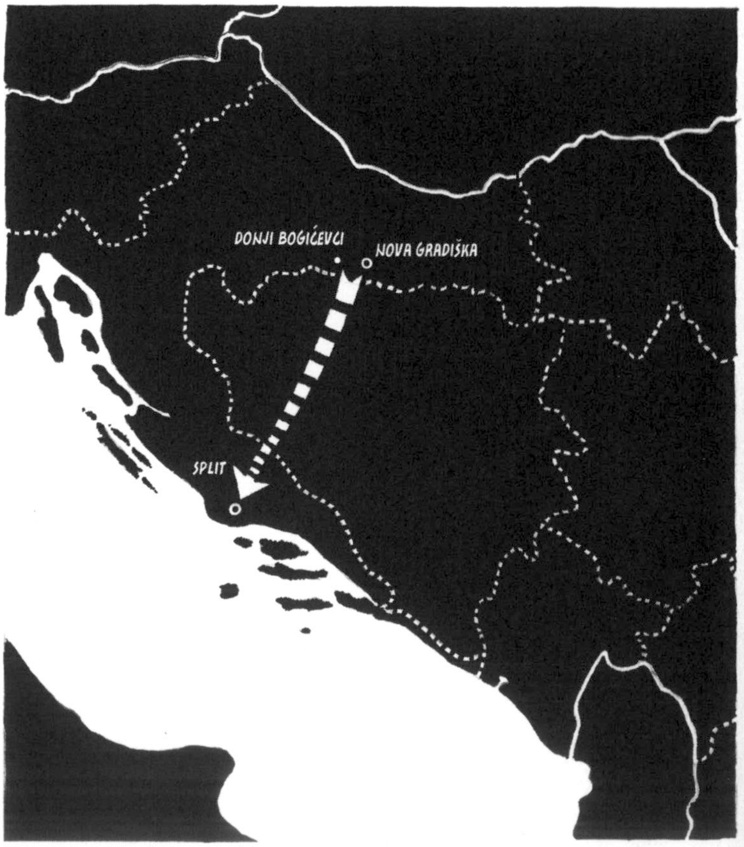
DONJI BOGIĆEVCI
NOVA GRADIŠKA
SPLIT

# DISSIDENT YEARS

ONE MAN'S IDEA OF LIBERTY IS ANOTHER MAN'S IDEA OF TYRANNY.

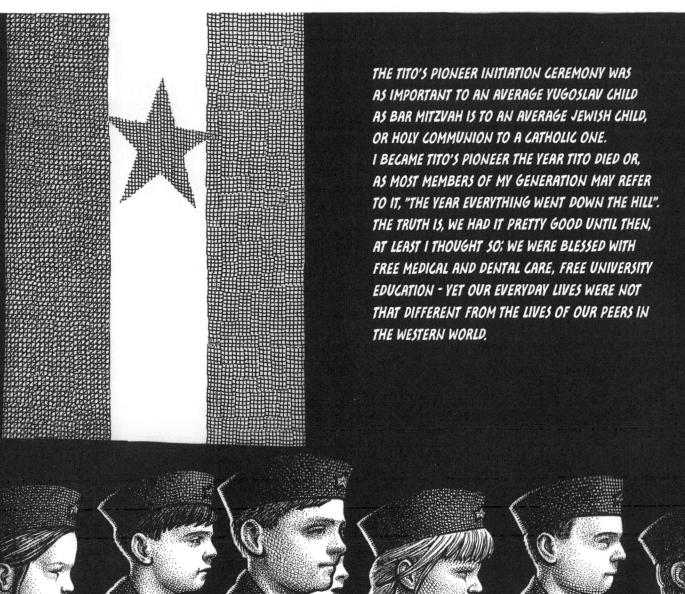

THE TITO'S PIONEER INITIATION CEREMONY WAS AS IMPORTANT TO AN AVERAGE YUGOSLAV CHILD AS BAR MITZVAH IS TO AN AVERAGE JEWISH CHILD, OR HOLY COMMUNION TO A CATHOLIC ONE. I BECAME TITO'S PIONEER THE YEAR TITO DIED OR, AS MOST MEMBERS OF MY GENERATION MAY REFER TO IT, "THE YEAR EVERYTHING WENT DOWN THE HILL". THE TRUTH IS, WE HAD IT PRETTY GOOD UNTIL THEN, AT LEAST I THOUGHT SO; WE WERE BLESSED WITH FREE MEDICAL AND DENTAL CARE, FREE UNIVERSITY EDUCATION - YET OUR EVERYDAY LIVES WERE NOT THAT DIFFERENT FROM THE LIVES OF OUR PEERS IN THE WESTERN WORLD.

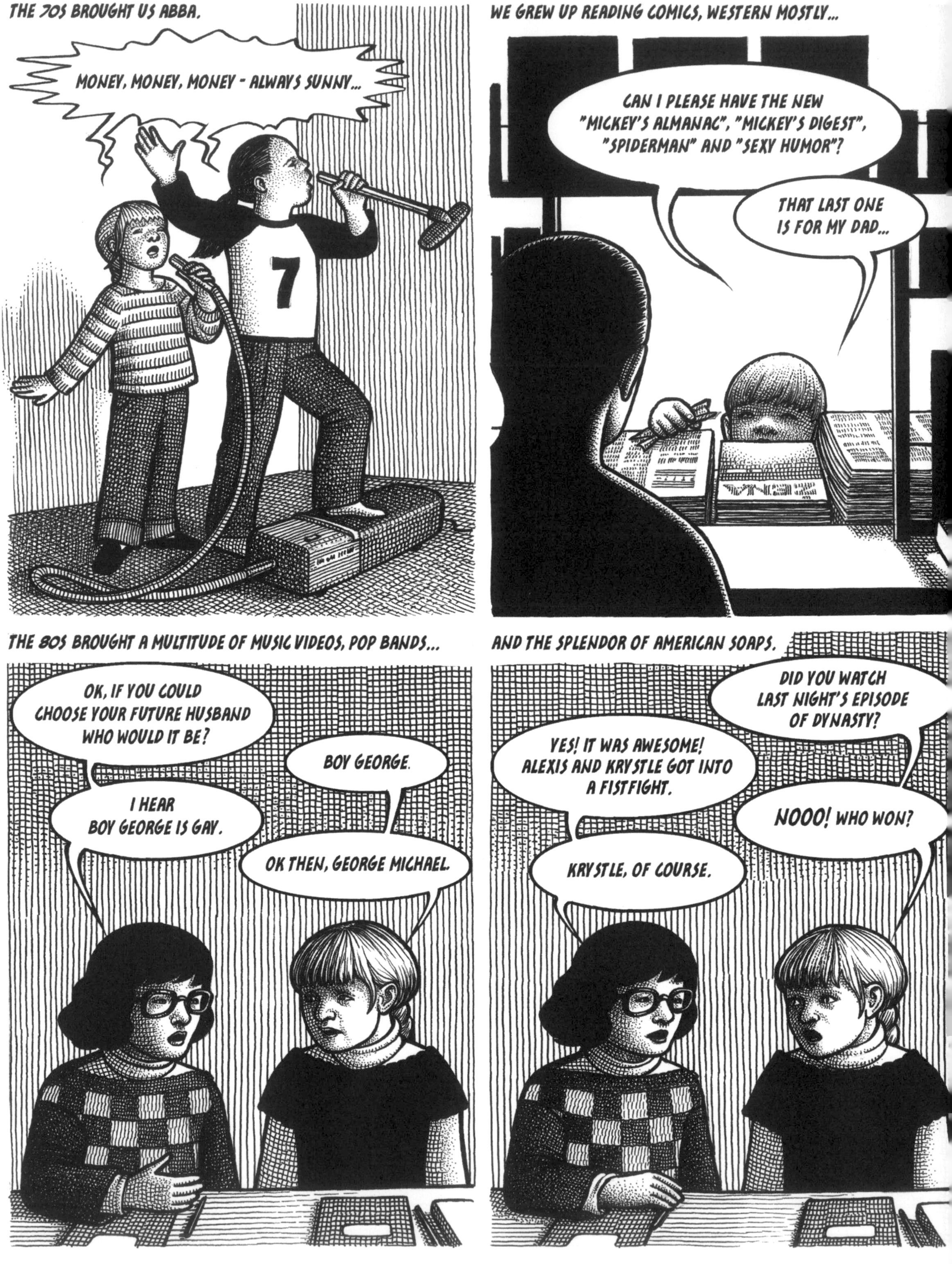
THE 70S BROUGHT US ABBA.
MONEY, MONEY, MONEY - ALWAYS SUNNY...
7
WE GREW UP READING COMICS, WESTERN MOSTLY...
CAN I PLEASE HAVE THE NEW "MICKEY'S ALMANAC", "MICKEY'S DIGEST", "SPIDERMAN" AND "SEXY HUMOR"?
THAT LAST ONE IS FOR MY DAD...
THE 80S BROUGHT A MULTITUDE OF MUSIC VIDEOS, POP BANDS...
OK, IF YOU COULD CHOOSE YOUR FUTURE HUSBAND WHO WOULD IT BE?
BOY GEORGE.
I HEAR BOY GEORGE IS GAY.
OK THEN, GEORGE MICHAEL.
AND THE SPLENDOR OF AMERICAN SOAPS.
DID YOU WATCH LAST NIGHT'S EPISODE OF DYNASTY?
YES! IT WAS AWESOME! ALEXIS AND KRYSTLE GOT INTO A FISTFIGHT.
NOOO! WHO WON?
KRYSTLE, OF COURSE.

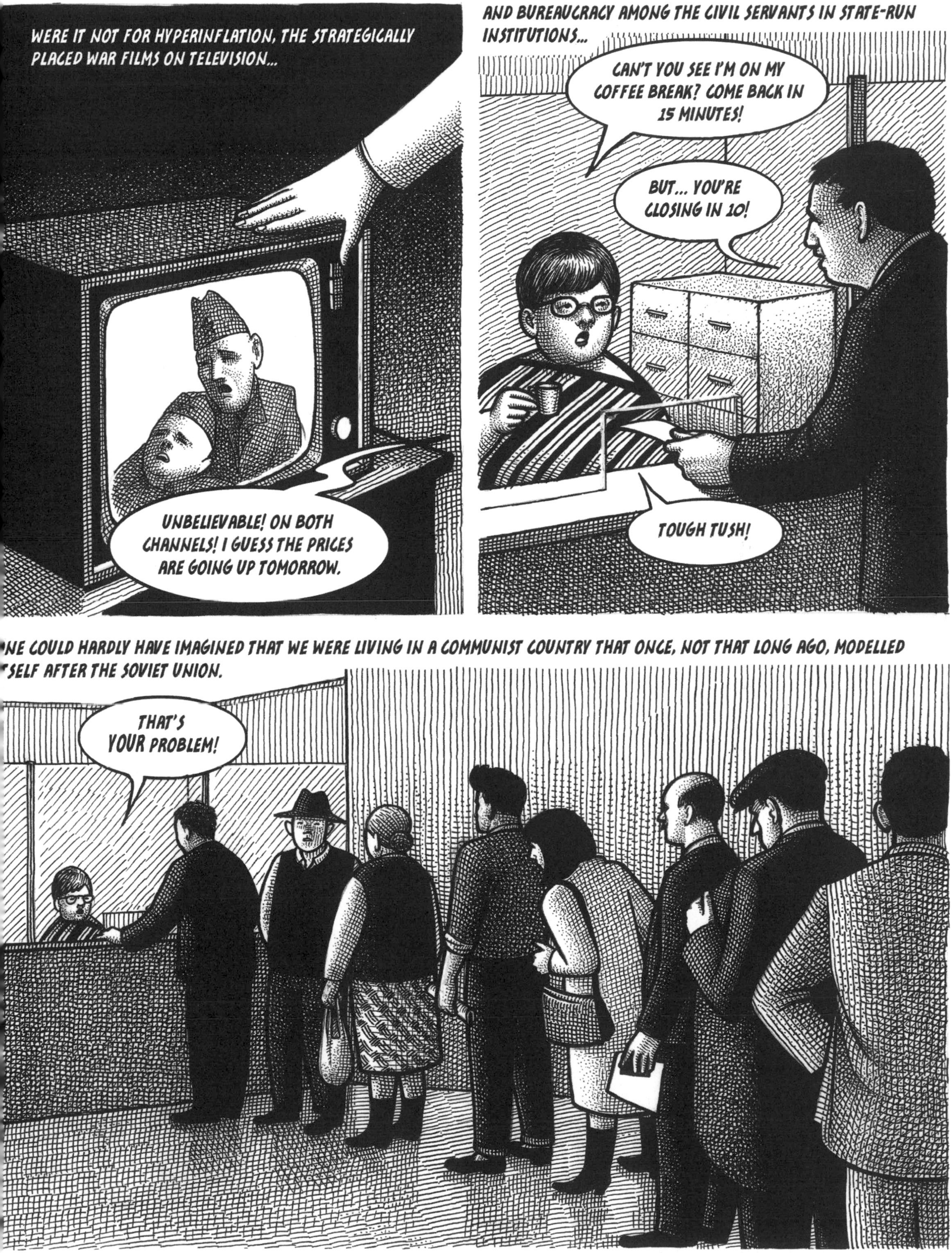
WERE IT NOT FOR HYPERINFLATION, THE STRATEGICALLY PLACED WAR FILMS ON TELEVISION...
UNBELIEVABLE! ON BOTH CHANNELS! I GUESS THE PRICES ARE GOING UP TOMORROW.
AND BUREAUCRACY AMONG THE CIVIL SERVANTS IN STATE-RUN INSTITUTIONS...
CAN'T YOU SEE I'M ON MY COFFEE BREAK? COME BACK IN 15 MINUTES!
BUT... YOU'RE CLOSING IN 20!
TOUGH TUSH!
NE COULD HARDLY HAVE IMAGINED THAT WE WERE LIVING IN A COMMUNIST COUNTRY THAT ONCE, NOT THAT LONG AGO, MODELLED
SELF AFTER THE SOVIET UNION.
THAT'S YOUR PROBLEM!

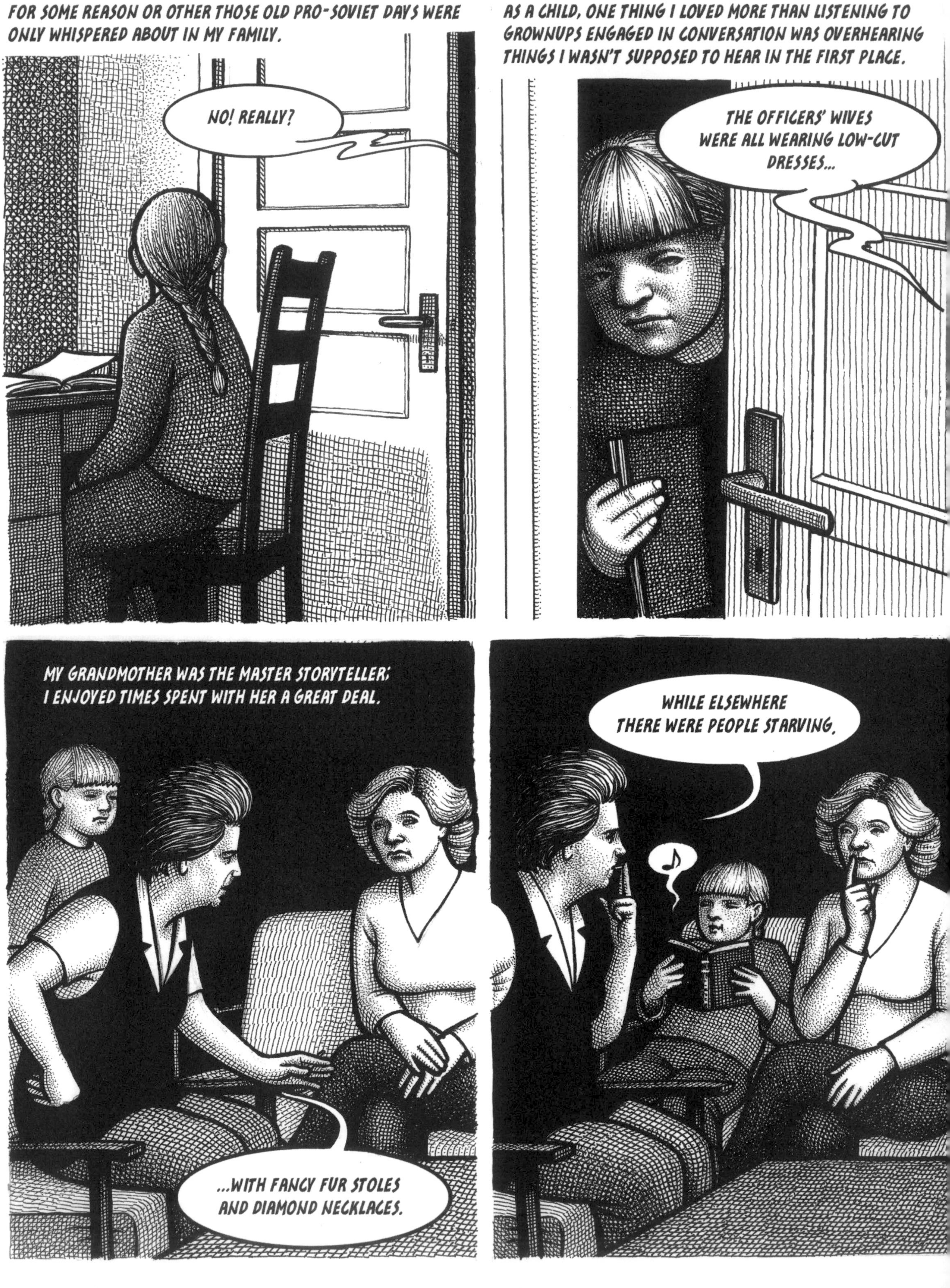
FOR SOME REASON OR OTHER THOSE OLD PRO-SOVIET DAYS WERE ONLY WHISPERED ABOUT IN MY FAMILY.
NO! REALLY?
AS A CHILD, ONE THING I LOVED MORE THAN LISTENING TO GROWNUPS ENGAGED IN CONVERSATION WAS OVERHEARING THINGS I WASN'T SUPPOSED TO HEAR IN THE FIRST PLACE.
THE OFFICERS' WIVES WERE ALL WEARING LOW-CUT DRESSES...
MY GRANDMOTHER WAS THE MASTER STORYTELLER; I ENJOYED TIMES SPENT WITH HER A GREAT DEAL.
...WITH FANCY FUR STOLES AND DIAMOND NECKLACES.
WHILE ELSEWHERE THERE WERE PEOPLE STARVING.

IT WAS BY EAVESDROPPING ON THESE CONVERSATIONS THAT I LEARNED ABOUT YUGOSLAVIA'S DARK HISTORY, CIRCA 1945-1948, A PERIOD WHICH WAS OTHERWISE MARKED BY OPTIMISM, REBUILDING, AND UNBRIDLED UTOPIAN ENTHUSIASM.

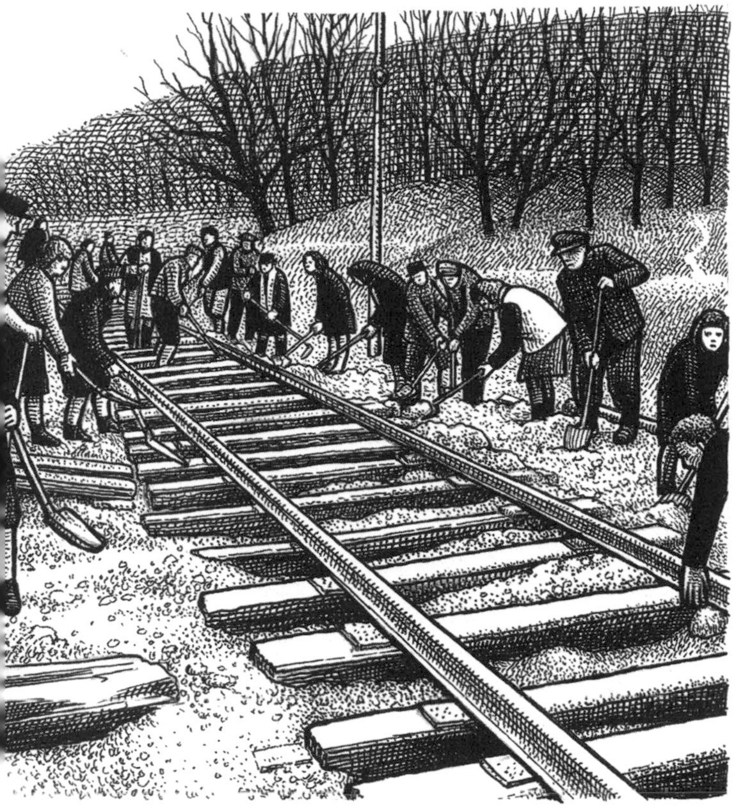

IT WAS AT THIS TIME THAT THE COUNTRY ADOPTED THE SOVIET ECONOMIC DEVELOPMENT MODEL BY INTRODUCING FIVE-YEAR PLANS...

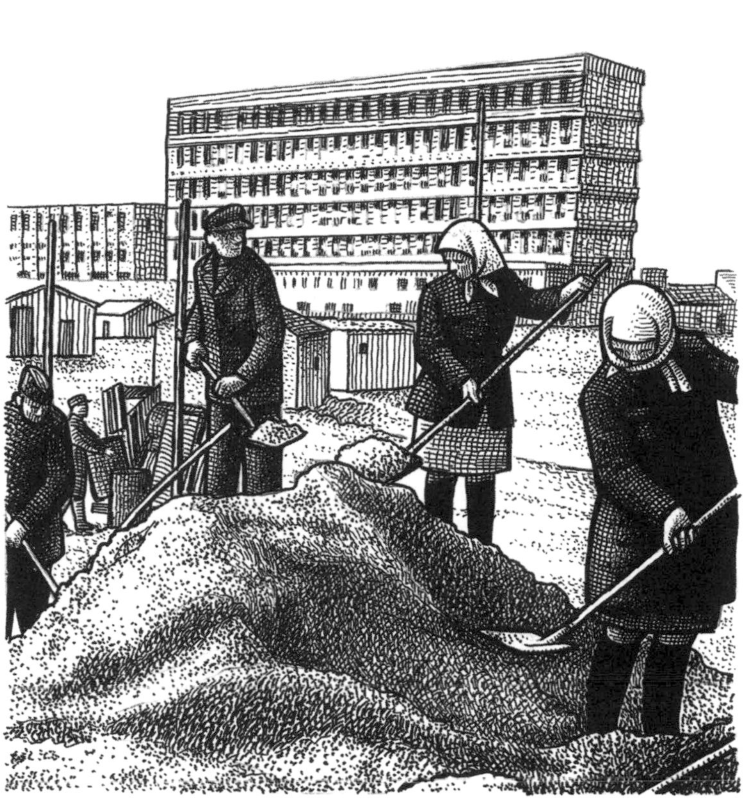

BY IMPLEMENTING COLLECTIVIZATION OF AGRICULTURE AND INDUSTRY...

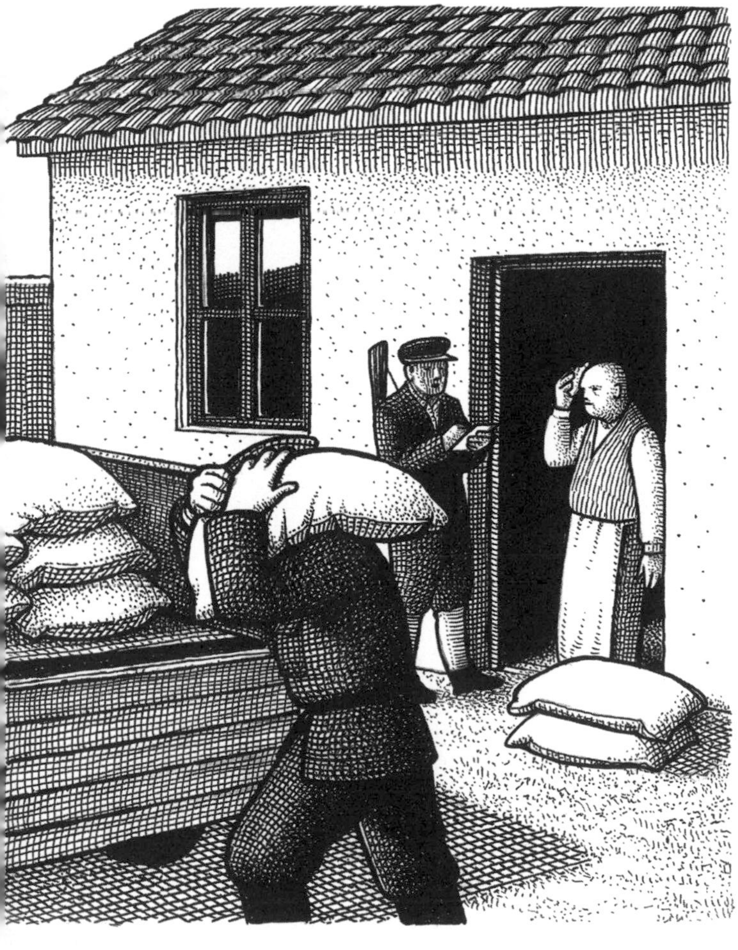

...AND ELIMINATION OF THE BOURGEOIS ELEMENTS BY ANY MEANS NECESSARY.

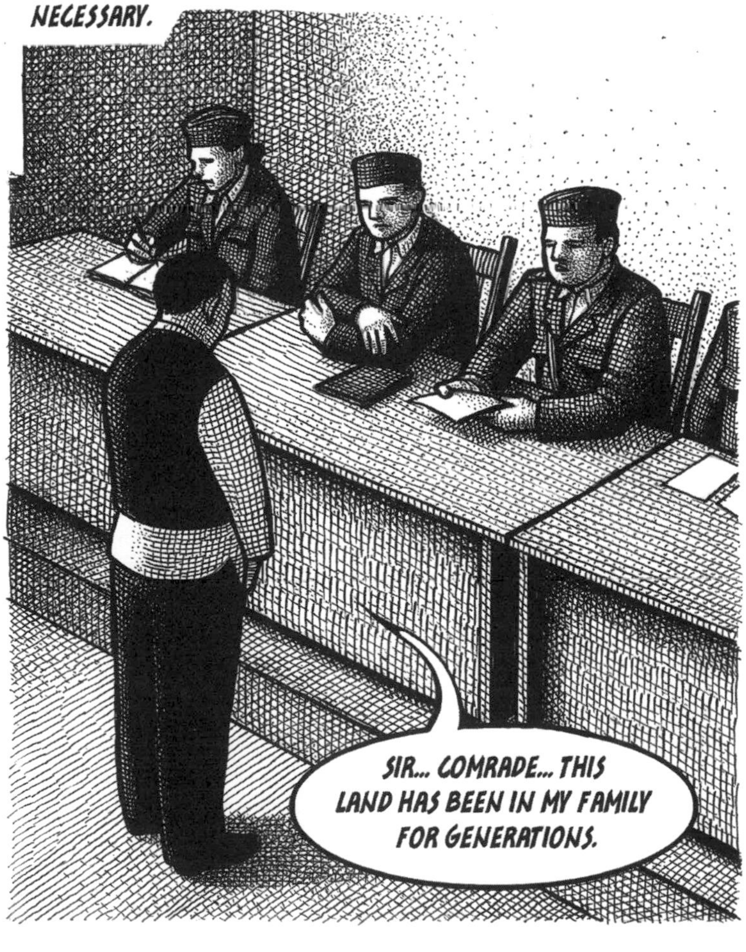
SIR... COMRADE... THIS LAND HAS BEEN IN MY FAMILY FOR GENERATIONS.

WAR-PROFITEERING AND COLLABORATING WITH THE ENEMY WERE PUNISHED MOST SEVERELY. CONVICTIONS WERE SWIFT AND OFTEN RELIED ON NO MORE THAN SINGLE-WITNESS ACCOUNTS. THE POLITICAL CLIMATE OF THE POST-WAR YEARS CREATED THE PERFECT ATMOSPHERE FOR OPPORTUNISM AND EXECUTION OF PERSONAL VENDETTAS.

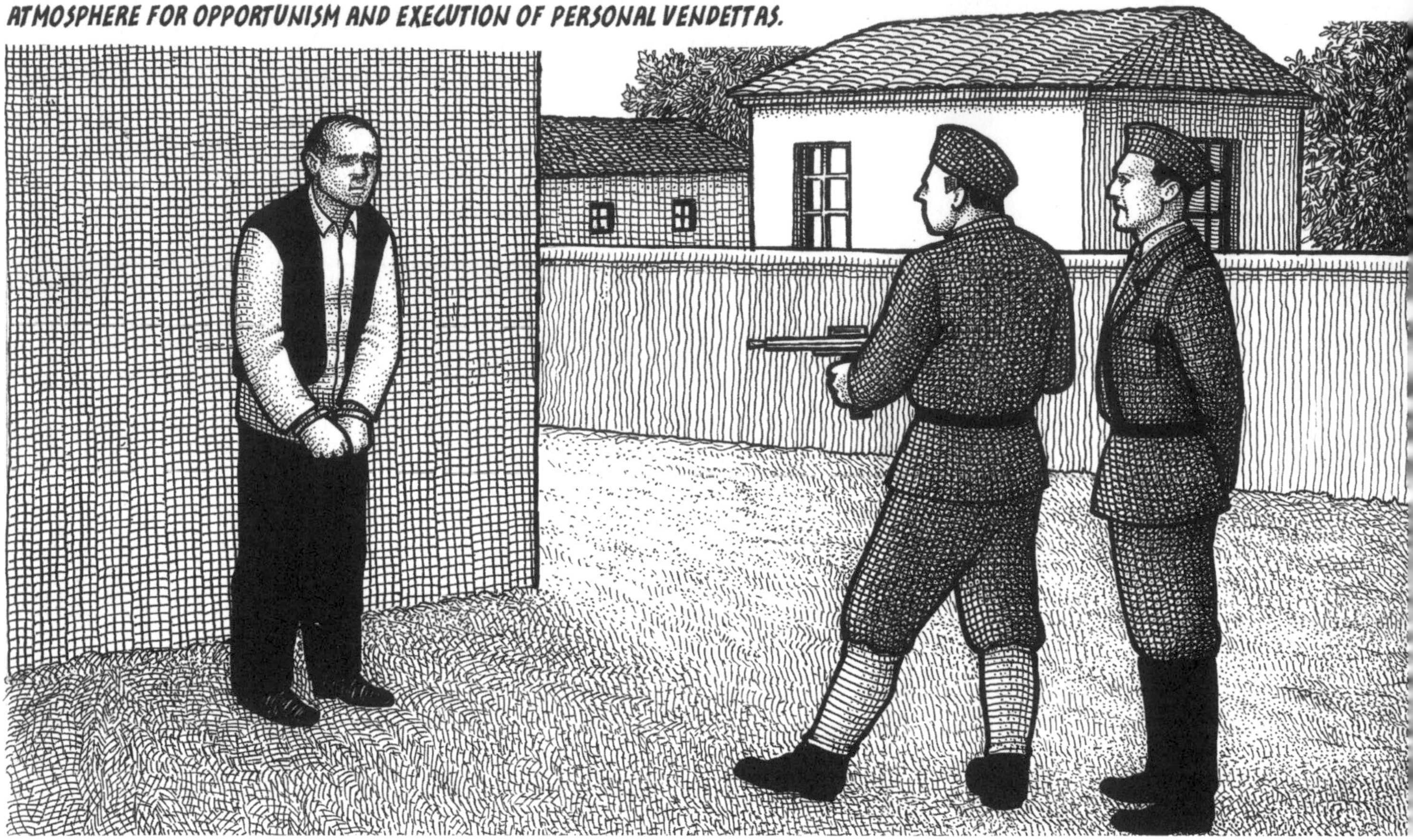

SAY YOU WERE COVETING YOUR NEIGHBOR'S WIFE.

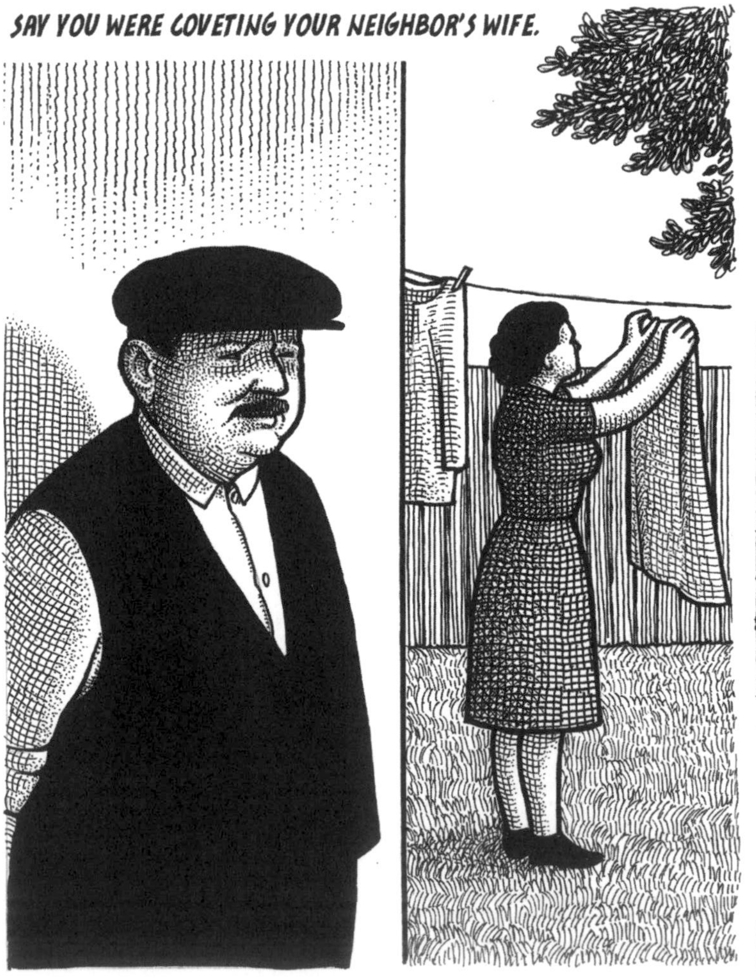

ALL YOU HAD TO DO WAS POINT YOUR FINGER IN HIS DIRECTION, MAKE UP A LIE AND THE OBSTACLE TO YOUR HEART'S DESIRE WOULD DISAPPEAR FOREVER, COURTESY OF THE STATE.

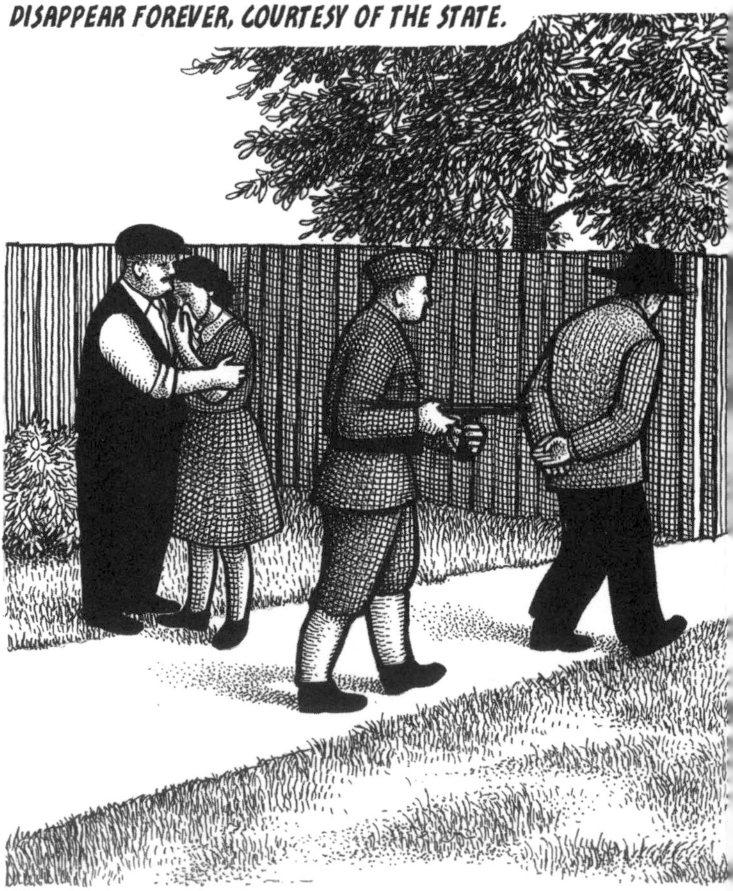

THE SITUATION ESCALATED IN 1948 WHEN YUGOSLAVIA GOT EXPELLED FROM THE COMINFORM FOLLOWING THE TITO-STALIN DISPUTE ABOUT AIDING THE COMMUNIST UPRISING IN GREECE AND THE POTENTIAL UNIFICATION OF YUGOSLAVIA AND BULGARIA.

WHAT FOLLOWED WAS AN ECONOMIC EMBARGO IMPOSED BY OTHER MEMBER COUNTRIES OF THE COMINFORM.

A BLESSING IN DISGUISE, THE EMBARGO WOULD NUDGE THE COUNTRY TO REDEFINE ITS FOREIGN POLICY AND DEVELOP ECONOMIC TIES WITH NON-COMMUNIST COUNTRIES.

YUGOSLAVIA WOULD EVENTUALLY EMBARK ON THE SOCIALIST PATH, BUT NOT BEFORE HAVING TO DEAL WITH THE "SOVIET ELEMENT" WITHIN ITS OWN BORDERS FIRST.

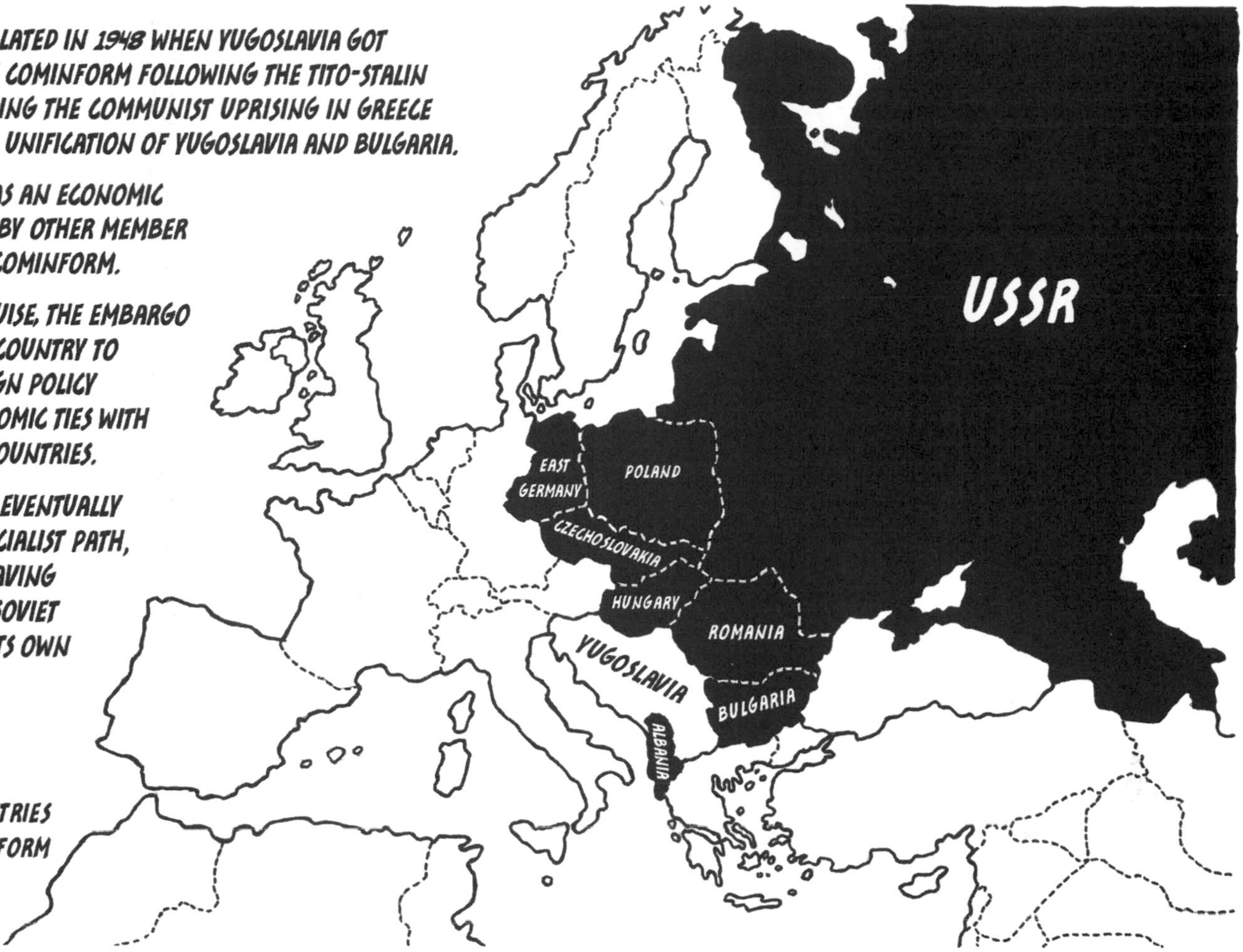
USSR
EAST GERMANY
POLAND
CZECHOSLOVAKIA
HUNGARY
ROMANIA
YUGOSLAVIA
BULGARIA
ALBANIA
MEMBER COUNTRIES OF THE COMINFORM

THE HOLY "LENIN-STALIN-TITO" TRINITY WAS BROKEN. SYMPATHIZING WITH STALIN WOULD HAVE ONE PEGGED A "STALINIST", AN ADDITION TO AN ALREADY LENGTHY LIST OF THINGS "ONE DARE NOT EVEN TALK ABOUT".

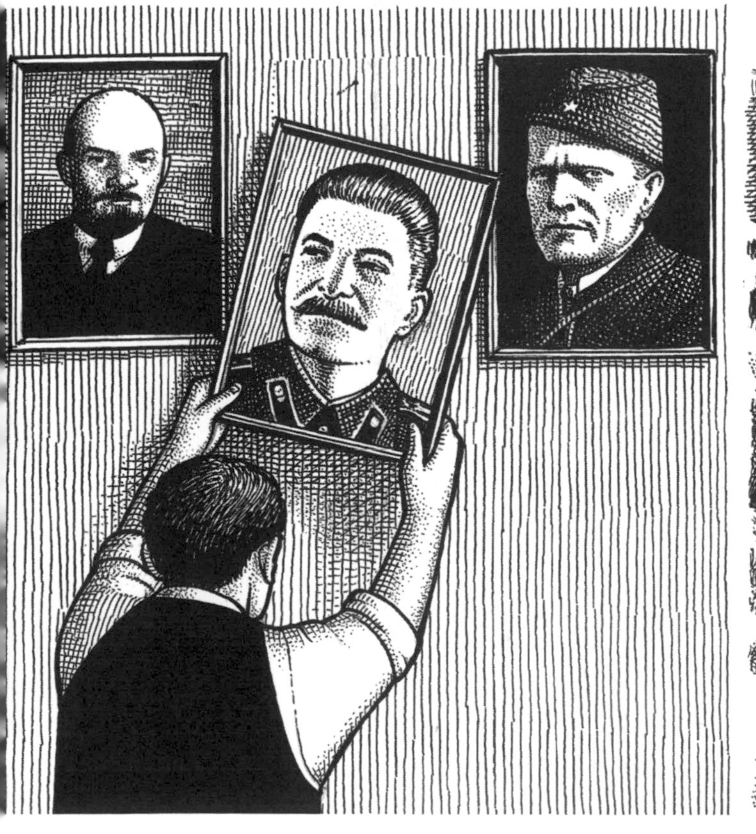

STORIES WERE TOLD ABOUT "GOLI OTOK" - THE PRISON WHICH WAS BUILT FOR THE SPECIFIC PURPOSE OF DEALING WITH THE ENEMIES OF THE STATE - AND THE SEVERE AND INHUMANE TREATMENT OF ITS INMATES.

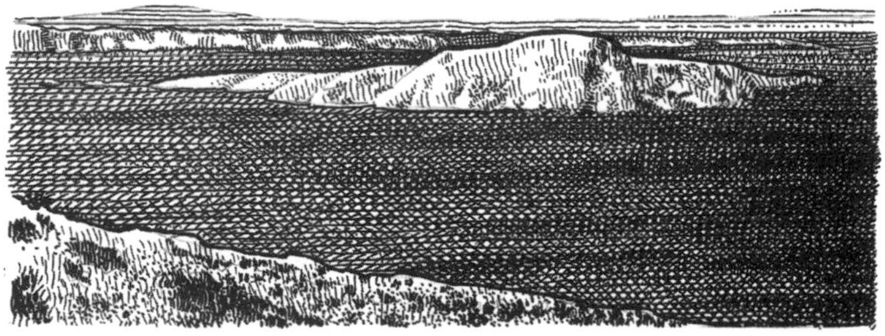

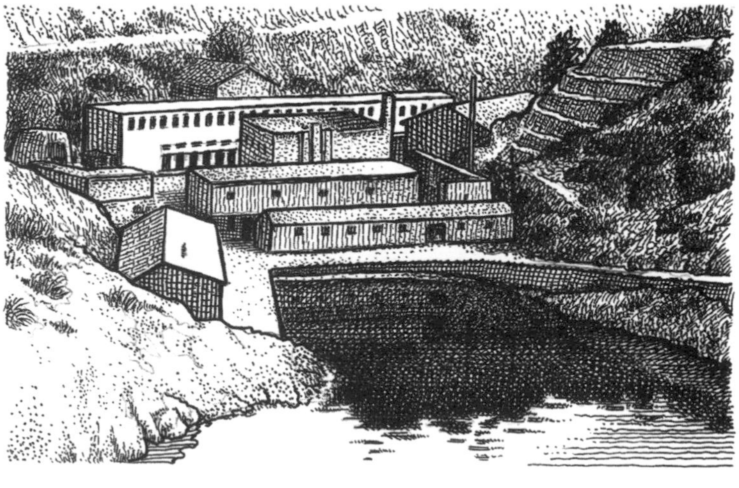

WHAT WAS WHISPERED ABOUT THE MOST, AND WHAT SEEMED TO BOTHER MY GRANDMOTHER IMMENSELY WAS THE INTERNMENT AND EXPULSION OF ETHNIC GERMANS FROM THE NORTHERN PROVINCE OF VOJVODINA. ALTHOUGH A LARGE PERCENTAGE OF THE GERMAN POPULATION DID SUPPORT AND JOIN THE WEHRMACHT DURING WWII, MANY INNOCENT PEOPLE PERISHED ALONG THE WAY BETWEEN 1945 AND 1948, SOLELY BY VIRTUE OF THEIR ETHNICITY.

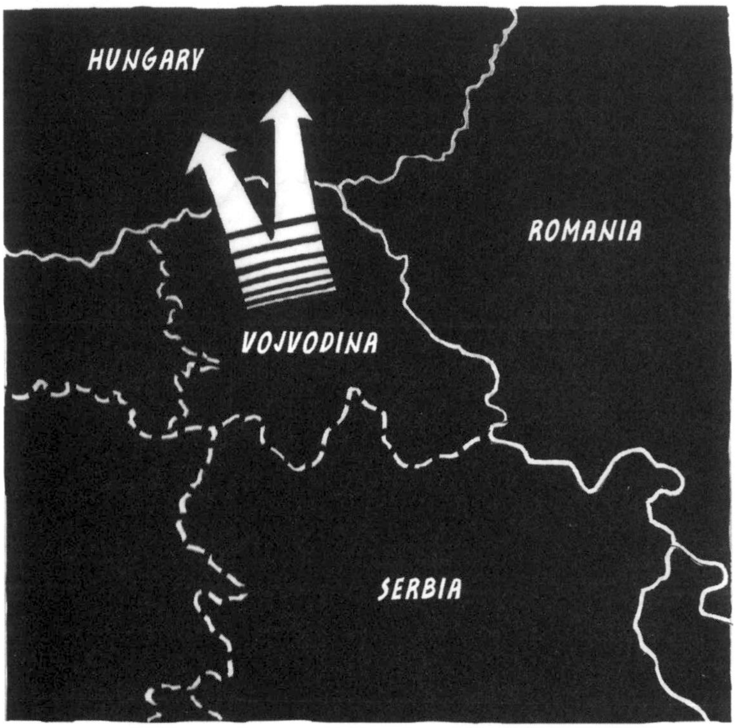
HUNGARY
ROMANIA
VOJVODINA
SERBIA

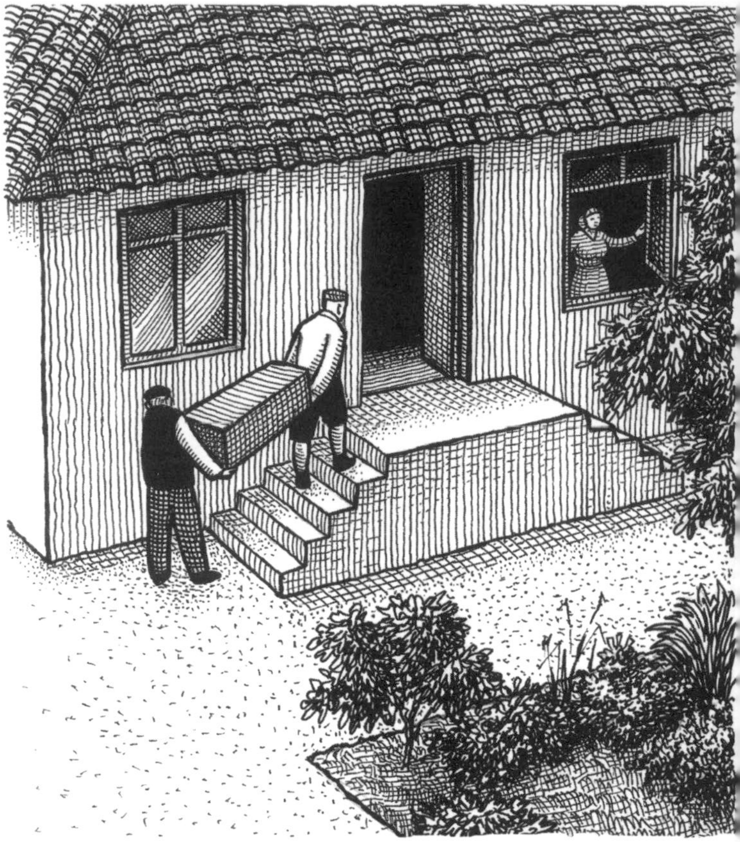

CONFISCATED PROPERTIES THAT ONCE BELONGED TO GERMAN FAMILIES WERE THEN GIVEN TO DESERVING MEMBERS OF THE COMMUNIST PARTY; IN MOST CASES FORMER PARTISANS.

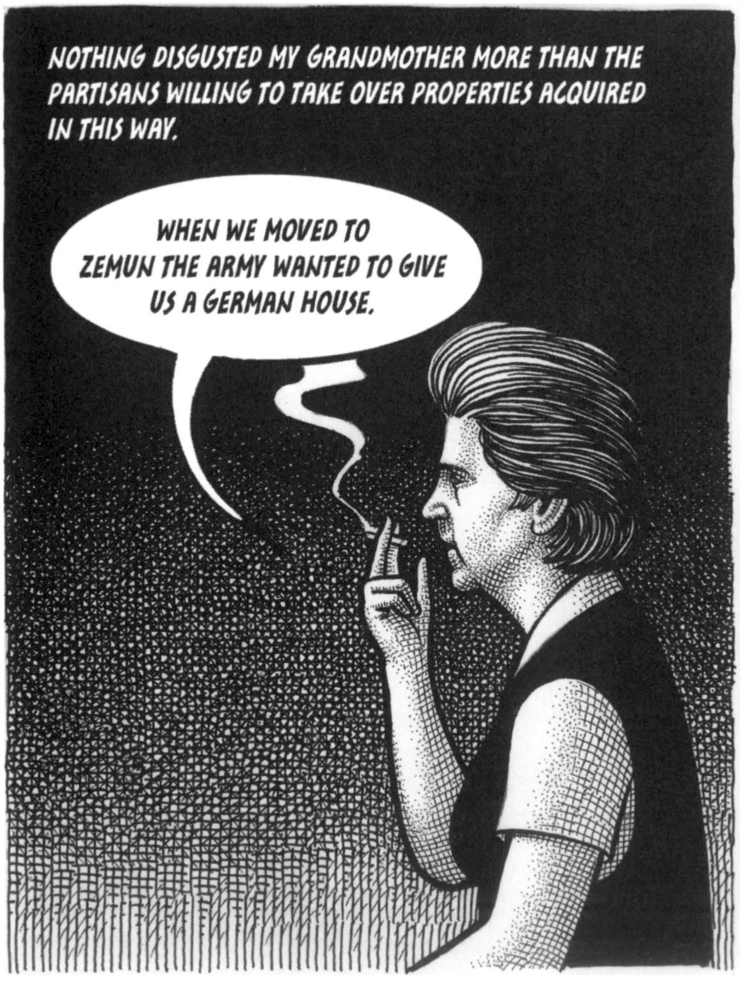
NOTHING DISGUSTED MY GRANDMOTHER MORE THAN THE PARTISANS WILLING TO TAKE OVER PROPERTIES ACQUIRED IN THIS WAY.
WHEN WE MOVED TO ZEMUN THE ARMY WANTED TO GIVE US A GERMAN HOUSE.

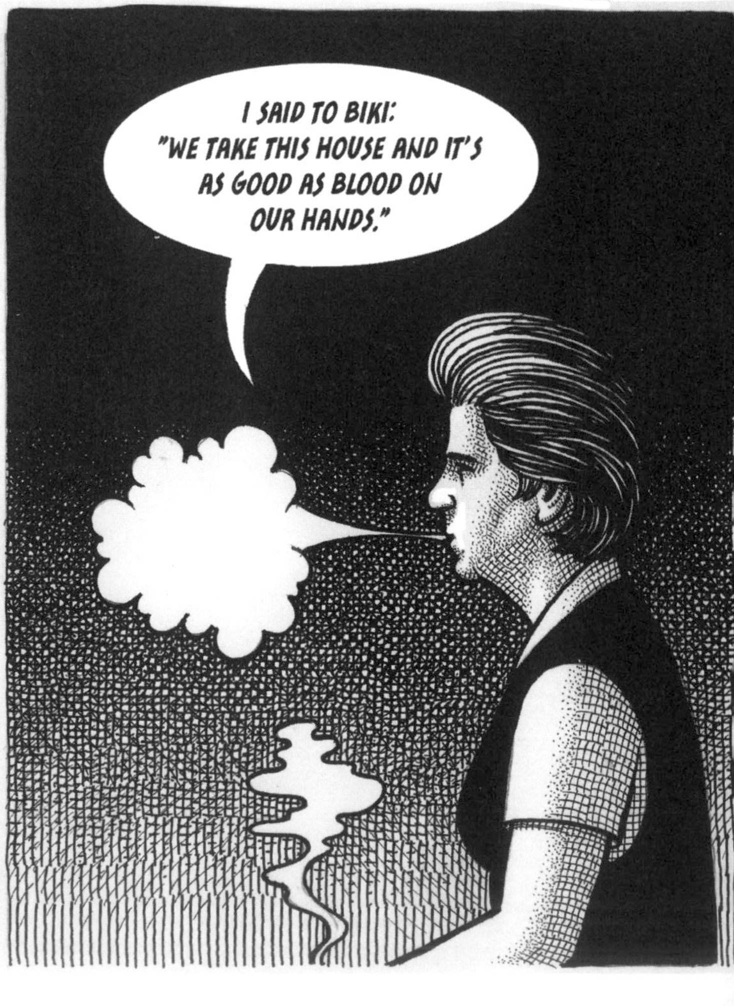
I SAID TO BIKI: "WE TAKE THIS HOUSE AND IT'S AS GOOD AS BLOOD ON OUR HANDS."

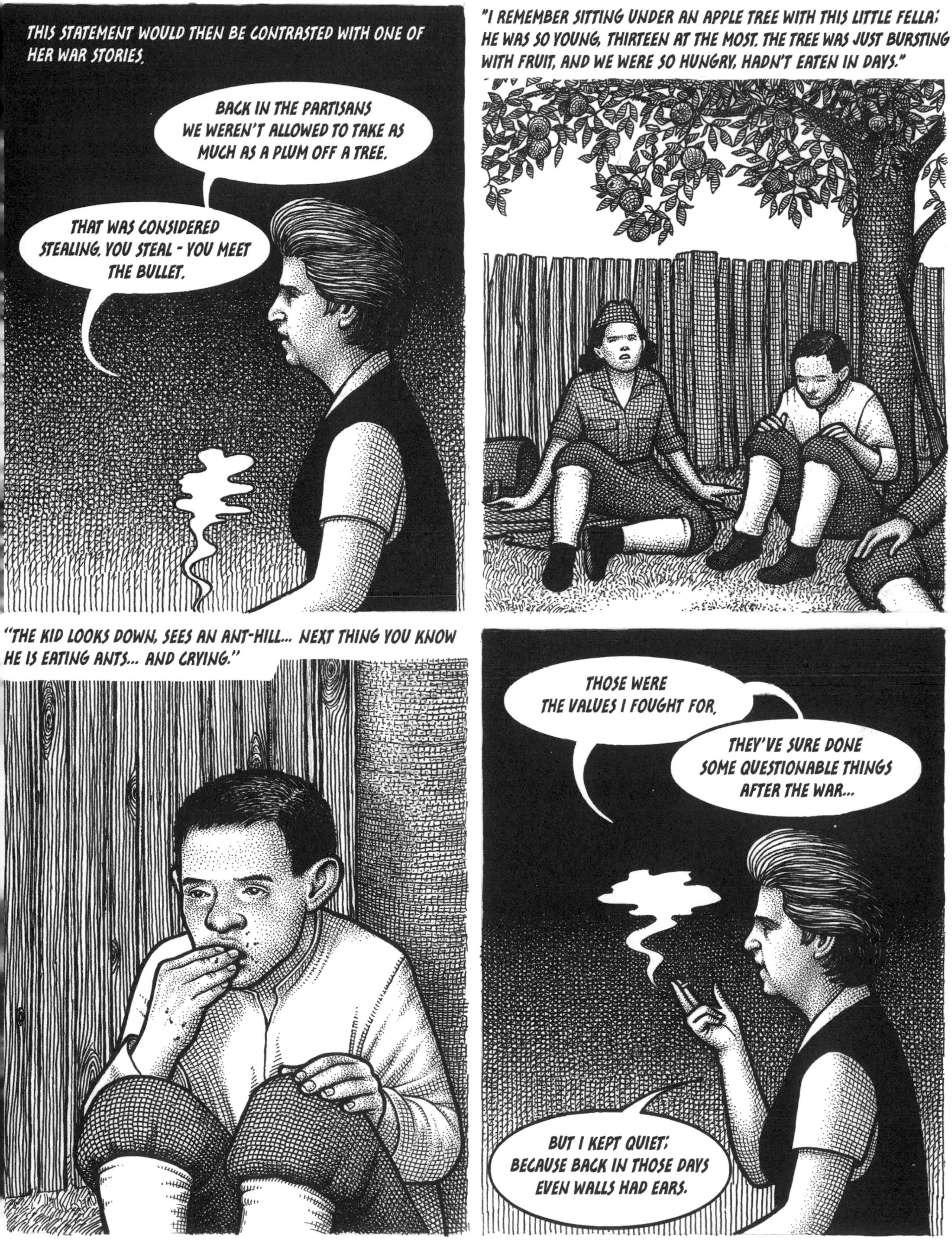
THIS STATEMENT WOULD THEN BE CONTRASTED WITH ONE OF HER WAR STORIES.
BACK IN THE PARTISANS WE WEREN'T ALLOWED TO TAKE AS MUCH AS A PLUM OFF A TREE.
THAT WAS CONSIDERED STEALING. YOU STEAL - YOU MEET THE BULLET.
"I REMEMBER SITTING UNDER AN APPLE TREE WITH THIS LITTLE FELLA; HE WAS SO YOUNG, THIRTEEN AT THE MOST. THE TREE WAS JUST BURSTING WITH FRUIT, AND WE WERE SO HUNGRY, HADN'T EATEN IN DAYS."
"THE KID LOOKS DOWN, SEES AN ANT-HILL... NEXT THING YOU KNOW HE IS EATING ANTS... AND CRYING."
THOSE WERE THE VALUES I FOUGHT FOR.
THEY'VE SURE DONE SOME QUESTIONABLE THINGS AFTER THE WAR...
BUT I KEPT QUIET; BECAUSE BACK IN THOSE DAYS EVEN WALLS HAD EARS.

SHE WAS WISE TO KEEP QUIET, FOR CRITICIZING THE GOVERNMENT WAS NOT TOLERATED ALL THAT WELL, EVEN IF THE CRITICISM CAME FROM TOP PARTY OFFICIALS. SUCH WAS THE CASE OF MILOVAN DJILAS, ONE OF THE KEY FIGURES IN THE COMMUNIST RESISTANCE, A MAN SECOND ONLY TO TITO. DJILAS WAS SEVERELY CRITICAL OF THE EMERGENCE OF A NEW CLASS IN WHAT WAS ESSENTIALLY A NO-CLASS SYSTEM.

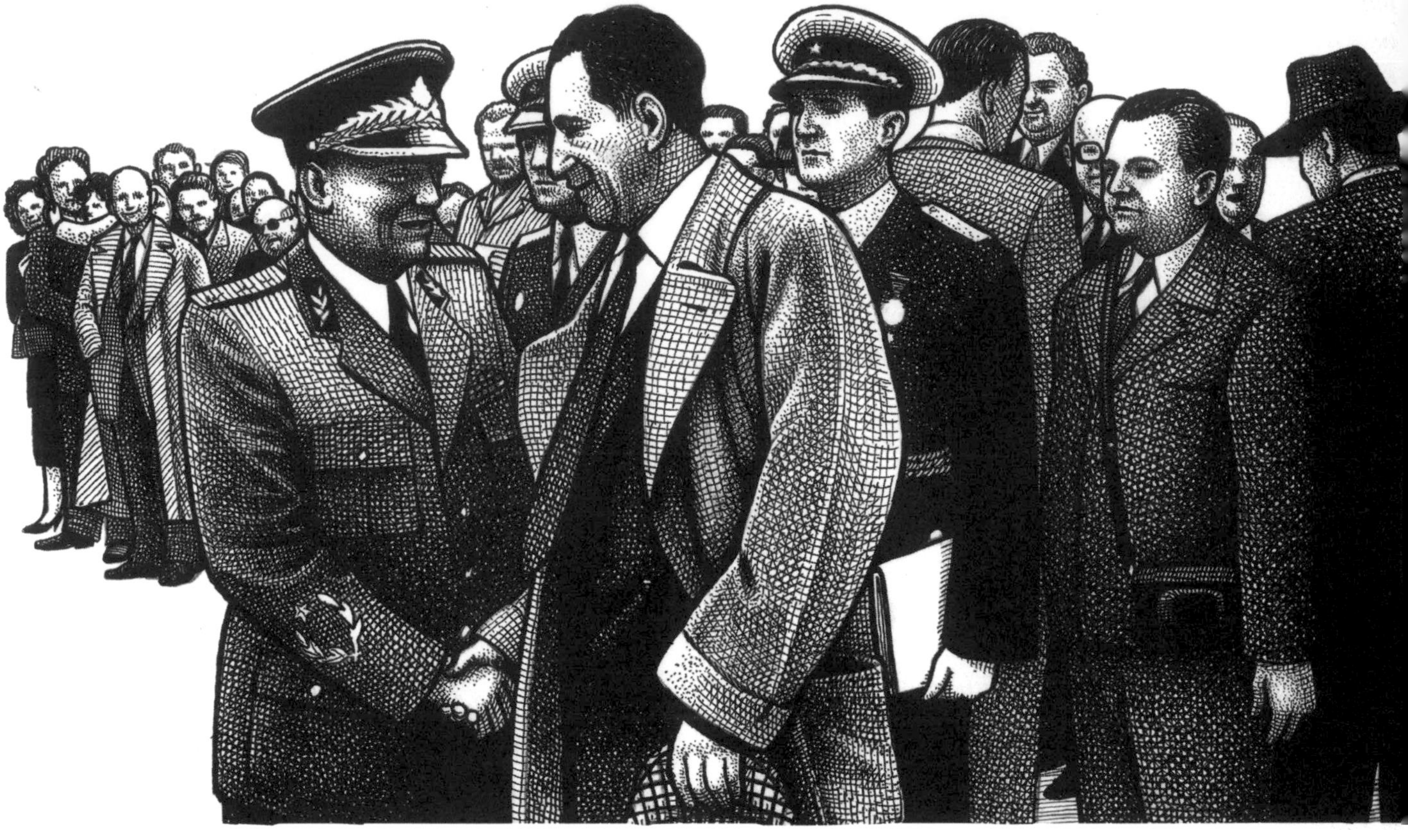

WHAT HE WAS REFERRING TO WAS THE LAVISH LIFE-STYLE ENJOYED BY THE ELITE PARTY MEMBERS, WHILE MOST PEOPLE LIVED WELL BELOW THE POVERTY LINE.

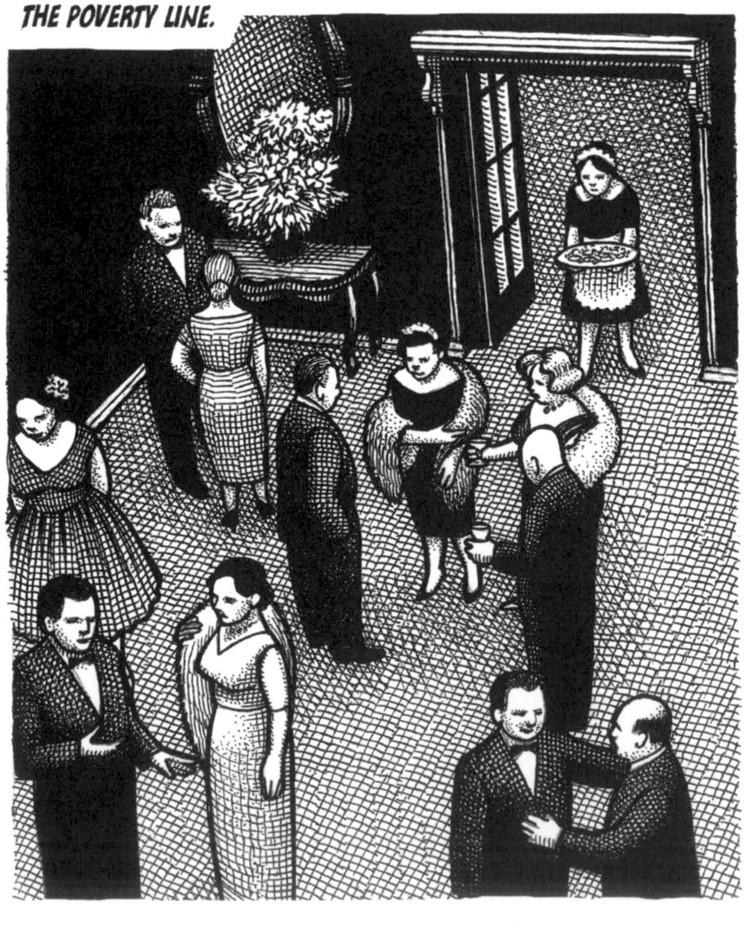

IN 1954 DJILAS PUBLISHED OVER A DOZEN ESSAYS ON THAT VERY SUBJECT IN *BORBA*, THE OFFICIAL PAPER OF THE COMMUNIST PARTY. ALTHOUGH WIDELY READ AND POPULAR, DJILAS'S WRITING WAS SEEN AS A GESTURE OF DISLOYALTY TO THE PARTY, AND WOULD EVENTUALLY CAUSE HIS EXPULSION FROM THE CENTRAL COMMITTEE.

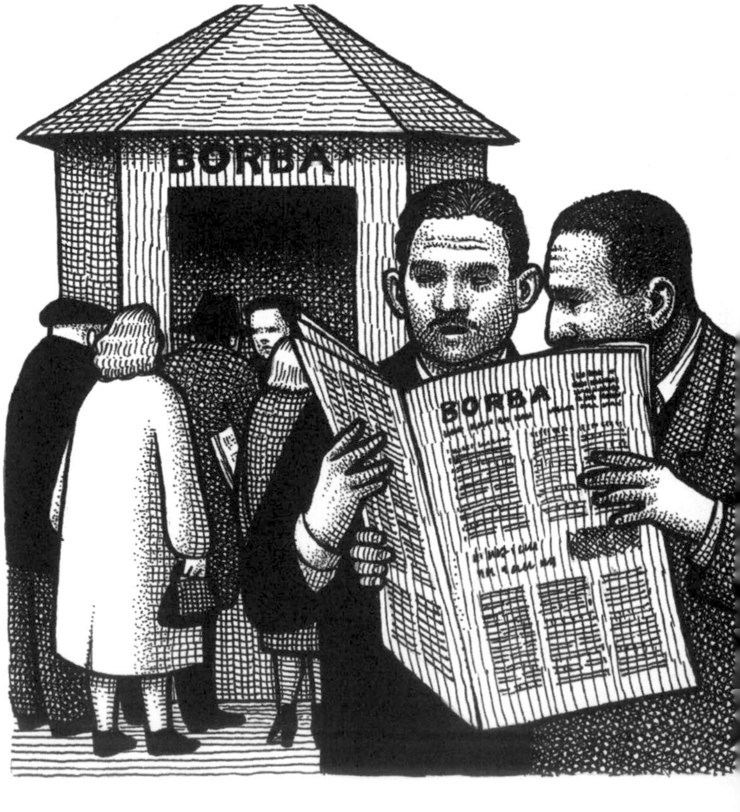
BORBA
BORBA

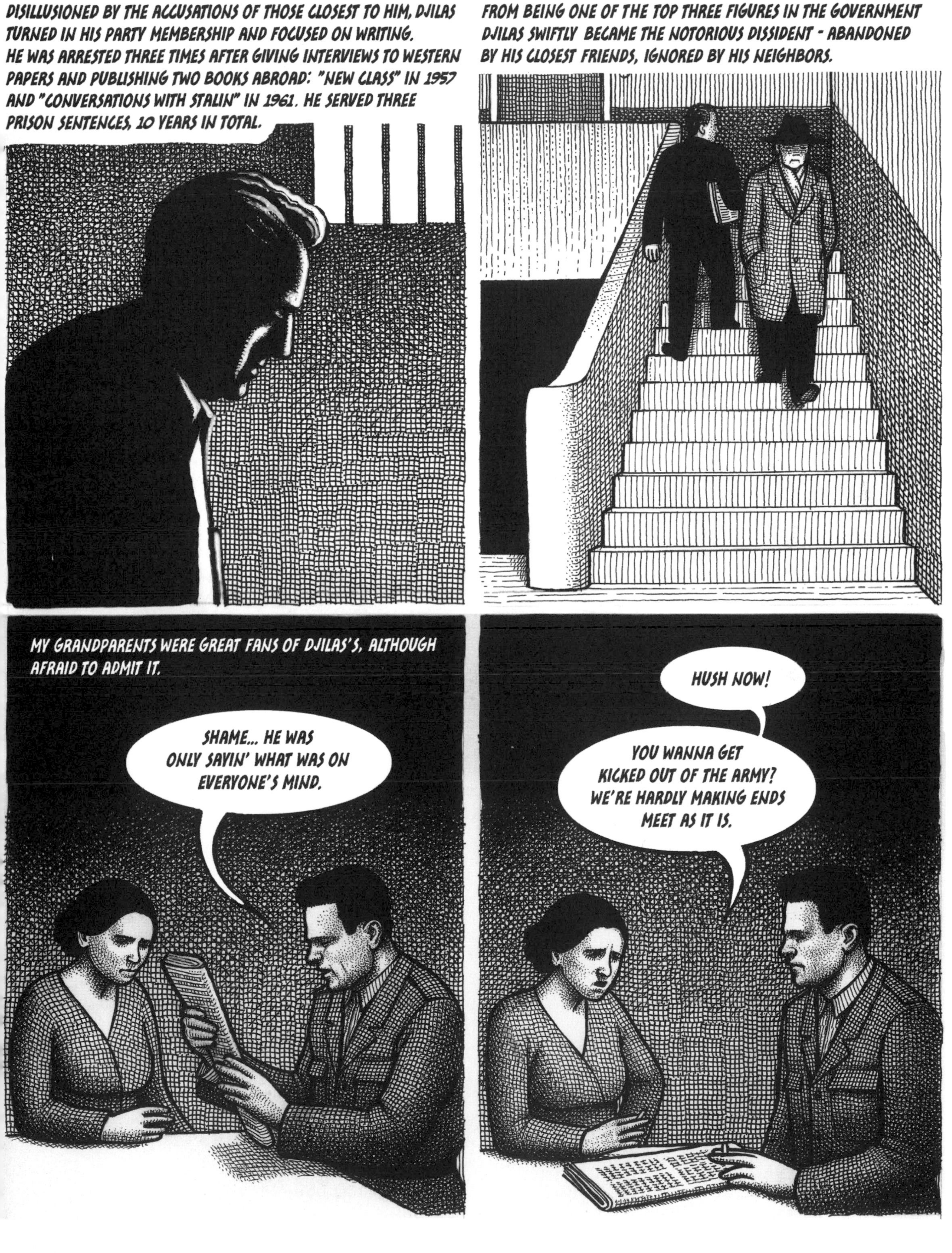
DISILLUSIONED BY THE ACCUSATIONS OF THOSE CLOSEST TO HIM, DJILAS TURNED IN HIS PARTY MEMBERSHIP AND FOCUSED ON WRITING. HE WAS ARRESTED THREE TIMES AFTER GIVING INTERVIEWS TO WESTERN PAPERS AND PUBLISHING TWO BOOKS ABROAD: "NEW CLASS" IN 1957 AND "CONVERSATIONS WITH STALIN" IN 1961. HE SERVED THREE PRISON SENTENCES, 10 YEARS IN TOTAL.
FROM BEING ONE OF THE TOP THREE FIGURES IN THE GOVERNMENT DJILAS SWIFTLY BECAME THE NOTORIOUS DISSIDENT - ABANDONED BY HIS CLOSEST FRIENDS, IGNORED BY HIS NEIGHBORS.
MY GRANDPARENTS WERE GREAT FANS OF DJILAS'S, ALTHOUGH AFRAID TO ADMIT IT.
SHAME... HE WAS ONLY SAYIN' WHAT WAS ON EVERYONE'S MIND.
HUSH NOW!
YOU WANNA GET KICKED OUT OF THE ARMY? WE'RE HARDLY MAKING ENDS MEET AS IT IS.

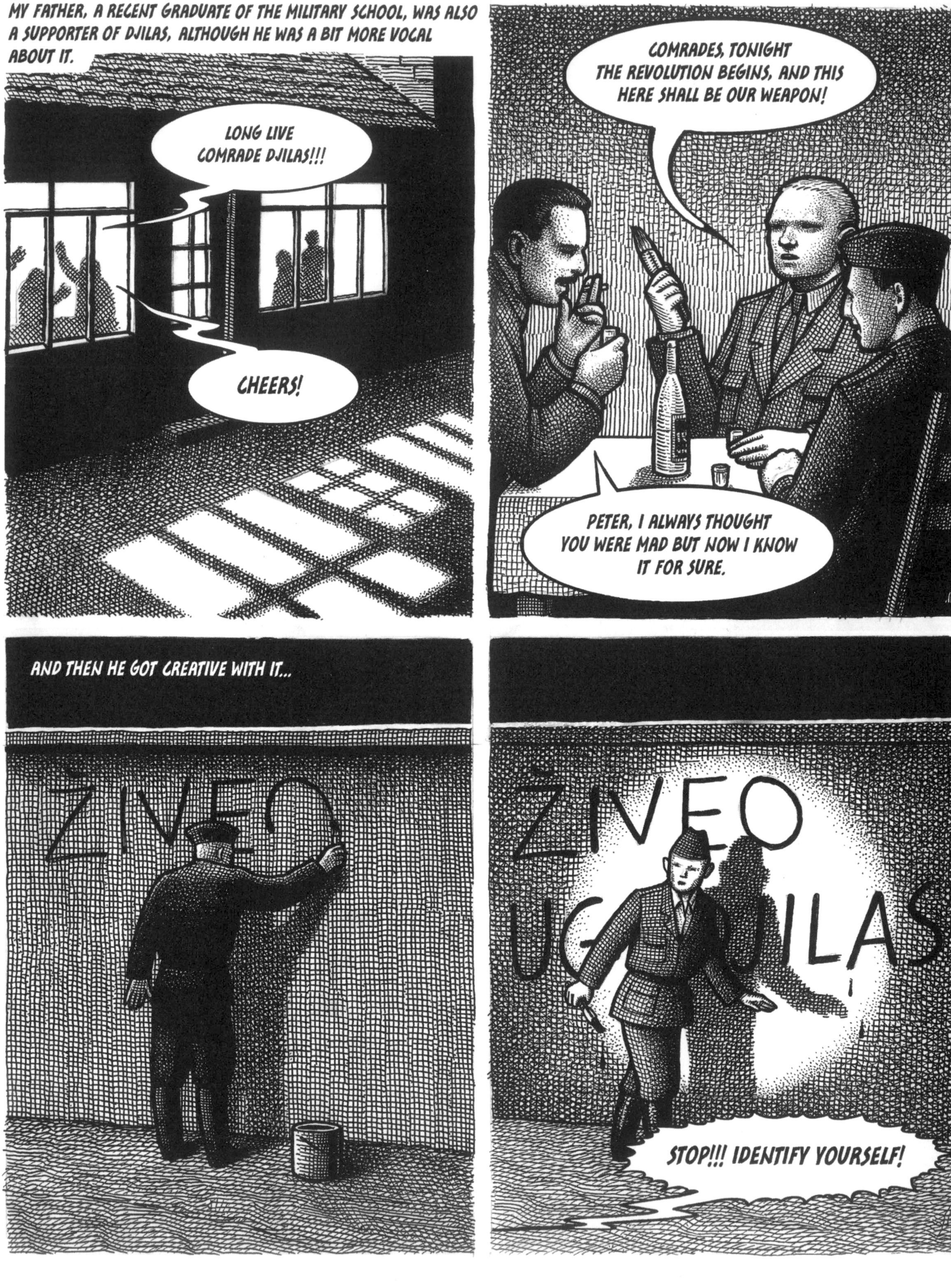
MY FATHER, A RECENT GRADUATE OF THE MILITARY SCHOOL, WAS ALSO A SUPPORTER OF DJILAS, ALTHOUGH HE WAS A BIT MORE VOCAL ABOUT IT.
LONG LIVE COMRADE DJILAS!!!
CHEERS!
COMRADES, TONIGHT THE REVOLUTION BEGINS, AND THIS HERE SHALL BE OUR WEAPON!
PETER, I ALWAYS THOUGHT YOU WERE MAD BUT NOW I KNOW IT FOR SURE.
AND THEN HE GOT CREATIVE WITH IT...
ŽIVEO
ŽIVEO
STOP!!! IDENTIFY YOURSELF!

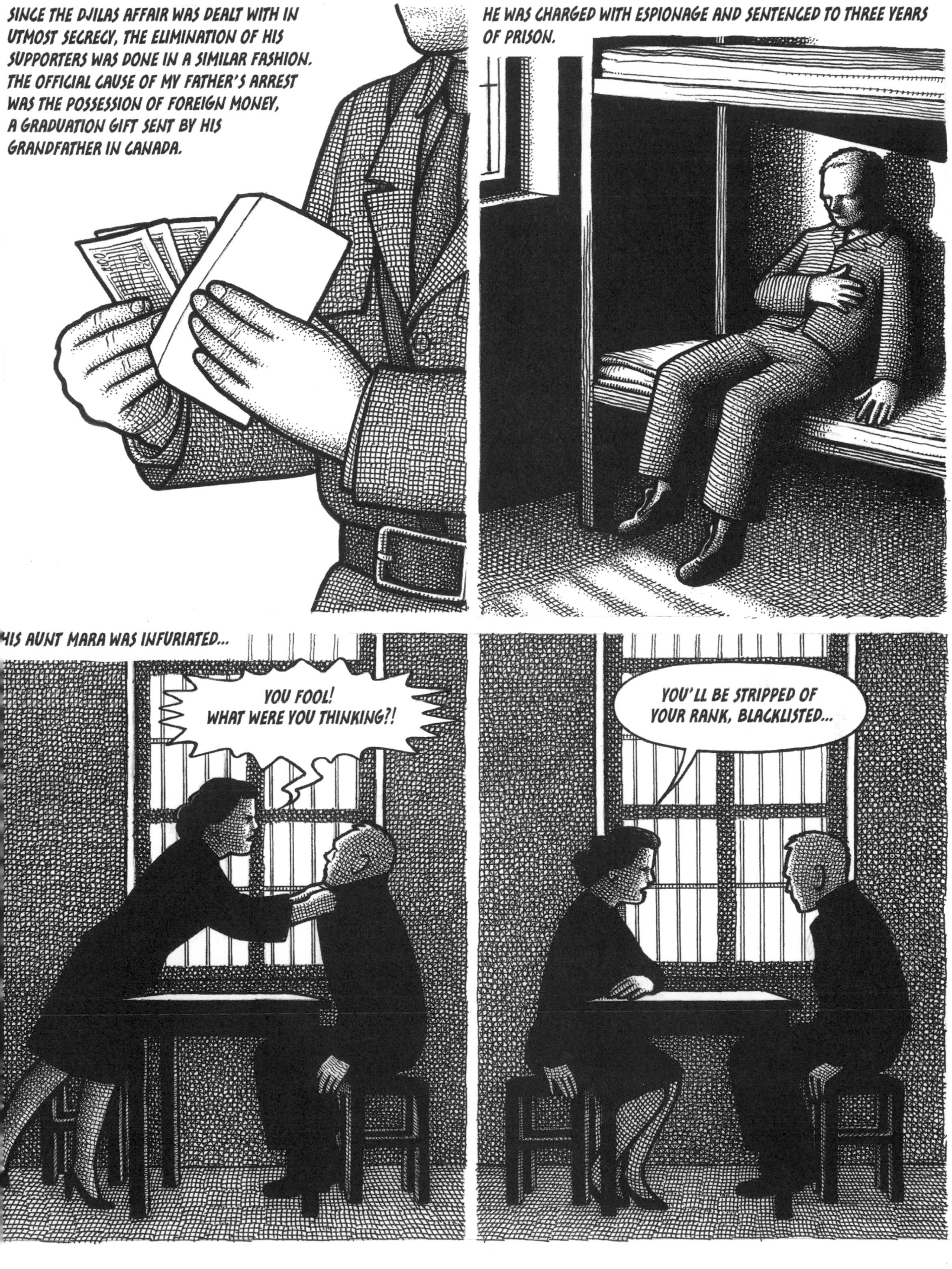
SINCE THE DJILAS AFFAIR WAS DEALT WITH IN UTMOST SECRECY, THE ELIMINATION OF HIS SUPPORTERS WAS DONE IN A SIMILAR FASHION. THE OFFICIAL CAUSE OF MY FATHER'S ARREST WAS THE POSSESSION OF FOREIGN MONEY, A GRADUATION GIFT SENT BY HIS GRANDFATHER IN CANADA.
HE WAS CHARGED WITH ESPIONAGE AND SENTENCED TO THREE YEARS OF PRISON.
HIS AUNT MARA WAS INFURIATED...
YOU FOOL! WHAT WERE YOU THINKING?!
YOU'LL BE STRIPPED OF YOUR RANK, BLACKLISTED...

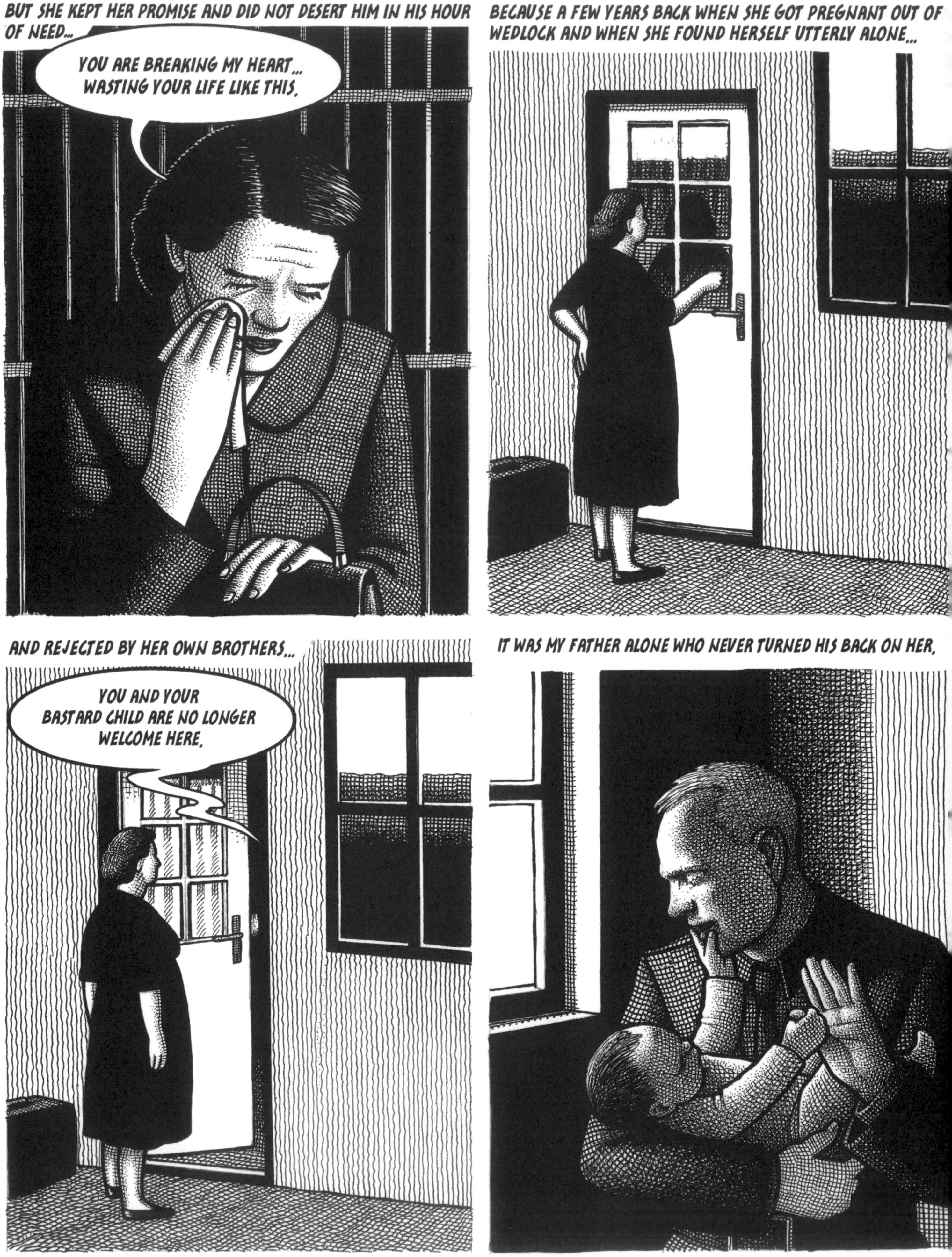
BUT SHE KEPT HER PROMISE AND DID NOT DESERT HIM IN HIS HOUR OF NEED...
YOU ARE BREAKING MY HEART... WASTING YOUR LIFE LIKE THIS.
BECAUSE A FEW YEARS BACK WHEN SHE GOT PREGNANT OUT OF WEDLOCK AND WHEN SHE FOUND HERSELF UTTERLY ALONE...
AND REJECTED BY HER OWN BROTHERS...
YOU AND YOUR BASTARD CHILD ARE NO LONGER WELCOME HERE.
IT WAS MY FATHER ALONE WHO NEVER TURNED HIS BACK ON HER.

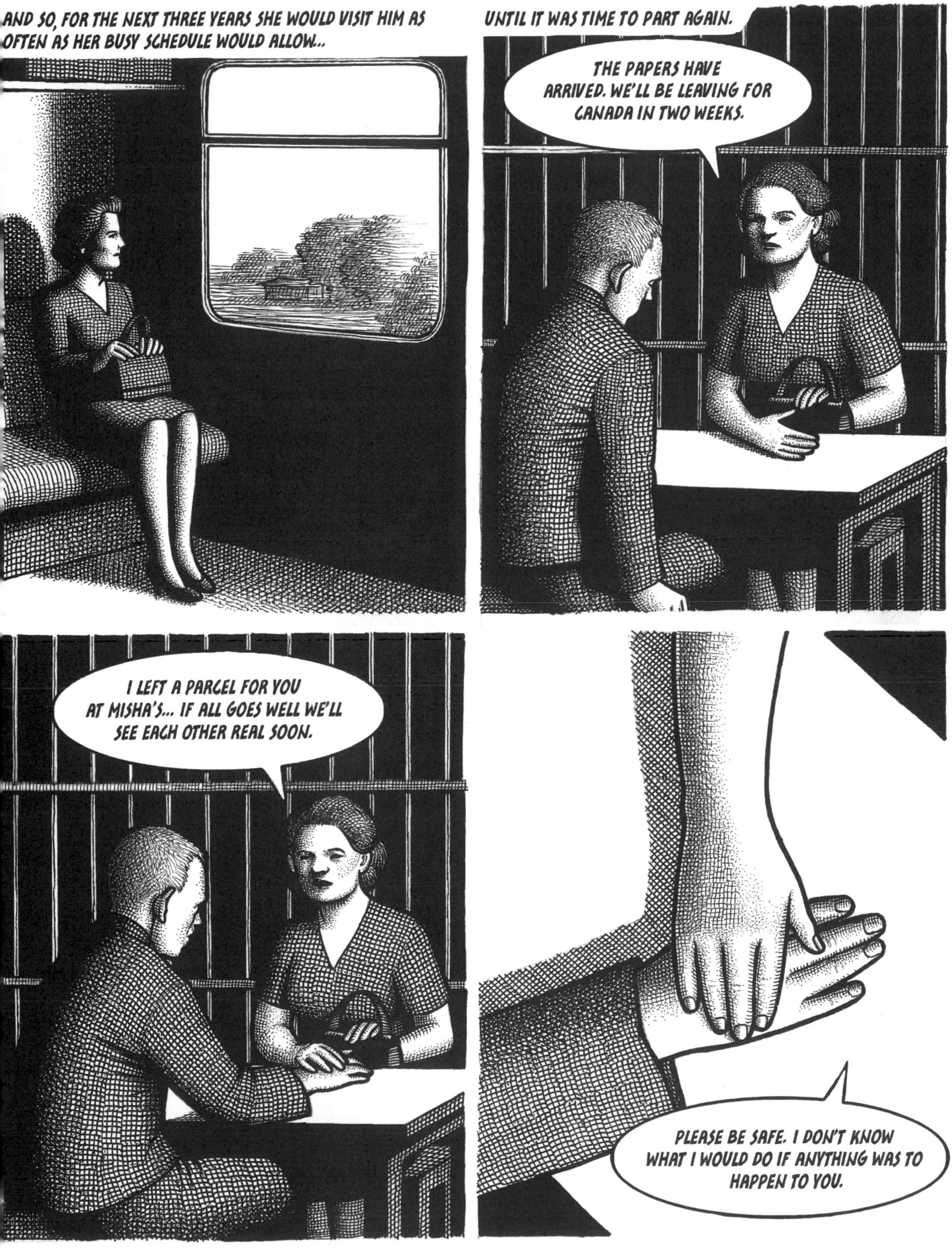
AND SO, FOR THE NEXT THREE YEARS SHE WOULD VISIT HIM AS OFTEN AS HER BUSY SCHEDULE WOULD ALLOW...
UNTIL IT WAS TIME TO PART AGAIN.
THE PAPERS HAVE ARRIVED. WE'LL BE LEAVING FOR CANADA IN TWO WEEKS.
I LEFT A PARCEL FOR YOU AT MISHA'S... IF ALL GOES WELL WE'LL SEE EACH OTHER REAL SOON.
PLEASE BE SAFE. I DON'T KNOW WHAT I WOULD DO IF ANYTHING WAS TO HAPPEN TO YOU.

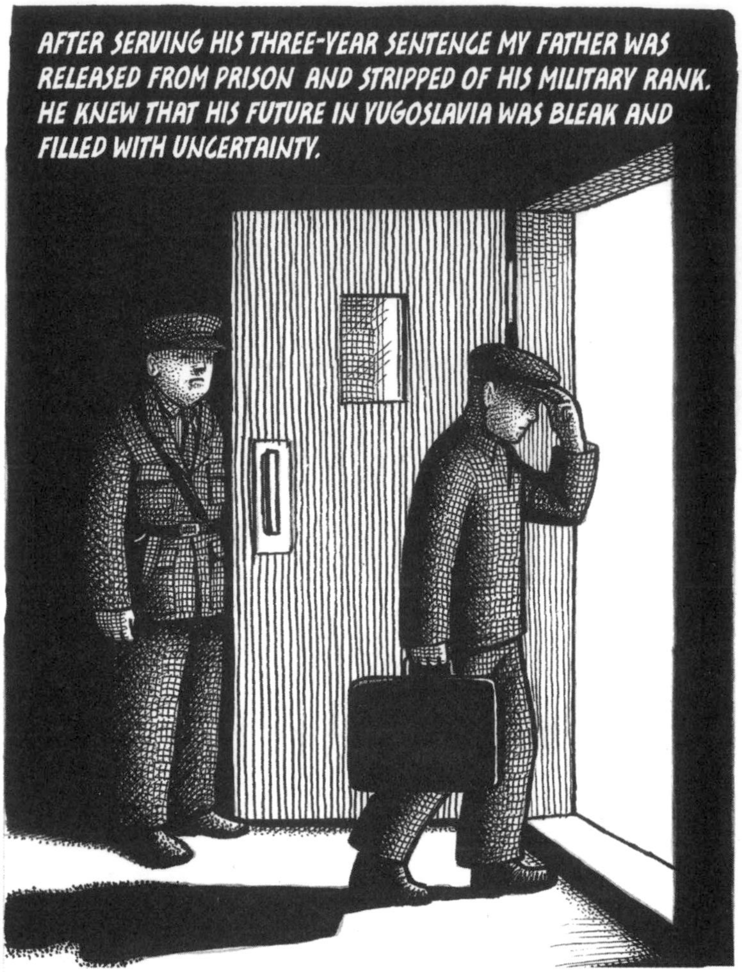
AFTER SERVING HIS THREE-YEAR SENTENCE MY FATHER WAS RELEASED FROM PRISON AND STRIPPED OF HIS MILITARY RANK. HE KNEW THAT HIS FUTURE IN YUGOSLAVIA WAS BLEAK AND FILLED WITH UNCERTAINTY.

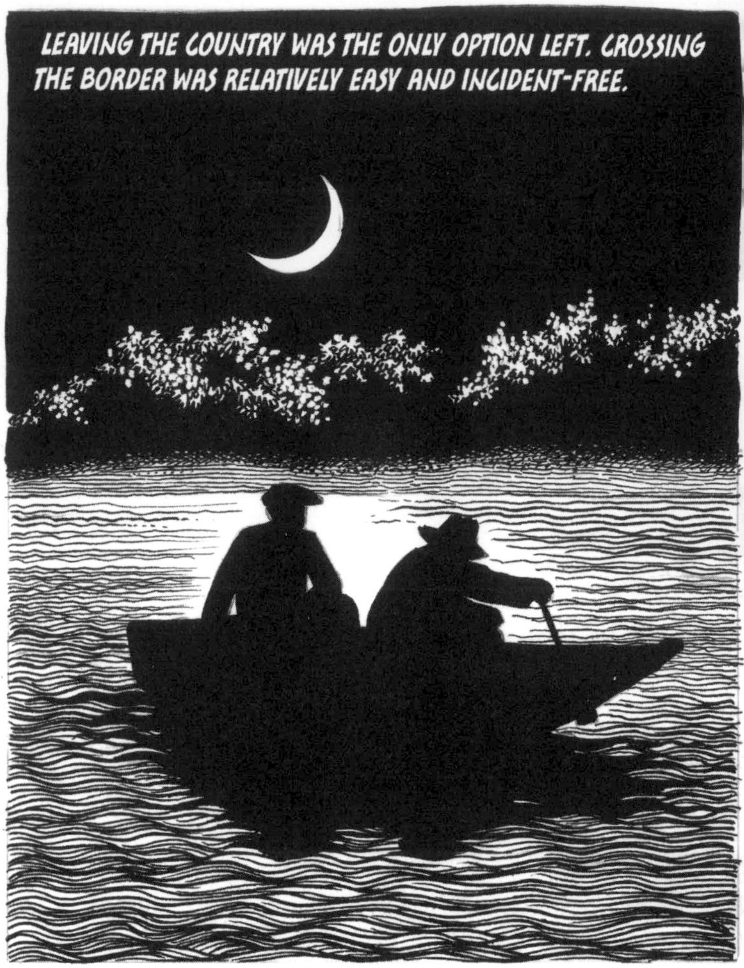
LEAVING THE COUNTRY WAS THE ONLY OPTION LEFT. CROSSING THE BORDER WAS RELATIVELY EASY AND INCIDENT-FREE.

WAITING FOR PERMISSION TO ENTER CANADA WAS A THREE-MONTH ORDEAL, DURING WHICH HE REMAINED AT THE INTERNMENT CAMP IN UPPER AUSTRIA...

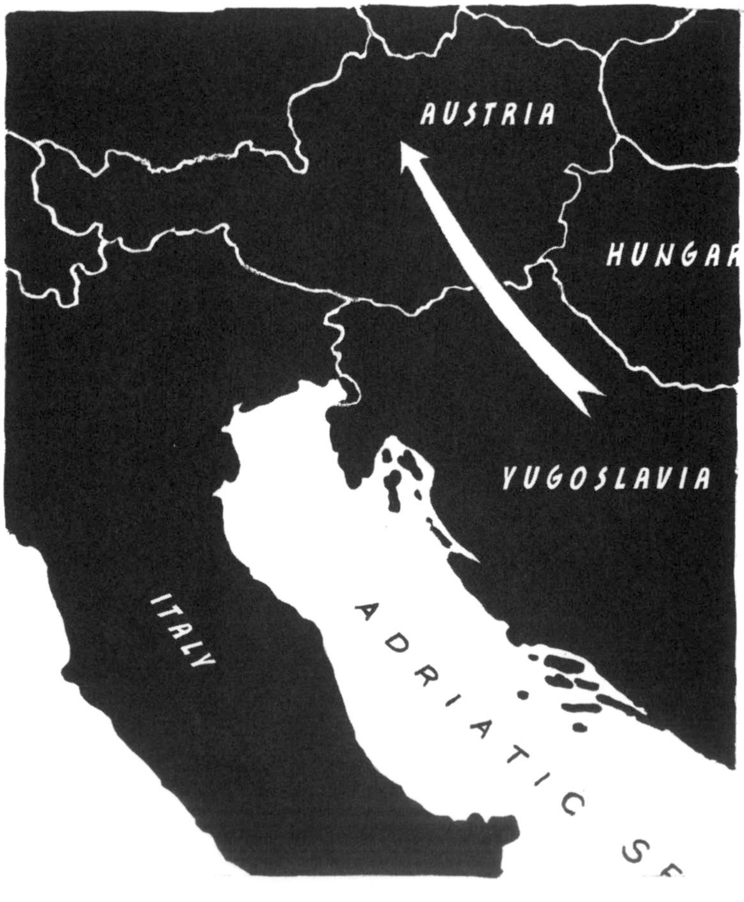
AUSTRIA
HUNGAR
YUGOSLAVIA
ITALY
ADRIATIC SE

CONCURRENTLY WITH NIKOLA KAVAJA, AN EXILED MILITARY OFFICER MUCH LIKE HIMSELF, WITH A SIMILAR BONE TO PICK. THIS MEETING WAS TO INFLUENCE MY FATHER POLITICALLY AND IDEOLOGICALLY MORE THAN ANY OTHER BEFORE.

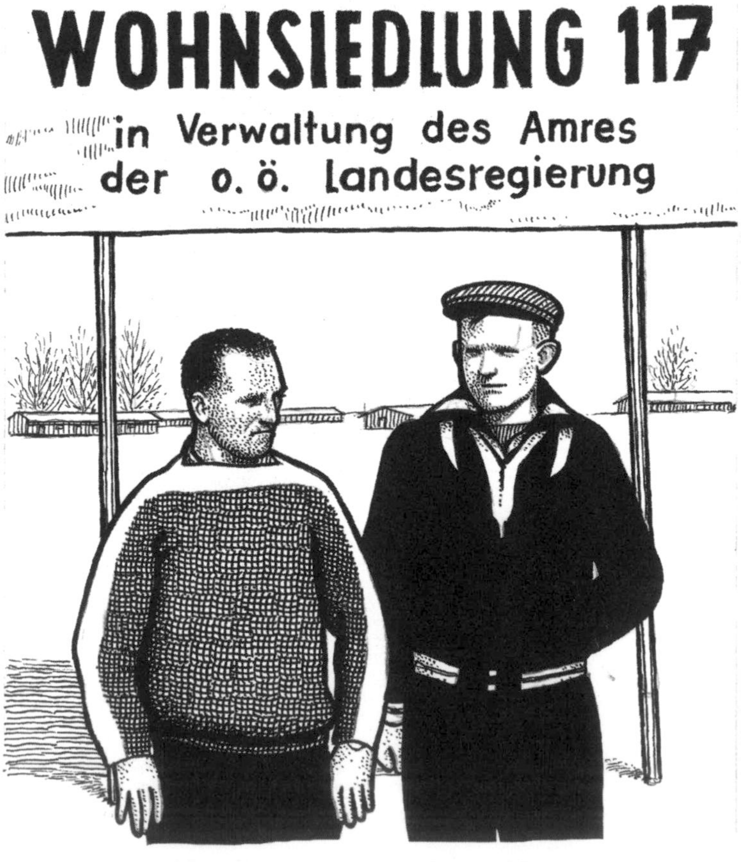
WOHNSIEDLUNG 117
in Verwaltung des Amres
der o. ö. Landesregierung

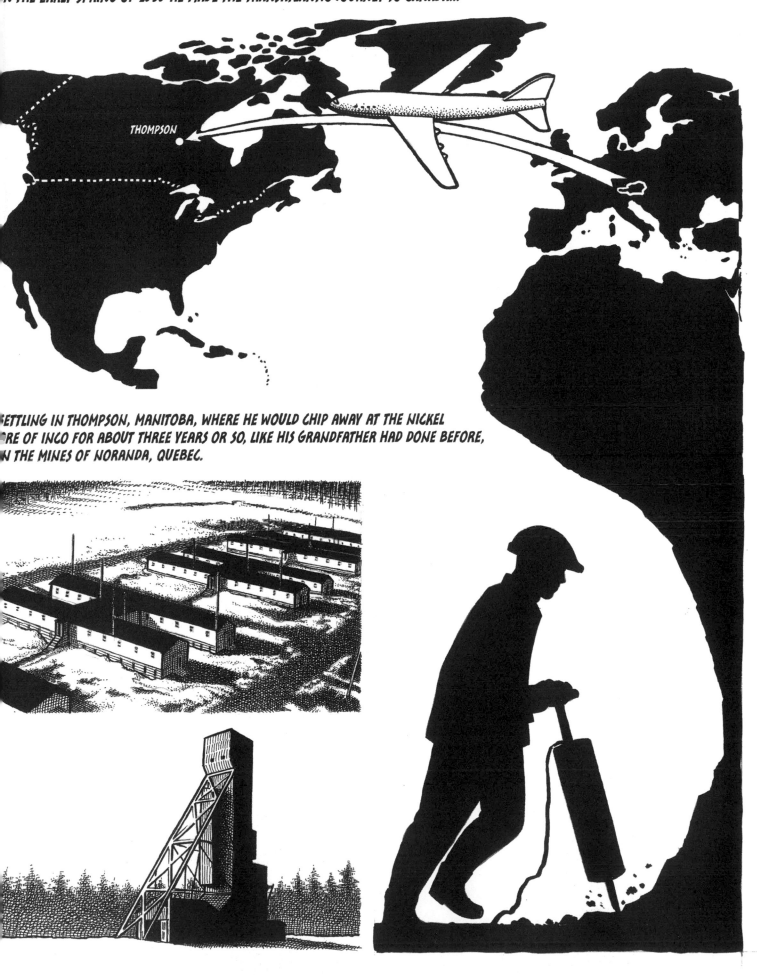

IN THE EARLY SPRING OF 1959 HE MADE THE TRANSATLANTIC JOURNEY TO CANADA...

THOMPSON

SETTLING IN THOMPSON, MANITOBA, WHERE HE WOULD CHIP AWAY AT THE NICKEL ORE OF INCO FOR ABOUT THREE YEARS OR SO, LIKE HIS GRANDFATHER HAD DONE BEFORE, IN THE MINES OF NORANDA, QUEBEC.

# EXILE

961 IT IS MY FATHER'S SECOND YEAR OF LIVING AND WORKING IN THOMPSON, MANITOBA; HE IS LONELY, OVERWORKED AND HOMESICK. THE CITY IS BASED PRIMARILY AROUND ITS MINING INDUSTRY AND, AS SUCH, OFFERS LITTLE IN TERMS OF ENTERTAINMENT AND LEISURE ACTIVITIES.

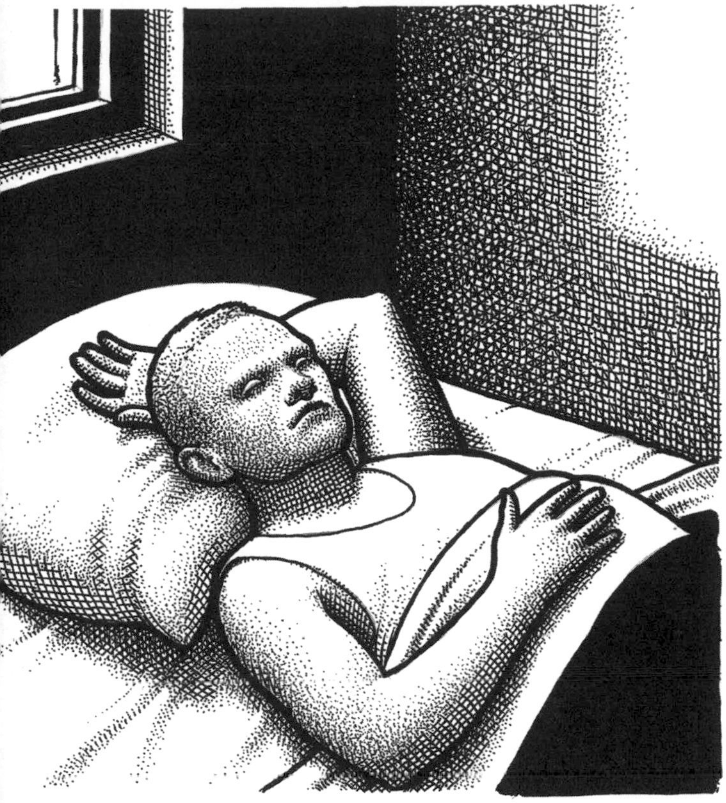

LEAFING THROUGH AN OLD ISSUE OF A BELGRADE-BASED SPORTS MAGAZINE HE COMES ACROSS THE ADVERTISING SECTION. HE SEES SEVERAL ADS PLACED BY YOUNG PEOPLE SEEKING PEN-PALS AND DECIDES TO DO THE SAME.

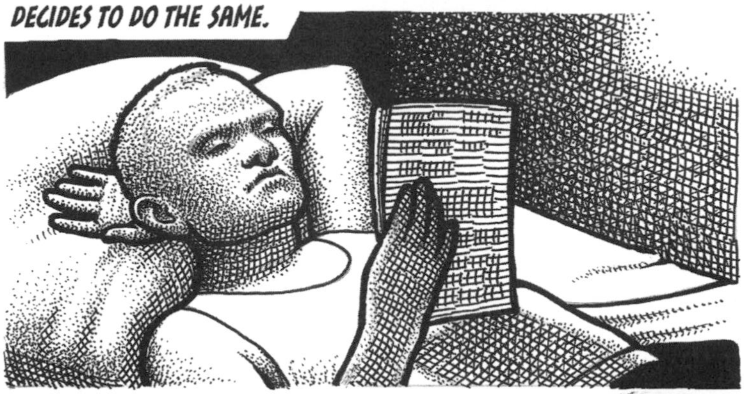

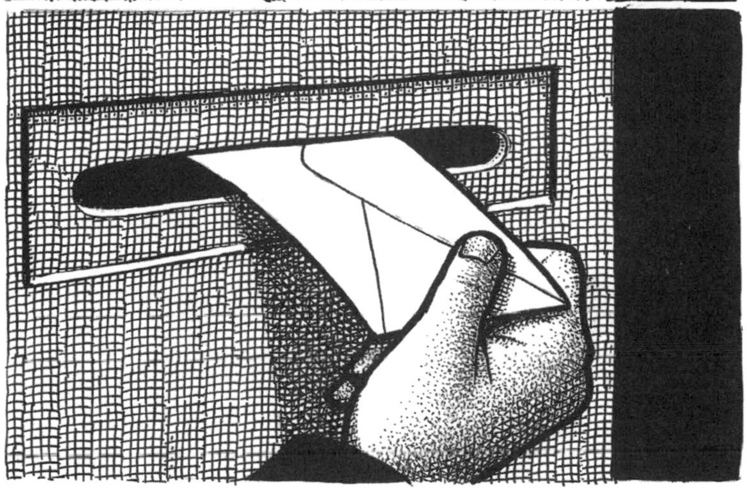

THE MAGAZINE RUNS HIS AD WITH A TYPO. IN MONTHS TO COME DAD WILL RECEIVE HUNDREDS OF LETTERS AND POSTCARDS, ALL ADDRESSED TO: INCO, THOMPSON, MANITORA.

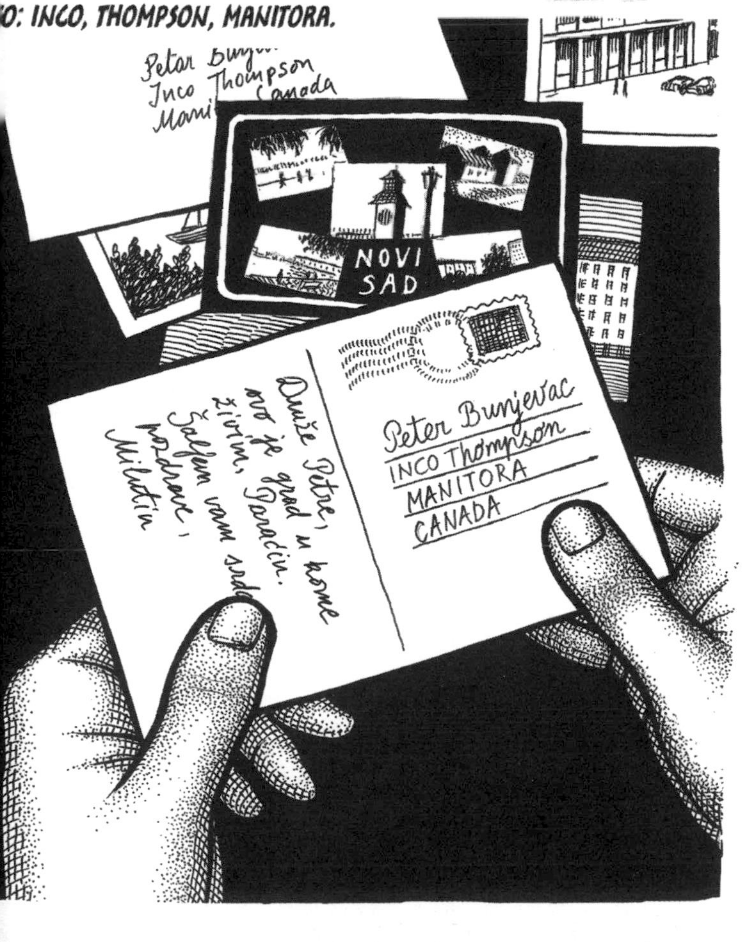
NOVI SAD
Peter Bunjevac
INCO Thompson
MANITORA
CANADA

THE POSTCARDS ARE TAPED TO THE WALL OF HIS BARRACK, LIKE SMALL WINDOWS ONTO THE LAND HE WILL NEVER BE ALLOWED TO SET HIS FOOT ON AGAIN.

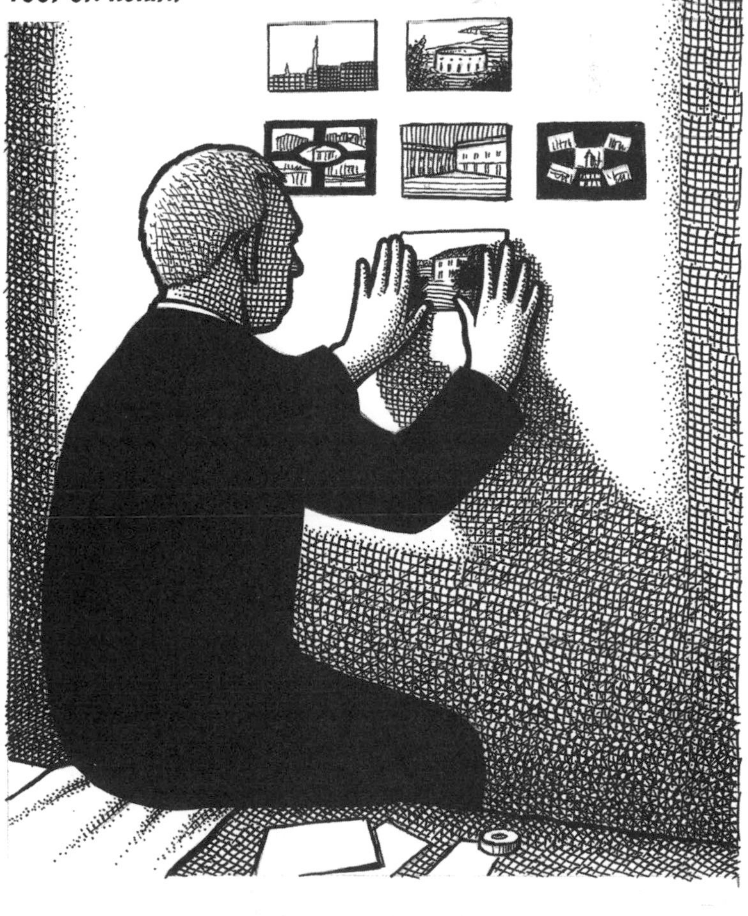

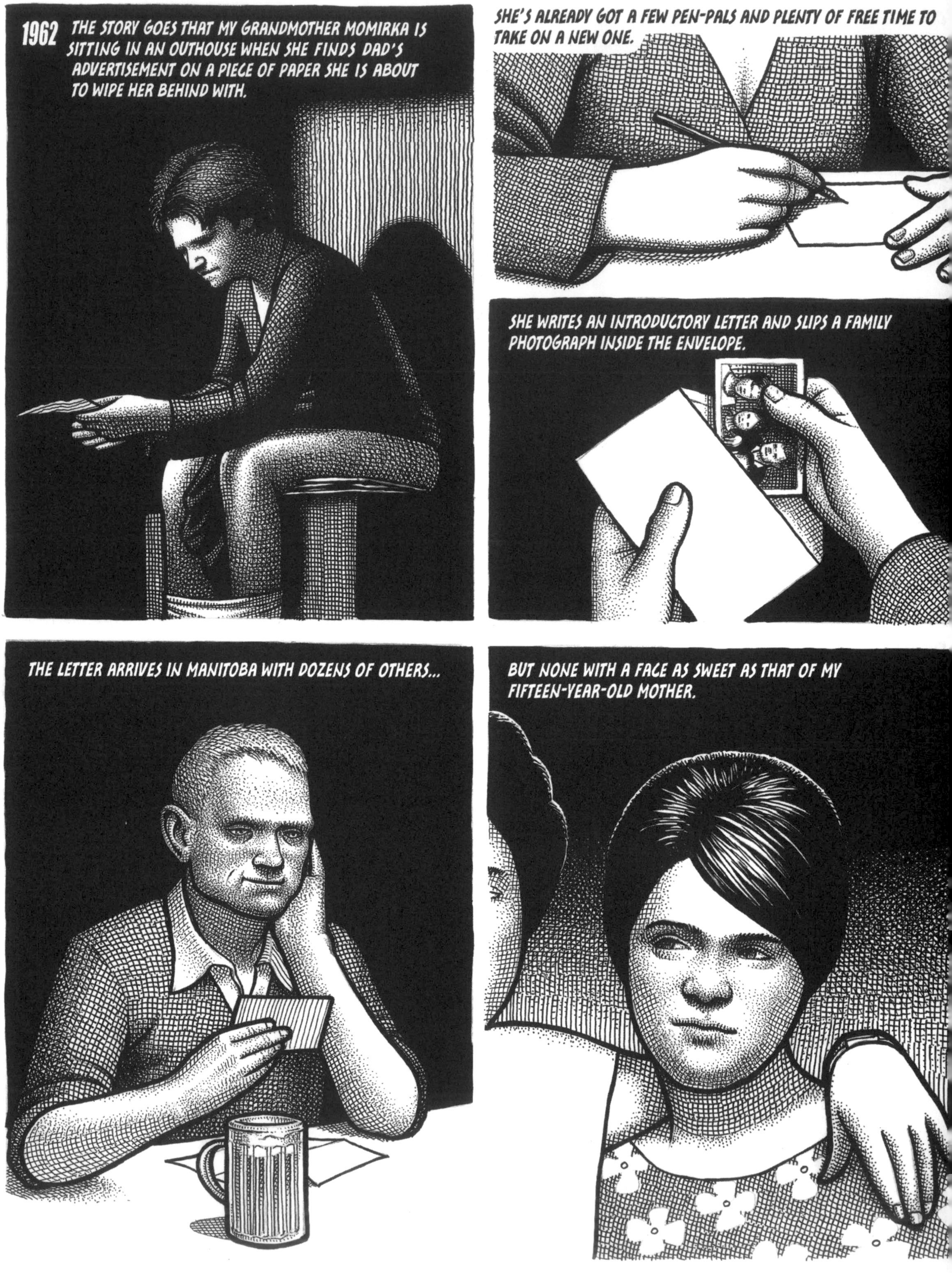
1962 THE STORY GOES THAT MY GRANDMOTHER MOMIRKA IS SITTING IN AN OUTHOUSE WHEN SHE FINDS DAD'S ADVERTISEMENT ON A PIECE OF PAPER SHE IS ABOUT TO WIPE HER BEHIND WITH.
SHE'S ALREADY GOT A FEW PEN-PALS AND PLENTY OF FREE TIME TO TAKE ON A NEW ONE.
SHE WRITES AN INTRODUCTORY LETTER AND SLIPS A FAMILY PHOTOGRAPH INSIDE THE ENVELOPE.
THE LETTER ARRIVES IN MANITOBA WITH DOZENS OF OTHERS...
BUT NONE WITH A FACE AS SWEET AS THAT OF MY FIFTEEN-YEAR-OLD MOTHER.

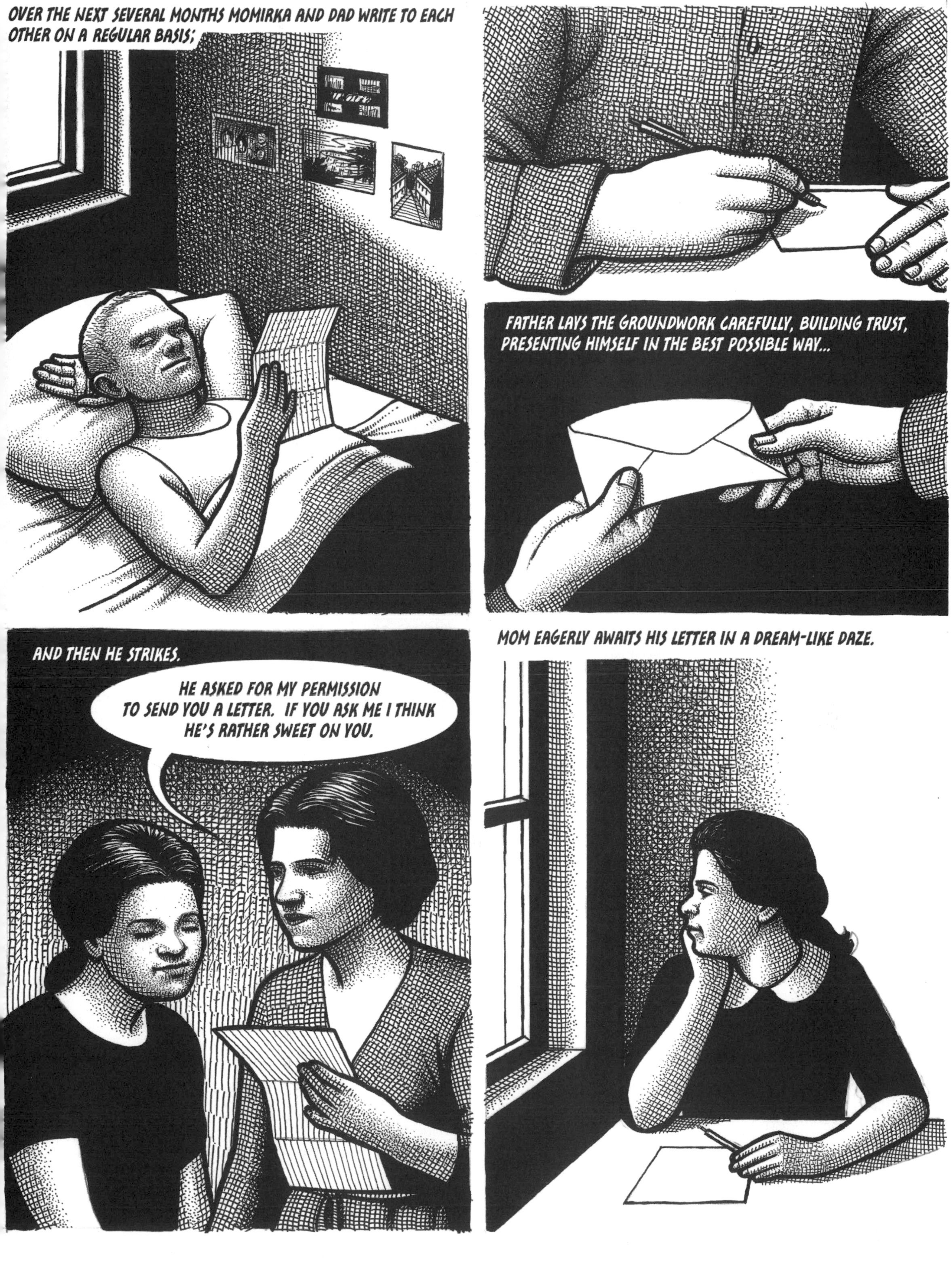
OVER THE NEXT SEVERAL MONTHS MOMIRKA AND DAD WRITE TO EACH OTHER ON A REGULAR BASIS;
FATHER LAYS THE GROUNDWORK CAREFULLY, BUILDING TRUST, PRESENTING HIMSELF IN THE BEST POSSIBLE WAY...
AND THEN HE STRIKES.
HE ASKED FOR MY PERMISSION TO SEND YOU A LETTER. IF YOU ASK ME I THINK HE'S RATHER SWEET ON YOU.
MOM EAGERLY AWAITS HIS LETTER IN A DREAM-LIKE DAZE.

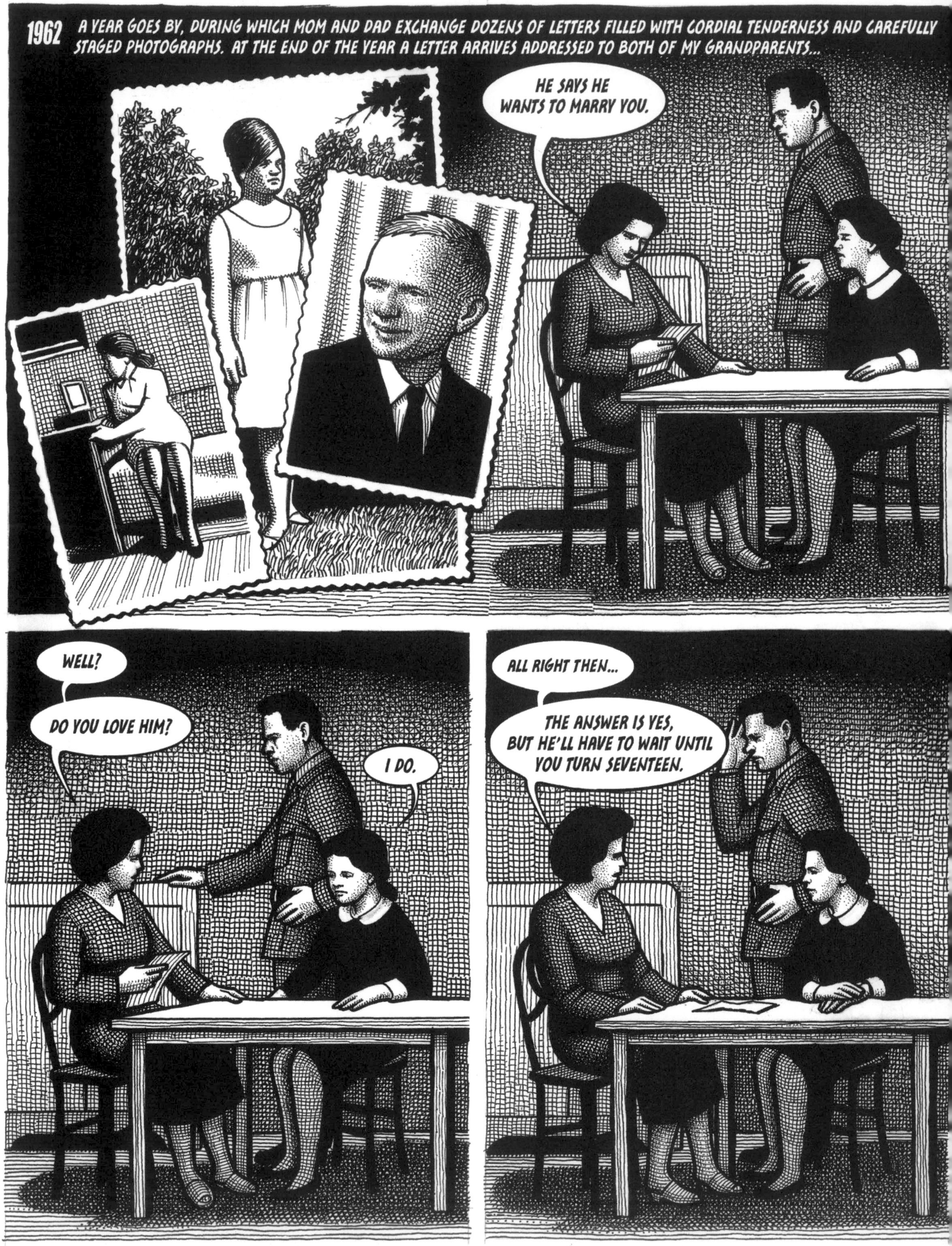
1962 A YEAR GOES BY, DURING WHICH MOM AND DAD EXCHANGE DOZENS OF LETTERS FILLED WITH CORDIAL TENDERNESS AND CAREFULLY STAGED PHOTOGRAPHS. AT THE END OF THE YEAR A LETTER ARRIVES ADDRESSED TO BOTH OF MY GRANDPARENTS...
HE SAYS HE WANTS TO MARRY YOU.
WELL?
DO YOU LOVE HIM?
I DO.
ALL RIGHT THEN...
THE ANSWER IS YES, BUT HE'LL HAVE TO WAIT UNTIL YOU TURN SEVENTEEN.

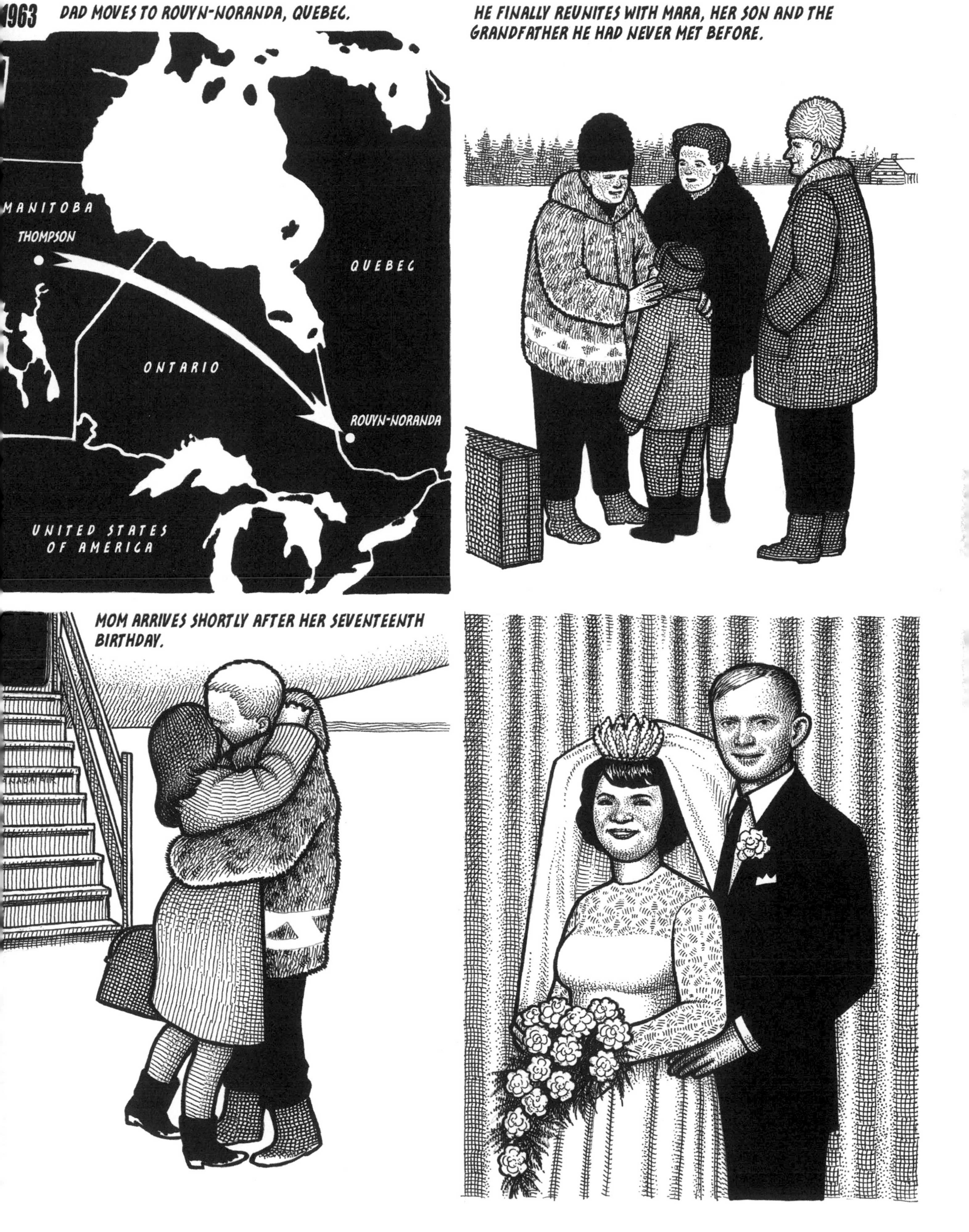
1963
DAD MOVES TO ROUYN-NORANDA, QUEBEC.
MANITOBA
THOMPSON
QUEBEC
ONTARIO
ROUYN-NORANDA
UNITED STATES OF AMERICA
HE FINALLY REUNITES WITH MARA, HER SON AND THE GRANDFATHER HE HAD NEVER MET BEFORE.
MOM ARRIVES SHORTLY AFTER HER SEVENTEENTH BIRTHDAY.

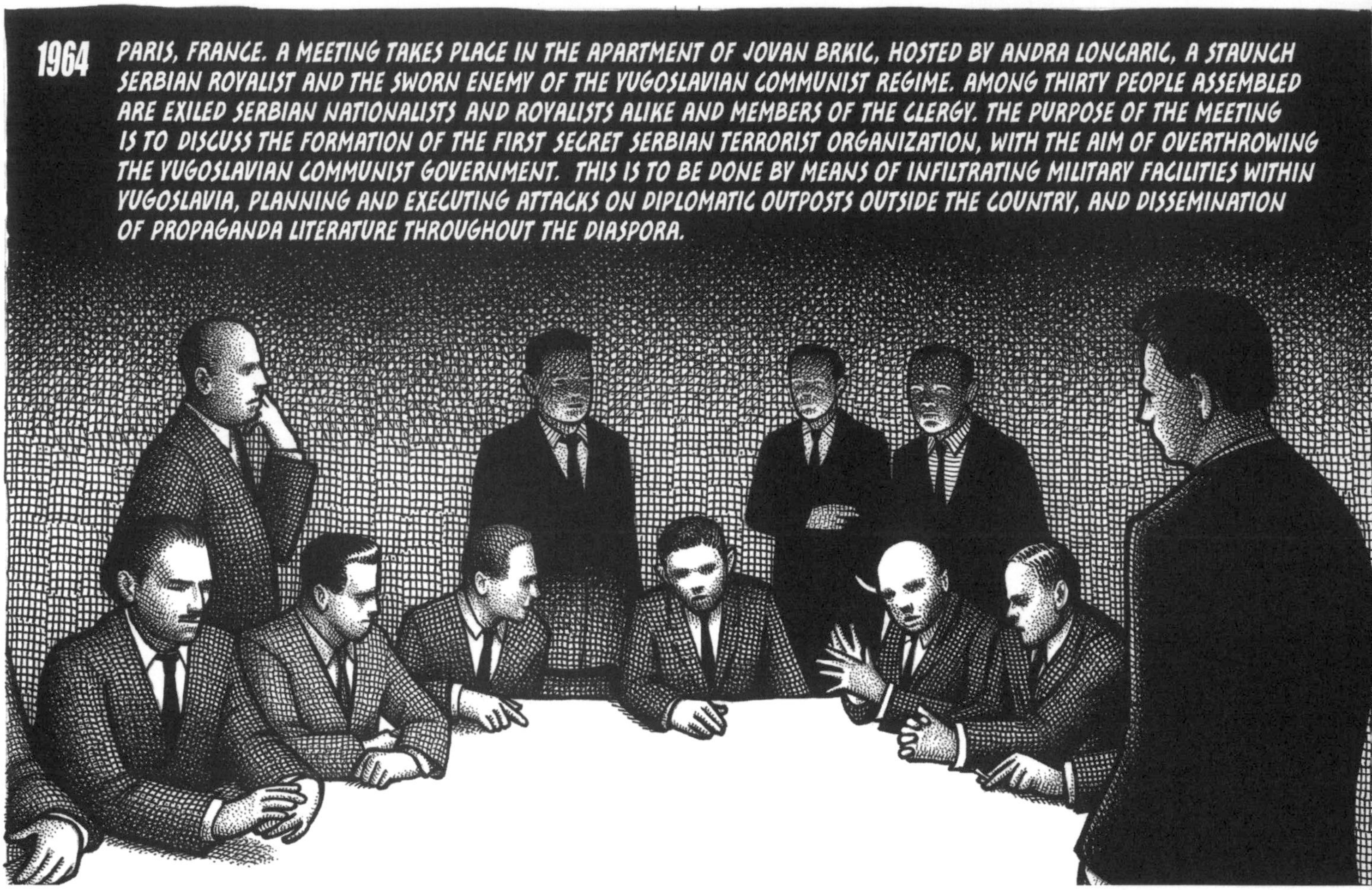
1964
PARIS, FRANCE. A MEETING TAKES PLACE IN THE APARTMENT OF JOVAN BRKIC, HOSTED BY ANDRA LONCARIC, A STAUNCH SERBIAN ROYALIST AND THE SWORN ENEMY OF THE YUGOSLAVIAN COMMUNIST REGIME. AMONG THIRTY PEOPLE ASSEMBLED ARE EXILED SERBIAN NATIONALISTS AND ROYALISTS ALIKE AND MEMBERS OF THE CLERGY. THE PURPOSE OF THE MEETING IS TO DISCUSS THE FORMATION OF THE FIRST SECRET SERBIAN TERRORIST ORGANIZATION, WITH THE AIM OF OVERTHROWING THE YUGOSLAVIAN COMMUNIST GOVERNMENT. THIS IS TO BE DONE BY MEANS OF INFILTRATING MILITARY FACILITIES WITHIN YUGOSLAVIA, PLANNING AND EXECUTING ATTACKS ON DIPLOMATIC OUTPOSTS OUTSIDE THE COUNTRY, AND DISSEMINATION OF PROPAGANDA LITERATURE THROUGHOUT THE DIASPORA.

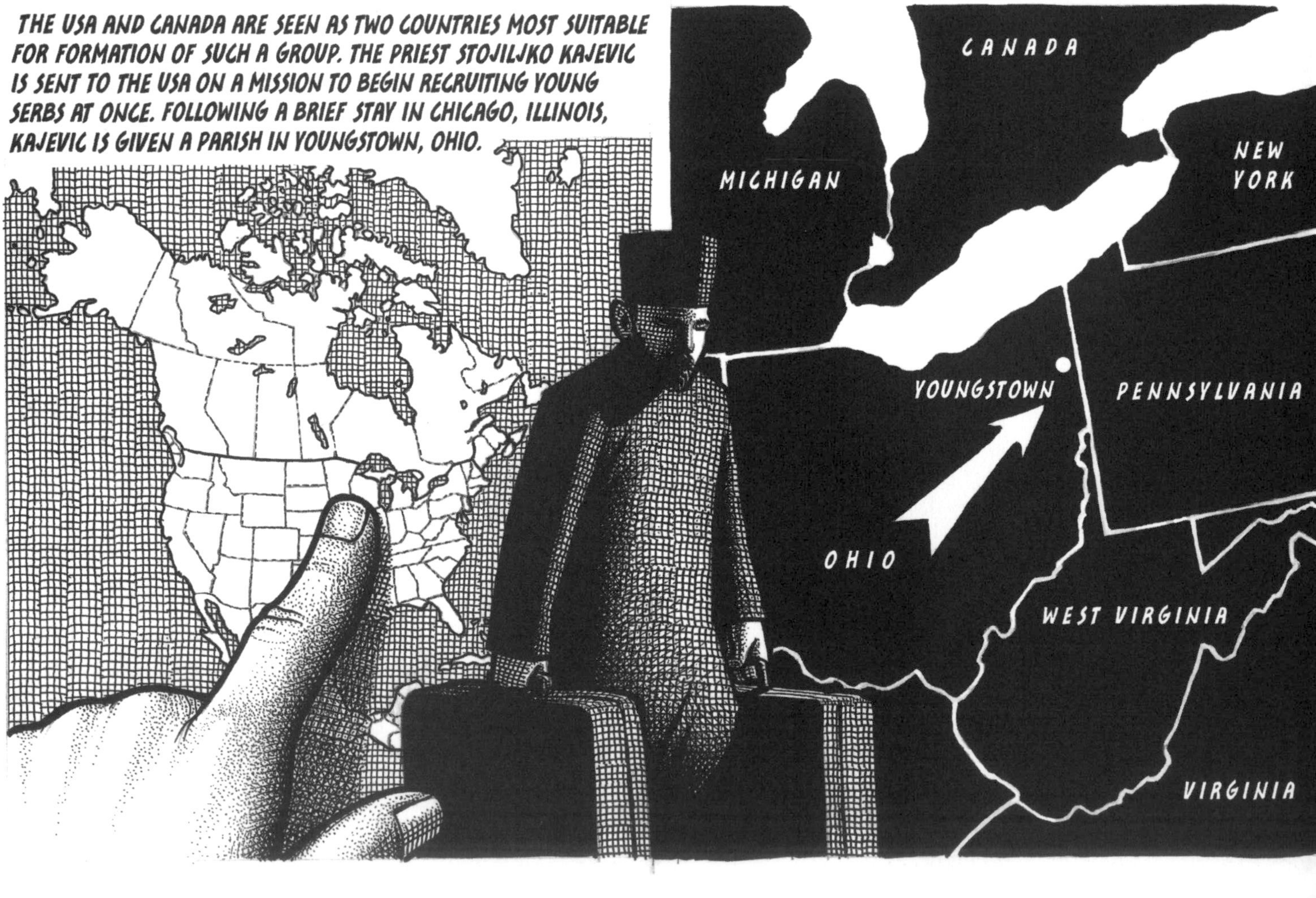
THE USA AND CANADA ARE SEEN AS TWO COUNTRIES MOST SUITABLE FOR FORMATION OF SUCH A GROUP. THE PRIEST STOJILJKO KAJEVIC IS SENT TO THE USA ON A MISSION TO BEGIN RECRUITING YOUNG SERBS AT ONCE. FOLLOWING A BRIEF STAY IN CHICAGO, ILLINOIS, KAJEVIC IS GIVEN A PARISH IN YOUNGSTOWN, OHIO.
CANADA
MICHIGAN
NEW YORK
YOUNGSTOWN
PENNSYLVANIA
OHIO
WEST VIRGINIA
VIRGINIA

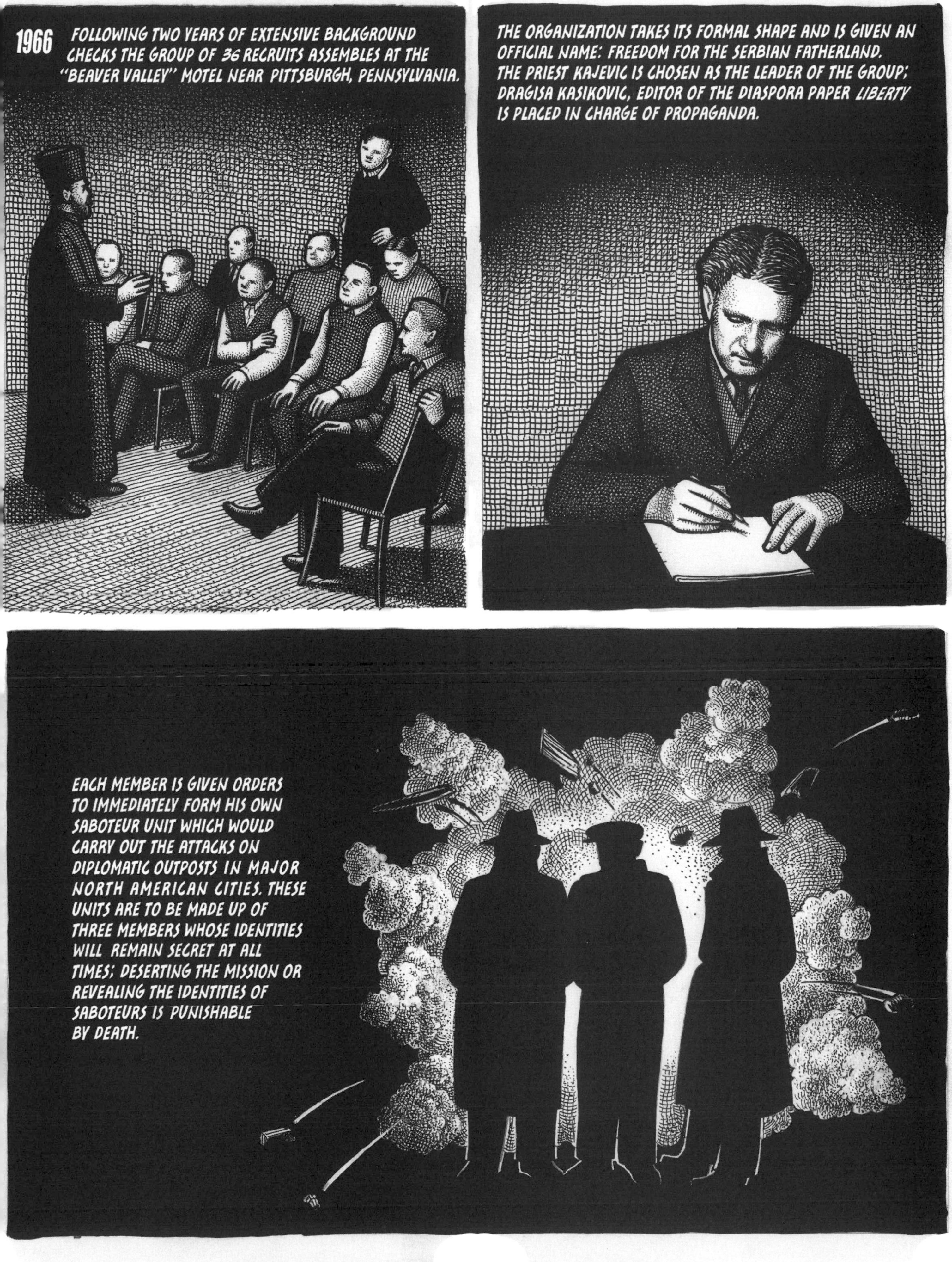
1966 FOLLOWING TWO YEARS OF EXTENSIVE BACKGROUND CHECKS THE GROUP OF 36 RECRUITS ASSEMBLES AT THE "BEAVER VALLEY" MOTEL NEAR PITTSBURGH, PENNSYLVANIA.
THE ORGANIZATION TAKES ITS FORMAL SHAPE AND IS GIVEN AN OFFICIAL NAME: FREEDOM FOR THE SERBIAN FATHERLAND. THE PRIEST KAJEVIC IS CHOSEN AS THE LEADER OF THE GROUP; DRAGISA KASIKOVIC, EDITOR OF THE DIASPORA PAPER *LIBERTY* IS PLACED IN CHARGE OF PROPAGANDA.
EACH MEMBER IS GIVEN ORDERS TO IMMEDIATELY FORM HIS OWN SABOTEUR UNIT WHICH WOULD CARRY OUT THE ATTACKS ON DIPLOMATIC OUTPOSTS IN MAJOR NORTH AMERICAN CITIES. THESE UNITS ARE TO BE MADE UP OF THREE MEMBERS WHOSE IDENTITIES WILL REMAIN SECRET AT ALL TIMES; DESERTING THE MISSION OR REVEALING THE IDENTITIES OF SABOTEURS IS PUNISHABLE BY DEATH.

**1967** JANUARY. FREEDOM FOR SERBIAN FATHERLAND CARRIES OUT A SERIES OF SYNCHRONIZED BOMB ATTACKS ON YUGOSLAVIAN EMBASSIES AND CONSULATES IN NEW YORK, CHICAGO, SAN FRANCISCO, WASHINGTON, TORONTO AND OTTAWA. SOME ARRESTS ARE MADE BUT NO CHARGES ARE LAID DUE TO AIR-TIGHT ALIBIS. DRAGISA KASIKOVIC IS GIVEN IMMUNITY IN EXCHANGE FOR THE TESTIMONY; ONCE HE TAKES THE STAND KASIKOVIC USES THE OPPORTUNITY TO MAKE A STATEMENT: "HISTORY WILL REVEAL THAT THE SIX-BOMB ATTACK CARRIED OUT ON JANUARY 27TH WAS A JUST DEED."

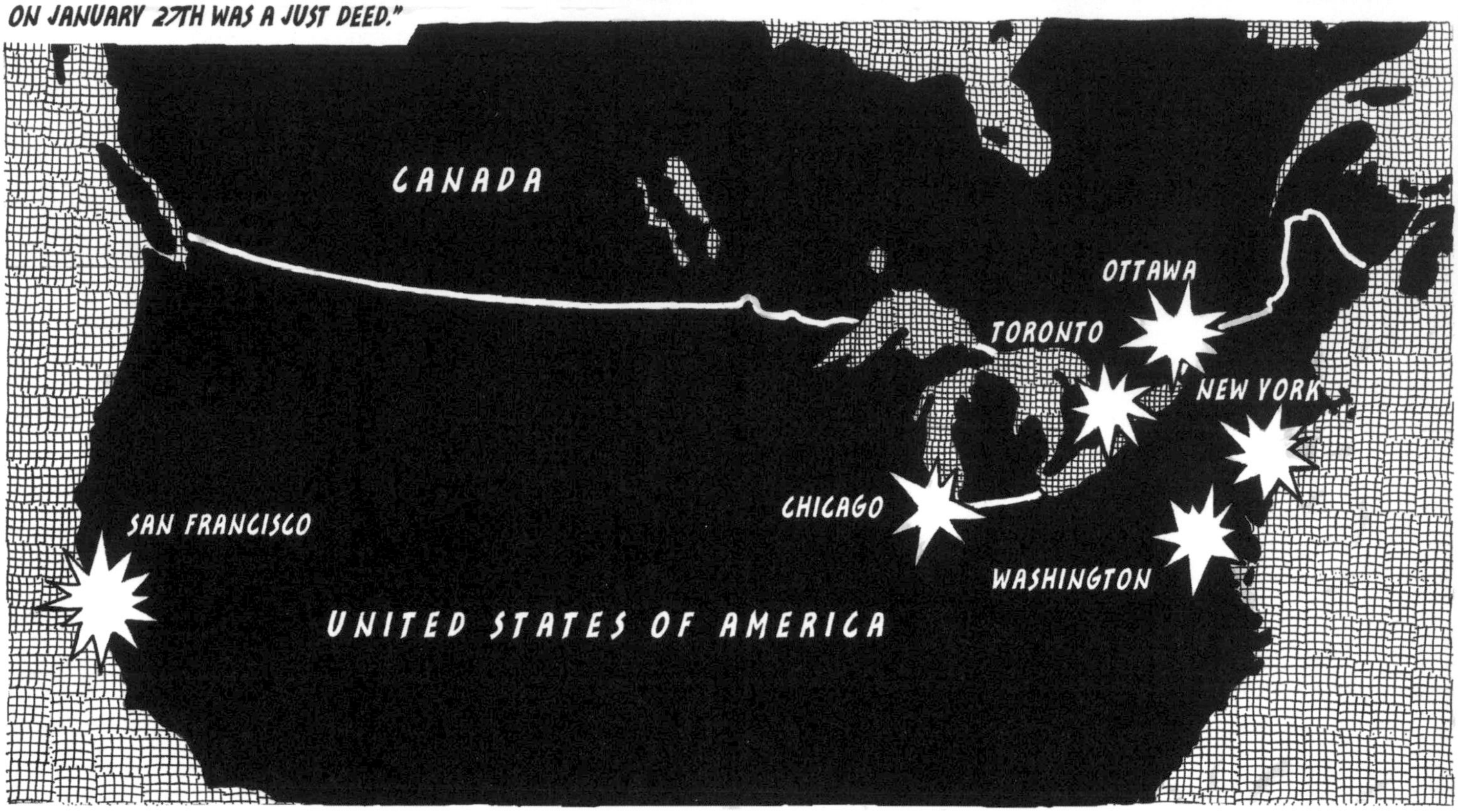
CANADA
OTTAWA
TORONTO
NEW YORK
CHICAGO
SAN FRANCISCO
WASHINGTON
UNITED STATES OF AMERICA

THAT SAME YEAR MOM AND DAD MOVE TO PORT COLBORNE WHERE DAD BEGINS WORKING AT THE INCO NICKEL-PLATING PLANT.

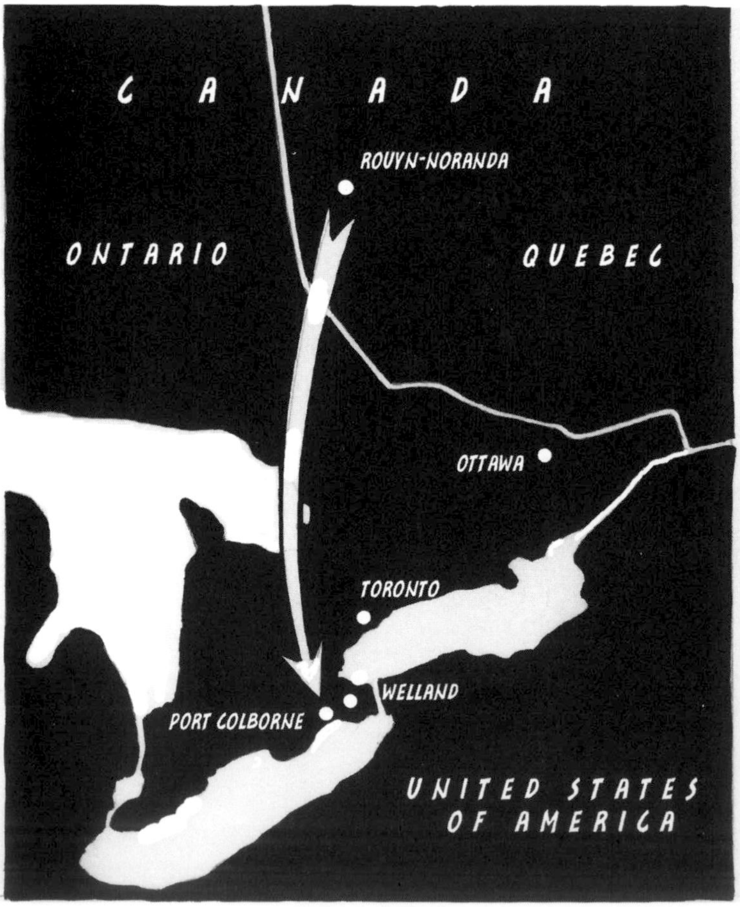
CANADA
ROUYN-NORANDA
ONTARIO
QUEBEC
OTTAWA
TORONTO
WELLAND
PORT COLBORNE
UNITED STATES OF AMERICA

THEY MOVE IN WITH DAD'S COUSIN VIOLET AND HER HUSBAND TETA

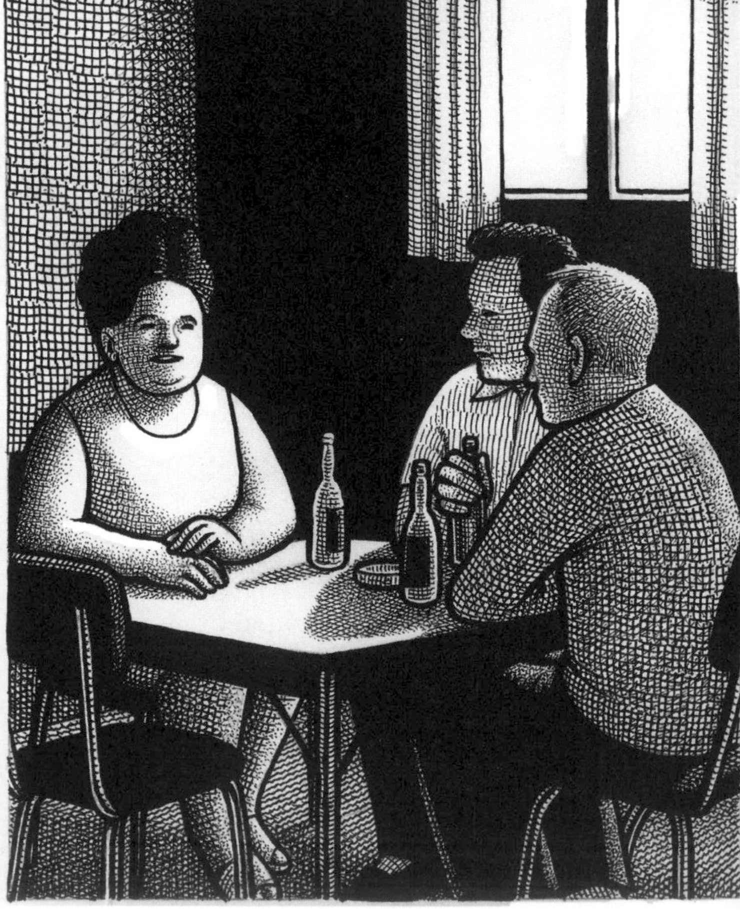

1968 MY BROTHER'S ARRIVAL BRINGS HOPE AFTER THREE FAILED PREGNANCIES. THE COUPLE IS ON TOP OF THE WORLD.

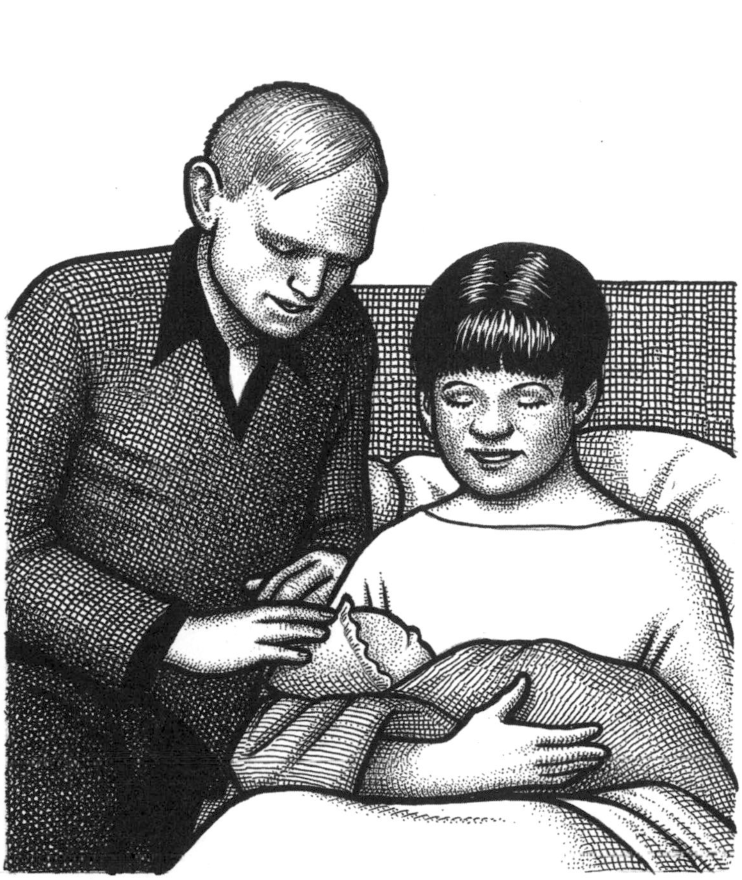

THEY PURCHASE A SMALL WHITE HOUSE ON BROADWAY STREET IN WELLAND...

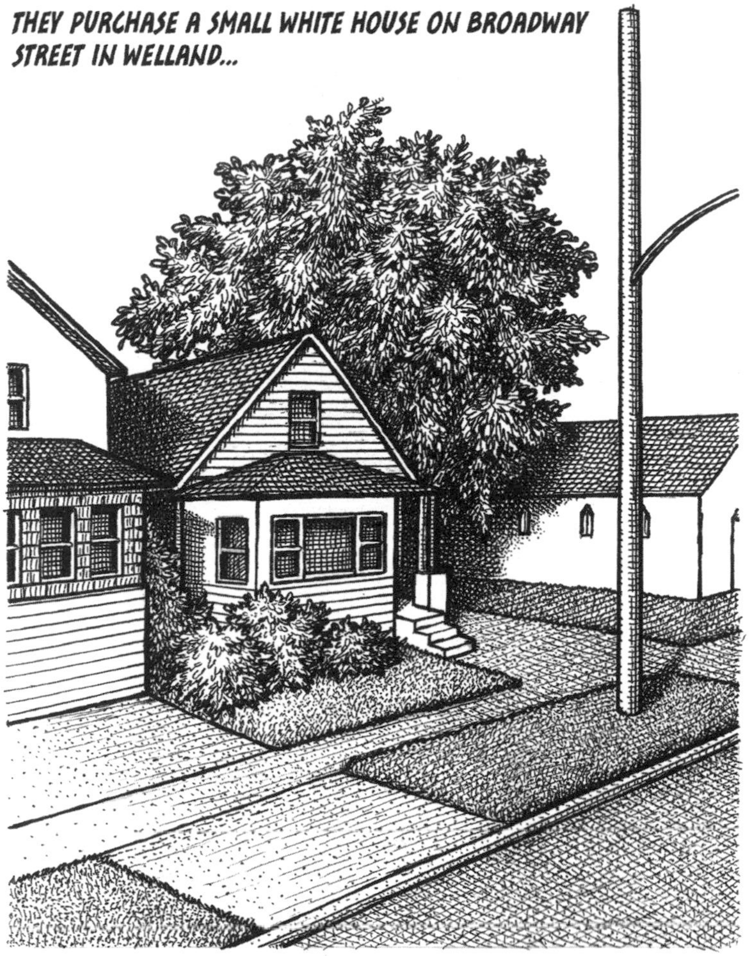

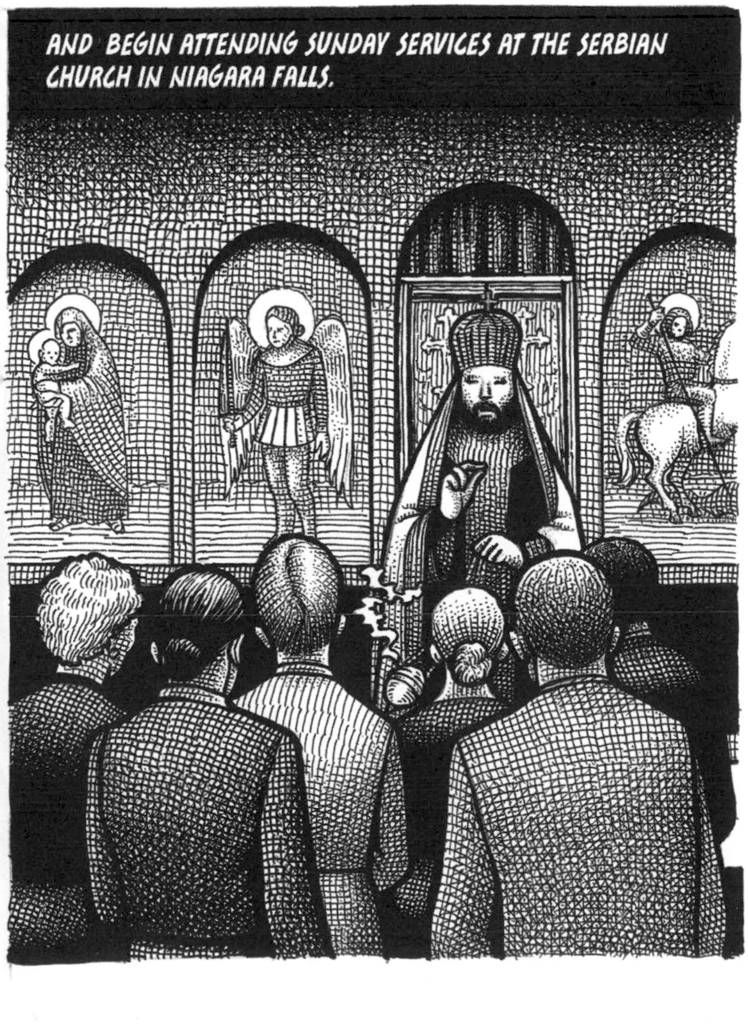
AND BEGIN ATTENDING SUNDAY SERVICES AT THE SERBIAN CHURCH IN NIAGARA FALLS.

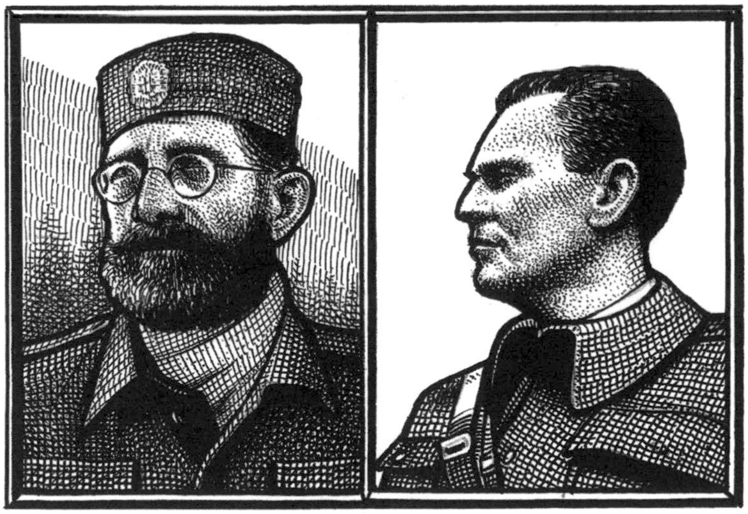

THE SERBIAN POPULATION IN THE NIAGARA REGION IS RATHER LARGE, AND IS GENERALLY DIVIDED INTO TWO GROUPS: ROYALISTS AND COMMUNISTS.

IN HOMES OF ROYALISTS ONE MAY EXPECT TO FIND PORTRAITS OF EITHER KING PETER, THE CHETNIK LEADER DRAZA MIHAILOVIC OR BOTH. THOSE STILL LOYAL TO THE PARTY CAUSE WOULD PROUDLY DISPLAY THE PORTRAIT OF TITO.

MY FATHER JOINS THE FIRST GROUP.

MY GRANDMOTHER MOMIRKA COMES TO VISIT.

SHE IS AGHAST AT THE SIGHT OF HER WAR ENEMY, SO CLEARLY DISPLAYED IN MY PARENTS' LIVING ROOM.

WHAT IS THAT DOING IN HERE?

FATHER SAYS:

"THAT" IS A BUST OF A TRUE HERO.

HERO MY ASS!

DO YOU KNOW WHAT THE CHETNIKS DID TO US DURING THE WAR?

SHE REMEMBERED THE "SHAMING OF THE PARTISAN WHORE" RITUALS THE CHETNIKS WOULD PERFORM OVER CAPTURED FEMALE PARTISANS - AFTER PUBLICLY SHAVING THEIR HEADS THEY WOULD TORTURE OR BEAT THEM TO DEATH.

WELL, IF YOU DON'T LIKE IT YOU KNOW WHERE THE DOOR IS.

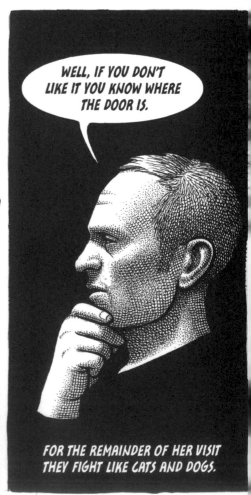

FOR THE REMAINDER OF HER VISIT THEY FIGHT LIKE CATS AND DOGS.

**1969** ANDRA LONCARIC IS BRUTALLY MURDERED IN HIS PARIS APARTMENT.

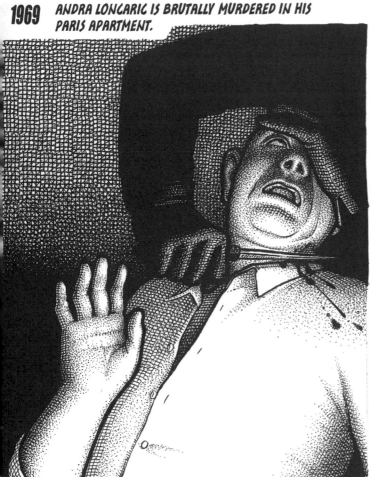

FREEDOM FOR SERBIAN FATHERLAND UNDERGOES INTERNAL RESTRUCTURING. SOME NEW FACES ARRIVE ON THE SCENE. NIKOLA KAVAJA, MY FATHER'S FRIEND FROM THE AUSTRIAN INTERNMENT CAMP, JOINS THE ORGANIZATION.

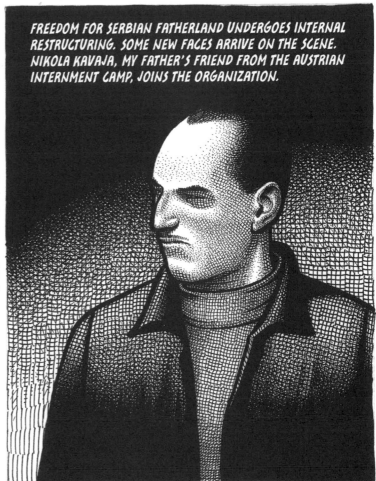

IN ONE OF THE ISSUES OF *LIBERTY* FATHER READS ABOUT AN UPCOMING MEETING OF SERB NATIONALISTS IN NIAGARA FALLS. HE FEELS COMPELLED TO ATTEND.

AT THE MEETING HE RUNS INTO HIS OLD FRIEND.

PETER! JUST THE MAN I WAS HOPING TO SEE!

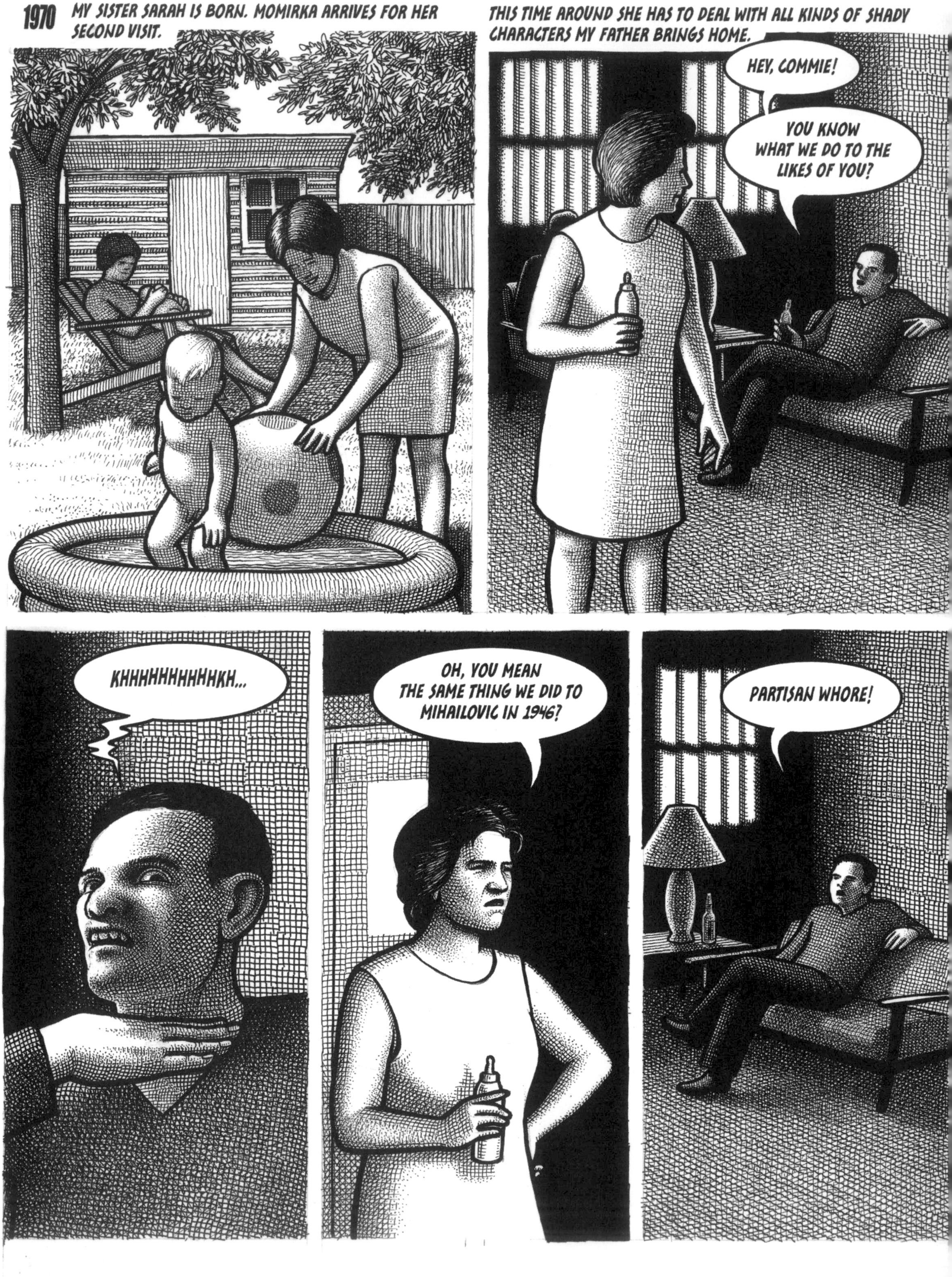
1970 MY SISTER SARAH IS BORN. MOMIRKA ARRIVES FOR HER SECOND VISIT.
THIS TIME AROUND SHE HAS TO DEAL WITH ALL KINDS OF SHADY CHARACTERS MY FATHER BRINGS HOME.
HEY, COMMIE!
YOU KNOW WHAT WE DO TO THE LIKES OF YOU?
KHHHHHHHHHHKH...
OH, YOU MEAN THE SAME THING WE DID TO MIHAILOVIC IN 1946?
PARTISAN WHORE!

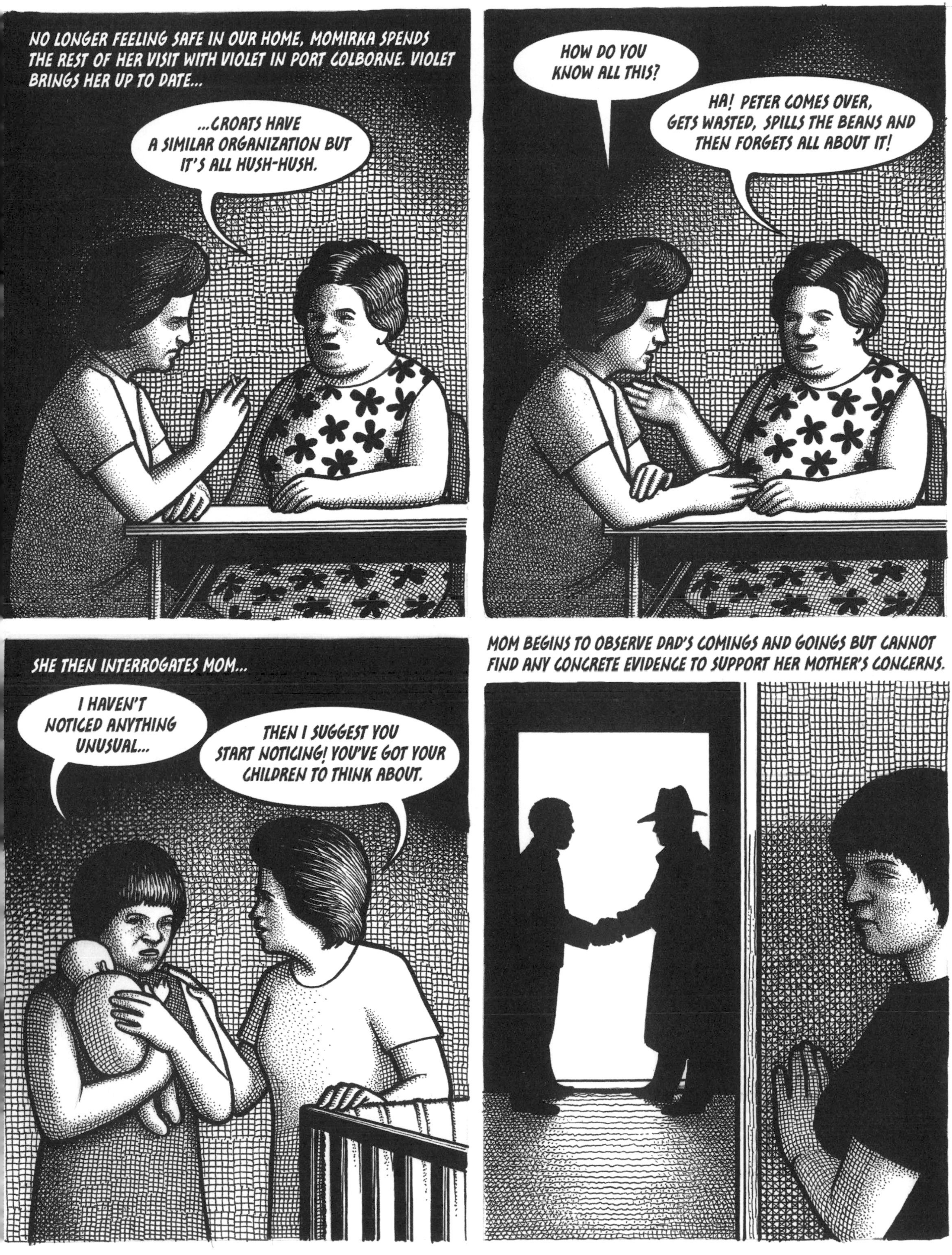
NO LONGER FEELING SAFE IN OUR HOME, MOMIRKA SPENDS THE REST OF HER VISIT WITH VIOLET IN PORT COLBORNE. VIOLET BRINGS HER UP TO DATE...
...CROATS HAVE A SIMILAR ORGANIZATION BUT IT'S ALL HUSH-HUSH.
HOW DO YOU KNOW ALL THIS?
HA! PETER COMES OVER, GETS WASTED, SPILLS THE BEANS AND THEN FORGETS ALL ABOUT IT!
SHE THEN INTERROGATES MOM...
I HAVEN'T NOTICED ANYTHING UNUSUAL...
THEN I SUGGEST YOU START NOTICING! YOU'VE GOT YOUR CHILDREN TO THINK ABOUT.
MOM BEGINS TO OBSERVE DAD'S COMINGS AND GOINGS BUT CANNOT FIND ANY CONCRETE EVIDENCE TO SUPPORT HER MOTHER'S CONCERNS.

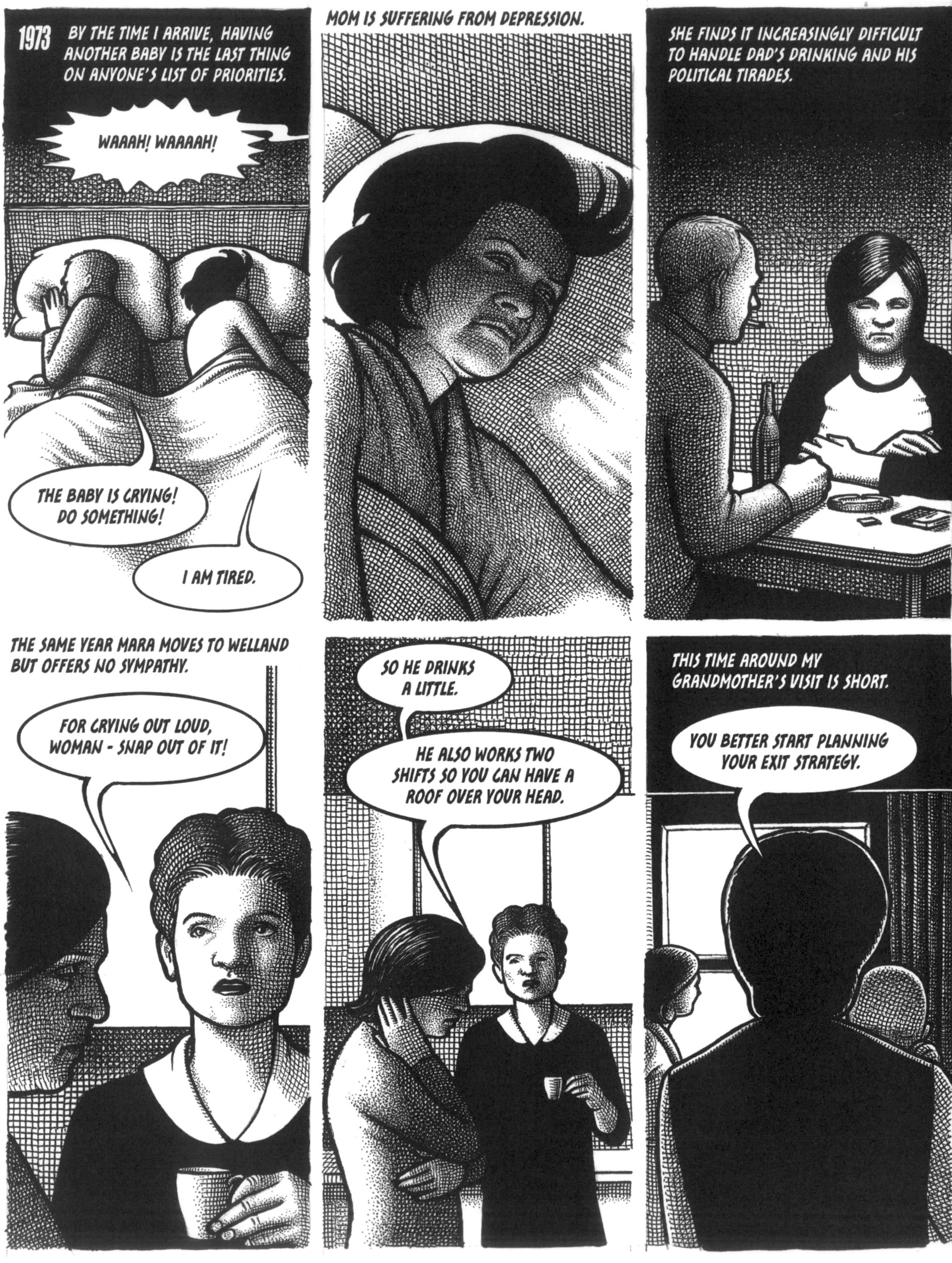
1973
BY THE TIME I ARRIVE, HAVING ANOTHER BABY IS THE LAST THING ON ANYONE'S LIST OF PRIORITIES.
WAAAH! WAAAAH!
THE BABY IS CRYING! DO SOMETHING!
I AM TIRED.
MOM IS SUFFERING FROM DEPRESSION.
SHE FINDS IT INCREASINGLY DIFFICULT TO HANDLE DAD'S DRINKING AND HIS POLITICAL TIRADES.
THE SAME YEAR MARA MOVES TO WELLAND BUT OFFERS NO SYMPATHY.
FOR CRYING OUT LOUD, WOMAN - SNAP OUT OF IT!
SO HE DRINKS A LITTLE.
HE ALSO WORKS TWO SHIFTS SO YOU CAN HAVE A ROOF OVER YOUR HEAD.
THIS TIME AROUND MY GRANDMOTHER'S VISIT IS SHORT.
YOU BETTER START PLANNING YOUR EXIT STRATEGY.

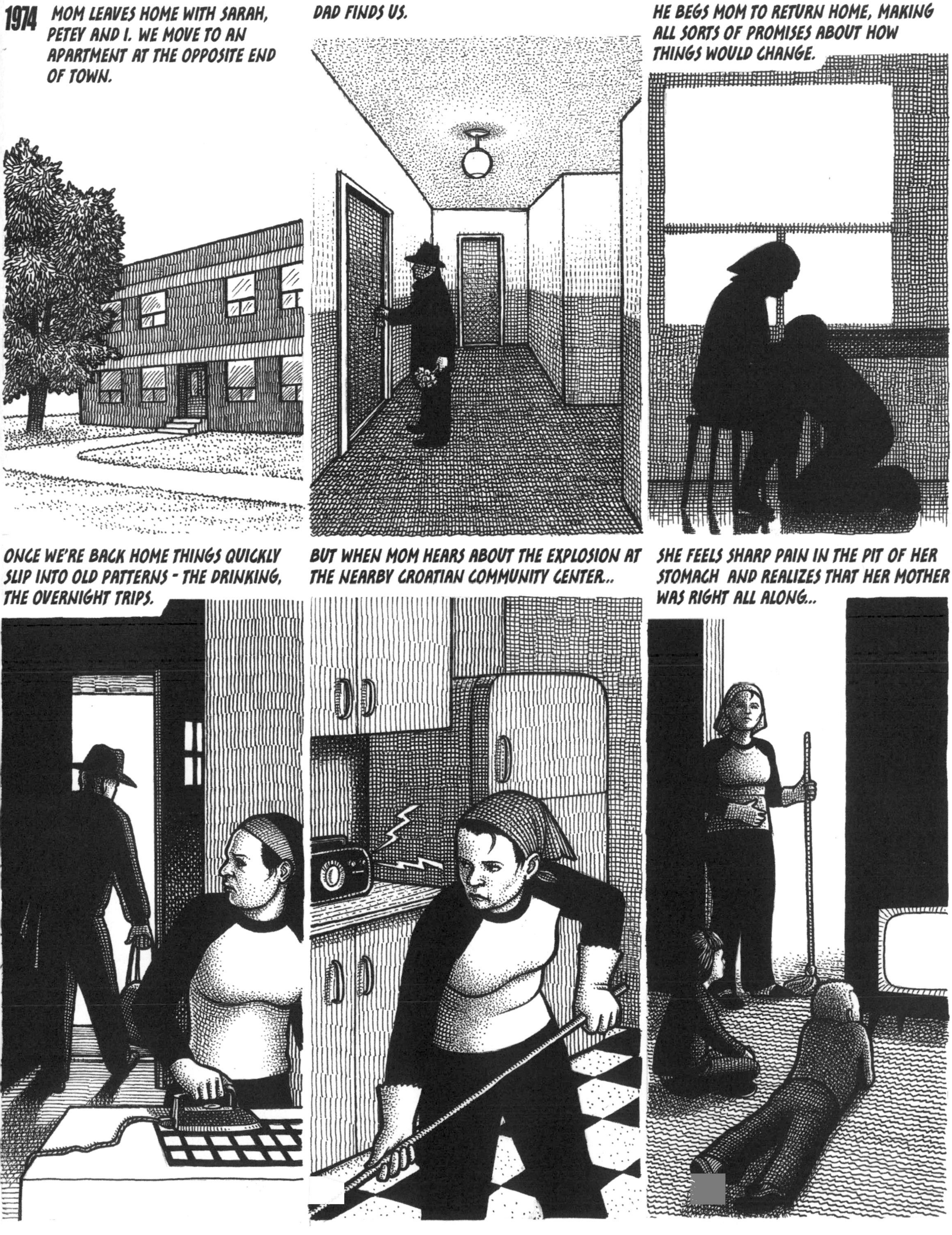
1974 MOM LEAVES HOME WITH SARAH, PETEY AND I. WE MOVE TO AN APARTMENT AT THE OPPOSITE END OF TOWN.
DAD FINDS US.
HE BEGS MOM TO RETURN HOME, MAKING ALL SORTS OF PROMISES ABOUT HOW THINGS WOULD CHANGE.
ONCE WE'RE BACK HOME THINGS QUICKLY SLIP INTO OLD PATTERNS - THE DRINKING, THE OVERNIGHT TRIPS.
BUT WHEN MOM HEARS ABOUT THE EXPLOSION AT THE NEARBY CROATIAN COMMUNITY CENTER...
SHE FEELS SHARP PAIN IN THE PIT OF HER STOMACH AND REALIZES THAT HER MOTHER WAS RIGHT ALL ALONG...

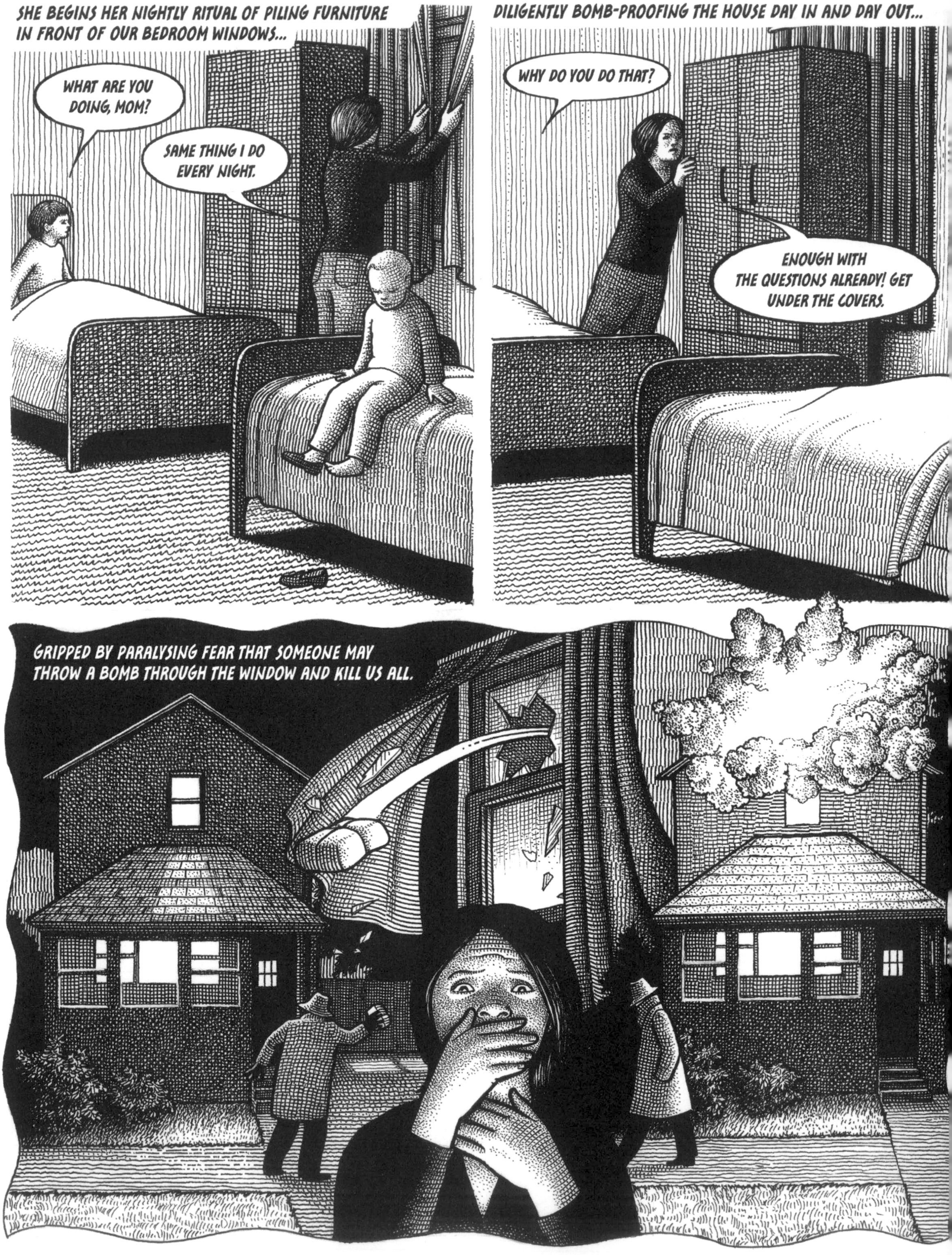
SHE BEGINS HER NIGHTLY RITUAL OF PILING FURNITURE IN FRONT OF OUR BEDROOM WINDOWS...
WHAT ARE YOU DOING, MOM?
SAME THING I DO EVERY NIGHT.
DILIGENTLY BOMB-PROOFING THE HOUSE DAY IN AND DAY OUT...
WHY DO YOU DO THAT?
ENOUGH WITH THE QUESTIONS ALREADY! GET UNDER THE COVERS.
GRIPPED BY PARALYSING FEAR THAT SOMEONE MAY THROW A BOMB THROUGH THE WINDOW AND KILL US ALL.

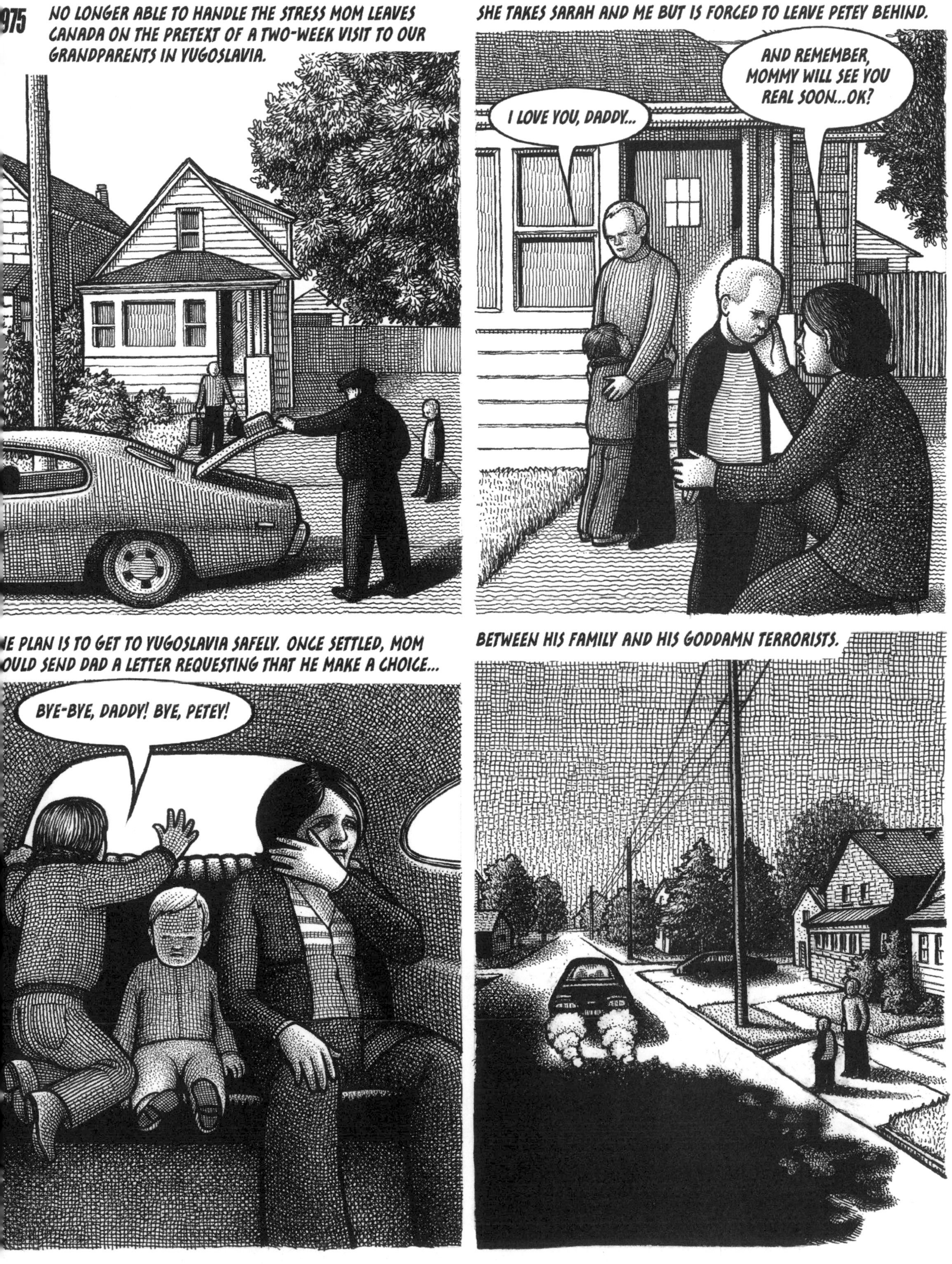
975
NO LONGER ABLE TO HANDLE THE STRESS MOM LEAVES CANADA ON THE PRETEXT OF A TWO-WEEK VISIT TO OUR GRANDPARENTS IN YUGOSLAVIA.
SHE TAKES SARAH AND ME BUT IS FORCED TO LEAVE PETEY BEHIND.
I LOVE YOU, DADDY...
AND REMEMBER, MOMMY WILL SEE YOU REAL SOON...OK?
E PLAN IS TO GET TO YUGOSLAVIA SAFELY. ONCE SETTLED, MOM OULD SEND DAD A LETTER REQUESTING THAT HE MAKE A CHOICE...
BYE-BYE, DADDY! BYE, PETEY!
BETWEEN HIS FAMILY AND HIS GODDAMN TERRORISTS.

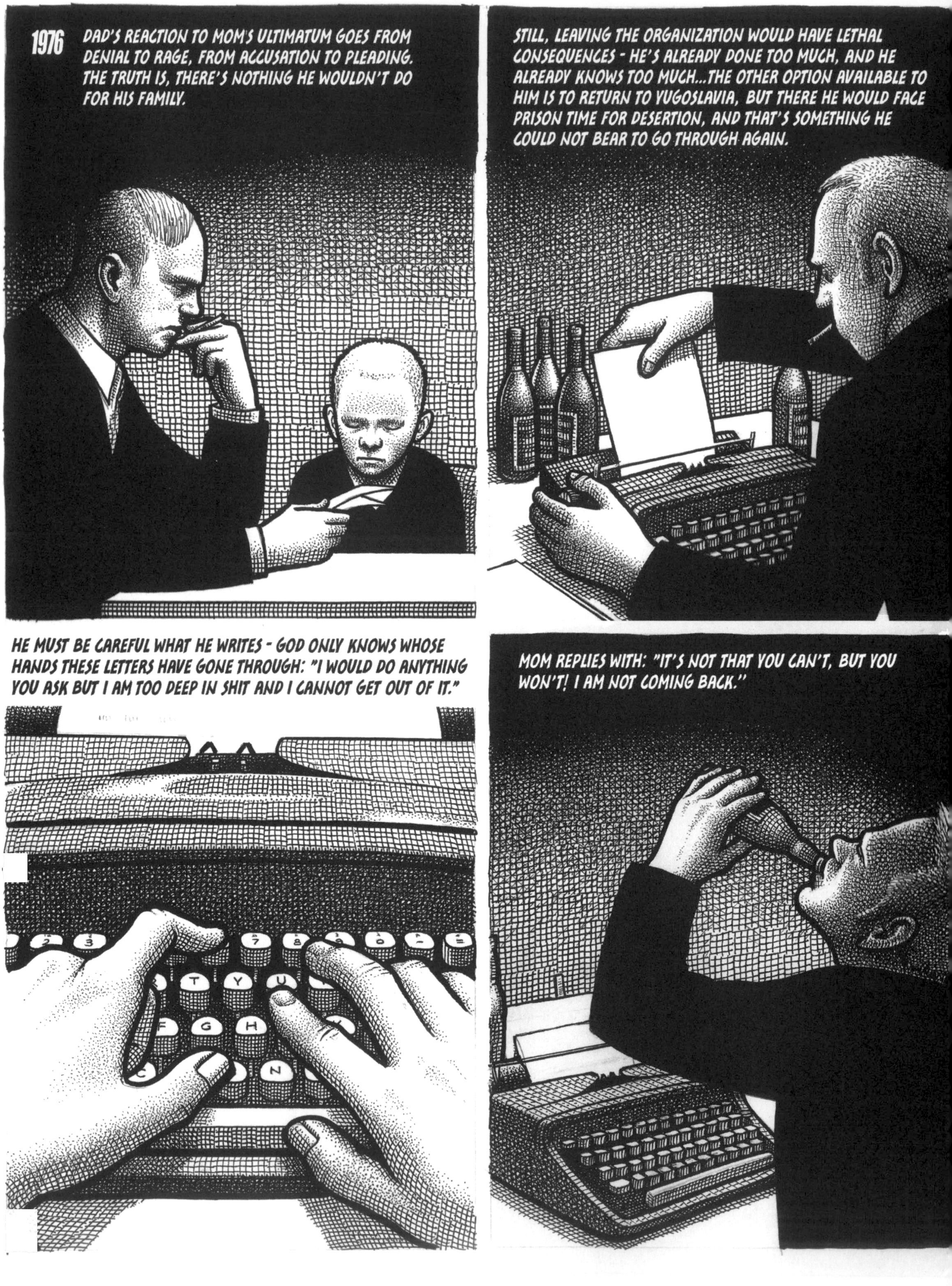

1976
DAD'S REACTION TO MOM'S ULTIMATUM GOES FROM DENIAL TO RAGE, FROM ACCUSATION TO PLEADING. THE TRUTH IS, THERE'S NOTHING HE WOULDN'T DO FOR HIS FAMILY.
STILL, LEAVING THE ORGANIZATION WOULD HAVE LETHAL CONSEQUENCES - HE'S ALREADY DONE TOO MUCH, AND HE ALREADY KNOWS TOO MUCH...THE OTHER OPTION AVAILABLE TO HIM IS TO RETURN TO YUGOSLAVIA, BUT THERE HE WOULD FACE PRISON TIME FOR DESERTION, AND THAT'S SOMETHING HE COULD NOT BEAR TO GO THROUGH AGAIN.
HE MUST BE CAREFUL WHAT HE WRITES - GOD ONLY KNOWS WHOSE HANDS THESE LETTERS HAVE GONE THROUGH: "I WOULD DO ANYTHING YOU ASK BUT I AM TOO DEEP IN SHIT AND I CANNOT GET OUT OF IT."
MOM REPLIES WITH: "IT'S NOT THAT YOU CAN'T, BUT YOU WON'T! I AM NOT COMING BACK."

A YEAR HAS GONE BY SINCE WE LEFT. DAD IS DESPERATE. MARA AS ALWAYS OFFERS EMOTIONAL SUPPORT.

LEAVE THE BOY HERE FOR THE NIGHT AND GO GET SOME SLEEP. YOU LOOK EXHAUSTED.

UPON RETURNING HOME DAD HEARS MY CRIES FROM THE UPSTAIRS BEDROOM. HE RUSHES UP THE STAIRS...

WAAAH! WAAAAH!

ONLY TO FIND THE HOUSE EMPTY.

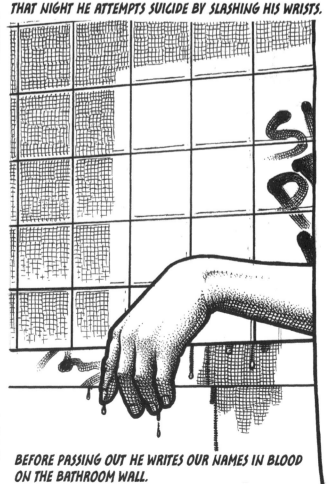

THAT NIGHT HE ATTEMPTS SUICIDE BY SLASHING HIS WRISTS.

BEFORE PASSING OUT HE WRITES OUR NAMES IN BLOOD ON THE BATHROOM WALL.

**1977** JUNE. DRAGISA KASIKOVIC AND HIS NINE-YEAR-OLD STEPDAUGHTER ARE FOUND MURDERED. HIS BODY IS DECAPITATED; BOTH BODIES SHOW MULTIPLE STAB WOUNDS TO CHEST, NECK AND FACE.

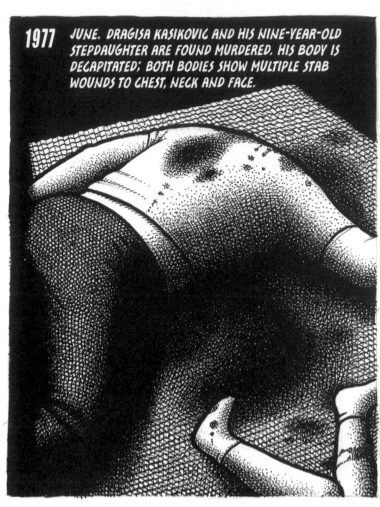

IT IS ASSUMED THAT TITO'S SECRET POLICE IS RESPONSIBLE FOR THIS VIOLENT ACT. THE ORDERS ARE GIVEN TO AVENGE KASIKOVIC'S DEATH BY BOMBING THE YUGOSLAVIAN CONSULATE IN TORONTO.

DAD IS A NERVOUS WRECK. AT THIS TIME HE IS CERTAIN THAT HE'S BEING FOLLOWED.

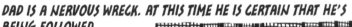

ON AUGUST 28 HE TAKES PETEY TO MARA'S FOR AN OVERNIGHT STAY.

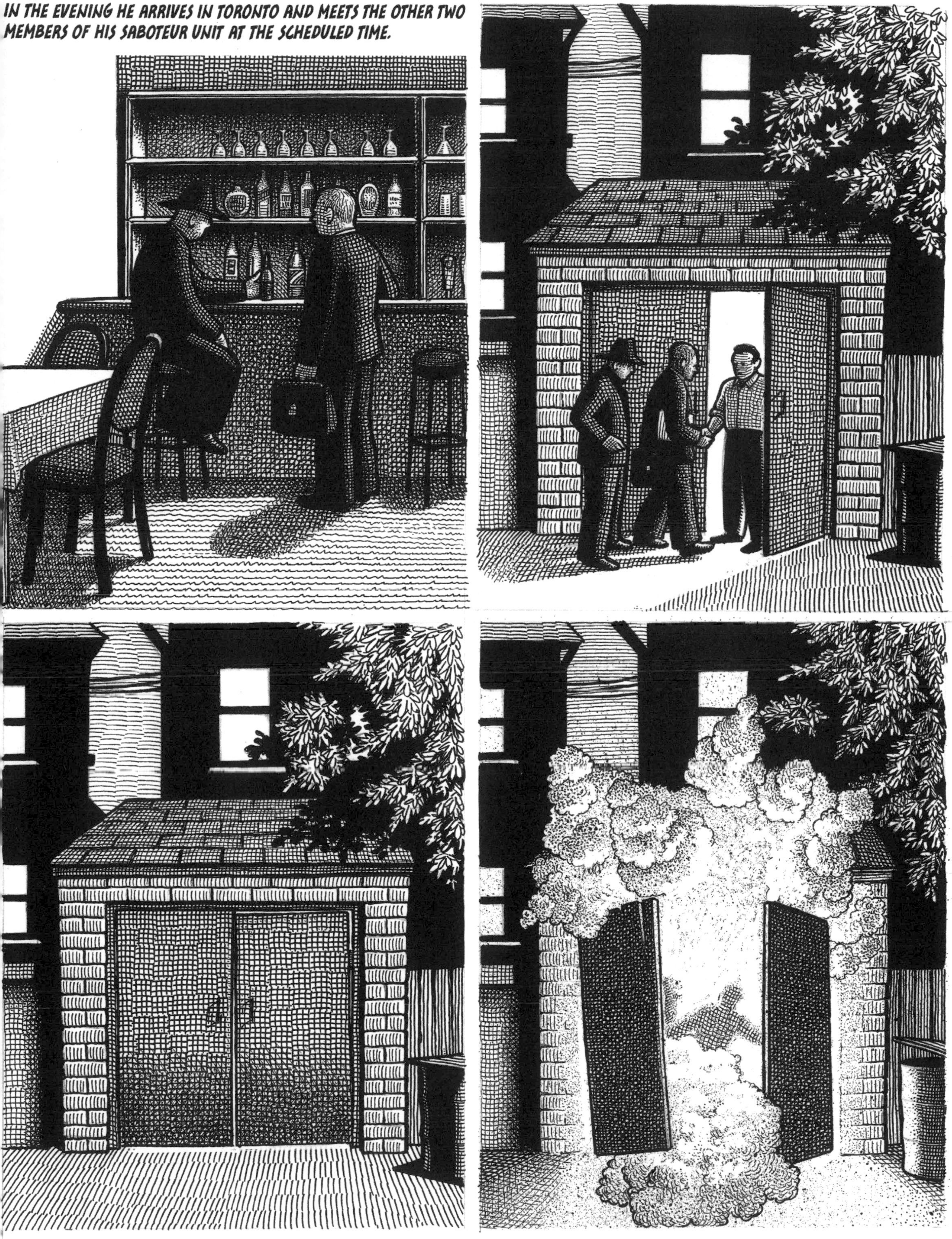
IN THE EVENING HE ARRIVES IN TORONTO AND MEETS THE OTHER TWO MEMBERS OF HIS SABOTEUR UNIT AT THE SCHEDULED TIME.

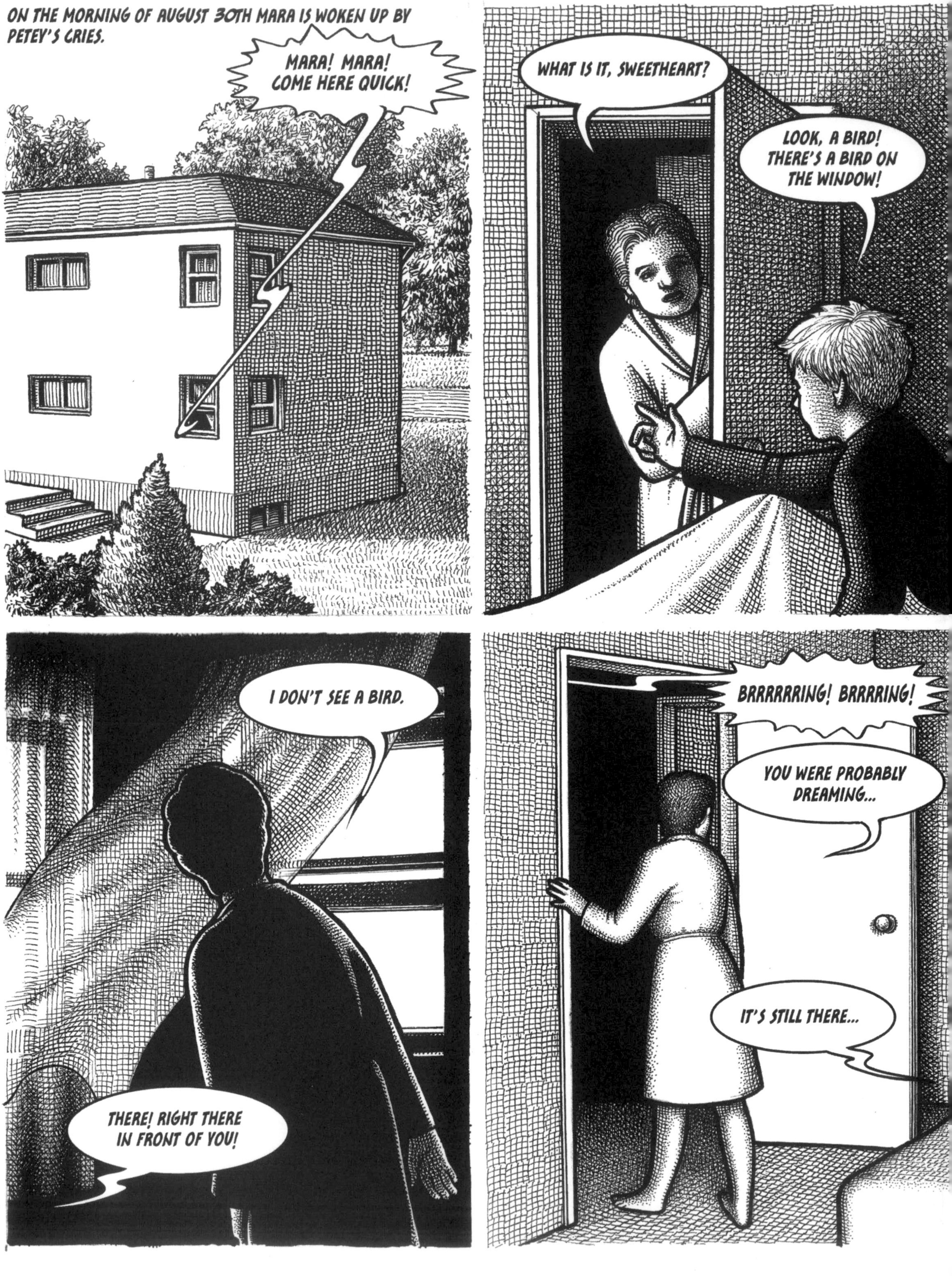
ON THE MORNING OF AUGUST 30TH MARA IS WOKEN UP BY PETEY'S CRIES.
MARA! MARA! COME HERE QUICK!
WHAT IS IT, SWEETHEART?
LOOK, A BIRD! THERE'S A BIRD ON THE WINDOW!
I DON'T SEE A BIRD.
THERE! RIGHT THERE IN FRONT OF YOU!
BRRRRRRING! BRRRRING!
YOU WERE PROBABLY DREAMING...
IT'S STILL THERE...

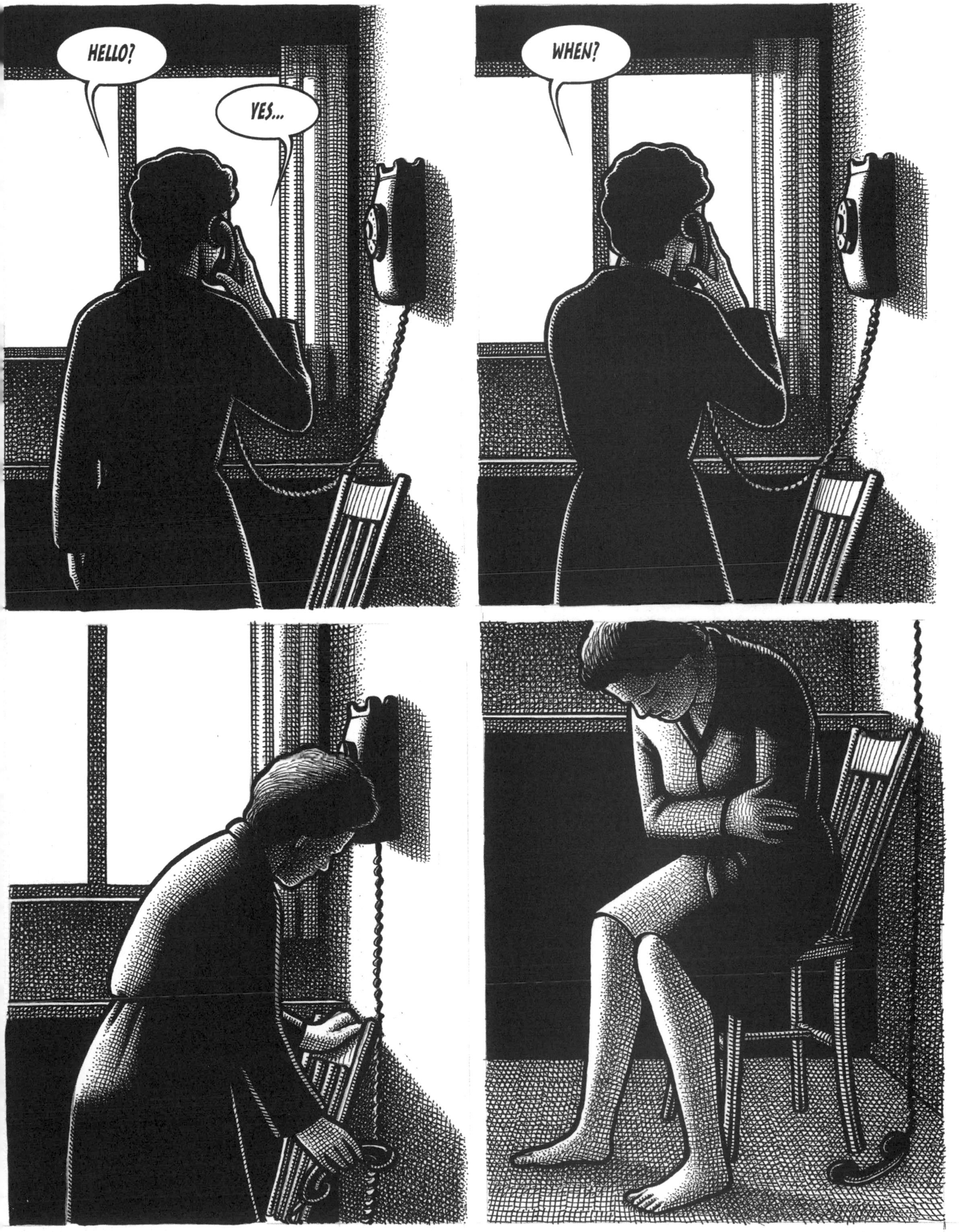
HELLO?
YES...
WHEN?

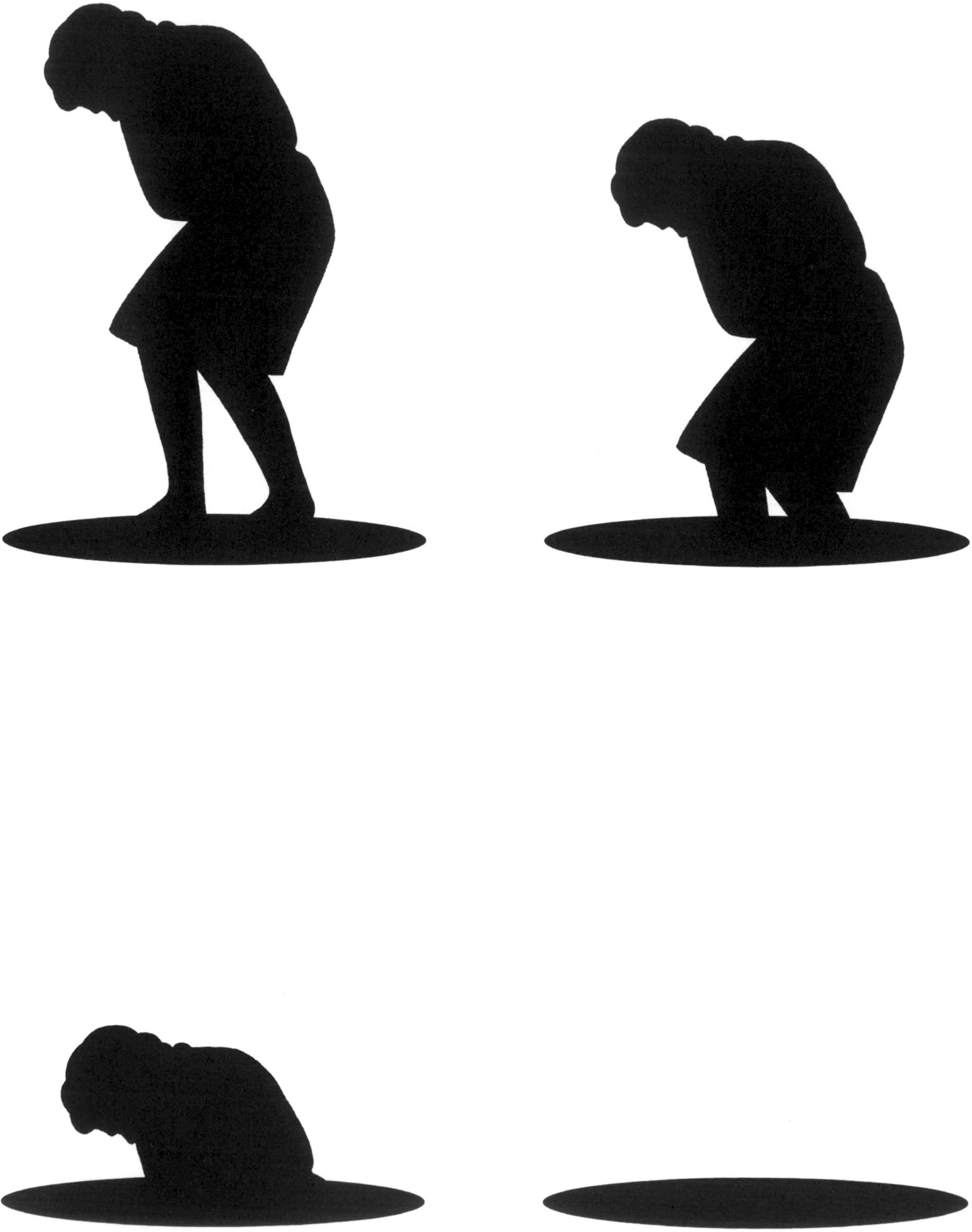

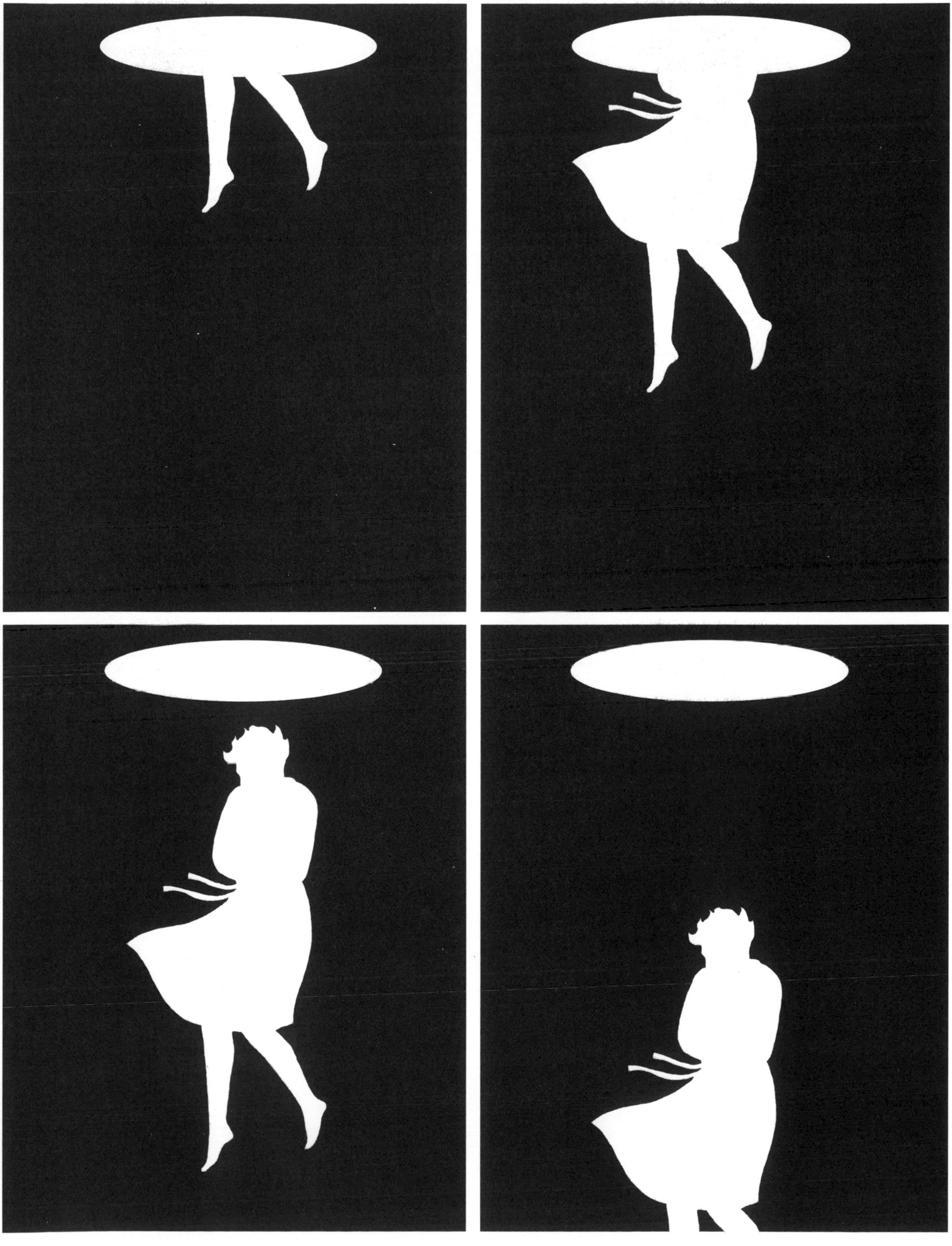

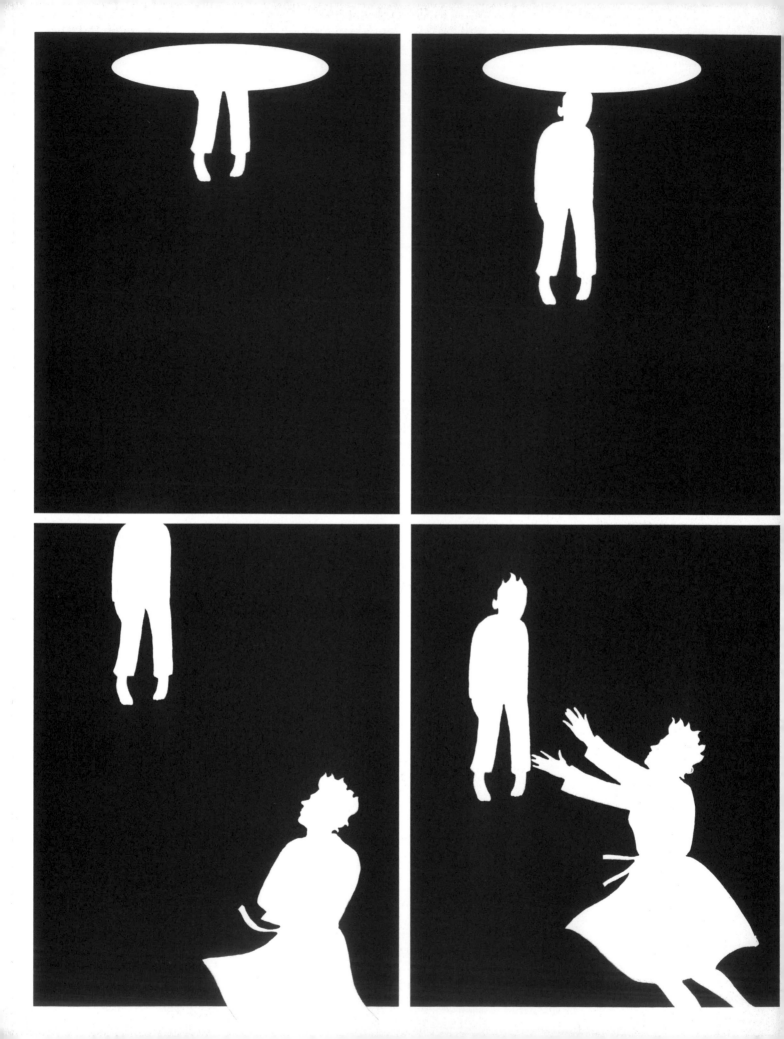

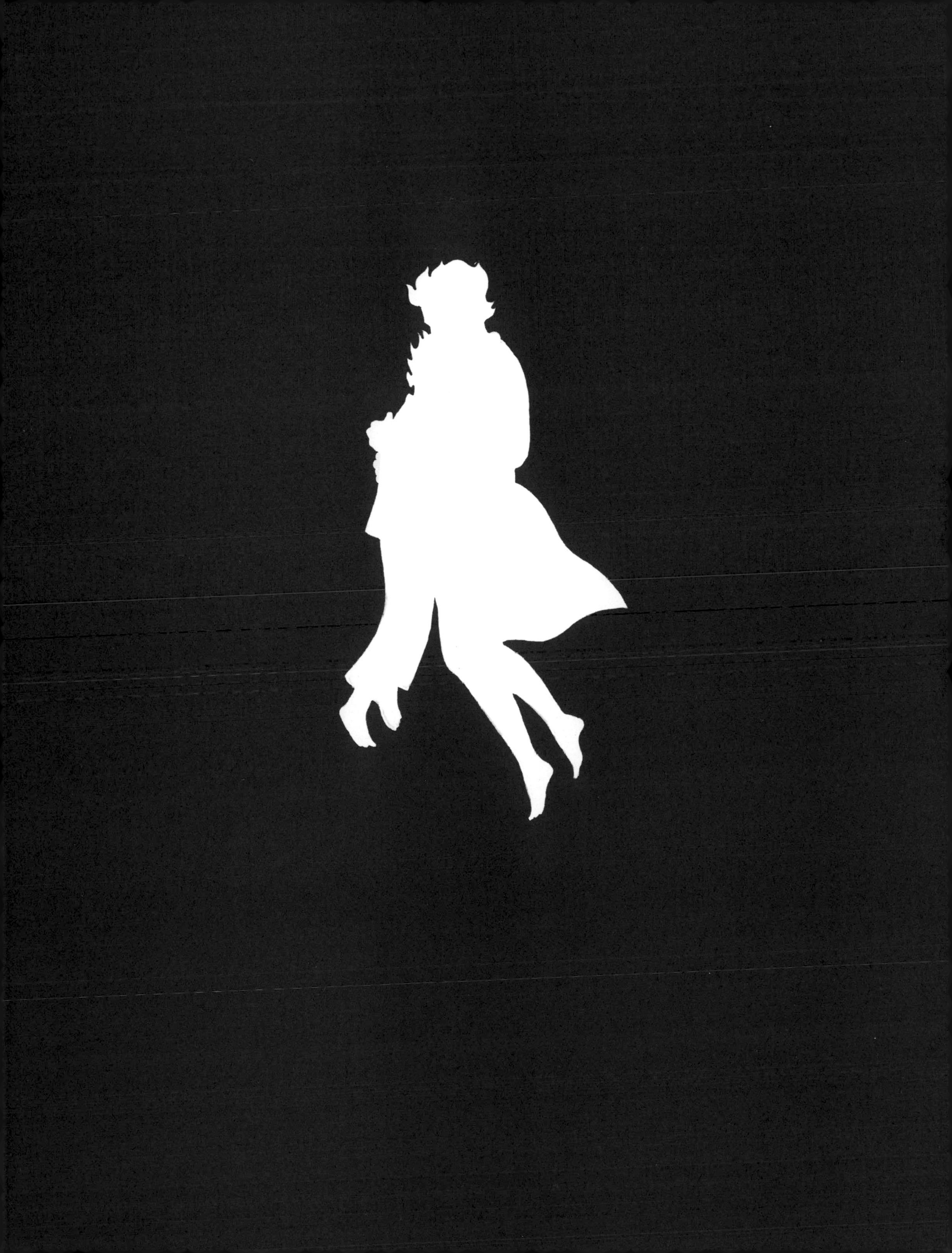

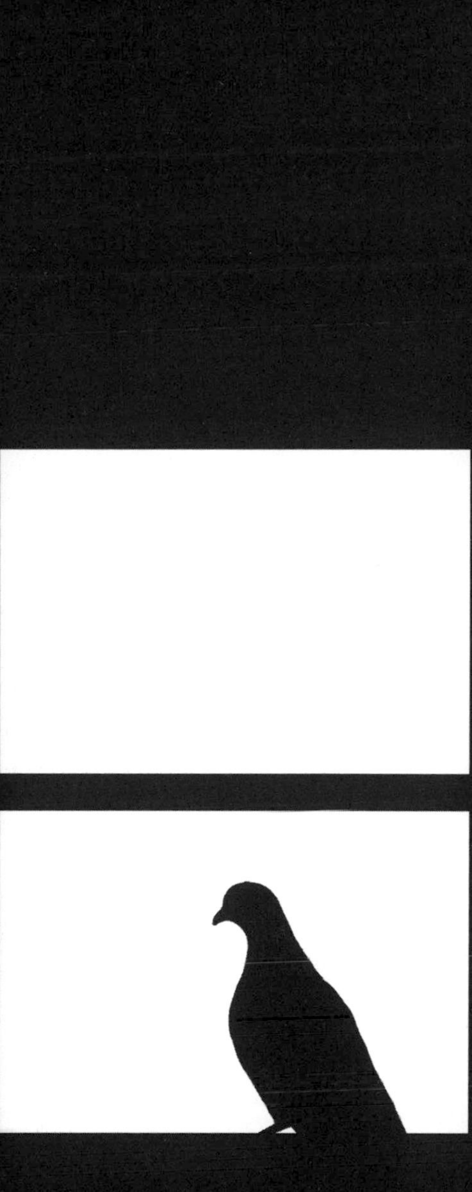